H A

One of a group of four night pictures first establishing the beauty

к K!

and accuracy of the camera and flashlight in big-game photography.

HUNTING WILD LIFE WITH CAMERA AND FLASHLIGHT

A Record of Sixty-five Years' Visits to
the Woods and Waters of North America

By

GEORGE SHIRAS, 3D

Volume II

Wild Life of Coasts, Islands,
and Mountains

NATIONAL GEOGRAPHIC SOCIETY

WASHINGTON, D. C.

Table of Contents

This publication of the important wild-life researches of George Shiras, 3d, is made by the National Geographic Society as a contribution to its purpose—the increase and diffusion of geographic knowledge.

Introduction

THE preceding volume is devoted mainly to my observations during parts of many years in the Lake Superior region. The present volume goes farther afield and includes localities along the Atlantic coast from Newfoundland to Panama. My study and photography of wild life also led me along the Rocky Mountains of the West to the upper Yellowstone Lake region and to the Kaibab Plateau of northern Arizona. I also made visits to the southern coast of Alaska.

From 1876 to the present I have passed a part of each year in some section of the eastern seaboard of North America between the subarctic plains of Newfoundland, where ranges the caribou; and the rain-forest jungles of Panama, frequented by tropical spotted cats and monkeys. Coastal indentations taken into account, this region stretches more than 7,000 miles in length, and includes the fauna and flora peculiar to the several life zones from the Hudsonian of northern Newfoundland through the Canadian, Transition, and Upper and Lower Austral to one of the most strongly characterized parts of the Tropical.

From the time of the arrival of the early colonists, whether on the shores of Canada, the United States, Mexico, or Panama, to the present day, the chronicles of these regions have contained many references to the abounding wild life. The middle part of this coastal area has become the most densely populated section of the New World. Here are located numerous great cities and a well-settled countryside, but a study of the results of occupation of the region by civilized man for centuries shows surprisingly small effect on the face of nature as a whole.

It is true that the newcomers have cut down the forests, from vast areas, and have utilized the ground for agriculture, and that a number of large and noteworthy species originally inhabiting the region have disappeared, but these are species that apparently are unfitted to adapt themselves and survive in populous section. Among them may be mentioned the bison, elk, wolf, and mountain lion, which once roamed the forests of the eastern United States. With them have gone from this general region the great auk, Labrador duck, heath hen, passenger pigeon, and Carolina parakeet. Moose and caribou still hold their own in some of the wilder places, and a large number of species of wild creatures have adapted themselves to share their world with civilized man.

The white-tailed deer is probably now more numerous in some sections than at any previous time in its history. Within a radius of 300 miles of New York City, with its approximately 7,000,000 inhabitants, sportsmen during each yearly hunting season take more than 40,000 of these deer. In Pennsylvania their increase has been so great that on account of lack of sufficient forage the entire stock of deer has been threatened with starvation.

Probably the total number of small birds now found in the region has increased vastly since the days of the Pilgrim Fathers. This phenomenon is due to the increase of available food on farms and in second-growth forests. Millions of migratory wild fowl still troop southward every fall to winter in the coastal waterways and marshes, but unwise drainage operations and years of excessive drought have affected their welfare throughout this continent.

Many small creatures of field and forest have developed such an insight into man and his ways that they outwit him at times when their interests conflict. Cottontail, swamp, and snowshoe rabbits, squirrels, muskrats, beavers, minks, otters, skunks, foxes, raccoons, wildcats, and other small mammals, and even the black bear are common in many places. Doves, wild turkeys, ruffed grouse, and bobwhites continue to lure the hunter afield.

So far mention has been made only of the creatures of more northern latitudes, but excursions to the southward have brought me in contact with such tropical beasts as monkeys of several kinds, the jaguar, ocelot, yagu-aroundi cat, coati mundi, peccary, tapir, prehensile-tailed porcupine, and anteaters, as well as with parrots and many other strange birds and a plant life so different that it constitutes almost a new world to the northern visitor. Here untamed nature surrounds man with a wall of persistent life ready to move in and supplant him wherever he ceases the constant efforts necessary to maintain his supremacy.

With so much of the original capital in wild life to go on, it is especially pleasing to note the awakening that has taken place among the people of the United States during the last 20 years in the recognition of the value of wild life as a great national asset that must be maintained and perpetuated. This change from a state of comparative indifference to one of interest has come about as the direct result of educational campaigns conducted for years by many organizations, among the most effective of which has been the National Geographic Society.

BIG GAME OF EASTERN CANADA

At the time of my visit to eastern Canada in 1906 and 1907, the amazing numbers of caribou in Newfoundland and their annual migration across the island each fall constituted one of the marvels of American wild life. At the same time, moose, white-tailed deer, and bears were extraordinarily abundant in New Brunswick.

Although this region had long been accessible to settlers, its unsuitability to agricultural development had resulted in vast areas being so sparsely occupied that they remained true wildernesses in which the native animal life thrived. There the sportsman or the photographer of wild things could establish his camp in ideal surroundings and feel himself in the midst of conditions almost like those of primitive days.

Conditions during the World War led to a period of intensive pursuit of big game in all this region for its value as meat. This slaughter of the moose, and especially of the caribou, dangerously lowered their numbers.

The migratory herds of caribou will probably never again troop across the barrens of Newfoundland in anything like their former numbers.

With well-enforced protection, however, the caribou in Newfoundland and the moose in New Brunswick and Maine may be maintained in fair abundance. Caribou seem to be disappearing forever from Maine, New Brunswick, and Nova Scotia, the white-tailed deer having taken their place in many districts.

Accounts of some of my experiences with the moose in the wild, forested parts of New Brunswick, and with the caribou on the lakes and barrens of Newfoundland, have appeared in articles in the NATIONAL GEOGRAPHIC MAGAZINE. My second trip to Newfoundland was for the special purpose of photographing migrating caribou as they swam across the large Sandy and Little Deer Lakes, which lay in the path of their regular route.

The survival of so much wild life along the eastern coast and its bordering hinterland is due chiefly to the physical characteristics of the country. To the north, in Newfoundland, Nova Scotia, New Brunswick, and Maine, are vast, thinly peopled, forested areas abounding in streams and lakes. There travel is still so largely by rough roads and small boats that conditions remain favorable to wild life. The rock-bound coast and outlying islets also provide homes for countless sea birds, just as do similar conditions on the shores of the North Pacific.

ONE COASTAL PLAIN

Beginning near the mouth of the Hudson River is a great coastal plain that extends southward to eastern Mexico. In the northern part it has a width of only a few miles; southward it broadens to 250 miles in places and narrows again near Tampico. In this entire area there are no outcroppings of metamorphic rocks and apparently none of sedimentary formation except the coquinas of Florida.

This plain is fronted by sand beaches penetrated here and there by bays, sounds, inlets, and the mouths of rivers. Back of the exposed beaches lie many great marsh areas and shallow bays, with numberless sand bars, low islands, and mud flats. In such places thrive aquatic plants and myriads of fishes, crustaceans, and other food that in winter sustain millions of swans, geese, ducks, gulls, waders, and other wild fowl.

Fortunately for these birds, the broken shore line and the extensive stretches of submerged lands have prevented the opening of highways, and have limited agricultural development. Large areas in Maryland, Virginia, North and South Carolina, Louisiana, and Texas are occupied only by fishing villages or by hunting clubs.

From Tampico, Mexico, south to Panama the coastal region is completely tropical, consisting mainly of an indented coastal plain broken here and there by mountains that sometimes rise abruptly from the sea, but usually stand at varying distances back in the interior. All this tropical region is sparsely occupied, the chief cultivated areas being the sugar and banana plantations of Mexico and Central America. Much of the land is covered with forests in more or less primitive condition, some consisting of stunted arid tropical growth and others of the luxuriant rain-forest vegetation.

My five trips to the Rocky Mountain area were brief, but they gave me a much desired opportunity to become acquainted with the general characteristics of a region of superb scenic grandeur, with a flora and fauna so new to me that they were of absorbing interest.

Several trips to the Yellowstone Lake region, beginning in 1904, enabled me to see the southern part of that wonderland while it was still an almost unknown wilderness. There it was my good fortune to discover moose in surprising abundance, and I brought to the attention of scientists a previously unknown geographic race of this noble animal.

My visit to the Kaibab Plateau was for the purpose of investigating one of the best object lessons conservationists in this country have ever had of the results of the long-continued protection of large game animals in a large isolated area with no plan for eliminating the surplus. For years the mule deer were under rigid protection; then with the inevitable outcome of overstocking came the ultimate starvation of thousands of helpless victims.

My two visits to Alaska were first to secure photographs of the giant moose and the white mountain sheep of the Kenai Peninsula, and the second, made with my son, to become acquainted with the big bears for which the southern coast of that Territory is famous. Both trips were successful and the big bear secured proved to be a species new to science.

GEORGE SHIRAS, 3D.

A LITTLE WHITE, OR SNOWY, EGRET FLIES ALONG DAYTONA BEACH

Until steps were taken for its protection, this species seemed doomed to extinction, but now with plume hunters forbidden to kill it, it is slowly increasing in numbers.

WITH WHIR OF COUNTLESS WINGS THEY LEAVE A POOL IN LOUISIANA

On the bays and marshes of this State, Virginia, and North Carolina, a great proportion of the ducks, geese, and swans of North America pass their winters. Refuges have been provided for them, and they are quick to learn where safety lies.

CHAPTER I — PART I

Author's First Visit to Newfoundland

THE FALL migration of the great caribou herds in northern Newfoundland had become widely known. For many years hunters lined up along the railroad near Sandy River, intercepted the animals as they came southward, and killed them in great numbers. This easy method of destruction led to so serious a condition that to protect the herds from threatened extermination the Government closed to hunting an area extending five miles north of the railroad.

For some years I had felt a great desire to see and photograph these interesting animals and, in 1906, accompanied by several friends, I made a trip to the island to study their migration, as well as to try the famous trout fishing.

Newfoundland is the oldest British colony in North America, and it still maintains a colonial form of government. Its early history is involved in some obscurity, but trustworthy records show it was discovered in 1497 by John Cabot. During the 17th and part of the 18th centuries its history is little more than a record of feuds between the English and French fishermen.

In shape the island resembles an almost equilateral triangle, about 315 miles on each side, and it contains an area of about 40,000 square miles. It is separated from Labrador on the north by the straits of Belle Isle. Since 1909 a part of the Labrador coast and the Island of Anticosti have been included within the jurisdiction of the Newfoundland Government.

A LAND OF RIVERS AND MOUNTAINS

The surface of the island is diversified by mountains, marshes, barrens, ponds, and lakes, some of the mountains towering to 2,000 feet. It is estimated that one-third of the surface is covered with fresh water. The coast line is everywhere deeply indented with bays and estuaries, many of them spacious enough to harbor the whole British navy. Most of the narrow, winding rivers flow from interior lakes, and are navigable only for small boats.

While much of the soil is sterile and unproductive, there is considerable arable land along the seaboard. The best timber grows in the interior, and consists of pine, fir, poplar, and birch, with a lesser growth of willow. There are no decided extremes in climate, the temperature varying from about zero during the coldest winter to 80 degrees at the height of summer.

Most of the people are employed in the fisheries and live along the coast, where cod, salmon, and herring are abundant. The main fisheries are on the "Banks" offshore, which form the greatest submarine plateau known, and constitute one of the most famous fishing grounds in history. The seals afford an important fishing industry of the island, the season on them beginning usually about the first of March.

BY RAIL TO SANDY RIVER

Our party of four arrived at Port-aux-Basques, at the southwest corner of the island, on the morning of September 6, 1906, and we were soon traveling away from the rock-bound coast on the narrow-gauge railway, which crossed Sandy River, our immediate destination. En route we were joined at Bay of Islands by two sturdy guides, who as erstwhile fishermen were experienced in handling small craft on swift waters. At the river crossing our party was increased by two additional guides, each famous as a trapper and caribou hunter.

The journey by rail disclosed scenery new to most of us familiar with a more forested and occupied country; for the train wound its way through valleys through which dashed streams notable for their salmon pools, or over rolling hills and across tundras dotted with high mounds and pinnacles of jagged rocks which often served as landmarks in a vast interior lacking trails or human habitations.

We left the railroad and camped the first night on Sandy River, a short distance above Grand Lake, the largest and most beautiful body of water on the island. It is 56 miles long, 5 miles wide, and more than 300 feet deep, and contains an island 22 miles long. From this point a trip by canoe would take us through streams and lakes to within a few miles of the northern boundary of Newfoundland, where some small islets, a short distance offshore, were the last haunts in America of the great auk.

THE PAUSE FOR LUNCHEON WAS IN DELIGHTFUL SURROUNDINGS
Many inviting places for landing were seen as the party ascended Sandy River (see text below).

From the first camp on Sandy River we were to ascend the river to an upper chain of lakes in three canoes and a bateau manned by local guides to carry our camp equipment and supplies. While the boats were being loaded, my Michigan guide, John Hammer, and I took our own canoe and started on the way.

UP THE RAPIDS TO CAMP AT LITTLE DEER LAKE

The river was swift in many places, requiring strenuous paddling, but it was not until we reached the foot of a long, tumultuous rapid that we had any doubts as to the result. Halfway up, our headway decreased until the canoe became stationary, and every prospect pointed to our drifting back when we should become exhausted. With some effort we worked the canoe ashore, where in the eddy below a large boulder we awaited the arrival of the others.

As they came to the foot of the rapids, they substituted poles for paddles and came steadily upstream, apparently with no great exertion. When they arrived abreast of us, the guides showed much amusement at our predicament, saying that no one had ever succeeded in paddling up these rapids and that we should have used our poles.

On being told that our canoe contained none, they supplied them. We reached the head of the rapids in a state of exhaustion. Except possibly in New Brunswick, there are no more skillful canoeists than those of Newfoundland.

On our return several weeks later we shot down the rapids at high speed. At their foot we found an overturned canoe that had capsized when two visiting sportsmen, trying to use poles on the way down, had thrust them into deep water at the foot and, finding no bottom, had gone overboard. Aside from the ducking, they had suffered no injuries, but had lost a part of their outfit, including a camera and two guns. We had tried paddling up, and they had improperly used poles in going down, a procedure that showed that each party had something to learn in navigating new waters.

We camped for a week at the southwest corner of Sandy Lake. Back of camp a long stony ridge was bright with blueberries, and a small stream nearby supplied the camp with brook trout. This lake marked the center of the caribou country,

NAVIGATION AT THE FOOT OF THE RAPIDS ON SANDY RIVER REQUIRES SKILL

On the trip into caribou country the camp equipment was carried in a stout skiff (see text, page 2).

but as the migration at this date was limited to a few does, fawns, and yearlings, I had little expectation of much success with the camera.

Only one member of the party had taken out a hunting license, since at that season the large stags had not started on their migration, nor were their antlers fully developed. It was our intention to make use of this permit later, on a trip to be made in November, but the holder of it agreed to shoot a young stag for camp use. With this object in view he went out one afternoon on the extensive barrens near the lake.

A PERSISTENT ORPHAN

After an hour or two we heard a shot, and since this was the first big-game hunt this man had ever undertaken, we waited expectantly. When the hunter returned, he seemed much flustered. He told us that he had shot what appeared to be a two-year-old stag, but on examining the body he had found it to be a doe bearing small antlers. He had been unaware that most female caribou in Newfoundland and elsewhere have this usually masculine emblem.

A few minutes later a fawn had come out of the brush and had begun whimper-

ing over its mother's form. Much distressed at this sight, he had driven the little creature away, but it had persisted in following him most of the way to camp.

While telling the story he suddenly exclaimed, "There it is now!"

The little orphan seemed more curious than alarmed, until we all joined in a chase to relieve our friend of its unwelcome presence. For several days the waif was seen near camp, and then we were pleased to see it adopt a foster mother, a doe that came swimming near the beach upon which it stood.

Two months later our despondent companion killed several fine stags, and this served to lessen his chagrin over the tragedy of his first hunt. These he shot on November 15 near the southern end of the island, where he saw about 400 adult caribou stags temporarily consorting together after the close of the mating season. The larger antlers were being shed as evidence of an armistice between former rivals. This occurrence takes place from one to two months earlier than is the case with moose, white-tailed deer, or elk.

The female caribou, however, carry their small antlers throughout most of the win-

THIS CARIBOU MADE AN AGONIZED RUSH TO ESCAPE THE CANOE

The animals swim slowly in deep water, but go ashore with great speed (see, also, illustration, page 6).
They are of the species known in Europe as reindeer.

ter. In connection with previous observations of the shedding of the velvet, it should be stated that these caribou do not "horn" the trees and bushes until after the antlers are free from velvet. Additional evidence is thus presented that the rubbing of trees is a sexual manifestation, and that it is not for the purpose of removing the velvet, an effort that would have proved futile, considering the massive and intricate character of the antlers of these animals.

The caribou use the long sharp hoofs of the forefeet for digging down into the snow after ground vegetation, although the animals are largely dependent in winter on a dark gray lichen that festoons many of the conifers. The hoofs, when spread open, support the caribou on the crusted snow or, in the summer, on bogs that would mire any other large quadruped.

Whenever we paddled close to a swimming caribou, as we journeyed together across the lake, the animal displayed little apparent concern, but it became very evident that deep down in its heart was an inherent dread of man. Upon finding footing in the shallow water near the shore it would plunge forward with all its remaining strength in a deluge of spray that sometimes concealed it from the camera. Since caribou are lacking in facial and vocal expression, their emotions can be discerned only by their quick and nervous movements when confronted with danger or when suffering pain.

NEWFOUNDLAND CARIBOU AND KIN

Caribou is the American name for the member of the deer family known in the Old World as the reindeer. Beyond the northern boundary of the United States, caribou are found in most of the Canadian Provinces, in Alaska, and on nearly all the larger arctic islands. At one time there was a considerable number of them in New Brunswick, in Maine, along the northern shore of Lake Superior, in Minnesota, and in the more northern Rocky Mountain States; but the ease with which these animals are killed, and the recent occupation of their more southeasterly range by moose and white-tailed deer, have almost eliminated them from those areas.

Scientists have described a number of so-called species of caribou in different parts of northern North America; but from

YOUNGSTERS AND FEMALES BEGIN THE FALL MIGRATION

These two yearlings were photographed while crossing the lake. A small band of does and fawns was landing on the opposite shore.

the information now available it seems probable that eventually it will be proved that there exists on this continent only one species, which has been modified by environment into numerous geographic races, or subspecies.

One of these is the caribou that occurs in Newfoundland. The term "Woodland Caribou" is loosely applied to the animals that live in the forested regions of the northern United States and Canada to distinguish them from those called Barren Ground Caribou that inhabit the treeless Arctic tundras of the North. No definite boundary can be found between the two forms.

CARIBOU VARY WIDELY IN SIZE

Caribou vary in size in different regions. Those found in Newfoundland belong to one of the larger races. The stags weigh from 200 to more than 300 pounds; the does are much lighter. The antlers of the stags are large and widely spread, making handsome trophies. These animals, however, are smaller than the great caribou of the northern Rocky Mountains of British Columbia, and have smaller antlers. The caribou is the only member of the deer family in North America in which the does grow antlers, but these are very small and slender compared with those of the stag.

Newfoundland caribou live almost continuously in open country, over which their trails extend in all directions. In summer, when bothered by flies, they hunt the seclusion of arboreal thickets during the day and come into the open only at night. When not driven to cover by insects, they feed mainly on reindeer "moss" and other plant growth of the open tundras. On several occasions in the fall I saw caribou bed down there at nightfall and found them in the same places in the early morning.

Those who know the Newfoundland caribou only in the fall hunting season may gain the impression that they are always gregarious, since at that time most of them move south in herds of various sizes, sometimes numbering 100 or more, and on the winter feeding grounds they are often massed, not unlike elk. After the spring migration the herds separate, and the caribou may be found singly or in little family parties.

HOWEVER SLOWLY HE SWIMS IN OPEN WATER, HE GOES ASHORE FAST

At the approach of the author's canoe, this caribou made for land with frantic speed (see, also, illustration, page 4).

On several nights I skirted the shore of the lake at the Little Deer Lake camp, hoping to get flashlight pictures of the animals, which I knew were nearby in considerable numbers, but I encountered not a single one. This failure to feed at night appears in strong contrast to the habits of other deer which feed so commonly at night, especially on aquatic plants on the shores of lakes.

Bot flies are terrible pests to Newfoundland caribou in summer. Apparently two species of these insects attack them, one filling the skin of the back with grubs, which perforate it, and the young of the other infesting the animals' throats.

So far as I could learn, the main rutting season of the caribou on the island occurs between October 1 and 25; the single fawn is born in June, eight months later.

MIGRATION OF CARIBOU

The seasonal migration of caribou almost throughout the American range of this animal is more marked than that of any other game animal. These migrations occur independently in different regions, some of them involving the movements of hundreds of thousands of animals. Al-though the area traversed in Newfoundland is much more circumscribed than that in some of the continental regions, and although the seasonal differences in temperature there are unusually limited, the migration is pronounced.

THEY THRIVE IN RIGOROUS CLIMATE

The equable climate and moist winds from the surrounding ocean produce a good growth of varied vegetation, including conifers, willow, birch, poplar, mosses, lichens, grasses, and many herbs and aquatic plants. The subarctic climate and prevalence of boggy country seem especially suitable for caribou; and it is doubtful that any other members of the deer family would thrive there, except possibly the moose, in the southern half of the island. There, however, the dampness of the climate might prove a serious obstacle to their welfare.

One day in September we saw a well-antlered doe and her fawn swimming diagonally across Sandy Lake on their migration. We paddled swiftly to head them off before they landed. As the canoe sped along, the two did not change their course, but continued straight ahead. They would necessarily have to pass directly in front of our craft.

When we were within a hundred feet of them, the fawn became restless and finally rose half out of water and struck the mother's flank with its front feet. Thereupon the doe half turned her head and then redoubled her speed.

When we were close enough to take a picture, we saw that the right eye of the doe had been destroyed. Doubtless this injury had been caused by the thrust of a dead branch.

On reaching the shore the doe easily jumped over the sagging trunk of a mountain ash, which had been pulled down by bears feeding on the berries; but when her offspring attempted the same feat, it hung partly suspended for several minutes.

A MOTHER CARIBOU DESERTS HER FAWN

Meanwhile the mother continued on her way and disappeared in the forest, apparently indifferent to the plight of her young. On regaining its footing and finding itself deserted, the fawn returned to the lake shore, where it was seen wandering about aimlessly for several days.

When a white-tailed doe is separated from her young, she will circle again and again until she finds the fawn. This apparent indifference of the caribou doe may account partly for the scarcity of fawns in Newfoundland.

At one time timber wolves were a menace to the caribou in Newfoundland; for on such an island there was no escape from these persistent pursuers, either in summer or winter. A large bounty having been placed on them, the trappers soon reduced their numbers, and at the date of my visit they were supposed to be extinct. A nature fictionist, who was salmon fishing in Newfoundland about the time I was there, devoted much space to describing his adventures with the wolves on the island, some of which he declared he had followed day after day.

These animals are known to be almost wholly nocturnal. My guide, Squires, told me that no bounty had been paid for scalps in 15 years, and that during his guiding and trapping in the interior, where he lived throughout the year, he had seen no wolf tracks for many years, and believed the last one had been trapped or poisoned.

On the other hand, silver-gray, black, cross, and red foxes were frequently seen in the daytime, following the shore in search of sticklebacks cast up by the waves. After the wolves had been exterminated, poisoning was prohibited in the taking of other fur-bearing animals, for it had long been recognized that a large percentage of the poisoned animals were never found. To this wise law may be credited the abundance of foxes.

Once, when seated on a knoll back from Little Deer Lake, hoping that a caribou would pass on the trail just below, I observed four silver-gray foxes feeding on blueberries at the foot of the slope. Although my companion had a rifle, we left these beautiful animals undisturbed in the hope that one or more might come within photographic distance.

Finally three of them departed for their burrow, but we knocked over the fourth with a rifle ball as it started to leave, and later presented its handsome pelt to the Biological Survey in Washington. The following day I saw a fox on the beach, and by hiding behind a rock obtained its picture.

On a stream not far from camp was a large beaver house with a dam just below it. While I was trying for a picture of these wily animals, Squires told me of his own original method of taking many beavers. On the opening of the season he would secrete himself close to a beaver house and, after waiting a few minutes, would lean forward in the bushes and strike a resounding blow on the surface of the water with a paddle, exactly duplicating the sound made by a beaver's tail when the animal used it to signal alarm.

BEAVERS MORE ALARMED BY TRAPPING THAN SHOOTING

After a few minutes of silence up would come the head of an inquiring member of the resident beaver family intent on driving away any intruding beaver. These animals do not cultivate friendship among their neighbors. A shot through the head would instantly kill the curious animal. After its body had been recovered, the performance would be repeated until sometimes four or five would be killed at the same place in the course of a few hours.

Squires explained that beavers are not frightened by rifle shots in the vicinity of their lodge. When one is trapped, however, its death struggles in the water may alarm the remaining members of the family

LITTLE DEER LAKE, SANDY RIVER DISTRICT, NEWFOUNDLAND, IS TYPICAL

Here and at Sandy Lake the author had opportunity on his second trip to study the habits of caribou in swimming such bodies of water lying across the course of their migration.

SUNLIGHT MAKES A GOLDEN PATH ACROSS THE LOWER END OF SANDY LAKE

The stony ridge shown in the background was a much used route for migrating caribou, which crossed the river at the outlet of the lake. The set camera, placed on the animals' trail on the ridge, caught several pictures.

to such an extent that they may permanently desert the house.

Once we saw a bear working in and out of the bushes along the shore of Sandy Lake and heading toward the trail leading from our tent to the water's edge. Leaving the guide to watch, with instructions to whistle whenever the bear came near, I retired to continue an interrupted luncheon.

In a short time I heard a low whistle and hurried out, only to find that I had been deceived by the call of a Canada jay. Again I retired from view.

TRICKED ONCE BY A JAY, THE AUTHOR MISSES A BLACK BEAR PICTURE

Within a few minutes the whistle sounded several times. I attributed it to the bird and ignored it for some time; then peeping out of the tent, I saw the guide crawling along the trail, waving his arms excitedly. Running down to the shore, I came upon the bear where it was sniffing at the canoe. I was so close that he dashed into the bushes and escaped a shot from the camera, evidently believing that the usual bullet was in store for him. The bear had come out of the brush only about 100 feet away, and the guide had whistled repeatedly as instructed without receiving any response on my part.

The disappointing experience recalled to my mind several others I had had with the mischievous Canada jay. But there are many difficulties in camera hunting not occasioned by such deceptions.

Once, in the western United States, I found the carcass of a buck that had been killed and partly eaten by wolves on the shore of a small lake. As I paddled back down the lake some time later, I saw a large black bear feasting on the remains, its head and shoulders showing plainly above the antlers of the deer. It was a remarkably fine opportunity for a picture and I drew the slide and made a hasty focus and exposure.

Quick as I was, however, the bear was quicker. It sensed the approach of danger and scuttled for cover.

The picture, unfortunately, recorded only a view of the animal's broad posterior as it disappeared in the bushes. Every wild-life photographer sooner or later has such exasperating disappointments; but if success were always assured, the sport of hunting with the camera would lose much of the appeal of its uncertainty.

THE CAMERA CAUGHT A BLACK REYNARD

Red foxes were common about Sandy Lake, and black and cross varieties appeared repeatedly (see text, page 7).

Passing much of the time on or near the water, we had a chance to see the Canada geese that, in family groups, visited the neighboring hillsides for blueberries, which at that time of year seemed to be their mainstay. Because of the moist climate of this region, great clusters of berries remain on the bushes until October, at which time the hunters dig them out of the snow for camp use.

ANIMALS ENJOY BLUEBERRIES

These berries, the toothsome morsels enjoyed particularly by black bears, are sought eagerly by many wild creatures. In Alaska native eskimos preserve in seal oil large quantities of a similar wild fruit, the huckleberry, which grows in profusion on hillsides and in mountain valleys near the coast.

Earlier in the season, when the adult geese were moulting, it was the custom of the natives to drive them ashore, where they were easily captured. I observed a number of such captives about cabins, where they were fattened for a Christmas feast or for selling as live decoys to the wildfowler from the States.

MIGRATING CARIBOU SWIM SANDY LAKE, NEWFOUNDLAND

Because of their heavy coat of long, tubular hairs, they ride high in the water, but not so fast as either moose or white-tailed deer. In the water they carry their tails erect.

MIGRATING CARIBOU FOLLOW A SET SCHEDULE

Young and old, singly or in squads, the animals travel between 9 a. m. and 4 p. m. In order to detect danger ahead, they move against the wind (see text, page 13).

CHAPTER I — PART II

Second Newfoundland Trip

AS MENTIONED in the account of my trip in 1906, I passed pleasant weeks with congenial companions, fishing, canoeing, and camping on the interior lakes and rivers of Newfoundland.

It was not until the latter part of September, 1907, however, that I made a special trip to that island to study the caribou, and particularly to obtain photographs of them as they were crossing several lakes on their route when migrating.

CAMP ON A CARIBOU MIGRATION TRAIL

Accompanied only by a native guide, William Squires, who had been with me on my previous visit to Newfoundland, I traveled by canoe up Sandy River to Little Deer and Sandy Lakes. Our camp was located at the outlet of Little Deer Lake, which, with Sandy Lake, formed an east-to-west base line of more than nine miles across the southerly line of migration.

Here, on the day following our arrival, a fine stag, an antlered doe, and a fawn plunged into the water, and, looking neither to the right nor the left, began their long swim across the lake. In a few minutes our canoe was by their side. Raising their heads, previously held close to the water, they made a gallant effort to outstrip us, their stubby white tails held erect like flags of truce. After photographing them, we permitted them to continue their travels.

While studying the caribou in this locality, I was surprised to note the small number of fawns, compared to the adult does, as disclosed by my own close observations and those of several others. My records of more than 300 does show an average of only one fawn to four does.

This condition is in striking contrast to the case of the moose and the deer in other regions, which, though they usually have two young each, are more or less harassed by the timber wolf and cougar. In Newfoundland man is the sole enemy of the caribou, for the wolves, once numerous, were extinct at the time of my visit.

This proportion of caribou fawns held true under a great variety of circumstances. Three does out of every four were barren. In a group of four does there would be only one fawn or none; in one band of 16 does

crossing the lake in single file, I counted only four fawns, and in larger herds the young were equally scarce. While this may be due to the extremely damp and rigorous weather in the spring when the fawns are born, or to the peculiar habit of single stags of rounding up great herds of does each fall, the fact seemed to be that the Newfoundland caribou fawns are far below the average of the young of other antlered game on this continent.

It may be, however, that during migration females with young fawns prefer to make a detour about the lakes instead of swimming across them, and thus where we located, barren does, yearlings, and stags were more likely to be seen. Moreover, the fact that many does migrate to the southern end of the island a month in advance of the rest necessarily curtails the opportunity for mating.

If my inferences are correct, the great necessity for proper game laws on this island is obvious, for once these great herds of caribou become greatly reduced in numbers, the process of restoration will be extremely slow.

SWIMMING SPEED OF CARIBOU

Another matter upon which I may express an opinion, although it differs from statements made by F. C. Selous and other well-known sportsmen who have hunted on this island, concerns the supposedly great speed of caribou in swimming. When undisturbed, a single caribou crossing a large lake makes about three miles an hour, and a fair-sized herd is somewhat slower.

When first sighting a pursuing canoe, the animal springs half out of the water, and then, with head erect, tries to distance the paddlers. For the first one hundred yards its speed varies between five and six miles an hour; then, the caribou becoming somewhat exhausted by the extreme exertion, slows down to about three and one-half miles an hour—a rate that a single paddler in a loaded canoe has no trouble in exceeding. The swimming speed of this animal, as I have observed it in the wilds on many occasions, is below that of the moose and the white-tailed deer.

A STAG, A HORNED DOE, AND A FAWN SWIM SANDY LAKE

About one in two or three female caribou in Newfoundland have antlers. These animals were so strictly diurnal in habits that they did not give any opportunity for flashlight pictures.

IN UNION THERE IS STRENGTH

Caribou in groups usually swim compactly; the suction helps those in the rear. It must not be supposed, however, that such close companionship is the rule with these animals on land.

THIS CARIBOU STAG HAS FINE ANTLERS

Swimming high, as is the custom of his species, he keeps them out of the water.

I saw no caribou enter the water before 7 o'clock in the morning, or later than 5 in the afternoon; the migration was at its height between 10 a. m. and 3 p. m. These animals, as a rule, are not nocturnal, either when migrating or when feeding, although during the fly season they feed at night, and late in the fall under the stress of heavy snowstorms they sometimes travel night and day.

CARIBOU DIFFER FROM DEER IN HABITS

In color the caribou so closely resembled the water as they swam the lakes under dull autumnal skies that the heads and bodies were not visible at a great distance, the gleaming white of their stiffly upright tails often appearing at first glance like a little flock of gulls. Unlike the other members of the deer family with which I am familiar, caribou, when they come to a body of water on their travels, sometimes burst through the bordering bushes and plunge into the water with a splash so great that it may be seen more than a mile away.

It is characteristic of Newfoundland caribou to depend on scent rather than on sight or hearing to detect danger. Because of this, during the fall migration they nearly always move south against a south wind. Generations of experience have taught them that they can discover and avoid any danger that may threaten them up the wind when they follow this course, whether the danger be from the dreaded wolves that were once numerous or from the hundreds of hunters who lie concealed along the trans-island railway or in the passageways between numerous lakes.

Most of these hunters are islanders out to lay in a supply of much needed winter meat, but others, often from the United States, are after the prized antlers of big bulls for trophies. The caribou, being headed up the wind, the telltale scent of an enemy can be detected at a long distance, but without such aid the animals may pass within a few yards of a man who is only slightly concealed.

It is this dependence upon scent that impelled the migrating animals to persist along their up-the-wind course even when headed off by a pursuer in a canoe when they were crossing water. They would try to pass the boat on one side or the other, or would coast along shore until they could get back again on the course. Their persistence in this was greater than I have ever seen exhibited elsewhere by man or beast.

A NEWFOUNDLAND COW CARIBOU PHOTOGRAPHS HERSELF WITH HER CALF

The camera was set with a string crossing the trail used by these animals in their fall migration. It was here that the French trappers sprang the apparatus and thought it was a set gun (see text, page 17).

Newfoundland is visited each fall by numerous nonresident sportsmen in quest of stags with fine heads, and it is difficult to estimate the amount of meat abandoned each year on account of the remote location or because of the rankness of the flesh of the stag.

On my second trip to the island, I met three young collegians from the "States," who several days previously, on the barrens east of Grand Lake, had encountered a number of migrating caribou, and by good judgment and accurate shooting had, in a single day, picked out and killed nine large caribou stags—the three apiece allowed by law. They candidly admitted that, owing to the toughness of the flesh of the stags and the distance from their camp, they had abandoned every ounce of the flesh, aside from the heads, thus wasting a total of more than 3,500 pounds.

Yet these young men had come thousands of miles for caribou hunting and were in every respect a manly set of fellows. After seeing some of my caribou pictures and hearing incidents connected with the obtaining of them, they seemed to realize that big-game hunting with the camera is an ideal method and one that they hoped to try thereafter.

HUNTERS LEAVE LARGE QUANTITIES OF FLESH TO ROT

As with the caribou stags, so it is with bull moose, bull elk, and gigantic grizzly bears. Year after year their decaying flesh is left to pollute the air of some beautiful valley, simply because the antlers or the hide was all that could be saved when these great animals were stricken in their remote haunts.

While I was at Little Deer Lake on this trip, a weasel in its brown summer coat came almost daily to the camp, looking furtively about, and carrying off scraps of meat. The day following the first snowfall a weasel of the same size appeared in a dainty white coat. This indicated an extraordinarily rapid change of color, if it was the same animal.

A passing Indian trapper declared a weasel can change its color overnight. His accuracy is doubtful, for these seasonal changes are known to be gradual and due to a moult. The process may be hastened, however, by favorable weather.

PROTECTIVE COLOR PROBLEM DIFFICULT

The theory of concealing and revealing coloration has always been controversial, extremists on either side falling into error through an insufficient understanding of a complicated problem. Unquestionably, color and shape often become important factors for defense or offense.

In the north the seasonal color changes of the varying hare, certain species of lemming, the weasel, and the willow and the rock ptarmigans seem to be of a purely protective character, the dark colors suiting the summer and the white the winter season. In accord with its usual surroundings of snow and ice, the polar bear remains white throughout the year.

The chameleon and certain tree frogs and fishes afford good examples of color control to blend in harmony with their surroundings, this faculty being useful in capturing their prey and in avoiding their foes. In the temperate regions of America most of the large game animals are not protectively colored, possibly because their original foes were the wolf and the puma, the former hunting by scent and the latter by dropping on its victim from an elevated vantage point or by other catlike methods.

The invention of the gun has been too recent for nature to provide its victim animals with anything of a protective character. Many animals and game birds, however, have changed their habits to meet new conditions. The wild fowl now often feed at night; the ruffed grouse seldom sit rigidly in a tree on the approach of the hunter, but take flight; and the bears, wolves, foxes, and antlered game avoid the daylight hours or feed in the seclusion of forests and swamps.

The caribou of Newfoundland are visible for miles in the open, and have neither a sensitive ear nor a discriminating eye. As has been indicated, they depend upon scent to detect man or wolves, which once roamed the island in large numbers.

From the viewpoint of the big-game hunter, caribou are stupid animals, and until they have learned to depend upon vision they cannot be expected to thwart the gunner. Their security now lies mainly in their occupying the remote and wilder portions of the country, their chief peril arising during the southern migration. Most of the larger stags no longer migrate, preferring safety to a change of scenery or surroundings. The trophy hunter must seek them in their remote recesses if he desires to obtain an exceptionally fine head.

When the limited range and the mildness of the winter climate throughout Newfoundland are considered, the instinctive habit of the caribou to migrate each spring and fall does not seem justified, unless it is necessary on account of food. With a diminution in their numbers, these animals may eventually avoid the perils of such seasonal movements by remaining throughout the year in secluded areas.

As noted previously, such a cessation in migration occurred in 1885 in the case of the white-tailed deer along the southern shore of Lake Superior.

NO FLASHLIGHTING OF CARIBOU

On most of my trips after pictures of animals, big or little, I had come to rely largely on the flashlight as a necessary adjunct when paddling about in a canoe at night or when using the set camera in places frequented by prowling animals after dark. This made available most of the 24 hours and thus greatly enlarged the opportunities.

Except during the fly season, the caribou, unlike the rest of the deer family, are diurnal, rarely moving about at night even to feed. Consequently, my flashlight apparatus could not be utilized in this northern region.

During this second visit the sun was low on the horizon even at midday, and there were only about six hours of light sufficient for photographing rapidly moving animals. Time, therefore, often hung heavily on my hands. Night excursions on placid waters, beneath twinkling stars, and amid shifting shadows of the bordering forests had always been entrancing, regardless of luck with the camera, and I greatly missed them.

Though I felt rather positive from previous observations that caribou do not migrate across the lakes at night, I deter-

THE CAMERA WAS SET FOR CARIBOU

At this spot several excellent pictures were obtained (see, also, illustration, page 14). The migrating
animals took their own photographs by touching a string stretched across their trail.

A NEWFOUNDLAND WEASEL IS A WARY FELLOW

These quickly moving little animals are difficult to photograph by day. The author encountered
an Indian trapper, who said they can change color overnight (see text, page 15).

mined this to my own satisfaction by obliterating each evening all tracks of animals that had come ashore in the day. The following morning I never found any fresh tracks.

Being thus satisfied that there was no chance for flashlight pictures, I set out a daylight automatic camera on a long, stony ridge that formed the southern boundary of Sandy Lake, where a well-used caribou trail offered prospect of success.

TRAPPERS TRAPPED

Any opportunity to obtain a photograph the first day was spoiled by two French trappers who walked into the string connected with the concealed camera. On their return to our camp that night they related their misadventure. It appeared that they had sprung the automatic camera as they traveled along the trail.

The pressure of the string and the click of the metal shutter had suggested to them a set gun that had fortunately missed fire. Terrified, they had fled precipitately, with the string entwined about their legs. On returning to investigate, they had discovered the cause of their alarm.

Such an incident seemed to indicate that these swarthy trappers were entirely familiar with the use of the set gun, a reprehensible method that has been practically outlawed in all countries, it being regarded as equally dangerous to man and beast.

The following day I was rewarded with a good picture of a doe and a fawn traveling the runway. Their heads were lowered and they were sniffing the ground, a circumstance that suggested that they had perceived a trace of human scent in the vicinity of the camera.

On the next day, when the sky was overcast, the camera was sprung by a caribou, so dark in color by reason of insufficient light, that it resembled a domestic cow. It was difficult to determine from the antlers whether it was a young stag or an old doe.

The next day we moved our camp, but not before it had been satisfactorily determined that the set camera could be used in the daytime for obtaining pictures of caribou migrating on some of the many trails to supplement those of the swimming caribou that had so largely engaged my attention.

One of the special objects of my second trip to Newfoundland was to obtain photographs of the herds of great antlered stags as they brought up the rear of the fall migration. For some days late in October, as the time for my necessary departure approached, we looked for a snowstorm that would start the big fellows on their way south. The continuation of moderate weather was discouraging, and with only two days left before taking the steamer from the island my chances of seeing a migration of large stags seemed slight.

A heavy snowstorm, however, began at noon on the next to the last day of my stay, and Squires prophesied that the next day I would use my last plate. He felt certain that the caribou would come through by the hundreds.

On the following morning I arose expectantly and dug out a trail to the lake shore, where I sat all day without seeing a single caribou. Since the snow was nearly two feet deep, my guide expressed the opinion that with all the runways obliterated, the animals were probably delayed in opening up the trails they had followed for centuries.

REASON FOR THE HALTED MIGRATION

His conclusion seemed reasonable, except that a north wind was blowing at the time, and I felt certain that these caribou migrate in fall only against a south wind. That the direction of the wind had halted the migration appeared to be the real explanation; for the next morning the wind came again from the south, and while we were breaking camp and loading the canoe in a heavy rain we saw the moving caribou crowding the opposite shore.

The fixed date of my departure and the heavy rain argued against any change in plans. I have ever since regretted this decision.

During the several hours required to go down the river I saw more caribou than the total number observed previously on this and my former trip. The heavy rain rendered successful use of the camera impossible, and it was most provoking to see dozens of caribou swimming within a few yards of our canoe.

At one point on the river we noticed smoke curling up in front of a small tent. Going ashore, I was pleased to find my old friend, A. Radcliffe Dugmore, who even at that time stood in the fore front of wildlife photographers. His mission was the same as mine had been, and I assured him that he had come at exactly the right time. With this he agreed, adding that for several

SHE FOUND A SAFE HAVEN

This doe caribou is going ashore at Little Deer Lake. The photograph shows a typical wooded belt bordering the water in northern Newfoundland. It was taken after a late September storm when the snow quickly disappeared.

hours hundreds of caribou had been crossing the river in sight of his camp, and that he was ready to begin the bombardment the next morning should the rain cease.

When I met him several months later, he spoke of his trying experiences. In an effort to use a motion-picture camera and a still-life one from the same blind he had suffered "buck fever," so that his results had proved unsatisfactory. He said he was going back the following year with the expectation of doing better.

That trip he made just before going to Africa, and obtained a series of caribou pictures surpassing any ever taken before. His successful endeavors are recorded in a volume entitled "The Romance of the Newfoundland Caribou," the text of which is as informative, as the pictures are accurate and beautiful.

At the railroad track I met a Boston sportsman preparing to start up the river. He asked if I had obtained any good heads, and I answered in the affirmative. Thereupon he looked in the canoe but saw no evidence of any such success.

Knowing what was passing in his mind, I explained, with some hesitation, that I had been photographing, not shooting, caribou. Upon hearing this, he called me by name, and when asked how he knew it, replied, "Why, you are the only darned cuss who would come so far for game pictures." Then, apologizing for such a greeting, he added that he also had a camera and would prefer to bring back pictures rather than heads and hides.

THE WHISKEY-JACK

For the caribou hunter, who often spends much time searching through binoculars for the roaming game, one diversion is observing the Canada jay, sometimes called camp-robber, meat-bird, or whiskey-jack. In color, shape, and habits it often reminds me of the Florida jay. It is bold and extremely tame, sometimes eating from one's hand on first acquaintance. Nevertheless, it prefers the wilderness, away from the permanent habitations of man.

No sooner is the hunter's tent erected in the haunts of these birds than one appears, followed soon by others. In Newfoundland

THE AUTHOR SNOW-CAUGHT IN CAMP AT LITTLE DEER LAKE, NEWFOUNDLAND

The first snowfall of the season caught the party late in October and started the main migration of caribou stags, which occurs later than that of the does and fawns. The tent to the left was the temporary quarters of two French trappers.

I took pictures of the Canada jays as they perched on the camp tables or on top of the tent, and of one as it was lifting a piece of venison from a sizzling frying pan. A special eating place consisting of a tin plate on the end of a box by the camp kitchen was provided for these birds. The plate had to be replenished frequently (see page 21).

A saddle of caribou proved to be a great attraction for a pair of jays and their three young, which kept busily at work filling their bills with suet and concealing it in crevices in the bark of trees for a winter cache. In later years I renewed my acquaintance with these entertaining camp companions in the Rockies and in parts of Alaska.

Both in Alaska and in Newfoundland trappers told me that the Canada jay nests in February. Although their nests are warmly lined, continuous incubation of the eggs and brooding of the nestlings until they are well feathered are necessary. Just why these birds should select for nesting zero weather when the food supply must be greatly restricted, is one of many difficult problems of bird life.

When we reached the railroad crossing, the rain had nearly ceased, and preparations were made to put up our tent for the night, for the train to Port-aux-Basques did not arrive until morning. This tent, of heavy coarse canvas, was thoroughly saturated inside and out, having been used for covering the outfit on the run down the river, and the ground near the railroad embankment was soft and muddy.

Squires suggested that we continue a mile down the river to the place where it entered Grand Lake, at which point there was a large and comfortable log cabin we could occupy, and return after daybreak in time for the train.

DEMOCRACY OF AMERICAN SPORTSMEN

On reaching the cabin we found a tent alongside it occupied by two guides, and within the cabin a titled Austrian sportsman. He greeted me pleasantly and invited me to share the cabin, which was owned by a hotel company for the use of its guests. My guide, he said, could put up the tent for his own use.

This large cabin had comfortable accom-

A CANADA JAY APPROPRIATES A HAUNCH OF VENISON

In the north country of Newfoundland the "whiskey-jack," or camp robber, makes himself free in almost every woodland camp. He is an arrant freebooter, and his confident and tricky ways cause amusement and sometimes exasperation. In the photograph above one has taken possession of a haunch of venison hung at the end of the tent.

I might add that when the exclusive scion of the Old World ascended the river the next day he was watched by a local warden, and was caught shooting a large caribou stag within the five-mile protected area north of the track. As a result, his trophy was confiscated and later he was heavily fined, much to the gratification of my guide.

Because of the class distinction so generally prevailing abroad, this happening was, of course, understandable, however much it was out of place in the American wilderness. In other respects I have no doubt this particular individual was a man of attractive parts, and intended no offense by his actions.

SOME NEWFOUNDLAND BIRDS

On my trips to the Island I was disappointed at seeing so few birds in the interior, where conditions seem not to be favorable for the support of many species. I saw a few ravens, thrushes, sparrows, nuthatches, northern horned larks, pipits, ptarmigans, and a superabundance of Canada jays. The only water birds noticed were herring gulls, two pairs of American mergansers, and a large number of Canada geese. Doubtless I missed other birds on account of my confinement in limited areas when watching for migrating caribou.

This island is too far isolated in the northeast to invite transient visitors on their flights to and from the easterly Canadian provinces, which, aside from barren Labrador, are the nesting grounds of a great variety of wild fowl. Many migrate each fall in a southeasterly direction so as

modations for half a dozen or more persons, and included two large bunks for guides. Since we had come down the river to avoid putting up the tent on wet ground, the Austrian's suggestion irritated me. When I informed Squires of the situation, he flushed with anger, and I saw a gleam in his eyes that showed his deep resentment.

Turning to the Austrian, I said that we would return to the track. Since my guide and I had occupied the tent together during the previous two weeks, I did not wish to accept his limited invitation. In a few minutes we were again in the canoe and reached the track a little before dark.

CANADA JAYS APPRECIATED AN ALL-DAY CAFETERIA

At one of the camps in Newfoundland the whiskey-jacks so persistently hunted food that the author provided a table for their special delectation as shown above. It was well patronized (see text, page 19).

to reach the Atlantic coast at Nova Scotia, or much farther to the southward, where shallow waters and protected bays afford satisfactory fall and winter quarters.

The situation is entirely different about the rugged shores and indentations of Newfoundland, where there are to be found many of the most interesting of the northern sea birds. These nest in the vicinity or may be seen fishing up and down the coast. Among the tidewater birds are auks, murres, puffins, jaegers, gannets, shearwaters, dovekies, fulmers, petrels, and gulls.

On my journeys across the Gulf of St. Lawrence to Newfoundland I saw many sea ducks, including eiders, three varieties of scoters, and a few harlequins. The Labrador duck, like the great Auk, has been extinct for many years, the last specimen having been taken in 1878.

A number of the above sea birds go long distances down the Atlantic coast in midwinter, where they may be seen fishing several miles from offshore. The large white gannets, for instance, I saw each winter off the eastern coast of Florida where, high aloft, with half closed wings, they plunged into the turbulent waters after their prey. These gannets are the largest as well as the most northerly species of the Booby family, one of the more southerly of which, called the white-bellied booby, I describe hereafter in an account of a voyage to the Bahama Islands in 1907.

WILD GEESE IN NOVA SCOTIA

In the fall most of the Canada and other geese headed for the eastern seaboard to winter in the Virginia and Carolina waters, stop often en route in bays and ponds along the coast of Massachusetts or that of Long Island, the severity of the winter governing the choice. It will, therefore, be a surprise to many to learn that tens of thousands of geese winter in Nova Scotia waters.

On my several trips through Nova Scotia on my way to Newfoundland I admired the beautiful open country, the farms, lakes, and high ridges in this islandlike province which, although 375 miles long, is attached by a narrow isthmus of 11 miles to the eastern coast of New Brunswick. Its coast line is of a most varied and extraordinary

A DENIZEN OF THE NORTH WOODS SHOWS SCANT FEAR OF MAN

The Canada jay, living in the coniferous forests on the fringe or beyond the limits of civilization, is remarkably tame and bold. Despite an enormous capacity for food, he sometimes gets enough, and then stores his surplus in tree crevices. This reserve supply may enable him to sustain his young in early spring before good foraging is possible.

character, for on the west lies the Bay of Fundy, with an average tide of 45 feet, which surges against 125 miles of cliffs.

There are many deep and safe harbors, and a large number of shallow bays where large beds of eel grass provide an abundant supply of winter food for the geese, this being particularly true of Port Joli, and Port le Herbert, where the shoal waters prevent shipping activities.

FUNDY TIDES OFTEN AID THE GEESE

The tides, when the weather is unusually cold, sweep out the thin ice at intervals and give the geese a chance to get at the eel grass. Experienced hunters estimate the number of geese wintering in Nova Scotia as between 50,000 and 75,000, although these figures have often been much exceeded by uninformed persons making exaggerated statements.

The presence of so many geese during the winter in these northern waters only proves once more that the migration of birds south each fall is not entirely for the purpose of escaping cold weather, but because such weather destroys and puts beyond reach their customary supply of food.

Along streams in the Rocky Mountains, that are kept open by hot geyser springs or swift currents north to Alaska, may be seen mallard ducks. They are indifferent to the weather so long as they find green vegetation or other food.

CHAPTER II

The Wilderness of New Brunswick

THE Province of New Brunswick is within less than a day's travel from the great metropolitan cities of Boston, Philadelphia, and New York. Whoever leaves these busy marts for New Brunswick is amazed to discover a region so isolated by large forests, hills, valleys, lakes, rivers, and sea. Save in the fastnesses of the Rockies, few places can be found so unchanged by man as the wilder tracts in the northwestern part of the Province.

In July, 1907, I passed an enjoyable time in New Brunswick hunting moose and deer with the camera and flashlight. Although I had traveled through this famous game country a number of times while en route to Newfoundland, my plans on no previous trip had permitted a visit into its wilds.

AFTER MOOSE AND DEER WITH THE CAMERA IN NEW BRUNSWICK

Leaving the railroad at Plaster Rock, in company with Adam Moore, the famous guide, trapper, and philosopher of these woods, I ascended the Tobique River 70 miles to its headwaters, Nictau Lake. Heavy and almost continuous rains during the previous month had kept the banks of the stream full, or as Moore expressed it, at a "logging stage"—a most unusual condition for a midsummer month.

The Upper Tobique is peculiar in that it has no rapids, no falls, and no slack waters, excepting an occasional salmon pool, for some 60 miles; yet it is one of the swiftest streams I have ever attempted to paddle. I say attempted, for the grand rush of the current, combined with the unusually high stage of water, made the bow paddle virtually useless.

All our motive power was concentrated in a ten-foot pole shod with steel, which the giant Moore, standing erect in the stern of the canoe, wielded with an expertness and strength that slowly but surely overcame a current against which paddlers would have been helpless. Except when we made a sudden dash from one bank to the other to avoid stretches of water too deep for the shoving pole, no paddles were used during the three days required to ascend the stream.

Admiring Moore's deftness, I inquired whether he had ever fallen overboard.

"No," he replied, "but then you can never tell when such a thing will happen."

A few minutes afterward the bow of the canoe suddenly lowered and I heard a splash behind. Turning around, I saw Moore coming to the surface, holding his watch high in his hand, an indication of his alertness in a sudden emergency. In the abnormally high waters his pole had failed to reach the bottom, and he had headed into the stream to avoid capsizing the canoe, a catastrophe a novice could not have averted.

When, pausing for luncheon on a forest-bordered beach that showed many tracks of moose and deer, we opened a can of salmon, and I remarked, "Perhaps this very fish once swam the Tobique during the spawning season." Unlike the salmon of the Pacific coast, which die after spawning, those of the Atlantic return year after year to the same streams.

Tossing me the empty can, Moore said, "You will see by the label that you have missed your guess by thousands of miles. This was canned in southeastern Alaska."

Such "bringing coals to Newcastle" is explained by the known scarcity of the eastern salmon as compared with its western relatives.

AN AGED FOREST OF BIRCH

Extending for a mile or so along the left bank of the Tobique at one point was a magnificent forest of white birch, many of the trees about two feet in diameter. I remarked to Moore that I had never before seen a native forest of white birch, having always believed them to be second-growth trees. He replied that the stand we were viewing had sprung up after the great fire of 1825, at which time a large portion of the country was devastated and many hundreds of lives were lost. He added that the trees had passed maturity and were beginning to topple from the onslaught of heavy winds.

Much might be written about the beautiful scenery, the moose and deer crossing the river ahead of us beyond range of the camera, the slow contest with the current, and the attractiveness of the camp each night and the appetizing supper of trout that had enjoyed life in this spring-fed stream until

A FAMOUS GUIDE WAS A DOUBTING THOMAS

During the author's trip to New Brunswick he was fortunate to have Adam Moore as his guide. Moore was widely known for his unusual ability and for the effectiveness of his services. At first skeptical about the photographing program, he became intensely interested in the sport.

We soon reached Moore's cabin, at the lower end of the lake, in a secluded corner that afforded a view of the entire lake. Here, on a well-cleared bank, with a more or less continuous smudge, we were able to fight the sand flies, black flies, and mosquitoes and yet be in a position to enter the canoe in a moment should a moose appear.

IT RAINED MOOSE

The day following our arrival was dark, warm, and wet; and it fairly rained moose. The animals' utter disregard of dampness was evident, for they waded out into the deeper parts of the lake, into which they would sink entirely out of sight, in their search for the roots of aquatic plants. So dark colored are moose and so swift their movements when they are pursued by a person in a canoe, that I refrained from attempting to photograph them under such unfavorable conditions.

the blazing campfire told me it was time to cast a fly into its clear waters.

As we entered the narrow creek connecting Lower and Upper Nictau Lakes, Moore, carefully scanning the stream, remarked, "There were plenty of moose in the water today."

MOORE SEES HAIRS ON THE WATER

Although I had hunted moose for many years, I had not noted any disturbance in the muddy bottom or any tracks upon the bank. I had failed to observe floating here and there upon the current numerous gray-brown hairs shed by the moose as they fed on the aquatic plants in the adjoining lake.

The days that followed were more propitious, although showers fell occasionally. Several times a day we paddled silently along the dark-fringed shores until close enough to a feeding animal to overtake it by rapid paddling after it had finally discovered us.

Like all the deer family, the moose has a poor and undiscriminating eye, and depends for protection upon its keen nose and ears; therefore, frequently when the animal has its head submerged, it is not difficult for a person to approach it in a canoe. In the succeeding five days I obtained a dozen or more photographs by taking advantage of this fact (see pages 28, 30, 32).

When I returned to camp each afternoon, I made preparations for a much more exciting camera hunt when darkness should shroud the little lake. Substituting smaller lenses for the large ones used in daylight work, we would enter the canoe about 9 p. m. with the jacklight in the bow and the flashlight apparatus within easy reach, and paddle along the dark and silent waters, while the single blazing eye of the canoe sought for some nocturnal denizen along the shore or out in the deeper waters of the many bays.

NIGHT ADVENTURES WITH BULL MOOSE

Until his first experience with the jacklight, Adam Moore had considered hunting with the camera merely an interesting but not unusual pastime. For many years he had studied these animals in the waters and in the forest of his native

A MONARCH PAUSES IN NICTAU LAKE

On quiet summer days pictures like this may often be seen through openings in the bordering forest. The country is dotted with such bodies of water. The moose find good forage in them. The author's guide was adept at finding likely places for camera hunting on this trip.

place. On the first night hunt, when his keen ears detected the wallowing of a moose at the edge of a small bog, and when later he saw its bright, translucent eyes and finally its massive body illuminated by light from the jack, he grew intensely interested (see opposite page). When the flash was fired and the great beast struggled about, blinded but not really alarmed, by what it thought was a flash of lightning, Moore laughed loud and long. Every night thereafter he was first in the canoe.

Hunters have told so many tales of attacks upon human beings by moose that many people believe such happenings actually take place. The real explanation of

the supposed belligerency of moose at night became apparent to me on this trip.

One evening, Adam in the stern, his son in the middle, and I behind the light, paddled toward a large bull feeding in the center of the shallow lake. We were only 30 feet away when the head sank out of sight. The canoe could have passed over the large, submerged antlers. When the flash was fired, the moose showed no concern. We kept our position, and I prepared and fired a second flash. This again eliciting no response, I prepared a third charge, but when I pulled the trigger, the cap alone exploded with a sharp crack. In a mighty swirl, the big animal, alarmed at the snapping sound

AN EARLY VISITOR STARTLED THIS LADY

On starting trout fishing one foggy morning, the author found a cow moose taking a bath. The foggy background made a picture possible.

THE AUTHOR CAUGHT A "TIP-UP" NESTING NEAR NICTAU LAKE

This bird is characterized by its solitary habits. It is a species frequently seen in Northern States, its bobbing tail and plaintive notes attracting attention as it feeds or flits along the streams.

A BULL MOOSE GOES FORAGING AT NIGHT

After flashlighting this fellow in deep water the author again snapped it near shore. Unlike deer, moose are not alarmed by the glare and roar of the explosion when they are photographed, apparently regarding these phenomena as natural, like thunder and lightning (see text below).

behind the light, swam rapidly away toward the inlet of the lake.

I recapped the flash, and we paddled in the direction he had gone. We soon saw him standing in about two feet of water close by some bushes and facing the light. Again I fired the flash. Displaying a little concern this time, he began walking up the stream.

While the paddler kept in sight of him, I prepared the fourth flash. Just as the moose entered a broad trout pool, and while he was facing the bushes a few yards ahead, his big antlers only partly visible over his body, I fired the charge. Never before had I been given a chance to photograph the retreating form of a moose at night.

In the smoke-filled atmosphere in front of the jack I heard a great splash and then another. At the same time a deluge of cold water drenched me and the cameras. There within four feet of the jack, his big head towering seven feet above the canoe, stood the bull, looking not down into the light, but beyond, as if preparing for another spring.

It certainly seemed time to do something.

Half rising, I waved my cap before his astonished eyes and gave a yell that could have been heard a mile or so away. This was sufficient. With an easy lope he entered the bushes upon our immediate left and disappeared.

Moore, howling with delight, made some remarks about the penetrating quality of my voice. This, I told him, might be accounted for by my position in the canoe at the time. Since my lively bombardment of a subject of King Edward took place on the night of July 4, it might be considered my contribution to the pyrotechnic celebrations that were occurring the same evening throughout the States.

My adventure confirmed what I had long suspected. The moose perceived the vivid flash only by its reflection on the bushes ahead; hence its sudden retreat. The cow that apparently charged our light in Canada, as the picture shows, was at first facing away from us. The bull that my old hunting companion shot at was standing, stern toward us, gazing at the diffused light of the jack reflected on the bushes beyond, and the sudden rifle shot caused him to swerve

ALL POWER ON

This New Brunswick moose was photographed from a canoe as he surged across Nictau Lake at such a rate that it required the best efforts of two good paddle men to take the camera within range.

A COW AND CALF MOOSE APPROACH SALT LICK

These animals were caught as they walked unsuspectingly before the flashlight camera under the shelter of midnight. The presence of the youngster was not noted until the plate was developed two weeks later (see text, page 39).

A PANIC-STRICKEN BULL MOOSE MADE A HURRIED LANDING
This photograph was taken on Nictau Lake in daylight; at night he would not have fled.

THIS MOOSE WAS CAUGHT BY FLASHLIGHT AND DAYLIGHT
Development of the plate and that shown on page 32, upper, proved that the same subject had been photographed twice.

A YOUNG MOOSE WAS INTERESTED IN THE APPROACHING JACKLIGHT

He appeared unconcerned, probably wondering at the rising of a sun in the middle of the night.

from the apparent source of danger in front and thus to plunge down upon the canoe.

I recalled that in the five or six instances that white-tailed deer had thrown water into the boat when dashing madly by us, they had all been looking into the forest at the wavering light of the jack upon the trees or bushes. When the explosion came, they instinctively rushed into the water away from the terrifying reflected lights and shadows of the forest. On the other hand, in the hundreds of cases in which I fired the flashes directly into the faces of deer, moose, elk, and other wild animals, they never, in a single instance, charged forward after the explosion.

The hunter should avoid firing a flash or discharging a rifle at a moose at close range when it is facing away from him. If he does so, he should be prepared for a possible collision more or less dangerous because of the great weight of the animal. If the hunter cannot swim, he should not risk a shot at all.

Another misconception equally common in regard to the moose concerns its savage character in the fall. Many articles have been written on this subject, most of them by honest, well-meaning sportsmen of somewhat limited experience, describing their narrow escapes from the sudden charges of these big animals when they are fired upon.

The explanation is simple. When a moose is suddenly shot at from behind by an unseen hunter and is not wounded, it almost invariably takes its back track. This frequently brings it face to face with the surprised hunter, who may or may not then succeed in shooting it down.

When a moose is fatally hurt, or very badly wounded, by a shot from an unobserved hunter in front of it, it generally rushes madly forward 25 yards or more in the agony caused by its unexpected injury, and thus, once more, the animal is close upon the hunter with a suddenness that is somewhat terrifying to those who see in its glaring eyes an overpowering desire for revenge. In either case the animal has every appearance of charging the hunter. Hence originate the tales of the tenderfeet.

Some contend, also, that the bull moose

DAY OR NIGHT, HE LOOKED THE SAME

Comparison of this daylight photograph with the flashlight on page 30, lower, reveals how characteristic of the subject was the pose.

A BEDRAGGLED OLD COW MOOSE OFFERS CONTRAST

Her lethargy was probably due to her poor physical condition. Not all of the females of the species
were thus spiritless (see lower picture on opposite page).

A MAGNIFICENT BULL GOES INTO ACTION

He did not tarry as the canoe approached, but made for shore at breakneck speed. The greatest
spread of New Brunswick moose antlers range between 66 and 69 inches.

FOR ONCE IN HER LIFE SHE WAS ALMOST GOOD LOOKING

Rusty brown, long legged and short necked, with a huge nose and mulelike ears, the cow moose is
usually unattractive. This one, however, has assumed an admirable attitude of alertness.

MOOSE ARE LUSTY SWIMMERS

This bull was photographed by daylight as he was making for shore to escape the canoe.

THIS COW MOOSE SHOWED SPIRIT

Unlike the bedraggled specimen shown on page 32, lower picture, she went into action quickly as the canoe approached. Note the hump with bristling hairs on her shoulders and also on the shoulders of the bull above. Both pictures were taken on the same day on a lagoon near Nictau Lake.

his most feared and deadly enemy, man. As a matter of fact, however, just one faint whiff of human scent will send the biggest bull into headlong flight, his massive body quivering with fear.

ANOTHER NIGHT ENCOUNTER WITH A BULL MOOSE

Exactly one year after our experiences flashlighting moose in New Brunswick, I received from Adam Moore a letter in which he described a scrimmage he had had with a bull moose when he was using a jacklight. It was his opinion that the animal had become frightened by the fluttering light on the bushes, and had changed its course with no intention of charging down upon the canoe or its terrified occupants.

His letter, dated July 31, 1908, was in part as follows: "We had a change in our Provincial government last spring, and in July Charlie Cremins and I took the new Premier and the Surveyor-General out to see what we were doing. The former had with him his son and daughter, and the latter his daughter, and they stayed ten days, the same period that you were there last year.

"One quiet, dark night on Nictau Lake, I took out one of the large canoes with Charlie behind the jacklight you gave me, the two young ladies next, side by side, and the Surveyor-General behind them, while I wielded the paddle in the stern. We went

is particularly dangerous during the mating season, even if not being hunted. It is true that he is then more indifferent to his safety. When in some remote forest wilderness his feverish eyes mistake the distant skulking figure of a man for his lady love or his rival, he approaches with a bellow. It is easy to understand how some persons may interpret such impetuosity as a desire on the part of the animal to give combat to

RECONNAISSANCE

Coming out of the dense forest the deer looks carefully about, its reflection showing in the water.

DEER AND MOOSE HAVE DIFFERENT SCHEDULES

The whitetails visited the lick only by day, coming at all hours. The moose, with a single exception, came throughout the night, first appearing at dusk. This indicated the incompatibility between the two animals.

A WHITE-TAIL BUCK APPROACHES SALT LICK

Before 1895 this lick was frequented by many caribou, which were often killed there. With the coming and increase of whitetails and moose, the caribou deserted their once favorite resort and since then have almost vanished from New Brunswick.

out to look for big bulls across the lake from camp. The first seen was a small one, and then came a dandy big bull. We played with him for some time until he took to the middle of the lake. Then we sighted another small bull feeding near shore.

"Passing on to the upper end of the lake, we saw a good-sized bull in the inlet standing near shore in a little cove. Hearing what seemed to be a larger bull beyond, we passed close behind the first animal while it was looking at the bushes, Charlie carelessly keeping the jacklight on it as we passed.

"Seeing only the light and shadows on the bushes, the bull turned in our direction and in two jumps was upon us, jumping over the canoe between the girls and the surveyor, knocking the latter down, and injuring him in one arm and shoulder as it passed over. The boat was nearly filled with mud and water, but I don't think the moose did this. The boat tilted partly over when those in it shifted their positions.

"The boat was taken ashore and emptied, and soon we were on our way back to camp, with the young women so delighted with

their adventure that afterward we went out nearly every night, but we carefully avoided letting the moose see the light on the bushes. I agree with you that when the animal is scared and runs the other way, it doesn't know there is a canoe concealed beneath the little jacklight.

"Of course it was a good joke on the surveyor, for he had charge of the game and fish laws, and to have a bull moose jump over him made a headliner for the daily press. Many think the story was a lie because they don't understand it and we let it go at that, but you and I know how such a thing can happen."

A NEW BRUNSWICK SALT LICK

On leaving Nictau Lake, we descended the river about 17 miles to Red Brook, where we camped a couple of days in a little cabin located about a mile upstream, well up on a steep hillside. This cabin was used by trappers in winter and at other times by hunters or by photographers of game, and near it, a hundred yards below at the base of the hill, was a natural salt lick. Close

SATISFIED THAT HE WAS SAFE, THE BUCK WADED TOWARD THE BLIND

On reaching the stream, the animal drank of the cold, clear water before it gulped down the muddy mixture in the lick. This is the deer shown on page 35, upper picture. He was so confident that both photographs were taken in broad daylight without his being frightened.

by flowed a small creek that emptied into the Tobique a mile down the valley. This salt spring, as usual in this region, issued from beneath a sandstone ridge, resembling those of the Lake Superior region.

A large and comfortable log blind had been built above the edge of the lick, affording concealment for the hunter, as well as protection from the mosquitoes. Originally the lick had been frequented only by caribou, but with the increase of deer and moose in the region, the caribou appeared to lose interest in their old resort.

Seldom have I passed a more interesting time in any kind of blind than I did there, for deer and moose came frequently, some of them even too near to be photographed. Among the white-tailed deer that visited this salt lick were a pair of semi-albino yearlings, the white circles about the eyes and the splotched faces giving them a comical expression. Each day we had many opportunities to observe the difficulty the moose, with their long legs and short necks, had in reaching the surface of the lick to drink without spreading their forelegs.

On the first afternoon of our stay I no-

ticed several hundred large yellow butterflies on the mud about the lick. Shortly afterward a big white-tailed buck, with its antlers in the velvet, entered the lick and started up the butterflies, which arose in such a cloud as almost to conceal the animal's body. I was about to photograph this extraordinary scene when the deer, evidently even more surprised and startled by the butterflies than I had been, made a long leap and disappeared among the bushes. In northern Michigan a dark blue species of butterfly was often observed at salt springs.

I thought it quite possible that flashlight pictures could be taken at night from an opening in the blind, and that we might thus profitably occupy our time during the early evening hours. I therefore arranged a camera so that it would cover the main part of the lick and fastened the flashlight apparatus to the outside of the blind where it could be fired by pulling a string.

After a late supper we went down to the blind, hoping for success. Soon after dark we heard a heavy animal coming down the hillside. After it had passed, we could hear it gulping down the muddy waters.

A PAIR OF YOUNG WHITE-TAIL DEER COME DOWN TO SALT LICK

They show distinct traces of albinism, the one to the right particularly, its white markings giving it a comical masklike appearance. This photograph was taken in a heavy rain on a dark day.

Turning on the electric hand flash, I saw a moose standing too close for a picture. I waited until it had moved farther out, and then fired the flashlight. Soon afterward, we heard another animal walking along the creek and, judging from the sound that it was in front of the camera, I fired the flash again.

Up to this time on the trip I had not obtained a picture of a moose calf and had about given up hope of getting one. When I developed the negative of this second flash, some two weeks later, I was greatly pleased to find on the plate the photograph of a cow moose with a little calf trudging along behind (see page 29).

The next morning a young white-tailed buck lay down in the grass opposite the blind and gave me one of my few opportunities of witnessing a deer chewing its cud. At noon we left the blind and the cameras and went up the hill for luncheon. While we were seated at the door of the cabin I remarked to Moore that some animal was coming up the trail.

Looking over my shoulder he exclaimed, "Why, that is a caribou! The first I have seen in several years."

As the animal ambled by a few yards away, we suffered the disappointment so often experienced when one leaves one's gun or camera out of reach.

PHOTOGRAPHING A FAMOUS GUIDE

That night it rained so hard that the creek overflowed the salt lick, so diluting its waters that no animal was likely to come to it for several days. The following morning, therefore, we packed our outfit down the creek to the river. Floating down the swift and swirling waters, we came soon to a more open country occupied largely by small farms. One plate had been left in reserve in case an animal might be unexpectedly seen, an event which I hoped would not happen, for I wished to take a photograph of my famous guide. This I did as Moore was standing at the foot of a small cascade (see page 24).

A mile farther on we noticed a picnic party peering through the bushes at something on the other side of the stream. The object of interest proved to be an old cow moose nibbling unconcernedly on the brush. I did not regret, however, having pictured the giant form of the guide instead of a vagrant animal that should have known better than to be consorting with a holiday party of humans instead of remaining within the family circle farther up the river amid the forests and beautiful lakes of the northern wilderness.

When I parted from Moore on the lower Tobique, he said: "In my varied experience and with many scenes before me, I can only say in all sincerity that the hunt of the last week has proved more interesting, more exciting, and of more real value in the study of animal life than any that has gone before."

Thus spoke a man who has looked at game over a rifle barrel for more than forty years!

INCREASE OF MOOSE IN NEW BRUNSWICK DUE TO WISE GAME LAWS

Prior to 1885, moose were extremely scarce in New Brunswick, but, as a result of the gradual disappearance of the Indian trapper and hide hunter and the passage of an effective buck law, this noble animal was at the time of my visit more widely distributed and more abundant in parts of this Province than in any other area of equal size on the American continent, except on the Kenai Peninsula, Alaska. Since no cows or calves can be legally killed, thousands of females then formed great breeding herds capable of supplying more than the number of bulls killed annually and of adding many more each year to the permanent breeding stock. In more recent years I fear these conditions have changed and moose are less numerous.

With the increase in the number of the moose came also an increase in the white-tailed deer, and they likewise are abundant. Their availability saved many a big moose or caribou that otherwise would have been sacrificed to meet the temporary needs of the pot-hunter or trapper. Formerly the caribou were also plentiful locally in New Brunswick as in Maine, but from both these areas they now have nearly or quite disappeared. In practical game management, where the producing animals are carefully protected and the increment is made the basis of a restricted killing, we find here a splendid example of good judgment and concurrent rewards.

Photograph by A. A. Allen

CANVASBACKS ONCE ABOUNDED NEAR CORNELL UNIVERSITY

Every fall and winter ducks of this species, scaups, and golden-eyes frequent Cayuga Lake. It was near here that a dangerous crossing on the ice one night was made by the author.

THEY ARE WINTER RESIDENTS OF LONG ISLAND SOUND

This group includes two nearly adult ring-billed gulls with an adult in the center. The ring-bills are generally distributed with the herring gull, which they resemble in color, but they may be distinguished by their smaller size. On the coast their habits are like those of the herring gull, but in the interior they sometimes feed on insects as well as fish.

CHAPTER III

At Cayuga Lake, on Long Island Sound, and Sandusky Bay

UNTIL the fall of 1877, when I went to Cornell University, at Ithaca, on the south shore of Cayuga Lake, I had never done much duck shooting. I had, however, hunted small game, including grouse and the wild pigeon, and had shot many deer in northern Michigan, where I had gone year after year since 1870. The south shore of Lake Superior affords very poor duck hunting, for most of the migratory wild fowl seem to avoid crossing this wide, deep, cold body of water, and pass either through Minnesota or to the east, along the St. Clair flats and Lake Erie.

In talking with some local hunters at Ithaca, I learned that the duck shooting there was rather satisfactory, marsh-frequenting species being found at both ends of the lake, and the redhead, canvasback, broadbill, and golden-eye on the open water.

Aside from a few incidents, it is not my purpose to give an account of my many pleasant days on Cayuga Lake, except to say that if I had devoted the same amount of attention to my studies I might have received a *cum laude* degree from the university.

Once, when Cayuga Lake was frozen over at the south end, I planned to join a few companions to shoot ducks along the edge of the ice. It was agreed that, on the night preceding the hunt, I was to walk some distance down the railroad track on the eastern shore, and then cross the lake on the ice to a cottage on the opposite side, where a lighted lantern would guide my course. On reaching the proper point, I could see the lantern about two miles away and began my journey on the ice.

The night was dark, and I could not even see the hills against the sky. When I had gone about halfway across, a great flapping of wings and a loud quacking of ducks startled me. Less than ten yards in front of me was open water. Had not this open water contained some black ducks, I should have plunged in and, loaded down with ammunition, gone to the bottom.

How far this open water extended and where I could get around it, there was no means of determining. With palpitating heart I began to retreat; but this was not

HE STOOD NEAR THE BLIND AT SANDUSKY BAY

This greater yellowlegs was the first shore bird the author bagged with the camera.

easy, for there was no lantern to guide me. When I had nearly reached the shore a light snow began falling, and this changed the whole situation. Dark as was the night, the light snow showed plainly on the ice, and I was able to complete the trip across the lake without further trouble.

Next day I refused, despite tempting chances, to shoot at any black ducks, for among those that passed there might be, I thought, some of those that had warned me the night before.

STILL-HUNTING THE GOLDEN-EYE

It was on Cayuga Lake that I first witnessed a still hunt for diving ducks. In Ithaca I had often seen an old trapper peddling a basketful of dressed ducks whose plumpness would appeal to most housewives. They were golden-eyes, which, when deprived of their feathers, resembled closely some of the more edible species.

HE SEIZED A BLOODLESS VICTIM

By a fortunate chance the camera in the author's blind, near Sandusky Bay, was trained on his wooden decoys in expectation that some passing duck might make a call. When a duck hawk darted in and seized one of the smaller decoys in his talons, a quick shot with the lens recorded this scene.

half a dozen birds. They were fine-looking when dressed, and he did a thriving business.

When broadbills were numerous this market hunter would toll them within close range of his blind by having his spaniel run up and down the shore as an enticement. He told me that on several occasions he had fired both barrels into the closely packed flock and killed about 25 birds with a shot. The Federal Migratory Bird Law has stopped this form of market hunting.

TWO YEARS ON LONG ISLAND SOUND

From Ithaca, where Cayuga Lake had proved such an attraction, I went to the Yale Law School in 1881, intending to devote a little more attention to my studies than heretofore. The proximity, however, of Long Island Sound renewed my interest in duck shooting, and I passed many weekends at the mouth of the East Haven River,

Since these birds are wary, feed alone, and seldom fall victim to the fowler, I asked the vender how he obtained so many every week. He said that on any day that the weather was moderate he rowed along the shore of the lake, looking carefully around each bend for golden-eyes feeding on crayfish in gravelly bays, where they were usually within gunshot of the shore. When he saw one he would land and, as the duck dived, run about 50 yards toward it, sinking to his knees when it was about to appear. As the duck came to the surface, he would kill it on the water or as it was taking wing. I went with him one day and saw him kill

where I was allotted a room as the only winter guest in a summer boarding house, and soon acquired a great liking for Mr. and Mrs. Dennis Mansfield, its owners.

About that time I purchased a "Barnegat sneak-boat," one of the most seaworthy types of small, rough-water boats ever constructed. It was only about ten feet long and three wide, but apparently no gale could sink it. Built of Spanish cedar, it had a sharp bow edged with brass, which curved into a rounded bottom extending nearly to the square stern. Because of its construction, the bow cut the waves and the body of the boat was lifted up, riding the water

THIS GREATER YELLOWLEGS WAS SOCIABLE

One day he came in and alighted in the shallow water by some duck decoys near the shore of Sandusky Bay, where the author was awaiting the arrival of ducks.

BLUEBILL OR LESSER SCAUP DUCKS ARE COMMON IN THE EAST

In the fall and winter this duck is widely distributed in open waters from Long Island Sound to Florida and the Gulf coast. This photograph shows two drakes with black heads, light backs, and white sides, and four females in somber grayish brown plumage except for a white band back of the bill. The broad, blue bills of these birds account for their common name bluebills, or broadbills.

SHE WAS FIRST OF HER KIND TO POSE

On Sandusky Bay the author began wild duck photography with this female mallard and the drake shown in the picture on the right.

like a duck. It had a cockpit with a four-inch railing, and in all my experiences in the winter weather on Long Island Sound, and later on Lake Superior, it was never necessary to bail it out. It carried a leg-of-mutton sail for use when needed, and had a metal centerboard, so that long trips could be made with speed and comfort.

HOW THE AUTHOR'S BOAT GOT ITS NAME "CERTAIN DEATH"

Mansfield, who had a large number of flat-bottom rowboats for the use of his summer boarders, eyed my craft with great suspicion and called it *Certain Death,* which name it still bears on its bow in my camp garden at Whitefish Lake, Michigan, where, filled with flowering plants, the mast entwined with vines, it has left the water forever, but serves as a pleasant reminder of 50 years ago.

The form of duck hunting on the Sound that interested me most was line shooting. This was done from a line of boats anchored off a point dividing two good-sized bays. The boats were placed about 90 yards apart, and sometimes extended out into the

Sound half a mile, the length of the line depending, of course, on the number of shooters.

The boats, when anchored, headed up into the wind, while the shooter, reclining in the cockpit, faced down wind, from which direction the birds almost invariably came. Wild fowl coming out of either bay or following an offshore course, would not notice these boats, with their subdued colors, until they were within about 150 yards, when they would rise a little higher and pass midway between two of them. This gave each sportsman therein a shot at not more than 45 yards.

WOE TO THE DUCKS THAT BREAK THROUGH THE LINE

When a number of ducks broke through different places in this line, there was a great bombardment, the spent shot often rattling about the nearest boats. To recover the dead or wounded ducks, the fowler had only to unsnap a line running to the anchored buoy. If uncertainty prevailed as to which hunter killed the duck, the best oarsman settled the question.

Though this form of shooting was exciting when many birds were on the wing, the culinary value of the game was of a low order, since most of the victims were old squaws, white-winged coots, and loons, with now and then a broadbill or some other deep-water duck. When line shooting was not possible, I would row out to some large exposed boulders known as the "Cow and Calf," where I would place decoys according to the prevailing wind and pull up the sneak-boat on the opposite side.

One bright, still day that held little prospect of any shooting, I heard a "ping" to the right, and then the crack of a rifle on shore. The would-be duck hunter had a high-power repeater, and I thought his efforts amusing until one of the bullets was deflected from a wooden decoy and fell at my feet. While he was reloading, I stood up, waved my hat, and fired off both barrels of my shotgun. The long-range hunter hurried back into a patch of woods.
sundown, when I thought the wind might in a violent offshore gale. I waited until sundown, when I thought the wind might subside, but instead it seemed to grow more violent. Had the boat been less heavily loaded, it would have been possible to row quarteringly toward the shore, but since

most of the decoys I had out were fastened on a collapsible frame, it was impossible to reach shore with such a load.

I started down the Sound with the wind off my quarter, hoping to make a landing farther along. I managed to get ashore at Thimble Islands, some ten miles distant, and in a buckboard drove back to the East Haven River. It was then about midnight, and I saw a light in the barn, where Mansfield was hitching up his horse to carry the news to my friends that I had been drowned in *Certain Death,* as he had always predicted.

A PREDICTION THAT CAME TO NAUGHT CAUSED DISAPPOINTMENT

At my unexpected return he seemed quite disappointed, appearing, for a moment, to value his predictions above the loss of a friend for whom he had mourned half the night to no purpose.

On October 16, 1901, I went from Pittsburgh to the Winnous Point Club, Sandusky Bay, on Lake Erie, to make one of my first efforts in photographing ducks. I was accompanied by an artist-sportsman who wished to make sketches of marsh scenes for some of his water-color pictures. Since the shooting season did not open for several weeks, we could occupy any pond or blind that the weather permitted. Although I was using a long-focus lens, the shutter was not rapid enough for taking wing pictures of ducks, and I had to content myself with photographing swimming birds, some in groups, and others singly and close to the blind.

Conditions at Sandusky Bay have long been favorable for wild fowl, and practically every species of duck frequenting the waters east of the Mississippi River resorts there, the black duck, mallard, and the two kinds of teal predominating. Here also during migration may be found occasional flocks of wild geese and large numbers of whistling swans.

At the time of our visit an extraordinary condition prevailed in these great marshes, which, for more than 50 years, had been the favorite hunting resort of many sportsmen from Cleveland and other cities of the region. Formerly most of the shallow bays there had produced a large variety of duck-food plants in such abundance that birds had been drawn to the feast from far and near. Then some misguided person introduced German carp into these waters. As

THE DRAKE FLOATED NEAR THE DUCK

He and his consort on the left obligingly "posed" near the blind on Sandusky Bay for the author to make his first pictures of waterfowl.

they increased rapidly in numbers, these fish, with their hoglike feeding habits, had almost completely destroyed the plant growth.

So thorough was this destruction by the time of our visit, that all wild-fowl shooting would have ended for lack of birds except that the shooting clubs had resorted to the costly expedient of baiting the shallow waters with grain. So far as I am aware, this was one of the first instances of this practice that has now become so general.

SANDUSKY BAY CARP WROUGHT HAVOC IN MANY WAYS

So destructive and pernicious were the carp that during periods of high water they ate the bark from the willows along the bank to such an extent that the trees were girdled and killed. They ate the spawn of any other fish breeding there, and kept the waters so continuously roiled that the formerly abundant bass were driven out into the clear water of Lake Erie.

On the second day of my visit to the Sandusky marshes, I saw a duck hawk flying toward me a short distance in from the shore, where it was ready to seize any duck that should flush from the shallow waters. Hoping that the hawk might pass over the teal decoys I had out, at a speed slow enough to be pictured, I awaited its coming.

On seeing the decoys, the hawk swung out over the water, and as it passed over the first decoys I prepared to take a snapshot, but the hawk suddenly dropped on one of them and submerged it by the force of the attack. As the hawk attempted to rise with the decoy in its talons, I obtained a picture of the unusual scene (see page 42).

The captor struggled aloft with its prize, the long cord and lead anchor trailing behind. When the hawk was halfway across the pond, the decoy slipped from its grasp and plunged beneath the surface for a moment after striking the water. The hawk then flew to a near-by muskrat house, on which it sat, evidently trying to figure out what had happened, for there on the water floated its desired victim showing no evidence of harm nor of alarm.

After a few minutes the bird of prey went its way and I rowed out and recovered the kidnaped dummy. On its back were deep scratches, and the sides and bottom showed punctures like those made by small shot.

Two days later I was occupying a blind on a larger body of water, and this time the decoys were divided into two sets, with an opening between for any visiting duck. I had been in the blind for only a short time when I observed a large bald-head eagle flying low over the water, and wondered whether it, too, would make a visit to my decoys. The eagle alighted on a snag about one hundred yards away, and watching it through the glass I could see that it was intently eyeing the decoys. I swung the camera to the left to be ready when the bird should pass over the first set.

Just as I had done this, the eagle drew near, but instead of dropping down on one of the first group of decoys, it continued on to my right, and seized from the second group a decoy representing a drake mallard. I hurriedly swung the camera in that direction, but the motion was observed by the eagle, which dropped its prey and hastened away.

The bird may have passed the first decoys expecting that they would spring into the air in alarmed flight, and that it could easily capture one, as frequently happens in such cases; but when they did not flush, it tried to make certain of a capture among those beyond. Hawks and eagles every now and then appear to be completely deceived by the painted wooden decoys, and commonly they pay the extreme penalty exacted by the irate hunter for a capital crime committed against his property.

On one occasion a friend of mine was looking away from duck decoys set before his blind on Henry Lake, Idaho, when he heard a splash and, turning quickly, saw a bald eagle carrying away the wooden image of a canvasback. A quick shot brought down the marauder, killed instantly, the decoy still held firmly in its talons; a rather ignominious end for such a royal bird.

GREEN-WINGED TEAL ARE GRACEFUL SWIMMERS
These handsome little ducks were rather numerous in marshy ponds near Sandusky Bay.

CHAPTER IV

Birds of the Nation's Capital

SINCE 1926 I have passed each spring, fall, and the early winter at my suburban home in Wesley Heights, Washington, D. C. The rolling hills and the valleys in this area are largely covered with forests, so that the clearings about residences, where scattered trees remain, and shrubs and other vegetation have been planted, provide favorable places for birds. The feeding boxes, the bird bath, and the top of a rounded slope beneath my library windows daily attract feathered visitors.

Although we are surrounded by other residences, the birds that come vary in size from humming birds to crows, and include the sharp-shinned hawk, the Carolina dove, and the wood thrush.

LIST INCLUDES 42 SPECIES

During the 10 years of my stay there I have kept a careful record of the birds observed on the premises. The list of species is being gradually increased each season, but lacks the several small flycatchers, vireos, and warblers that undoubtedly visit the plum tree near by during every migration. Their movements are too elusive to permit me more than a glimpse of tiny flitting forms. At the time of this writing, in the spring of 1935, my list contains the following species:

1. Bob-white; 2. mourning dove; 3. sharp-shinned hawk; 4. sparrow hawk; 5. hairy woodpecker; 6. downy woodpecker; 7. red-bellied woodpecker; 8. flicker; 9. chimney swift; 10. ruby-throated humming bird; 11. great-crested flycatcher; 12. blue jay; 13. fish crow; 14, starling; 15. cowbird; 16. purple grackle; 17 goldfinch; 18. white-crowned sparrow; 19. white-throated sparrow; 20. chipping sparrow; 21. slate-colored junco; 22. song sparrow; 23. English sparrow; 24. towhee; 25. cardinal; 26. scarlet tanager; 27. loggerhead shrike; 28. yellow warbler; 29. yellow-rumped warbler; 30. mocking bird; 31. catbird; 32. brown thrasher; 33. Carolina wren; 34. house wren; 35. winter wren; 36. white-bellied nuthatch; 37. tufted titmouse; 38. Carolina chickadee; 39. wood thrush; 40. gray-cheeked thrush; 41. robin; 42. bluebird.

This seems to represent a fairly good cross section of the bird fauna of this district when one considers that it includes only the visitors to a lot 100 by 150 feet in area, located among other occupied lots in the midst of a closely built suburb. The main attractions to our feathered friends are the pool and the bird bath, combined with bread crumbs and seeds scattered on the ground or on an elevated platform, and suet placed beyond the reach of cats and dogs on a slender ten-foot pole, or on the window ledge.

The vicinity of Washington appears to be favored by birds, especially in places where they are provided with suitable cover, food, and protection. A careful census of the breeding birds taken one season at Wild Acres, the partly wooded five-acre tract where Dr. Gilbert Grosvenor has his suburban home, a few miles from town, totaled 135 pairs belonging to 40 species. It is believed that this record has not been excelled on any similar area anywhere in the country.

Our success in attracting birds to our home in Wesley Heights has been a source of constant interest and pleasure, for it has afforded an insight into their seasonal changes and their relations to one another that we could not have obtained otherwise.

CARDINALS

Our handsomest and most notable visitors are perhaps the cardinals. At first, only an individual or two appeared, but their numbers later increased. One winter especially, from 20 to 25 cardinals at a time came repeatedly, making a gorgeous display of color on the ground and in the leafless plum tree. Among these was a partly albinistic male, whose lovely shade of a very pale pink made it conspicuous among its fellows.

In contrast to this winter's abundance, another season was marked by the almost complete absence of cardinals, only one or two coming at considerable intervals, despite the varied repast that always awaited them. It was difficult to account for the rarity of the birds unless it was because the winter was an open one, and perhaps an abundance of their natural food supply was available.

The gentle manners of the cardinals are restricted to mated birds. At my winter

THE AUTHOR HAS A BIRD STUDIO AT WESLEY HEIGHTS, WASHINGTON, D. C.

From the living-room windows above, the many visiting birds can be studied and photographed at the feeding platform, the suet pole, and the bird bath. From the basement window such visitors can be pictured on the ground at close range (see, also, page 60).

home in Florida the males become very solicitous in their springtime attentions to their mates. The females commonly stand among the scattered bread crumbs, seeds, and other food, apparently as helpless as young birds, while the males hop about, select the best tidbits, and pass them to the bills of their mates, which complacently accept these devotions.

At Wesley Heights the same scenes of domestic felicity are observed among the cardinals six weeks later. This trait of the male paying such devoted attentions to the female early in the mating season is rare among birds, which usually express their emotions in such instances by singing or by other personal display. Except during the mating and nesting period, the cardinals visit the feeding places individually, and give no sign of any attachment that persists beyond the nesting season.

It was not until the grain was placed on an elevated platform in the winter instead of on the ground that I learned the disposi-

tion of the male cardinal to exclude any of its kind from the tray. This I noticed in January, 1933, when, for a second winter, we had an unusually large number of these handsome visitors. It seems strange that this pugnacious intolerance should be directed largely toward its kin, for often a dozen English sparrows, or a smaller group of starlings would jostle the lone cardinal without any signs of resentment on its part.

It was an interesting but mournful sight to see a dozen or more hungry cardinals, that had come separately from various directions, perched on the leafless limbs of the plum tree waiting their turn for the winter dole, their sharp and impatient *tsip, tsip, tsip,* in marked contrast to the charming duets of the mated pairs in the spring. To correct this situation, I scattered grain about on the ground, so that all might have an equal chance and avoid the provoking delay caused by the leisurely manner of the one in possession when satisfying its hunger.

This seasonal and contrasting mood of

the cardinal is a characteristic of most other non-gregarious land birds, such as the jay, mocking bird, catbird, and brown thrasher, which usually like to monopolize the feeding tray, after the sexes have separated for the greater part of the year. Each leads an individualistic life.

Cardinals are much later feeders than most other birds, often lingering until falling night renders them almost invisible. In contrast to this habit is the behavior of such gregarious visitors as the starling and English sparrow, which leave their feeding places while it is still broad daylight to seek some common roosting place with others of their kind, and often, as a consequence, become nuisances.

ENGLISH SPARROWS AND STARLINGS ARE NUMEROUS

The English sparrow appears to be the street urchin of the bird kind. Although it seems confident and unafraid about the streets, yet at the feeding place at Wesley Heights it is the most timorous of all the bird visitors. These immigrants have never been molested during the years they have had a bountiful supply of food provided for them there, but if a person approaches the closed window to look at them, they almost always whirr up into the top of a small neighboring tree as if expecting harm.

Many times when they are feeding they burst away in full flight in what appears to be causeless frights, but which must be due to some noise or slight movement their acute senses have detected. For many years every one's hand was raised against them, and this may have developed their attitude of supercaution.

Since the replacement of the horse and stable by the automobile and garage these sparrows have lessened in number and appear to have become more insectivorous. In the more northern States, because of scarcity of food in winter, except where friendly persons aid them, the majority of them die of starvation and cold. With their American ancestry dating from about 1850, more toleration should be shown these bustling, cheerful little birds which enliven our towns and villages.

At Wesley Heights I first became acquainted with the starling, a bird introduced into this country about 1890 near New York City by some well-meaning but misguided persons. It has thrived marvelously

A FEMALE STARLING FEEDS ITS YOUNG

These birds, introduced near New York City a comparatively few years ago, have spread over the eastern United States to beyond the Mississippi River. They are useful insect-eaters, but aggressively oust natives, such as bluebirds and others, from their nesting places. In Washington they have defied all manner of efforts to dislodge them from public buildings.

A PURPLE GRACKLE VISITS THE CAPITAL

To the author's suburban home at Wesley Heights in Washington come birds of many colors, sizes, and habits. The District of Columbia has a greater variety of land birds than almost any other area of similar size in the country.

ENGLISH SPARROWS ENJOY A FEAST AT WESLEY HEIGHTS

Presumably tame and fearless, these urban inhabitants have proved the most wary of visitors to the feeding trays provided by the author.

in its new home and has extended its range until it now occurs in all the States east of the Mississippi River and even in Texas and some other States.

Its only virtue is its destruction of a great variety of insects. Aside from this, the habits of this immigrant are pernicious, for it nests in holes in buildings, walls, or trees, and is ruthless in its destruction of the nests and eggs of the bluebird, house wren, and other native birds, of whose despoiled premises it takes possession. In view of the decrease of nesting sites in a thickly populated area, the general spread of the starling may seriously affect the future of the bluebird and other species.

From two to three dozen starlings and an even larger number of English sparrows come much of the time to our feeding places. These two immigrants are so energetic and businesslike in their methods that they consume more food than all the native bird visitors combined.

It was not until late in the spring of 1930 that I realized how greatly the starlings preferred insects to the bread crumbs, grain, and suet provided at our feeding station, to which, during the winter months,

they appeared to be so attached. At that season they were daily visitors, sometimes a dozen of them being present at a time.

Early in May they were often accompanied by their young, which stood or perched helplessly about while the parents picked up the food and placed it in their open mouths. The increased numbers of starlings at that time left little food for other birds and I came to look upon them as pests.

A CHANGE IN DIET

During the latter part of each May a marked change took place. In an entire week scarcely a starling approached the regular feeding place formerly so popular. Several of the birds were seen, however, industriously searching among the short grass of the lawn and in our flower garden, and others similarly engaged were noted on the lawns of our neighbors. They were obviously hunting for insects, for they rooted about in the loose topsoil with the points of their bills. Evidently they met with such success that they became completely indifferent to the food we provided.

These birds' persistent search for insects

HUNGER BRINGS UNUSUAL NEIGHBORS TOGETHER

While a family of starlings is feeding from the top of the piece of suet, a downy woodpecker is going up to sample it from below.

indicates their value in helping keep down the numbers of such pests, a fact that should be considered carefully by communities seeking the wholesale destruction of starlings on account of annoyance they may give in other ways.

THE CHICKADEE COMES UNAFRAID

From the near-by woods came many Carolina chickadees, their nervous movements in nowise indicative of fear. These little black-capped visitors, as expected, were very fond of suet, but we were amazed at the avidity with which they ate sunflower seeds, often carrying these large seeds away to their forest retreat, probably for winter storage.

When climbing up and down, or hanging suspended from beneath a limb searching in the bark for the eggs and larvae of insects, these cheerful little acrobats give animation to the woodland lots. Like their less diminutive associates, the nuthatch, they are in continuous action throughout the day, and it is hard to imagine them quiescent during the long hours of the night.

The chickadees belong to the numerous titmouse family, building their nests in holes of dead trees, and seldom straying away from their place of birth except in the more northerly ranges when severe weather may force a slow retreat. The habitat of the Carolina species lies between the latitude of Indiana and the Gulf coast, whereas the Hudsonian chickadee inhabits the Canadian provinces northward to the tree limits.

Observing the daily life of my feathered visitors as they gathered about the feeding box or on the ground below has afforded me much interest.

Early in the morning, before the people of the community had begun their daily activities, crows would drop in to skirmish for whatever they might find. Sometimes only a single one would appear, but often there would be several in the group. These feathered outlaws were averse to taking undue chances in their contacts with man and usually departed before the regular boarders came to their breakfast.

For several mornings early in the winter the crows departed as usual, but none of the smaller boarders appeared. This was quite a mystery until a female sharp-shinned hawk was seen perched in the

AN ALBINO CARDINAL IS A SURPRISE VISITOR

Whenever food is scarce, these birds come to the author's feeding places. Sometimes there are only one or two, but once 25 gathered, each coming alone. One season a partly white male, a very pale pink in color, haunted the premises. It is shown here in company with a normally colored specimen.

BLUE JAYS ENJOY THE AUTHOR'S OFFERINGS

Blue jays are among our regular visitors at Wesley Heights. The rough log feeding block shown here is on the sunny side of the house, and often, when the sun is hot, one of them, having satisfied his appetite, will sprawl there with spread wings for a sun bath.

middle of the top of the wild plum tree near the usual feeding place. There it sat motionless as a small image among the bare branches. Evidently the hawk had noted the gathering place for small birds and had selected the partly concealed perch as a convenient place from which to drop on its prey.

One morning a junco flew across the deserted lawn to a low branch of the plum tree. Almost at the instant it alighted there was a flash of brown and it was seized and carried off in the talons of its enemy, leaving some floating feathers to mark the way. When the hawk had flown up and alighted in a tall blue-gum tree near by, it was evident that in some way its victim had escaped. A closer examination of the hawk on its perch in the plum tree revealed that one of its legs hung helpless as if broken.

Before the arrival of the hawk and its attack on the junco half a dozen juncos were daily visitors to the feeding place, but

WHAT A PLEASANT PLACE!

The blue jay contemplates the good things on the author's feeding block at Wesley Heights. The bright colors and confident ways of these birds render them very attractive.

IN A MIXED PARTY, RACE AND AGE ARE DISREGARDED

A dove, a young starling, and several English sparrows, the latter the street urchins of the bird family, bold but always alert, dine together at Wesley Heights.

for five days after the attack not one appeared. Apparently the fellows of the injured bird had been informed in some way of the lurking danger.

From time to time after its first appearance in the plum tree, the hawk returned. Its presence seemed to be known to the birds of the neighborhood, and none would appear. As soon as it departed, blue jays and starlings would come to the feeding place; thus it seemed that these

larger and bolder birds actually kept watch of the hawk's movements from points of concealment.

I have commented elsewhere on the general understanding by different species of birds and mammals of the meaning of cries of fear uttered by one of them. The whistling snort of a deer at the edge of the water may send marsh ducks scuttling away, and the croaking of a heron, frightened from its station, appears to be understood by

A GRAY SQUIRREL BECOMES NEIGHBORLY

For several seasons these little fellows from trees near by have been regular and interesting visitors to the feeding places at the author's home.

many animals. Wild creatures are so constantly exposed to deadly peril that those that do not develop an alert consciousness of the meaning of all occurrences about them are promptly eliminated.

Most of the boarders enjoyed a varied diet, but the catbirds, bluebirds, and woodpeckers partook only of the suet, just as the cardinals and doves ignored everything but grain.

There can be little doubt that the dependable supply of food and water induced many of the birds to go to housekeeping on the limited premises. In one week late in May I saw the occupied nests of the blue jay, catbird, chipping sparrow, brown thrasher, and dove. Bluebirds were seasonal tenants of the little box put up for their use.

Thus the yearly cycle in avian life ends, and then begins anew with the younger generation ready to fill in the ranks broken by casualties resulting from accidents or from old age.

Sometimes we were entertained by visitors other than the birds that came to us. Two species of land turtles, one a specially handsome box turtle, often strolled in from the adjacent woods to wander deliberately about among the flower beds and sunshiny openings. Once a larger turtle was found in the pool of the water garden successfully hunting tadpoles and vainly trying to capture the goldfish. Large green frogs sat on lily pads in the pool, feeding on transient insects by day and performing solos and duets in basso as on twanging banjos by night.

GRAY SQUIRRELS DEPARTED WHEN THEIR
TREE FELL

For three years a family of gray squirrels boarded at the bird cafeteria under the windows. Then, suddenly, they disappeared and were not seen again for several years. In trying to ascertain the cause of the cessation of their visits, I learned that a large gum tree that had recently blown down in a neighbor's yard had contained a cavity in which the squirrels had lived and in which they had always been able to seek safety from raiding dogs and small boys armed with sling shots.

The disappearance of these squirrels indicated the necessity for providing shelter if these animals are to be encouraged in such localities. Nothing but the loss of their safe home would have caused them to leave a place in which the most capricious appetite could be so easily gratified.

PROWLING CATS

Objectionable four-footed visitors were the house cats of the neighborhood. They soon learned that our premises afforded a good hunting ground, and one or another of them came every day to the consternation of the more welcome guests. The cats found good shelter in a row of Japanese barberries at the foot of the slope, but because of the steep slope above on which the birds gathered these were not well located for successful raids.

The victims of the cats were chiefly young English sparrows and starlings, which frequented the slope as a kind of nursery. The young wandered about with open mouths and fluttering wings begging their parents

A CATBIRD ENJOYS A FEAST AT THE AUTHOR'S WINDOW

If, on arriving in the spring, one of these or a bluebird immediately finds and begins eating the suet, it is known for a visitor of the previous year.

A SONG SPARROW PAYS A CALL

It pauses for a bit of suet at the author's window in Wesley Heights, where also several of its cousins find refreshment.

for food and so became easy victims. I have always considered stray house cats and crows as the most destructive enemies of the nests and young of our birds.

In northern Michigan wandering and homeless cats cannot survive the combination of deep snow and severe cold, but in the south, especially in Florida, many of these animals, abandoned by their owners or voluntarily strayed from their homes, have taken to the wilds, where they find plenty to live upon throughout the year.

All the hunting skill of their wild ancestors being revived, these cats are a serious menace to most land birds living within their haunts.

Whether in the forest or in open country at night, even when aided by a full moon or a powerful jacklight, one rarely sees birds of diurnal habits. It is difficult to discover where they roost when darkness falls. In more than half a century of observations while canoeing along the shores of lakes and streams, I have seen few land birds at night.

THE RED-BELLIED WOODPECKER IS A RARE VISITOR

Only occasionally does one of these birds come to the author's window
ledge for a taste of the food offered there.

AN IMPROVED METHOD IN WINDOW-SILL PHOTOGRAPHY

A narrow board, covered with a strip of rough bark upon which grain
can be placed, is attached to the ledge at right angles, the suet being
placed at the base. This affords a fine perch. The pair shown here are
Carolina chickadees, the smallest of the author's feathered visitors.

the jacklight caused alarm, small birds could be heard and occasionally seen as they fluttered from their leafy retreats.

With few exceptions, land birds secrete themselves within a canopy of leaves, or in their nesting holes, if tree frequenters, or within the shelter of grass or reeds if they live on the ground. Even with such precautions they fall victims of the keen-eyed owls that, like ill-omened shadows, search for them on silent wings.

Many persons believe the attractive little screech owls with their mellow call notes are comparatively harmless mousers, but Dr. A. A. Allen's close observations of their habits near Ithaca, New York, have proved conclusively that they are exceedingly destructive to warblers and other little birds occupying the leafy coverts of treetops. Quail, ruffed grouse, and some of the larger small birds are destroyed by the barred and horned owls, which must have an almost microscopic vision to detect their prey, which supposedly is protectively colored and concealed. To aid in the struggle for existence, Nature gives each species special equipment.

The roosting places of some gregarious birds, both large and small, often become conspicuous because of the numbers of birds resorting to some chosen locality. Especially is this true in or near towns.

The aggressive immigrants, the starling

One was a kingfisher roosting on a bare limb partly canopied by foliage which projected over the margin of Whitefish Lake. It was startled from its perch when I flashlighted a deer in the water below it. Kingfishers commonly sleep in their holes in banks along watercourses or in similar places, but such shelter was not available in this locality. Sometimes when my canoe brushed against the bushes or the rays of

and the English sparrow, have strong gregarious instincts that are evident both by day and by night. They are especially numerous about towns, where they maintain themselves in a way unequaled by any native birds. In Washington, as evening approaches, hundreds of each species seek regularly frequented roosting places about the corners of buildings or in certain trees in streets or parks, often within the full glare of electric lights. They have little to fear from visiting owls, but become such a nuisance from their droppings and their noise that they are subjected to raids by the police or are mobbed by indignant citizens.

At one time the picturesque walls of the Smithsonian Institution building were overgrown by a wonderful mantle of ivy, but the English sparrows found this afforded them such an ideal roost and safe breeding place that they became intolerable. In order to banish them, it was necessary finally to destroy the ivy.

THE NUTHATCH LOVES SUNFLOWER SEEDS

Seeking them they come to the feeding perch at the author's suburban home in Wesley Heights, D. C.

THE TUFTED TITMOUSE IS EQUALLY FOND OF SUET AND GRAIN

It calls often at the author's window ledge and always does justice to the food offered. These little visitors soon learn that there is nothing to fear from their host. It is interesting to note, however, that some species avoid others, coming only when the feeding perch is deserted.

A sycamore tree, about 25 feet high, standing in the middle of the sidewalk on Pennsylvania Avenue in a brightly lighted spot almost in front of the *Washington Post* building, was chosen as a roost by a large number of starlings. The popularity of this nightly resort was attested by the condition of the sidewalk below it each morning. Many pedestrians passing below carried away unwelcome mementoes. All sorts of schemes were proposed to banish the nuisance without harsh measures, but it required a long campaign of rude assaults with the firehose and other weapons to convince the birds they were not welcome in their convention place.

Just as the country's capital is an attractive gathering place for our citizenry, so for the purple martins it is a good place for great conventions. After the breeding season is over, in summer and early fall, they congregate and roost in the midst of the city until the final migratory urge takes them to their winter homes far to the south. A visit to their nightly gathering places is an exciting and unusual experience too often missed by bird lovers.

During the nesting season purple martins are scattered in innumerable small breeding groups, varying from one to 20 or more pairs over most of the eastern United States and southern Canada. They are well known because of their friendly occupation of nesting houses or boxes set up near the habitations of man. Customarily in ancient times, as they do occasionally today, they nested in old woodpecker holes or other small cavities in dead trees.

When the young are grown some mysterious impulse causes the birds from great areas to gather by thousands at common roosting places in the tops of trees, usually in the midst of, or close to, towns or large cities. These roosts have been observed from Massachusetts to California.

MARTINS THRONG WASHINGTON ROOSTS

The first record of a martin roost in Washington was made in 1917 and they have appeared there with more or less regularity ever since. In each instance they have occupied the wide spreading tops of elms bordering busy streets. Two localities have been specially favored, one not far from the White House grounds, on 17th Street as it enters the Mall, and the other near the corner of New Jersey Avenue and L Street Northwest.

One season the number of birds in the Washington roost near the Mall was estimated to be about 35,000. In 1922 Doctor Oberholser estimated the number occupying the roost on New Jersey Avenue at 50,-000. This roost was in elm trees overarching the double tracks of a busy trolley line. It is usually occupied during July and August, but in the year mentioned it was tenanted throughout July and August and more than half of September.

The birds come in to their roosts from all directions and some from very high overhead as if arriving from a great distance. The noise of their wings and of the chattering cries from thousands of throats and the myriad dark forms descending from the evening sky makes a stirring event to witness. It is usually two hours or more

after dark before they become quiet for the night. Soon after daybreak they scatter to hunt their winged prey in the air over all the surrounding region, returning each evening. With them, but usually segregated at the edges of the occupied roost, there are sometimes thousands of grackles and starlings.

CROW ROOSTS ALWAYS IN WOODS

Virtually every one is familiar with the persistent habit of the common crows to seek food and to travel in straggling flocks almost throughout the year, but it is not so generally known that in the winter season throughout their range from the Atlantic to the Pacific coast, especially in the eastern half of the country, the crows in districts from about 40 to 80 miles in diameter gather nightly in great central roosts. The roosts are always in woods bordered by open country. There the birds mass until they blacken the treetops. As they come in from about sunset until dark, the increasing chorus of their loud cawing and gabbling makes a tremendous uproar, even more exciting than that of swarming purple martins.

One of the largest crow roosts on record was located for some years at Arlington, Virginia, across the Potomac from Washington. Dr. W. B. Barrows in the winter of 1886-87 estimated that from 150,000 to 200,000 crows came to it every night. About 1910 and for several successive years thereafter a great roost was in existence in one end of a small patch of woods on the border of the northeastern suburbs of Washington, about five minutes' walk from the nearest houses.

Many persons went out to watch the birds come in and always were well repaid by the stirring sight of tens of thousands of winged creatures in action. When this roost was in its decline in the winter of 1915-16, it was estimated to contain about 25,000 birds, but at its prime, about 1911-12, there were many more.

Fish crows sometimes join the common crows at these resorts from Washington southward, and in many places they have smaller roosts of their own, especially in Florida, where they gather nightly among trees bordering some of the numberless lakes or lagoons. When sharing a roost with common crows, they are segregated on the margin of the area occupied by their larger relative.

Before the passing of the neighboring roosts, the daily, long, straggling procession of crows passing over Washington mornings and evenings from and to their roosting places was such a familiar sight to all residents there that it passed almost or quite unnoticed, but at once attracted the attention of visiting observers. Today, in 1935, no crow roosts are known in the region about Washington.

THE CAMERA CAUGHT A GRAY SQUIRREL IN THE AIR
He was jumping from the plum tree to the author's feeding platform.

NATURE DECORATES A TREE FOR THE YULETIDE

The wild plum tree, beneath my living-room window in Wesley Heights, has a seasonal calendar all its own. By April 1 Nature bursts into activity, decorating the tree with a mass of white blossoms—the pride of the neighborhood. In early summer the dense foliage affords welcome shade and shelter for many birds, some of which nest therein in perfect security, all impatiently awaiting the opening of their cafeteria in the early autumn. In November the coming of Jack Frost plucks the leaves, baring the twigs and branches as perching places for the assembling boarders.

One late December night the ground temperature was below freezing and a light rain fell. In the morning every branch

A MOCKINGBIRD PAYS HIS RESPECTS
Perched at the author's window, he has a bite of suet and a chat.

A USURPER VISITS THE WINDOW LEDGE
Of course, the gray squirrel is welcome, but he keeps all the birds away until he departs. A pair of these animals deserted the premises when their tree home was blown down (see text, page 64).

WINTER COMES TO WESLEY HEIGHTS, 1935

Above on the left is the wild plum tree in its winter garb, in seasonal contrast to the fragrant, white blossoms of spring. On the upper right can be seen the feeding perches projecting beyond the window sill, which, when freed from snow, are open resorts for the hard-pressed birds. These feathered aviators follow their own air routes and, varying in color, size, and speed, resemble airplanes coming to a central landing field (see illustration, page 48).

and twig on the leafless plum tree before the library windows was coated with clear ice, and the tree sparkled like a structure of crystal in the morning sun. The refraction of the sun's rays produced a dazzling wealth of prismatic colors.

Into this beautiful setting came bright red cardinals and troops of brown sparrows. The whole ensemble created a veritable fairyland scene highly appropriate at the Yuletide.

A great mass of writings on the mentalities of wild things has been published without very satisfactorily determining their status and the exact relationship between

them. I have no desire to enter into this controversy, but wish to record some of my observations that bear on these subjects and to give my interpretations of them. I venture to add that in my opinion it is necessary to attribute to wild things the possession of similar mental processes to those of man when causes and reactions are essentially the same in the two groups of beings.

Furthermore, the fact should not be overlooked that the more completely man is dominated by the effects of civilization, the more his reasoning powers become developed and the more his instincts tend to become atrophied.

The instinct that helps guide a homing pigeon over unknown areas is improved by experience just as the inherited hunting instincts of dogs is further developed by training. It is common knowledge that by selective breeding almost any desired physical character may be developed into definite breeds of animals. To a certain extent I believe that special mental traits may be emphasized and increased, as has been done in certain strains of hunting dogs.

INHERITANCE OF TRAITS—ORIENTATION BY BIRDS

The same general process goes on in nature, but in an infinitely slower and more broken way. In trying to interpret hereditary characteristics in birds and mammals, I have often thought that to a certain extent the results of experience on the minds of individuals are inherited, and when such inheritance works to the advantage of the species it may develop into some more or less fixed characteristic or habit.

I am aware that many biologists doubt the transmission of such mental traits, but if inheritance of mental characteristics does not occur, whence comes the endless variety of peculiar habits, often of a complicated kind, especially in their nesting and feeding habits, among the many groups of birds? It is a general rule among birds for the female to do the incubating and care for the young, but in several species this task is taken over by the males. Such divergencies must have had an ancestral origin and have been passed down the line.

The faculty possessed by many birds of making long migratory flights in spring and fall to distant but more or less definite areas is primarily due to an instinctive urge. It is supplemented by keen observations of the land and water areas they pass over. Many birds migrate mainly during good weather and at night. The wildfowl travel either by night or day, according to weather conditions. Since practically all birds appear to lose their sense of direction in a heavy fog, it seems likely that observation of their course is essential.

Apparent local exceptions may be observed among the myriad sea birds which for several months fly out to their feeding grounds at sea and back daily through dense fog that covers the Fur Seal Islands and the adjacent parts of Bering Sea. This certainty of direction through the fog about

THE WHOLE FAMILY WAS ON RELIEF

A pair of bluebirds depended on the suet for themselves and young.

the Fur Seal Islands is no doubt assisted by the sound of breakers on the rocky shores and the voices of seals and birds, which may be audible for several miles.

It is known that those wandering oceanic birds, the shearwaters at Monterey Bay, on the coast of California, become completely confused as to the proper course of their flight when a heavy fog shuts down.

FORMER BOARDERS RETURN

When one interested in bird life maintains at different seasons and in different places a series of feeding stations, he has an excellent opportunity to become well acquainted with the varied beneficiaries of his bounties. At Wesley Heights, for instance, some of the birds, such as starlings, English sparrows, woodpeckers, and chickadees, remain throughout the year. Others, such as robins, mourning doves, catbirds, mocking birds, bluebirds, and grackles, come northward the last ten days in March to nest in this vicinity later and pass the summer and fall.

There are those that may be considered winter residents, numbering among them the blue jays and cardinals, which in the

THE YOUNG TURKEY BUZZARD HAS A WHITE BIB AND TUCKER

The cottony white down is worn early in life. This photograph was taken in a rocky niche in the gorge of the Potomac River, above Washington.

spring disperse in all directions to nest. Among the migrant birds are many that tarry at Wesley Heights for only a week or ten days on their way north or south. These include juncos, white-throated sparrows, and half a dozen species of warblers.

Whenever the seasons bring different birds to our premises, it is easy to single out those that have made this a boarding place previously, for such birds within a few minutes after arriving may be seen picking at the suet or eating grain from the tray or that scattered about on the ground.

It often takes newcomers a week or ten days to discover that their presence is welcomed by this household, and that the variety of food supplied is not only for their entertainment, but for the purpose of bring-ing them into close contact with their hosts for the benefit of both.

While it is well known that migrating birds follow the same general course in their dual movements, the fact that many of these return to our half-acre lot to nest or feed shows pretty plainly that they have retentive memories, and that these pleasant recollections have helped them find their former resort, small as it is. This involves a reasoning power quite apart from instinct.

The modern system of bird-banding has done much toward determining accurately the seasonal movements of many migrants, but one who maintains a bird cafeteria is also in a good position to single out, on their return, the old customers from the newcomers.

CHAPTER V — PART I

Eastern Shore of Virginia—Earlier Visits to Revels Island

REVELS ISLAND, partly marsh and partly a low ridge overgrown with pines and cedars, is surrounded by extensive salt marshes and shallow bays. It lies about a mile to the southward of Little Machipongo Inlet, and the same distance inland from the sand dunes along Parramore Beach, on the Atlantic coast.

It is one of a group bordering the eastern shore of Virginia, between the open beach and the mainland. The islands are in Accomac County, one of the two counties forming the eastern shore of Virginia, and terminating the peninsula that also borders the eastern shore of Chesapeake Bay.

ISLAND OWNED BY SHOOTING CLUB

Revels Island, owned by the Revels Island Shooting Club, of which I became a member in 1894, comprises several thousand acres. It contains two large, nearly land-locked bays, sufficiently shallow to form feeding-places for ducks, geese, and brant; a few fresh-water ponds which are visited by black ducks; and many mud flats and sandy beaches attractive to shore birds. Several navigable channels give access by motor boat to most of the property, and at times of high tides many creeklike waterways penetrate other parts of the island otherwise inaccessible by boat.

Just south of the clubhouse is a long, broad, sandy beach, extending a mile east, and terminating in a sandy point. Across the water a similar point on Sandy Island combines with it nearly to enclose Revels Island Bay, which is the best feeding-place for ducks, geese, and brant in this region.

Nearly a mile north of the clubhouse is a long narrow ridge covered with yellow pines, cedars, and several kinds of bushes. At intervals of two or three years a very high spring tide occurs, and all the property except the ridge is covered with a foot or two of water. Once when I visited the island, the clubhouse and cottages were surrounded by the tidewaters, and no land was visible for many miles except the pine ridge and the distant main shore.

Because of these occasional floods, predatory animals, as a rule, avoided the area, although once or twice a pair of foxes appeared and made a den on the ridge, from which place they were easily dug out by fox hunters. The ground-breeding birds, therefore, had no four-footed enemies, and those nesting in the trees apparently were rarely disturbed by owls. The only resident hawk was the osprey, which always lives on friendly terms with its neighbors. Bald eagles were not uncommon, but they lived mainly on fish taken from the ospreys, or on dead fish and dead or wounded ducks.

To the southward lies the long, ocean-washed Hog Island, which helps to enclose Broadwaters, a part of the eastern shore of a wide bay or sound that was once the favored shooting resort of Grover Cleveland.

The nesting birds had, however, one enemy that was present throughout the breeding season, and caused great havoc by destroying thousands of eggs and many of the nestlings. This was the fish crow. Members of the species apparently timed their coming to arrive on the island at the beginning of the period when food of this kind became abundant.

In May, under one tall pine, I found about 500 eggshells, most of them having a large puncture in one end. They were chiefly the eggs of the laughing, or black-headed gull, and the marsh hen, or clapper rail, but included, also, those of the green heron, grackle, red-winged blackbird, skimmer, and willet (see illustration, page 66).

EGGERS CAUSE SAD HAVOC

Other enemies of some of the breeding birds were the "eggers," including a large proportion of the natives of the Eastern Shore. Under local law it was permissible to collect newly laid eggs at the beginning of the nesting season. The eggs so taken were largely those of the laughing gull and the marsh hen. Gull nests were often closely grouped over several acres; consequently the eggs were easily collected.

One day I spoke to Jonah, the colored chore boy at the clubhouse, about a breeding colony of laughing gulls, and was surprised at the interest he displayed. I understood this a week later, when, on visiting the back yard at his request, I found a rounded heap of gulls' eggs, some four hundred in number. Dismayed at this sight, I voiced my disapproval.

THE FISH CROW GUARDS ITS OWN NEST BUT DESPOILS ITS NEIGHBORS'

On Revels Island these robbers are exceedingly destructive to the eggs of other birds. More than 500 empty shells of marsh bird eggs were counted under a tree where they had been dropped by them.

THE YOUNG ROBBER WILL SOON BE ON THE WING

In the nest in a cedar tree on Revels Island this fledgling fish crow awaits the time when he can join his parents at their piracy in other birds' homes.

REVELS ISLAND CLUB ADJOINS THE "SWASH" CHANNEL

The author's cottage stands in the foreground. The large open fireplace in the living room invited many an oyster roast. On such occasions the attendant guides deftly opened these delicious bivalves for those grouped about the cheerful hearthstone. A well equipped dark room promptly recorded the results of each day's camera hunt. To the right are the cottage of another member and the main clubhouse.

Whether or not such annual pillage has any serious effect on the number of young raised each season, the Federal bird law has outlawed the practice, although I do not doubt that eggs in considerable numbers are still collected each year.

When Jonah saw how annoyed I was by his raid on the gull colony, he sought to turn my thoughts elsewhere by asking if I had seen the big whale that was stranded on Sandy Island. I told him that I had not seen it, but that I thought it would afford a good opportunity for a modern version of Jonah and the whale, and that if he would sit in its mouth this could be accomplished.

Jonah replied: "Excuse me, boss, I don't want to go within 100 feet of that critter, for the smell is awful. Jes' wait till the wind comes from the west and you'll want to leave here and go home."

The clapper rails, called locally marsh hens, were abundant on Revels Island, but they lived such secretive lives in the tall grasses that, despite their harsh, cackling notes, they were rarely seen except when one made a painstaking search for them.

Each spring they returned from the South in extraordinary numbers, and skulked about among the grasses, rising and flying only a short distance when startled. At such times their weak flight makes them an easy target for the hunter. Their nests, neatly hidden under the overarching grasses, contain from 10 to 18 pale eggs that are comparatively large for so small a bird.

CLAPPER RAILS' EGGS PRIZED

As was the case with the black-headed gulls, thousands of the eggs of these rails were taken when they were freshly laid. Trained dogs were sometimes used to help find the artfully concealed nests. In seasons when heavy tides raised the water level of the marshes, an enormous number of eggs of the clapper rail floated from the nests and formed a drift line along the shores of the marshy areas. After the tide had receded, the birds lost no time in laying new clutches, and their great numbers appeared to continue undiminished.

The eggers argued with apparently demonstrated justification that a general

THE BLACK-HEADED GULL HIDES HER EGGS

Most of the nests of these birds on Revels Island were hollows made in drifted rushes and other vegetation along usually high-tide lines.

THE FISH CROW'S DUMPING PLACE REMINDS OF TRAGEDY

The eggshells shown here below a tall pine tree on Revels Island are a good example of the work of these destructive birds. These were stolen mainly from green herons, marsh hens, and black-headed gulls (see text, page 63).

robbery of the nests of the rails and the black-headed gulls for a short period under local regulation had no effect upon the numbers of the young birds reared each year. The robbed parents promptly proceeded to lay new sets of eggs. If the nests were repeatedly despoiled, the effect would unquestionably be harmful.

The wild-fowl shooting in the tidal waters close to Revels Island never equaled that in the sounds farther south. The peculiar shortage was due largely to the absence of fresh-water ducks, the black duck being the only one in this class found in abundance.

MANY AN OMELET, BUT TRAGEDY FOR THE BIRDS

In a few hours these 400 eggs of the laughing gull were collected for food by a native in eastern Virginia. This destructive custom is now being stopped under the Migratory Bird Treaty Act.

FLOATING BLINDS AND BOATS USEFUL

When I first visited Revels Island, many geese, brant, and broadbills (scaups), with occasional flocks of redheads, and a fair number of golden-eyes and buffleheads, or butter balls, frequented the region. This club was the first, I believe, to introduce floating blinds made of green cedar boughs stuck in buoyant wooden frames large enough to admit a ducking boat. Within these floating blinds a narrow, flat-bottomed scow was sometimes left during the shooting season for the use of the sportsmen.

Such a contrivance, when anchored, was always headed up wind, so that the decoys could be placed out to advantage. The hunter needed to watch only for the approaching birds, which, according to their habit, came in against the wind. Moreover, these floating blinds rose and fell with the tide; whereas it was difficult to shoot from stuck blinds at low tide, and an exceptionally high one exposed the boat and hunter. The floating blinds were set out before the arrival of the birds, which, in consequence, regarded the clump of cedars as a part of the landscape.

In those days no baiting was done, and it was essential to have the blinds located on good feeding-grounds or along narrow flyways. At first the shooting was satisfactory, but it gradually became poorer as the shallow bays were leased for oyster planting, and the near-by guardhouses, which were continuously occupied by watchmen in the fall and winter, became nuisances.

When naphtha launches, and later those propelled by gasoline, displaced the sailboats, these bays were kept in a state of continual disturbance, for with motor craft the lack of wind was no obstacle, but tended to increase activities.

FOWLERS HAVE AN INGENIOUS METHOD OF USING A BLIND

On the eastern shore marshes of Virginia, many of the black ducks have learned the danger of going to their feeding-places in fresh-water ponds by day, and seek them as the shades of night are falling. Taking advantage of this, the hunters have devised an unusual method of outwitting the wary birds. They make a high mound of marsh grass or seaweed near the side of the pond toward which the ducks usually come. Before the evening flight begins, the hunter, dressed in dark clothing, takes his place in

THE CATBOAT WAS FORMERLY USED ABOUT REVELS ISLAND

These craft are now replaced by motor boats.   Note the shore bird decoys placed on the point of land.

THE RUDDY TURNSTONE, OR CALICO BACK, IS AN EARLY BIRD

This common spring migrant comes, usually in flocks, to Revels Island. It is a handsome visitor that deserves protection (see, also, illustration, page 75).

front of the blind instead of behind it, for the approaching birds would see his projecting head if he were looking over the blind from behind. Sitting in front, he blends into it and is invisible.

For many years some market hunters on the marshes of the eastern shore of Virginia have used the destructive method of netting black ducks at night. Both the netting of the birds and their sale have long been outlawed, but persistent efforts to break up this nefarious practice have not yet become entirely successful.

DUCKS NETTED BY POACHERS

Nets have about a two-inch mesh, large enough to permit a duck's head to pass through, but not to be withdrawn easily, since the feathers catch on the sides of the mesh. The nets are staked horizontally along the surface of the shallow water of natural or artificial channels, leading out from ponds frequented by the birds. Corn is then scattered in front and under the nets. The ducks, following the bait heads down, swim slowly under the nets as they feed. When their heads are raised they slip through the meshes and are held fast. Sometimes almost an entire flock will be taken by this means. The outlaws who do this are so well acquainted with the marshes and work so slyly that they are difficult to apprehend.

The marshes and mud flats about Revels Island were famous for the number and variety of shore birds that visited them during migration. Even when an alarming decrease in the numbers of these birds was noticed along the greater part of the Atlantic coast,

THE BLACK-HEADED GULL APPARENTLY ENJOYS LIFE

This handsome species, often called the laughing gull on account of its cries, comes to the marshes of Revels Island from the south in April and later breeds there in large numbers.

these marshes were apparently the stopping place of all the survivors.

It is not strange that eventually a tremendous decrease in shore birds was observed during migrations; for in the spring when the local shore birds were either nesting or mating every clubhouse from Virginia to New Jersey was filled with members intent on hunting shore birds at a season when all other shooting was prohibited.

WHOLESALE SLAUGHTER WASTEFUL

Day after day I have seen otherwise reputable sportsmen bring in 200 birds, and when the weather was warm it was practically impossible to keep such birds from spoiling. In the later years, convinced of its wastefulness, I gave up spring shooting,

DECOYS ENTICE SHORE BIRDS AT REVELS ISLAND

A pair of greater yellowlegs are coming in to the wooden effigies placed in a good feeding ground for them and for willet. The blind of small bushes or of rushes overlooks this peaceful scene.

PECTORAL SANDPIPERS, OR GRASS SNIPE, WANDER FAR

These common fall and spring migrants breed far north on the Arctic tundras and winter south to the Argentine plains. They are transient visitors to the tidal waters of Revels Island.

ROBIN SNIPE COME DOWN TO THE DECOYS

They were among the favorite shore birds shot at Revels Island in former days, in the course of the spring migration. The set of their wings indicates that their flight is being checked preparatory to alighting. Unsuspecting, they were doomed to extinction by overshooting until saved by the migratory bird law.

REVELS ISLAND POND ATTRACTS MANY FEATHERED VISITORS

A typical scene is glimpsed here across a strip of marsh and cedars to the wooded ridge on the middle of the island, where many birds nest. A willet stands in the foreground.

but, having substituted the camera for the gun, I was doubtless less tempted than some of the others.

In an article published some years ago, I related an incident of one of my May hunting trips with a camera. I was accompanied by a shooting companion, who fired at a clapper rail as it arose. When the wounded bird was retrieved by the spaniel, a blood-splotched egg was laid in the sportsman's hand. The incident immediately made another convert to the creed opposed to spring shooting.

SHORE BIRDS AT NIGHT ON REVELS ISLAND

After watching for many years the shore birds in their daily flight along the beaches and mud flats or about marshy ponds, I often wondered how they passed the night. Undoubtedly in the breeding season most of these little waders are more or less concealed

about the nests, but during their migrations they remain near the open water.

To test this question on Revels Island, I made two trips with a jacklight to the places much frequented by these birds in the daytime. The Hudsonian curlews I found massed in considerable flocks on flats just above high tide, where at one time they were shot by natives with the aid of a kerosene torch or lantern. Flocks of sandpipers, turnstones, robin-snipe, and a few black-breasted plovers were seen squatting on the sandy shore, or on mud banks, while dowitchers were in the scanty grass a few yards farther back. Species that did not gather in large flocks by day, such as the yellow-legs, willet, ring-necked and semipalmated plover, were not seen. Being more or less solitary in habits, they were probably concealed in the vegetation back from the shore or about marshy ponds.

LITTLE JERRY, THE OX, WAS A COMICAL FELLOW

This dwarf was used for many purposes at Revels Island, where his odd ways made him an amusing local character (see text, page 81). Here he is hauling a load of cedar boughs.

THE OYSTER CATCHER SHOWS CLEVERNESS IN HIDING ITS NEST

This bird's artful placing of its eggs on bare sand among scattered shells and other small objects which serve as a natural camouflage renders them very difficult to find.

PECTORAL SANDPIPERS, OR GRASS SNIPE, ABOUND AT REVELS ISLAND

The camera bagged more than 125 birds at this shot as they flew over the decoys. Exposure for the picture was one-thousandth of a second. It is exceedingly difficult to photograph such small, swift flyers on the wing.

CALICO BACKS ARE SWIFT ON THE WING

These cheerful migrants, known also as the ruddy turnstone, come regularly to Revels Island in the spring. They are often seen standing on a rugged headland near surf (see, also, illustration, page 68, lower).

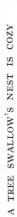

A TREE SWALLOW'S NEST IS COZY

The side of the dead tree was cut away to expose the white eggs and feather-lined nest of this common little bird. After the opening was closed, the birds went on with their housekeeping.

THE BLACK SKIMMER BUILDS NO NEST

It lays its eggs on the sand, where their protective coloring makes them difficult of detection. The casual passer would hardly distinguish them from pebbles.

THE COMMON TERN UNDERSTANDS CAMOUFLAGE

These birds were among the several waterfowl that used the sandy belt back of the tide line on Revels Island for a nesting place. It requires sharp eyes to find eggs so blending with the sand.

THE WILSON'S PLOVER IS A HANDSOME BIRD

This small coastwise migrant has always been common on the sandy beaches at Revels Island, which is near its northern breeding limit.

FOR ITS EGGS THE WILSON'S PLOVER HAS A NEST OF SORTS

It does not rely entirely upon the naked sand but chooses a spot a little secluded. Compare the nest of the common tern on the opposite page.

THE YELLOW-HAMMER, OR FLICKER, PAUSES AT THE DOOR OF ITS NEST

This picture was taken with a portrait lens in 1899, the camera being concealed in a bush four feet
away. The author, twenty yards away, pulled the string.

THE LITTLE GREEN HERON HAS AN AIRY HOME

A considerable number of these birds breed among the cedars in the interior of Revels Island. Many of their eggs and young become victims of the fish crows. No other heron bred there, but a colony of great blue herons was located on an opposite island.

THE BARN SWALLOW MISSES HIS OLD HAUNTS

This nest located under a little shelter in the wreck of an old building on Revels Island shows how ingeniously birds take advantage of favorable conditions. Barn swallows do not readily find in modern buildings the congenial nesting places old-fashioned barns provided. They do the best they can with such makeshifts as this.

A FLICKER MAKES A SECURE NEST

A pair of these birds made a hole for a home only about five feet from the ground in a dead stub near the Revels Island Clubhouse. An opening cut into the nest revealed two glossy white eggs. Then the opening was covered, leaving an entrance for the birds, and they continued using it.

In the course of my visit to Revels Island a marked transition took place in the oyster industry. In the early years I saw oysters dredged from the deeper waters of the small bays and channels, but these shell fish gradually decreased until the business was threatened. The wild oysters varied greatly in size, and it became increasingly difficult to find a sufficient quantity of the standard sizes to meet the requirements of the market.

OYSTER FARMING INTERFERES WITH WILD
FOWL

Finally the State of Virginia leased the best oyster grounds to individuals, although some of the beds were barren of oysters at the time. An abundance of old shells and some living oysters were strewn on the bottom to afford attachments for the oyster spawn, and this method of water farming soon proved so successful in producing desirable shell fish that a state of warfare developed between the lease holders protect-

ing their property and those called "oyster pirates," who believed they had an inalienable right to anything produced by the sea. In order to protect the planted oyster beds it finally became necessary to station guards armed with rifles along the shore during fall and winter. Small houses were built near by for their accommodation.

The establishment of the guards in all the best bays of the region had a disastrous effect upon the wild-fowl shooting. Geese, brant, and ducks were accustomed to feed and rest in the bays, especially in rough weather. No sooner did a flock of birds settle on the water, however, than the nearest guards would send rifle balls into their midst, driving them out to sea or into the big bays, where they would remain until darkness enabled them to return in safety. In the same period the few sailboats were displaced by many noisy motor boats that kept the birds in constant alarm.

THE AUTHOR REFRAINS FROM SHOOTING
INTO A VORTEX OF DUCKS

On the Eastern Shore there was as a rule no noticeable increased migratory flight on the approach of cold weather, but the birds arrived in easy stages from the North, as the waters there were gradually chilled. This was in contrast to the movement in spring when the wild fowl passed in almost continuous flights to their northern breeding grounds.

One afternoon in November, 1896, I was occupying a floating blind in Revels Island Bay. A strong, cold north wind, the first of the season, foretold the coming of freezing weather. Looking toward the north, I saw what appeared like a cloud in the otherwise clear sky. Soon it was apparent that an immense flock of ducks numbering thousands was approaching high in the air.

When the travelers sighted the broad shallow waters ahead, they swooped downward with a roar almost like that of a western cyclone. From a great height the birds descended in a graceful spiral. Three times this vast flock of scaups, for such they were, hurtled over the blind, dropping several hundred yards at each turn, making a sound with their wings resembling the sighing of a high wind in the treetops. Finally the visitors passed low over my decoys and alighted all about me with a tumultuous splashing, some almost striking the brush blind in which I sat.

Although tempted to shoot into the crowded ranks, with the prospect of dropping half a dozen birds, I restrained the impulse in order that the hungry and tired ducks could enjoy a period of rest, and thereby be induced to remain a day or two longer. It was a delightful experience to sit concealed in their midst. Some of the scaups splashed about vigorously, taking refreshing baths, some immediately began diving in search of food, and some faced the wind in little groups with heads drawn down on their shoulders, weary from the long flight.

No doubt among this flock were many ducks that were familiar with the attractions of this locality through visits during former seasons. They guided in the inexperienced youngsters of a new generation, even though they may previously have seen many a companion fall before the gun, an inevitable peril that these migrants must face wherever may be located their winter quarters.

As the wind and the tide forced the flock toward the opposite shore, I quietly withdrew, content in not having collected any toll from these newly arrived wanderers.

MEMORIES OF AUNT CAROLINE'S COOKING STILL LINGER

Aunt Caroline, a faithful and proficient colored cook, had charge of the club kitchen for more than a generation. She was always appreciated and was regarded as one of the club's valuable assets. Living in a State famous for its culinary art, she had few equals. The making of delicious clam chowder was one of her greatest accomplishments, and large clams were always available on a sandspit only about 100 yards away.

Early in the fall a goodly supply of oysters would be gathered from distant bays and placed in the shallow water on both sides of the long dock. Sometimes between meals a guide would wade out and get a basketful of them, which would be opened and eaten by us on the sunny side of the boathouse. Aunt Caroline served the oysters in several ways.

In the winter months, eels speared in their hibernating places in the mud at the heads of creeks were another delicacy on the bill of fare. In the hunting season Aunt Caroline produced the most appetizing dishes of perfectly cooked ducks and shore birds, besides stewed terrapin and

GREEN HERONS PERCH ON A BRANCH

These little birds are among the most cheerful and welcome of the visitors to Revels Island. Like many of their neighbors, such as the black-headed gull, the clapper rail, the grackle, the red-winged blackbird, the skimmer, and the willet, they are victims of marauding fish crows which rob their nests of eggs.

snipe potpies. The memory of her pastries, including apple and pumpkin pies, puddings, doughnuts, and other tasty products of her skill, still remains with me. Even the little tin lunch pails that were sent out to the blinds with us were like little Christmas boxes with their varied assortment of good things to allay the hearty appetites we had sharpened by hours in the open air.

LITTLE JERRY, THE OX, WAS A FAMOUS CHARACTER

One resident on Revels Island familiar to all the club members for many years was Jerry the ox. Although he was almost a dwarf of his kind, his black and white figure was considered an ornament to the flat landscape. He served us in many useful ways, and his doings afforded both exasperation and interest. Harnessed to a little cart, he hauled coal and wood from the dock and building material for new structures. He carted decoys and other material to ponds inaccessible by boat, and brought

YOUNG PURPLE GRACKLES COME OUT TO ENJOY THE SUN

Three little birds sit on a limb and wonder perhaps what the photographer is doing as he catches them with his camera.

vantage he was able to view the prolonged search with apparent enjoyment. When once harnessed to the cart, however, he was docile and energetic enough, so that his elusive ways were looked upon with tolerant amusement.

Because of the mild climate, no special shelter was provided for Jerry. When a cold wind blew, he would take refuge behind one of the buildings or amid the thickets of the little pine woods on the ridge.

His four-footed companions were the half dozen young hogs that each season grew fat on the swamp roots and other food they could gather in the marsh or along the shore until the time arrived when they were converted into ham and bacon in the smokehouse.

JERRY WAS A PHILOSOPHER

When the day of slaughter came, Jerry always looked on complacently as if approving such disposal of the grunting creatures, which had never appeared to pay the slightest attention to him. For a long time Jerry was regarded as one of the odd characters of the locality.

such produce as pumpkins, beets, turnips, and sweet potatoes from our productive garden on the higher ground to the root-house under the kitchen (see illustration, page 75).

None of these duties was to Jerry's liking, and whenever he saw the scow tie up to the dock, or noted any other occurrences that he had learned to associate with distasteful chores, he would quietly disappear. Later he would usually be found ensconced in a brushy thicket on the wooded ridge farther inland. Once the search for him seemed fruitless, and it was thought that he had probably crossed the channel to another island.

He was eventually discovered hiding behind the timbers of a wrecked schooner half a mile down the beach, from which point of

CHAPTER V — PART II

Last Days at Revels Island

LIKE many other members of the Revels Island Club, in the middle nineties, I visited the shore in the spring not so much for shooting at a time when other game was protected as for enjoying the beauty of Nature throwing off her drab winter garment and replacing it with green, swelling buds and unfolding leaves. This beauty, the gentle warmth of the sun, and the soft spring breezes constituted a welcome change to residents of more northern latitudes who loved the out-of-doors.

To Revels Island during these balmy days came nearly all the species of shore birds that inhabit our Atlantic coast. Some were en route from their winter homes in South America to their breeding grounds beyond the Arctic Circle. There were others that nest in less distant places, as well as those that remain to rear their young along the Eastern Shore. Though the different species arrived at different times, each form had its special schedule of arrival and departure.

First to appear were the jacksnipes, or grass snipes, which usually kept to the mainland, for the fresh-water meadows were to their liking. These were followed successively by Hudsonian curlews (many of which had wintered in South Carolina), willets, greater and lesser yellowlegs, numerous species of sandpipers, plovers (ring-necked, Wilson's, and black-breasted), turnstones, dowitchers, and knots or robin snipe.

In those days the wastefulness and cruelty of shooting birds that were already mating,

THE NEST OF THE CLAPPER RAIL IS ADROITLY HIDDEN

Built beside the tidal waters it was artfully covered with scraps of vegetation whenever the bird left it so that it resembled the surrounding drift matter. The eggs, proportionately large for the size of the bird, are very palatable and are gathered in great numbers by the natives of the Revels Island region.

THE CHUCK-WILL'S-WIDOW RESTS LYING DOWN

This picture was made by the author 35 years ago. It shows the bird in characteristic position crouching on a limb. The legs and feet are not visible until it rises for flight.

Sound, were millions of marsh and deep-water ducks, together with tens of thousands of greater snow and Canada geese and whistling swans.

An ample supply of wooden and tin decoys, shaped and painted to resemble the larger or more desirable species of shore birds, was available at the club. In a catboat with a large leg-of-mutton sail the gunner was conveyed by his guide from the clubhouse to a blind, which, the direction and force of the wind being considered, was best located for the purpose in view.

In hunting curlew, fowlers often dug a pit at the edge of a sand point in the marsh where the birds were accustomed to feed as the receding tide exposed the mud flats. When the tide was rising, the curlews followed the narrow channels through the island, alighting to rest on the grassy flats along either side. In such places, the hunters, well concealed behind grass blinds, could enjoy flight shooting.

or those that were actually in the midst of their nesting activities among the broken shells of the seashore or in tussocks of grass in the marshes, were not appreciated until several species were approaching extinction.

Because of the large number of species, each with its peculiar habits, shore-bird shooting at the island afforded a far pleasanter and more varied form of sport than did the wildfowling in the adjacent bays, where the salt water appeared to have attractions mainly for scaups, golden-eyes, geese, and brant. Comparatively few kinds of waterfowl were to be found in the vicinity of the island, although not much farther to the south, on Back Bay and Currituck

These birds were favorites with many sportsmen because of their size and slow, steady flight. Their large, compact flocks could be seen a mile or more away, as they came in to their feeding or resting places. If the hunter wished to shoot yellow-legs or willets, he would occupy a bush blind close to the edge of a little fresh-water pond, in the mud and shallow water of which the decoys would be placed in such spots as these birds commonly frequented when feeding.

The turnstones gathered on the mud banks bordering the larger bays in company

ITS EYES GLISTEN AT NIGHT LIKE A CAT'S (SEE TEXT, PAGE 179)

The chuck-will's-widow lies flat on the ground. This picture and that on the opposite page show the peculiar habit of this bird when it is resting.

with the smaller sandpipers that preferred the open shores. Because of the small size of these birds and their habit of flying in compact flocks, the gunners were able to bring them down in such numbers, sometimes a dozen or more at a shot, that they provided the material for many a delicious potpie, a welcome relief from the products of the frying pan.

CAMERA HUNTING BIRDS AND NESTS ON REVELS ISLAND

Toward the end of the season, about the middle of May, flocks of robin snipe frequented the exposed sea beaches, and for years they afforded excellent shooting. After a time I became seriously alarmed about the future of these handsome birds, for they began to decrease rapidly in numbers, and late in May, 1904, I made a special trip to Revels Island to obtain pictures of what I feared might be a doomed species.

All day I remained in a blind with my camera before a flock circled over the decoys. The marked difference between hunting with a gun and with a camera was here demonstrated. Had I discharged a gun at this flock, a few birds might have been dropped, and the rest would have hurried on in wild alarm toward their far northern home. As it was, I obtained a fine series of pictures of the entire flock as its members circled back time after time to satisfy their innocent curiosity concerning the strange wooden counterfeits.

During the days I passed in the blinds I was much interested in noting the skill with which some of the local guides imitated the notes of these birds. Often when the birds were passing on their northward flight, or were merely seeking new feeding grounds after having been disturbed by a rising tide, they would pass our decoys, which were strung out near shore, without paying them the least attention.

The guide at my side in the blind would imitate the note peculiar to the species that was passing, and very commonly the flock would respond by swinging in on a graceful curve that would bring them within gunshot. If we did not shoot, they would alight among the decoys, where we could photograph them at our leisure.

Nature photographers, especially beginners, find much enjoyment in picturing the nests and eggs of birds to be found so

A WILLET ON THE WING GOES FAST

The bird shown here is flying from its nest in a clumsy, grotesque manner to draw attention away
from its treasures. Such flight pictures are exceedingly difficult to take (see text, page 93).

THE WILLET HIDES ITS HOME WITH GREAT SKILL

The nests are concealed by overhanging grass that must be bent away to expose the eggs. If an
intruder approaches, the bird leads him away by awkward flight, as in the upper picture.

A CLAPPER RAIL SITS SNUGLY AT REVELS ISLAND

When incubating under cover of the canopy of marsh grasses, this marsh hen is almost invisible. On leaving the nest, it pulls over it the surrounding grasses (see text, page 94).

THE CLAPPER RAIL LAYS A LARGE CLUTCH

Even when the bird is gone the eggs, which sometimes reach 18 in number, are not seen readily except when the overhanging grass is pushed aside, as in this photograph.

ONLY A KEEN AND EXPERIENCED EYE CAN FIND IT

The meadowlark's nest is so well concealed by overarching grass that it is espied with difficulty.

CLEVER CONCEALMENT SPELLS SAFETY

The bob-white quail nest, filled to overflowing, is skillfully hidden. The photograph was taken on the mainland near Revels Island.

readily in most country places. The more ambitious of them photograph the parent bird on the nest, or when it is feeding its young. In many cases the notes made by these amateurs have proved of value to ornithologists concerned with the home life of our birds.

At first, being interested mainly in game animals and birds, I neglected opportunities to get pictures of the nests, even of rare birds. Moreover, I was seldom in the forests in May or June, my outings occurring usually at a time when the birds were already hatched and on the wing.

WILLETS HAVE BUILT AN ISLAND HOME

They have constructed their nest on a tuft in a marsh.

After many visits in spring to the island as a sportsman, I went there to make photographic records of the birds and their nests. Once on going to photograph the northern flight of the robin snipe, I found that the movement had not yet begun, and after waiting a day or two, I decided that it would be interesting to look for the nests of breeding birds. Such a search should result in a fairly complete census of the summer-bird residents of the Eastern Shore. How fascinating this endeavor proved.

On the first morning of my quest I left the cottage with a small camera affixed to a tripod for use in taking pictures of stationary objects at close range. This was the outfit that I had used in photographing fungi in the forests of northern Michigan. First I went down on the sand beach that extended for nearly a mile along the southern end of the island.

I had never hunted on this beach but had often walked its entire length for exercise after a day in the cramped confines of a shooting blind, and frequently had brought back a basket of clams for Aunt Caroline to convert into one of her famous chowders. In addition to sanderlings, turnstones, and other migrants, the birds that inhabited this beach in the spring included a number of species that remained to breed, and it seemed quite certain that on the sand above high tide some nests could be found.

After I had gone a few hundred yards along the beach, I saw the black and white figure of an oyster catcher near the edge of

the water, but it took wing as I approached. Closely examining the upper beach near the place where it had appeared, I found two heavily splotched eggs in a little hollow where the sand had been scratched out. The eggs were surrounded by a number of broken sea shells as if an attempt had been made to outline a crude nest or to camouflage the eggs. I photographed the eggs and continued my walk.

A TERN UTTERS PROTEST

Soon afterward I discovered three dark-colored eggs with dark spots in a depression in the bare sand, but no parent bird was visible in the neighborhood. As I was focusing the camera on this new find, the identity of the owner was established by the arrival of a common tern, which flew over my head protesting loudly.

As I approached the end of the sandy point, I observed a pair of black skimmers on the beach, but I doubted that they were nesting there, since these birds had a large breeding colony on Hog Island, on the opposite side of the channel. I was pleasantly surprised, therefore, to find their nest in this unexpected place.

After I had photographed it, I retraced my steps to the clubhouse along a line of small sand dunes covered with bunches of grass, from the direction of which the notes of Wilson's plover had sounded as I came down the beach. In that vicinity I had frequently seen these pretty little ring-

THE OSPREY SEEMS THE SPIRIT OF FREEDOM

Each year a pair of these fish hawks reoccupied their bulky nest of previous years located near the top of a large dead pine, where the lower quarters of the structure were occupied by blackbirds. They are heavy but skillful aviators, wheeling at apparently impossible angles, and darting down like arrows to capture the unlucky fish, which swims near enough to the surface to be detected by their keen eyes.

cated that their nest was close by. Careful search, however, failed to disclose the nest they were guarding.

These birds are remarkably skillful in concealing their eggs. I was probably led astray by the cunning maneuverings of the birds, which showed apparent anxiety first in one place and then in another. The willet is one of the few species of shore birds that nest as far south as Virginia. I saw many willets in Florida in winter. The migratory flights of some of these birds seem to be comparatively short.

Abandoning the search for the nest of the willets, I returned to the clubhouse, in the vicinity of which I hoped to obtain another picture. The buildings were surrounded by several acres of tall, thin grass that afforded some grazing for Jerry, the ox, in addition to harboring myriads of mosquitoes that could not be dislodged, even by the heaviest winds off the ocean. If a per-

necked plovers. After a considerable search I found a set of their eggs on the sand and added a photograph of them to my collection.

Two days later I returned, and by concealing the camera a few feet away, with a thread running about 75 yards to some sheltering bushes, I was able to release the shutter while the parent bird stood close by the eggs (see page 77). On my way back to the cottage, as I was crossing some low, wet ground covered with long grass, a pair of willets flew about close overhead, uttering cries of distress—behavior that indi-

son wearing black garments passed through this grass in the spring, in a few minutes the black on his back would turn to a uniform brown from the host of mosquitoes alighting on it. Fortunately, in the daytime these insects were not very vicious, and at night well-screened windows prevented them from being annoying.

This grassy locality was the resort of a pair of meadow larks that could be seen flying about at all hours of the day, and heard singing musically mornings and evenings. That these birds were nesting on this little island, surrounded by miles of salt marshes, and so far away from the mainland, would have seemed unlikely to me had not their actions indicated that they were housekeeping.

Several times I had observed one of the birds descend into the grass near a small cedar. Approaching the spot, I searched carefully and at length discovered a pyramid of grass tops, like a little Indian tepee, under which was a nest containing four eggs. Parting the grass, I photographed the cleverly concealed nest and then restored the canopy to its original position.

By this time I had photographed the nests and eggs of five quite different kinds of birds, and before attempting any further subjects, I decided to develop the plates to learn whether the camera was doing its duty. The developed plates proved to be satisfactory, and I started out the following morning to visit a breeding colony of laughing gulls.

IN AERIAL MANEUVERS THE OSPREY EXCELS

Rising, descending, soaring or reconnoitering, this bird is conspicuous along the shores. As a disciple of Izaak Walton, like the kingfisher, it may, in a practical sense, be regarded as a connecting link between land and water birds, for both live continuously along a water front and depend wholly upon fish taken on or near the surface by a skillful, arrow-like plunge from high above.

These birds had been seen circling about the marshy end of a bay situated about half a mile west of the clubhouse.

Before departing for the bay, I asked Jonah, the colored chore boy, whether the gulls had begun to lay. He replied that he had been down there a few days before, and that he thought that more than a hundred pairs were nesting.

Approaching the edge of this marsh, I found a place where the wind and waves had beaten down the bushes along high-tide mark, and where considerable debris had lodged. Wherever there was a flat surface

of rushes or other material a foot or more in extent, a pair of gulls had hollowed out a small depression and had laid their eggs. very little effort was expended in constructing a nest. I took several pictures of these crude nests.

As I returned to the clubhouse the sight of a flicker led me to try to locate the nest of the pair of these birds that had been seen flying about a little south of the houses. A short search revealed a dead pine stub containing a nesting hole only five feet above the ground. Placing the tripod and camera within a few feet of the tree, I fas-

LIKE A HUGE LEAF IS THE OSPREY

In flight it soars, wheels, and darts in graceful maneuvers, though it is rather slow awing. Any high treetop may be its momentary perch.

tened a string to the shutter and moved off a short distance. In a few minutes a flicker alighted on the side of the stub close to the entrance to the nest and helped me to a satisfactory picture (see page 78).

I next explored the pine ridge, where I expected to find the nests of many other species of birds. Low ground, through which ran a tidal creek, separated the grounds surrounding the clubhouse from the ridge, and across this an elevated board walk a quarter of a mile long had been built. This made it possible for one to visit the pine ridge even in times of high tides.

In a small bush close to the boardwalk I discovered a little nest containing four speckled eggs. It was impossible for me to identify the bird as it flew away, but later I was convinced that it was a seaside finch, a rather common bird in those marshes.

In an old clearing on the ridge stood the ruins of the first clubhouse, which had been built in 1885. In a sheltered nook of the ruined structure, a pair of barn swallows had built a nest. Close by, a pair of tree swallows was found nesting in the bottom of a hole in an old stub. With a little

saw I cut an opening to the nest and exposed the four beautiful white eggs on a soft bed of feathers. After taking a picture, I nailed the strip of wood back in place so that the birds could continue their housekeeping undisturbed (see page 77).

From this place I went westward to a patch of low cedars, which sheltered a dozen nests of the grackle. These structures, large and deep, were composed almost entirely of coarse swamp grass with a finer lining. After taking one photograph of a nest showing the eggs, I found another nest in which the young were nearly ready to fly. They were placed in a row on a neighboring branch on which they sat for their portraits, and appeared to be quite unafraid. Meanwhile, the mother bird protested vehemently (see page 84).

Beyond this point, at a place where deciduous bushes replaced the cedars, I saw a flash of brown and recognized the slender, graceful form of the brown thrasher with which I was so familiar in the winter quarters of the species in Florida, as well as during the spring and summer in the District of Columbia. A short search revealed that it also was nesting, and I took a photograph of its neat home. In some little bushes that grew among the heavy grass in damp open ground between the trees on the ridge and the open marsh a number of red-winged blackbirds were nesting, and these made easy subjects for the camera.

From the border of the marsh I turned toward the east to examine the wooded ridge near the site of the old clubhouse. As I approached some large yellow pines, several fish crows departed hurriedly and thus betrayed the presence of a half dozen nests. These were beyond reach, however, without the aid of a ladder or strips of wood nailed to the tree trunks.

Leaving these nests for later attention, I went on to another group of low cedars, very much like those in which the grackles were nesting, and here found many nests of the little green heron. They were flimsy structures, consisting of loosely built platforms of small sticks with saucer-shaped depressions in the tops for the eggs. One nest that I photographed held four greenish eggs, and another contained young birds four or five days old.

The green heron is the smallest and one of the most common of the true herons of North America. When perched in a tree, it usually sits with its head drawn down so that it has the appearance at a distance of a rather unattractive bird. But when standing alertly upright, it discloses all the grace of form usual to its kind. At a distance it looks dull and dingy in hue, but when held in the hand it reveals exquisitely blended variegated colors.

Although usually solitary in habits, during the nesting season the green herons gather in small groups or colonies in their chosen breeding places. The birds are so frequently seen as they rise and fly along the course of small wooded streams that in some parts of their range in the eastern States, the species is commonly called "fly-up-the-creek."

Not far from the colony of green herons stood a dead pine in which was an osprey's nest. Near this I built a blind of bushes and focused on the nest a camera equipped with a large lens. After a wait of only a few minutes the parent birds began flying about and I was able to obtain a series of photographs showing them circling about on outspread wings or perching on the nest.

Ospreys, or fish hawks, have long frequented the large salt marshes along the eastern shore of Virginia, where the meadows are penetrated by small bays and tidal creeks in which there are many fish that attract them. In many parts of the marshes, however, no woody growth is found other than bushes too frail to support the bulky nests, and the ospreys must carry their catches miles away to their young.

OSPREYS BUILD NESTS ON CROSSBARS OF TELEPHONE POLES

Several years after a life-saving station had been established on Parramore Island and a telephone line had been built across the Revels Island marsh, the ospreys began building their nests, precariously balanced, on the top crossbars of the telephone poles. These interfered so seriously with the working of the line that all the nests were destroyed. Sometimes the birds built nests on the roofs of cabins in the marshes.

I had not as yet located and photographed the nests of the willet and the marsh hen, two game birds in which I was particularly interested, and which were unusually abundant on Revels Island during the summer.

While I was taking the osprey picture, I noticed several willets flying back and forth over a little fresh-water pond, a short distance away in the marsh. As I approached the place, a willet sprang up from the tuft of grass on a little hummock surrounded by water. Although I looked carefully, I could see no nest, but when I parted the tall grass I discovered one containing four eggs. Pushing the grass to one side I took a picture and then restored the grassy cover (see page 91).

Soon afterward I obtained two additional pictures of the nests of the willet, but could not get one of a bird on the eggs. The bird would fly away as soon as I approached. It usually alighted in the grass at some distance and returned to its eggs under that cover so stealthily that I never knew just when it arrived.

PHOTOGRAPHING A WILLET IN FLIGHT

At one place I stuck a stick in the ground as a marker about eight feet from the nest. Then I focused the camera carefully ready for a shot later, and retired for half an hour. Setting the focal plane shutter at 1/1000 of a second, I stalked cautiously up to the marker and aimed the camera several feet above the nest. I had just got in the proper position when the willet sprang through the concealing grass, and the picture I obtained shows it hurtling through the air (see page 86).

The tall, stately willet is one of the handsomest of our shore birds. The variegated plumage of its back is brownish gray, black, and white, and the secondaries and part of the primaries in the long tapering wings are brilliant white. The bird is strikingly beautiful in flight. During the nesting season it incessantly utters loud ringing cries, *pilly-will-willet, pilly-will-willet*—as it flies about or hovers over the head of an intruder in its nesting ground. It is the only shore bird, so far as I am aware, that tries to protect its nest. I have found it nesting from northern Florida to Delaware, the breeding range on the Atlantic coast being comparatively limited.

Hundreds of marsh hens, or clapper rails, nested within a mile of the clubhouse. Their nests were usually built within fifty feet of the upper tide limits or about fresh-water ponds. Like the nests of the willet, they were well concealed from the keen-eyed crows that flew continually about the marshes in search of eggs. They were placed in thick grass or rushes and covered with grassy canopies.

I found that by zigzagging back and forth near the water, especially during high tide, I could easily flush the birds, or, if they were absent, could discover the nests by looking beneath every wisp of grass blade such as is woven above the eggs by the parent bird. At the time of my search the nest contained from four to 16 eggs. In those having 16 incubation had begun.

I parted the grass concealing one of these completed clutches of eggs and took the picture shown in the text. I then placed a small camera covered with grass in front of the nest where hatching had begun, and twisted back the concealing grass so as to expose the eggs or the setting bird. I attached a thread to the shutter so that by pulling on it I could take the picture when I was about 50 feet away.

After a short absence I cautiously returned, none too soon to get the desired photograph. The mother bird was sitting on the nest busily engaged in pulling back, with little jerking motions of her bill, the grass blades I had disturbed (page 89).

The next morning I returned with some slats to nail on a pine tree containing a nest of the fish crow, and had little difficulty in getting a satisfactory picture (see page 66).

FISH CROWS DRIVEN AWAY

The following year I was able to climb up the same tree and get a photograph of a nearly grown young crow, the two others having left the nest while I was focusing the camera. When the extent of the depredations of the fish crow on other nesting birds was fully realized, the superintendent of the club was directed to destroy all their nests found on the place. This was done with a shotgun, and most of these pests were driven away.

The last nest I photographed was that of a bob-white. It was located near tide water on the mainland opposite the island, and was well hidden in dense grass growing in a fence corner. It contained 15 eggs.

In the week I devoted to nest hunting I took photographs of 18 species, which were fairly representative of the birds most commonly living there during the breeding season. By concentrating one's efforts on a given area typical of the surrounding country, one can obtain a series of pictures that affords evidence of the birds nesting there, and that indicates their conceptions of what constitutes a desirable home. In many instances efforts apparently had been made by the birds to conceal or camouflage the eggs and later the young.

I often neglected to take the picture of a bird or animal when occasion offered, believing that this could be done, possibly more conveniently later. Delay, however, is poor policy when dealing with wild things, for they are subject to many more vicissitudes than are tame creatures.

PROCRASTINATION THE ENEMY

As a striking illustration, I might cite my failure to photograph the largest osprey nest I have ever seen. It was in the top of a tall dead pine on Revels Island, where during many successive seasons I saw the structure grow in bulk by annual additions. The tree was an outstanding one in a grove north of the clubhouse, and so large and elevated was the nest that it constituted a conspicuous landmark for visitors seeking the island.

Year after year I passed this tree always with the thought that some day I would photograph it with the osprey perching on its huge structure or circling over it. Time passed without my doing so, however, until one afternoon in the spring of 1902 I examined the locality to determine the best place in which to conceal the camera in order to obtain the long-desired picture which I planned to take the next morning.

An unusually heavy northeaster occurred that night. The club buildings creaked and rattled under the strain, but, comfortably sheltered, we enjoyed the rush and shrieking of the wind and the booming of the surf along the shore.

The following morning dawned clear and warm, and, shouldering my tripod and camera, I set out to photograph the osprey's home. Reaching the spot, I found the gaunt dead pine prone on the ground and the nest reduced to a great mass of sticks and other material. That the tree had sunk slowly to the earth under the force of the wind was indicated by the three unbroken brown-blotched eggs of the hawk that lay on the ground beside the nest. Among the debris were seven or eight smaller, bluish eggs of grackles, which had been unceremoniously ejected from their big, rent-free apartment house by the catastrophe that had overtaken their landlord.

Millions of shots are fired every season at ducks passing over decoys, or on flights to feeding or resting grounds. Unless a duck is shot through the head or other vital organ, or comes down with a broken wing, it may not be apparent that it has received a wound that will cause death in a few minutes by internal hemorrhage. Every gunner, therefore, should observe closely a departing bird that may have been hit, although it shows no evidence of injury.

Frequently a wounded bird will suddenly drop after it has flown several hundred yards, very commonly when the gunner is reloading his weapon or has his attention otherwise distracted. I recall an instance of retrieving two black ducks that if they had not been watched in their flight of about a mile would not have been found. This occurred during an unusually low tide in Revels Island Bay, when much of the bottom was exposed for a couple of hours.

Knowing that under such conditions black ducks were likely to come in considerable numbers to feed in the few places, I built a small blind at the edge of the marsh in the hope that some would pass within range. After a while a pair of black ducks headed in my direction, but dropped to a pile of seaweed nearly a hundred yards away.

Substituting for the cartridges in my gun others containing No. 3 shot, I stood up in the blind. As I expected, the pair arose almost perpendicularly, quacking loudly. I fired at the upper duck and then took a shot at the other.

I saw the birds leave, apparently unscathed. I could not be sure of this, however, and I watched them fly north toward the end of the bay.

A GROUP OF REVELS ISLAND GUIDES IN 1901

Leading simple lives in those days, they continued to honor the ancestral traditions of sturdy honesty in contact with visitors from the outer world. Unfortunately, at the time this picture was taken some of the older men who had grown gray in the service were absent.

When they were so far away that they looked like two tiny black spots, one of them turned and came back along the opposite shore. Its high and undeviating flight suddenly ended; it stopped abruptly and fell straight down with a splash on the surface of the muddy pool, directly in line with a distant stunted cedar.

By its actions I knew that the duck had died in mid-air before it fell. While pulling up my hip boots to go for it, I happened to notice that the surviving duck was returning along the same course as that followed by the first. Within a hundred yards of its dead mate it, too, collapsed and fell with a splash. A few minutes later I made the trip across the muddy flat and without difficulty found both birds.

Bald eagles were rather common about Revels Island. They seldom harmed the other birds, but one once caused great excitement at the clubhouse. Captain Wickes, then superintendent, was returning to the club through the "swash" channel in a small ducking boat when he saw one of these handsome birds flying overhead within easy gunshot. Thinking it would make a good specimen to mount as a trophy, he fired and dropped it near the boat.

OUR EMBLEMATIC BIRD MAKES A STIR

Picking up the apparently lifeless form, Captain Wickes stowed it between his legs and continued rowing toward the clubhouse. Suddenly one of his legs was gripped by the long talons of the bird, which sank into the flesh, causing great pain.

At such close quarters he could neither shoot the bird nor hit it with an oar. He did what seemed to be the best thing— leaped overboard, hoping to drown his assailant and thus cause it to release a grip that would only enlarge his wounds if he tried to pull the bird away while it was alive. As he came to the surface, he found the eagle had let go its hold and was standing erect on the bow seat of the boat.

No wind was blowing at the time, and the boat continued to drift with the tide toward the clubhouse. The captain swam ashore and limped along after the drifting boat for a quarter of a mile, expressing his feelings meanwhile in violent language.

The boat at length touched the bank at a bend, and the ousted skipper was able to get on board. Seizing one of the small oars, he gave the defiant bird a knockout blow, and it sank to the bottom of the boat, apparently with a broken neck.

On reaching his destination, the captain carried his trophy ashore, and threw it on the porch back of the kitchen.

While binding his bleeding wounds, for a small artery had been opened, he heard loud shrieks from the rear of the kitchen. Hastily tying on a temporary bandage, he hurried back to learn the cause of the uproar. A colored maid, with bare feet, while examining the bird, had given it a kick to turn it over for further inspection. Thereupon the apparently lifeless bird had sunk his talons deep into the calf of her leg. She shrieked and jumped about on one foot until she fell down the back steps to the

ground. Picking up a piece of stove wood, the captain finished the eagle.

There were days in the spring when the migrating shore birds were not in flight, and then I turned my attention to nesting gulls, skimmers, herons, and oyster-catchers, or to such land birds as the osprey, fish crow, flicker, brown thrasher, tree swallow, grackle, and bluebird. Seldom at this season of the year need the camera be laid aside for want of subjects, and thus the period lost by the devotees of hunting, now that spring shooting is necessarily prohibited throughout the country, can be utilized by the true lover of the out-of-doors.

The next to my last trip to the island was made to photograph the robin snipe and the Hudsonian curlew, for it seemed to me as if they were going the way of the wild pigeon and would soon be exterminated.

My last visit to the island was in May, 1923, at which time I was accompanied by Dr. E. W. Nelson, then Chief of the Biological Survey of the United States Department of Agriculture. The purpose of the trip was to check up on the reported increase of shore birds as a result of their protection under the Migratory Bird Law.

The launch had no sooner put out from the little town of Wachapreague, on the mainland side of Wachapreague Inlet, north of Parramore Island, than Hudsonian curlews began springing up on all sides, and we observed nearly a thousand on the six-mile trip. Yet this bird had nearly become extinct ten years before.

THE FEDERAL LAW HELPS

In our several days on the marshes and mud flats we found that the protection given the birds by the Federal law had resulted in an increase in the numbers of most of the shore birds, including the willet, the black-breasted and the smaller plovers, the knot or robin-snipe, dowitcher, calico-backs, or turnstones, and many varieties of sandpipers. The yellow-legs, however, were scarce, since an open season still permitted shooting of this species.

Subsequently the Advisory Board, of which I was a member, a committee of game commissioners and sportsmen appointed to offer recommendations for drafting regulations relative to the administration of the Migratory Bird Law, advised that the season be closed on yellow-legs. This suggestion was adopted by the Department of Agriculture in 1927.

CHAPTER VI — PART I

Wild Fowl on Currituck Sound of North Carolina

I HEARD so much years ago about the great gatherings of wild fowl in Currituck Sound that I longed to go there. The opportunity came through an invitation from W. Cameron Forbes, president of the Swan Island Club, to Dr. E. W. Nelson and me, suggesting that we might find that location a good one in which to study and photograph the assembled waterfowl.

On the evening of January 3, 1922, we left Washington on the boat for Norfolk on our way to the Currituck. The heaviest freeze of the winter occurred just at that time, the temperature dropping to 12 degrees Fahrenheit. During the first 20 miles the steamer had to break its way through the thin ice that extended from shore to shore on the Potomac River, and although this offered little obstruction to the steel hull of the large boat, we became concerned regarding the conditions that we might find at our destination.

Although the ice in the river delayed our arrival at Norfolk the next morning, we were in time to catch a little spur-line train for the village of Munden, on the western shore of the Sound, where the launch from the Swan Island Club was to meet us.

ICE LOCKED THE WAY

When we arrived at Munden we saw from the little dock a broad sheet of ice extending far offshore and no sign of the launch. A heavier launch from Monkey Island had just arrived, however, and the captain told us that he had experienced much difficulty in working his way through the ice and that he was certain that the lighter-draft launch from Swan Island would be unable to get through.

Because of these circumstances it was necessary for Doctor Nelson to return to Washington; the time he could give to this trip was definitely limited. I decided to remain, hoping that I might be able to get to the haunts of the birds.

As I sat on the dock in a somewhat disconsolate mood, talking over the weather prospects with some old fishermen, a powerful fishing tug forced its way in and tied up. The captain assured me that he could take me close to shore in front of the club so that I could land in a flat-bottomed boat.

This plan worked out successfully. The tug broke its way through the ice to within about 500 yards of the shore, and I slid ashore in a skiff pushed out on top of the ice. I was soon seated in the comfortable clubhouse, where the superintendent made me welcome.

Aside from the superintendent, I found the club deserted, for at the prospect of a freeze the members had hurriedly departed fearing that they might be marooned.

AT THE SWAN ISLAND CLUB

The Swan Island clubhouse was a long rambling building standing within a few yards of the water. A large window on one side of the living room overlooked the water and the wild fowl that gathered there except on the rare occasions when the bay was ice-bound. The part of the bay directly in front of the clubhouse has long been a favorite resort for wild geese and swans as well as for numerous species of ducks.

By a friendly understanding between the club members and the residents of the region no shooting was done within a quarter of a mile of the house. The birds as usual soon made free use of the sanctuary, and from the windows at the club one could study them in great detail. Almost immediately after my arrival my attention was attracted to several Wilson's snipe that were feeding with the utmost unconcern on the shore within a few yards of the living-room windows.

Late in the afternoon the ice broke, and a lane of open water appeared a little north of the house. Several hundred whistling swans soon gathered there and patiently awaited the disappearance of the ice so that their feeding places in marshes and bays would be unlocked. Realizing that they were not hunted by the gunners who created havoc among the other denizens of these waters, the swans had become unsuspicious.

Among the club decoys were half a dozen well-fashioned wooden swans, made much larger than the actual birds in order that they might be visible at a greater distance. With the assistance of a club attendant, I placed two of these decoys a few feet from shore opposite the flock of swans in the open lead. In a small blind built a short

EXCITED CURIOSITY BRINGS THEM SHOREWARD

This family of swans, the white parents and five grayish young, are examining some wooden decoys anchored a little farther inshore, and their expressive attitudes indicate their mental disturbance over the strange figures they see. The two pure white old birds, being wary of strange things, keep a little more aloof than the less experienced young.

distance back from the shore I remained concealed for several hours.

Although no swans came within photographic range, I passed my time profitably in studying through my field glasses a fine species that I had previously known only from books and hearsay. While I was in the blind, a blue heron stalked calmly about in the shallow water near at hand, apparently feeling secure in the presence of the two overgrown images of such usually watchful neighbors.

When I returned to the clubhouse, the superintendent, who had been watching my efforts to photograph the swans, expressed the opinion that one reason for my lack of success was my location back of a barren sand beach. The two decoys apparently had been unable to overcome the lack of attraction of water that contained no growth of food plants.

Next morning we built a blind in front of a slightly submerged sand bar south of the house, where Canada geese were awaiting the melting of the ice on their feeding places just as the swans had been doing the day before. From the concealment afforded by this blind I obtained a good series of Canada-goose pictures. I returned to Washington the next day, convinced that I must become better acquainted with the Currituck waters.

The superintendent of the Swan Island Club told me that when the first thin ice of this cold period had formed and put a stop to the wild-fowl shooting, one member had turned his attention to fish crows. With the

aid of wooden crow decoys and a crow call he had killed more than three dozen of these harmful birds. Wild-fowl hunters in general along the Atlantic coast might well follow his example and help destroy these black robbers.

Not long after I had been landed over the thin ice at Swan Island, two guides arrived from the main shore. They reported that they had experienced much difficulty in getting through the ice on the bay. On their way across they had noticed the body of an animal lying on the smooth surface. It had proved to be a dead wildcat or bobcat, and they had brought it with them.

A WILDCAT PERISHES FROM EXPOSURE

Although we examined it carefully, we could find no sign of injury. We were forced to the conclusion that for some reason it had entered the water, perhaps to escape dogs, and, surrounded by the newly formed ice, had died from exposure before it could reach shore (see illustration, page 102).

Its northern cousin, the Canada lynx, lives near the tree limit in Alaska and Canada, where the winter temperatures sometimes go down as low as 70 degrees below zero. Bobcats in some parts of their range in the United States can withstand very cold weather.

It is a fact not generally known that in parts of their range, at least, all the American cats, including the mountain lion and the lynx, are good swimmers, and take to the water rather freely when occasion arises. When in well-fed and healthy condition many mammals and birds can survive severe cold if they can find their accustomed shelter when not actually in action. Most species from a permanently warm region, however, suffer much and often die when subjected to prolonged cold. Such is known to have been the case with Mexican bob-whites introduced into some northern States.

Desiring to see Currituck Sound under favorable weather conditions, I made arrangements for another trip there the following year, in company with Dr. Frank M. Chapman. We left Washington on January 9, 1923, and proceeded to Monkey Island, in the northern part of the sound. There we were joined by the Federal game warden of the district, who was to take us with him on an official tour of inspection as far as Narrows Island, the home of the Narrows Island Club.

In the course of our passage down the sound in the warden's boat we observed several parties in motor boats hunting ducks. The warden approached each boat and warned the occupants that hunting migratory wild fowl from motor boats was illegal. He told them a repetition of the offense would mean arrest, appearance before the Federal court, and a heavy fine or imprisonment. The information spread rapidly and produced good results for that season at least.

AN EAGLE CATCHES A COOT

In a bay close by our quarters on Monkey Island was a large flock of coots, locally called "blue peters." Suddenly a bald eagle appeared from out the sky and headed for the coots. They exhibited great consternation as the eagle hovered over one end of the flock and then dropped down to within a few feet of the water.

Although not skilled in submerging, the coots dived out of sight. The eagle, thus foiled, mounted and again descended as the birds came to the surface. Again it drove them down. These maneuvers were repeated several times, but the eagle made no serious attempt to capture any of the birds.

After we had watched the birds for about five minutes we were called to lunch, and asked one of the guides to watch the eagle while we were away. The eagle maneuvered for a few minutes longer, then swooped and without difficulty seized one of the exhausted birds. When we returned, the marauder was seated on a channel post eating its victim.

A fish crow, flying by the busy eagle, saw a chance for a meal. It audaciously flew in behind and, beneath the eagle's tail, pulled away some of the remains of the coot. Apparently eagles do not "eat crow," for they might easily capture these slowly flying birds when they are crossing the waters of a wide bay.

Another odd sight that interested Chapman and me was a greater snow goose feeding with some tame white geese near the clubhouse. One winter the bird had noticed that regular rations were served to the tame geese, and it had deserted its fellows and joined them.

A SNOW GOOSE JOINS NEW ASSOCIATES

In the spring it went North with others of its kind to carry on its family duties, close to the Arctic circle, and no one expected to see it again. On the approach of cold weather, however, it reappeared, and parted from its kin to join again its adopted mates.

One day I threw out a handful of corn as bait and obtained a picture of this wise bird (see page 104, lower). Its alertness, both on foot and on the wing, was notable, and it gathered a large share of the grain while the tame geese were waddling about wholly unable to compete with their more active guest. The noise made by the focal-plane shutter caused the interloper to take wing in alarm. It did not return before I departed, apparently fearing the camera and its long tube of brass.

From Narrows Island Doctor Chapman returned to New York, but I remained for a few days' further work among the birds. Both of us enjoyed this expedition, which yielded many good photographs for my collection. My interest in this wonderful wintering place for wild fowl was so great that the following fall I became a member of the Narrows Island Club. The motion for my election was made by my long-cherished friend, Dr. George Bird Grinnell, dean of American sportsmen, and at that time president of the club.

The great flight of ducks, geese, swans, and other wild fowl that since time immemorial has swept down each fall through eastern North America from the northern breeding places occupies mainly two great wintering grounds. The most extensive of these includes the waters along the Atlantic coast from the head of Chesapeake Bay southward to Core Sound near Beaufort, North Carolina. The center of abundance

A FLOCK OF CANADA GEESE ARRIVES AT CURRITUCK SOUND

There is no more inspiring sight for a lover of wild creatures than the coming of wild geese from their far-northern breeding grounds. The ordered ranks of the flying birds and their clanging cries of greeting to their winter home stir one's pulse in sympathetic response. When migrating, far overhead, these geese usually travel in a wedge-shaped formation, with a leader at the head.

CANADA GEESE REST ON CURRITUCK SOUND

When these wary birds are preening themselves and resting in quiet places, one or another of the flock will raise its head and look about sharply for possible approaching danger.

THEY FIND GOOD HARBOR OPPOSITE THE SWAN ISLAND CLUB

When no shooting is permitted near the clubhouses, geese and ducks soon take advantage of these safety zones. On feeding places, a flock of geese presents an animated sight as the individuals continually up-end to gather food well below the surface.

A SOUTHERN WILDCAT WAS KILLED BY
A COLD NIGHT

When some guides crossed the new ice to the Swan Island Club, they found a wildcat lying dead on a floating cake of ice. Evidently it had perished from exposure (see text, page 98).

is in and about Currituck Sound on the coast of North Carolina. This haven is separated from the ocean on the east by long stretches of sand beaches and sand dunes and therefore well protected from violent storms.

Currituck Sound enters the eastern end of Albemarle Sound, which extends westward for 60 miles, and these combined waters connect with Pamlico Sound, which, with a width of 30 miles, borders the coast for nearly 100 miles, and joins Core Sound, the southern limit of the best ducking waters on the Atlantic coast.

The great extent of Pamlico Sound, combined with a favorable depth of water, makes it a congenial wintering haunt for large numbers of redheads, ringnecks, scaups, scoters, golden-eyes, buffleheads, and old

squaws. From Back Bay, in Virginia, to Core Sound, North Carolina, the inner, or western shore line, has an extent of some 300 miles, a distance somewhat longer than the outer, or eastern, coast, for the several shore-lines of Albemarle Sound are computed as a part of the inner lines. No other place on the American continent affords such a favorable winter home for our wild fowl, and here at an early day should be established large wild-fowl refuges that would be havens of security.

The birds that winter in this area come from two sources: (1) the great region of shallow lakes and ponds on the plains of Alberta and the neighboring provinces, the breeding grounds of central Canada, and (2) the breeding grounds of eastern Canada, including the Hudson Bay region, Labrador, and the neighboring Arctic islands to the northward. The birds that move down the Atlantic coast linger about Long Island Sound and Barnegat Bay until the coming of severe weather forces them southward, when they seek their accustomed winter quarters in these great sounds.

THE MISSISSIPPI IS A "FLYWAY"

The other great wintering ground includes the coastal and tidal marshes of Louisiana and Texas. The birds wintering there reach the Gulf of Mexico by following the broad flyway down the Mississippi Valley, in which they linger at favorable feeding grounds until driven South by the near approach of winter.

Since the eastern coast of Georgia and Florida has few shallow fresh-water bays and little wild-fowl food, these States separate almost completely the group of migrants that winter along the Atlantic coast from those that winter on the Gulf. A number of the species of geese and the swans so abundant in the Currituck Sound region are usually not found in such numbers farther south than the Carolinas.

Currituck Sound is an ideal home for wild fowl during the winter months. It is shallow and is surrounded by marshes, bays, and ponds of almost entirely fresh water, in which various kinds of excellent food plants for wild fowl abound. Fish, shellfish, and crustaceans favored as food by some of the species of waterfowl are also plentiful.

On the deeper and more open waters of the sound, therefore, thousands of canvasbacks congregate; and redheads, scaups, and golden-eyes are numerous. In the shallow bays and connecting ponds are great numbers of marsh ducks, such as the black duck, mallard, widgeon, pintail, and teal, which usually assemble in smaller flocks than the species that frequent deep water. Once, however, I saw a flight of pintails that probably contained more than 5,000 birds.

The geese are extraordinarily abundant in these waters. I have seen more of them in a single season on Currituck Sound than during a dozen years' visits to Revels Island, on the Eastern Shore of Virginia, where geese were not considered to be scarce.

THE WHISTLING SWAN

The whistling swan is to me the most interesting bird on the Currituck. Although local estimates of the numbers of these birds vary from 50,000 to nearly 100,000, the actual winter population probably does not exceed 20,000 or 25,000. Fifteen or 20 years ago the swans in this region were becoming dangerously reduced in numbers through overshooting, but protection has brought them back.

Although the whistling swan is found also on Chesapeake Bay and other neighboring waters, the main winter concentration is on Currituck Sound. I was astonished to learn from Doctor Chapman, who ranks among the leaders in American ornithology and has traveled extensively over this continent, that before this trip to the Currituck he had never seen one of these great birds in their haunts. This well indicates how local is the distribution of the species in its winter quarters as well as over its general range.

The increase in the numbers of swans that has resulted from the rigid protection afforded them has given rise to a troublesome problem. The concentration of these birds on waters occupied by great numbers of ducks and geese naturally decreases the food supply for all. Swans have the habit of pulling up the water plants, to eat the stems and some of the roots, and in places they destroy temporarily the available food crop over areas of considerable extent. Many sportsmen for this reason object to the presence of these birds on the ducking grounds and have urged that an open season be allowed in order that their numbers may be reduced.

A population even as low as 20,000 swans means approximately 8,000 breeding pairs. Since each pair produces from two to four young, it seems certain that, non-breeding birds and every form of casualty being taken into account, the young swans or cygnets must number several thousands annually.

Since a swan weighs from 12 to 16 pounds, the amount of food it consumes is considerable. The damage to the food supply is only temporary, however, for each summer there is a renewal of the growth on the feeding areas. Few sportsmen would care to shoot more than one swan a season, but the natives are very fond of them, especially the young ones, and under present conditions their increase is doubtless kept in check to some extent by illegal night shooting. Those who go forth to kill swans at night may be tempted also to shoot into flocks of geese and ducks if they should happen to come upon them.

Because of Federal regulations, the perpetuation of the whistling swan seems to be assured. Anyone who has witnessed the great white bands flying up and down the sound, or has seen the birds in large flocks in the quiet bays and has heard their clear, flutelike notes, often during the darkness of the night, will be ever ready to defend them.

Swans apparently mate for life, and the young during their first winter accompany their parents; so that whatever may be the number of birds that are congregated in one flock, the family is the unit. When the birds are on the water it is not difficult to pick out the small divisions based on kinship. The swans feed in the morning and late in the afternoon, and often at night if the weather is favorable. From 10 o'clock in the morning until 3 in the afternoon they can be seen drifting about in family groups, most of them sound asleep, with heads and long necks folded on their backs (see illustration, page 110).

DUCKS OF THE MARSHES AND OF DEEP WATERS

Ducks are divided roughly by their feeding habits into two large groups, each of which contains many species. In one group are the marsh ducks, which frequent the shallow waters in which reeds, rushes, wild rice, and other vegetation grow abundantly. Among these ducks, the best known are the mallard, black duck, pintail, widgeon, gadwall, and the several teals. The other group includes the deep-water ducks, species that commonly procure their food by diving. The most common of these, found in both fresh and brackish waters, are the canvasbacks, redheads, and scaups. With these may be included the heavy-bodied sea

THE SNOW GOOSE IS EVER WATCHFUL OF THE CAMERA

Wary wanderers of the heavens are these magnificent flyers that present a charming picture in
Currituck marshes.

THE WILD CAME TO DINE WITH THE DOMESTICATED

In the background is a snow goose which two winters in succession fed with the three tame
geese (foreground) on Monkey Island, Currituck marshes (see text, page 99). These geese breed
on Canadian Arctic islands and winter largely in Chesapeake Bay and the Currituck Sound region.

ducks, such as the eiders and the scoters, but the random notes here given refer little to them.

It is difficult to form any definite idea concerning the relative numbers of the marsh and the deep-water ducks. Marsh ducks pass so much of their time under cover of dense growths of vegetation that their numbers are indicated only when they mass to fly from one feeding ground to another, to migrate, or to escape from persecution by gunners. Deep-water ducks, on the other hand, appear daily in flocks on their feeding or resting places in open water offshore, so that the numbers occurring in a locality are much more readily estimated.

FLIGHT OF DUCKS

There are marked differences in flight between these groups of birds. Mallards, black ducks, pintails, and teals have proportionately longer and more pointed wings and proportionately slenderer bodies and are thus able to spring almost perpendicularly into the air; furthermore, many of the marsh-loving ducks can turn and twist in flight in a manner quite beyond the powers of others.

The deep-water ducks have proportionately shorter and more rounded wings and shorter and heavier bodies. Because of these physical characteristics they have greater difficulty in taking wing. They rise gradually, and perforce skim along the surface for some distance as they gain momentum.

The members of the two groups show similar differences in their methods of alighting. Gunners find the quick, erratic movements of teals, pintails, and black ducks on the wing a better test of marksmanship than is usually afforded by the steadier, less deviating flight of the deep-water ducks. A butter-ball, or golden-eye, however, when hurrying along, may call for the best shooting to bring it down.

Marsh ducks can usually drop abruptly to land where they desire in a way to fill any aviator with envy. Once, however, I saw an amusing miscalculation on the part of a dusky duck. I was ambushed in a blind near Sandusky Bay on the edge of a small grain-baited pool scarcely 10 yards wide, surrounded by a heavy growth of tall reeds. The bird was coming high overhead directly toward the spot.

When nearly above the pool, it dropped almost perpendicularly about 200 feet, and as it came near the surface of the water it changed its descent into a landing curve, vigorously back-stroking with its wings to check its speed. Its momentum was too great, however, and its impetus carried it with a loud rushing noise out of sight far into the reeds. A few moments later the discomfited bird came waddling back through the vegetation to the edge of the water.

A blind in a good marsh will afford the sportsmen a far more interesting variety of birds than will a shooting stand for deep-water ducks. In shooting deep-water ducks one usually obtains the best results from a battery, a floating blind, or a blind on the end of a long point separating two bays. The movements of these birds are largely governed by the weather, however, and one may sometimes sit in a blind for hours without firing a shot.

The plumages of the two groups of ducks display marked differences in color patterns. The colors of the marsh-frequenting species are much more broken and blend into a whole that fits readily into a background of marsh vegetation, whereas the deep-water ducks are characterized by having the colors distributed in strongly marked blocks or areas. In both groups the males are more strongly and handsomely marked than the smaller females.

The species of both groups of ducks have the power to deflate their bodies when wounded or even when alarmed, and can remain for long periods submerged with only the tops of their heads, their eyes, and the tops of their bills exposed. At such times they are very cunning in taking advantage of water plants or small floating objects to complete their camouflage.

KEEN SIGHT OF MARSH DUCKS

I am convinced that marsh ducks have a much keener sense of vision than the deep-water species. In their winter quarters these ducks have become even more closely familiar with the details of the landscape they frequent than man becomes with the streets he uses day by day in his home town. For this reason it is necessary that a shooting blind be constructed of material that blends closely with the background and that the occupant of this shelter wear clothing of the same generally inconspicuous hues.

It is well known that a hat or cap of an inharmonious color worn in the blind or any movements of the wearer will often alarm birds at a surprising distance. As they circle overhead, marsh ducks may be observed turning their heads at slight angles to get better views of the country below them. When they discover the enemy awaiting in the blind, the loud quacks of alarm that mallards sometimes utter are disconcerting to the sportsman.

In contrast to this alertness of the marsh ducks any hunter may recall the heedless manner in which canvasbacks, bluebills, and other deep-water ducks come sweeping in to decoys, giving little or no attention to the blind or its occupant even though the hunter may be imperfectly concealed.

DIALECTS OF THE MARSHES

Some species of ducks, especially those of the ocean, are usually silent or have low notes; some have loud, vibrant, and penetrating voices; and some give expression to their feelings in clear and musical tones. Often in the evening I have lingered on the border of a Virginia or Carolina shore marsh, or in the marshes of Louisiana, and listened to the gentle gabble of the different waterfowl as they fed in happy serenity without a thought of the deadly gun.

It sometimes was difficult for me to determine the identity of the birds, for they seemed to talk a language not used in the daytime. When wild fowl are migrating, consorting on the nesting grounds, or visiting feeding places by day, the different kinds may usually be determined by their notes, for each species has its characteristic language.

The black duck and the mallard, when alarmed, utter loud, resonant quacks, the voice of the female being the more strident; but when the birds are feeding amid peaceful surroundings, the notes are a softly modulated gabble. The gadwall, common in the interior but rare on the Atlantic coast, expresses its emotions by a quack that is higher in pitch but has less volume than the note of the mallard.

Both the European and the American widgeon utter a sort of *whew, whew,* while feeding or swimming, but are usually silent on taking wing. The green-winged teal is a noisier bird than the blue-winged, the male uttering a short, soft whistle and the female a quack that is high-pitched and often repeated. The shoveler, more common in the Mississippi Valley than on the Atlantic coast, is generally silent, but in the breeding season it is said to have a note like *took! took!*

The pintail, while going about its daytime activities, is usually silent, but at night "the hoarse muffled quack of the female, and the mellow whistle of the drake" can be singled out from among the voices of other ducks. During the mating season the drake has a low soft note, especially when performing its curious courting antics in the presence of its prospective mate.

Wood ducks, when alarmed in their woodland ponds or streams, spring from the water with a plaintive whistled *oo-eek*. This unsuspicious and most ornate of our woodland swamp ducks became greatly reduced in numbers until continuous legal protection throughout the country helped to increase its numbers in many of its haunts that had become almost depopulated.

The open-water, or diving, ducks are distinguished from those of the marsh by a broad lobe, or web, on the hind toe, a feature probably correlated with their habit of diving. They procure their food generally in deep water. This class may be further divided into those such as the canvasback and scaups that frequent the large lakes or the rivers and bays of fresh or brackish waters, and those such as the eiders, scoters, and old squaws that habitually occupy the ocean or the salt water estuaries.

VOICES OF THE DEEP

The ducks in the latter group use their wings as well as their feet in diving, and the several species are able to reach depths varying from 50 to more than 100 feet. The marsh ducks, on the other hand, have the "tip-up" habit of feeding and feed in the shallows with half of their bodies out of water.

With the exception of the old squaws, the deep-water ducks have notes not so loud or resonant as those of the marsh-dwelling species, and some that frequent the open sea seem to be voiceless. The canvasback, generally regarded in the East as the king of ducks, is found in large lakes or in shallow tidal waters. Often when I have had flocks of them under observation I have heard a harsh grunting note, which I attributed to the drake, for the female has a well-recognized quack and is reported when alarmed to utter a screaming *curr-row*.

The redhead I have also seen frequently on large bodies of open water and on the seacoast, but I have not heard its notes. The scaups, both the greater and the lesser, utter a purring note when excited, or when

LIKE A MASS OF TINY CLOUDS THEY RACE ON THE WINDS

Huge flocks of swans, geese, and ducks, sometimes numbering many thousands of birds, darken the sky over Currituck Sound. Above is shown a great flight of pintails opposite Swan Island.

PINTAIL DUCKS FEED IN CURRITUCK SOUND

Whenever a dainty morsel is located, down goes the bird's head and up comes its tail. The water presents a lively scene when these migrants arrive.

WHISTLING SWANS ARE MASTER AVIATORS

Tens of thousands of these noble birds winter in the region from Chesapeake Bay to Currituck and Albemarle sounds. Since they have been protected under the Migratory Bird Treaty Act, they have greatly increased in numbers. As they rise against the wind, they aid the launching into the air by vigorous use of their broadly webbed feet, as indicated by the spray shown in the photograph.

THE CAMERA REVEALS FLIGHT ATTITUDES OF WILD DUCKS

This series of individual pictures, taken from group views photographed on Currituck Sound, gives a varied presentation of wing motions of these mar dwellers rising from the water. The human eye cannot register positions which are held for only a small fraction of a second.

WHISTLING SWANS ENJOY PEACE AND QUIET

The typical swan family passes the winter in friendly companionship on Currituck Sound. The two pure-white parents and the grayer young may be distinguished readily. One of the young in this group is sleeping in a characteristic pose, its neck folded back against the bod and its head lying on the middle of its back, between the bases of the wings.

calling to their mates; but the note with which I am most familiar is a short rasping one that sounds like the word scaup, from which they have received one of their names. They are more generally known as bluebills, broadbills, blackheads, or raft ducks.

The American golden - eye, sometimes called the whistler from the sound made by its wings in flight, is a famous deep-water diver. When feeding alone or in small groups, members of this species are more watchful than are most of the deep-water ducks, which enjoy a fancied security when massed in large flocks. The note of the male golden-eye consists of a single *peep,* and that of the female of a sharp *cur-r-rew*.

The eiders and the several species of scoters, although the scoters nest mainly near fresh water, are typical sea ducks during their migration, ranging southward in winter along the eastern coast to Long Island Sound and the Carolinas, and on the western coast to Lower California. I have observed many of these heavy-bodied, sturdy ducks along the coasts of Alaska and Newfoundland in the summer and at the mouth of Chesapeake Bay in the winter.

Although at times they gather in great flocks, they often feed more or less alone, dotting the bays here and there with their dark forms, and ever intent on seeking on the sea bottom mollusks and crustaceans, a diet that renders their flesh strong and unpalatable. With the exception of man, they have few enemies in their winter home. I have never heard an eider or a scoter utter a sound; yet eiders, at least, are known to keep up a low guttural gabbling when in flocks about rocky points and islets.

The one duck of the ocean and salt-water bays of the North that has a loud and vibrant note is the old squaw. This is the only member of the duck family known to me that indulges in a vocal chorus and seems to enjoy it as much as does the springtime songster his utterances in the treetops. The notes are clear, musical, and penetrating, sounding like *ou-ou-wein,* or sometimes *south, south, southerly,* from which latter note they are frequently called south-southerlys.

At times, when half a dozen of these birds cry in chorus, the sound resembles the musical baying of distant hounds hot on the trail

A WHISTLING SWAN EXAMINES SOME DECOYS

This youngster swan has come in to visit some wooden effigies of his kind. Its dark-gray head and the dull white of the rest of its plumage indicate that it is a bird hatched the previous summer. It appeared to resent such clumsy images and swam up close to each one, pecking vigorously at its head.

of their quarry. All the tribes of natives in the North, where this duck is especially conspicuous during its migrations, have given to it names suggested by its loud ringing springtime song.

In the interpretation of duck talk, as in the speech of man, intonation plays an important part, for a word may have quite different meanings according to the stress. A black duck or a mallard, for instance, when suddenly flushed from the reeds, will utter a harsh quack, clearly expressive of alarm; whereas another quack from such a duck flying over the marshes and looking for some of its kin is interrogative in character, as if the bird were saying, "Where are you?" In response to this may come a friendly quack from below, indicating the whereabouts of would-be companions and meaning, perhaps, "The water's fine, come on in."

Here is a fertile field of study for the bird linguist, who by careful research may more fully understand the thoughts and actions of some of our most numerous and interesting forms of wild life.

In the Currituck region, where I have photographed many ducks, geese, and swans, there are three rest days weekly— Wednesday, Saturday, and Sunday—on which no shooting is permitted, and the waterfowl are thus given a chance to feed and rest.

This wise provision of the law naturally invites the use of the camera, and many sportsmen now occupy these otherwise idle days by taking pictures of wild fowl swimming about or speeding over the decoys, perhaps at 50 miles an hour.

In this kind of sport the customary hardships of wild-fowl shooting are largely avoided, for instead of arising at daybreak, the camera hunter may not go forth until the sun is well up, and should return early in the afternoon, before the time when the fading light makes rapid exposures impossible. If it is raining or blowing a gale, he may stay under a roof, awaiting better weather.

Satisfactory pictures of birds on the wing depend upon careful preparation and accurate handling of the camera. At first it may seem more difficult than wing-shooting, but in a short time practice overcomes the

MALE GREATER SCAUPS

A cameraman may shoot as many sitting ducks as he fancies without being a pot-hunter.

REDHEADS, MALE AND FEMALE

This picture and the others on this and the opposite page were taken on Currituck Sound.

MALLARDS, MALE AND FEMALE

The lord of the family precedes his consort as they swim along Currituck Sound.

principal troubles, and then the photographer can obtain greater numbers of wild fowl on his plates in a single hour than a crack shot could kill in several days.

The methods of locating the blind and setting out the decoys are the same as for shooting, except that there must be a small, low opening in the front part of the blind, where reeds or other obstructions are not permitted to interfere with a semicircular swing of the camera.

Of course, the greatest difficulty in taking pictures of flying birds is not in getting the birds on the negative, but in getting them in sharp focus. A badly focused bird is to the camera hunter as great a disappointment as a wounded one that escapes is to the fowler.

In a lane, between two sets of decoys, I place five especially marked decoys 10 feet apart, the nearest being 30 feet from the blind. These fixed distances should be shown on a temporary camera scale. It will be found difficult to release the shutter by the ascending mirror in time to photograph flying birds, if the graflex system is used, for the process involves much guesswork. By setting the shutter at time, however, one can dispense with the use of the mirror and operate the focal plane shutter successfully by a quick pressure on the upper catch.

HOW TO PHOTOGRAPH BIRDS IN FLIGHT

The shutter should be set at from 1/300 to 1/1000 of a second, as the quality of the light and the speed of the birds require. When a flock is seen approaching, a long lever on the side of the camera connected with the focusing disk is thrown to a point that brings the birds in focus, according to which one of the five decoys they happen to be nearest.

Whether the photograph is taken as the ducks are coming straight in, circling, dropping, or rising, it requires quick thinking and equally quick manipulation of the focusing apparatus and the shutter—exactly the same quickness of mind and body that is required in successful wing-shooting. The person hunting, however, has a distinct advantage with the camera, for if he misses or bungles, the birds are very likely to return to the silent blind.

Most of my pictures of swans were taken from a launch coming down wind toward feeding or resting birds; when they arose, quartering toward the boat, I could get satisfactory results, even at 100 yards, through the use of a long-focus lens. Several times I put out goose decoys painted white. The older swans eyed them with contempt; but sometimes cygnets, or young of the year, would swim in and at times even attack these poor counterfeits.

Canada geese rarely came to the baited blinds until after sunset, when shooting is forbidden. Apparently they soon became aware of this prohibition, and kept an eye on the declining orb. In 1927 a local regulation prohibited shooting after 4 o'clock in the afternoon, and the geese promptly advanced their feeding schedule. As a result of these circumstances I could enter the blind while there was yet sufficient light to get many pictures, much to the envy of my fellow hunters when they heard me tell that large flocks of geese swam back and forth in front of the blind paying no attention to the clicking camera.

GENEROUS LANDLORD NEEDED FOR OUR WILD FOWL

In recent years our wild fowl have been given increased protection. The outlawing of the market hunter, the prohibition of spring shooting, the marked reduction in the daily bag limit, and a shorter shooting season have all contributed toward the ultimate goal of protecting wild fowl from unreasonable inroads of the gun. It is now necessary, however, if desirable numbers of ducks and geese are to be maintained, that they have a better and more dependable food supply. To protect a bird from destructive shooting and then permit it to starve is poor policy.

It is easy enough in these days to pass game laws and create a demand for game refuges, but unless there is ample food on the reservations, the birds must leave them for maintenance elsewhere. This means peril from the gun or a visit to unsuitable sections in which they may come in contact with the death-dealing, mud-carried botulinus, which has already caused the death of many millions of ducks and other species of wild fowl.

Many well-meaning persons seem to think that because our wild fowl have markedly decreased in numbers during the past century, there must be ample feeding grounds for those that remain. Unfortunately, this is not the case, particularly in the winter homes of the ducks. There are now many millions of acres of marshland, shallow bays, and estuaries in which the aquatic food has

RING-NECK, MALE AND FEMALE
The camera caught them sitting on the quiet waters of Currituck Sound.

FEMALE WIDGEONS
Currituck Sound is a mecca for many interesting species of waterfowl.

BLACK DUCKS
Because of their color they stand out among the swimmers on Currituck Sound.

"ROCKED IN THE CRADLE OF THE DEEP"

This swan is peacefully asleep on a quiet, bright day, its long neck folded over its back.

ITS APPETITE BETRAYED IT

This young swan, suffering from lead poisoning and unable to fly, was caught near shore. The ailment comes from shot pellets picked up on the bottom and retained in the gizzard until destroyed by attrition.

to be a tendency on the part of wild fowl to migrate in larger flocks and to concentrate in waters having an insufficient food supply throughout the winter. In Currituck Sound I found that two-thirds of the so-called public waters were barren of plant food, although some of the diving ducks still had a scanty supply of crustaceans and other small animal life.

In this region thousands of bushels of corn and other grain scattered about on club properties contributed much toward preventing the starvation or the dispersal of the wild fowl throughout the waters of the sound.

The creation of large winter wild-fowl refuges has resulted in many birds being attracted to them at the beginning of the hunting season. These wild fowl soon destroy the bulk of the available food, and when they are thus fattened, they furnish to hunters in adjacent areas victims that are in prime condition. I once

been destroyed, sometimes by overfeeding on the part of the wild fowl, and sometimes by agencies for which man is responsible, such as oil or chemical pollution, the invasion of fresh waters through canals connected with tidal waters, the use for oyster culture of waters formerly monopolized by waterfowl, or the daily activities of fishermen with their nets and gasoline launches.

These difficulties are purely physical. Then, too, for several reasons there seems

noted a comparatively large fresh-water lake in the Louisiana marshes that at the beginning of the hunting season was so covered with the banana plant that the surface of the water was hidden. After the arrival of the canvasback by the tens of thousands this plant soon completely disappeared. Fortunately, the roots were not destroyed, and the next season's crop would be equally abundant.

What becomes of the ducks when they leave a protected area? This query may be

THEY HAVE THEIR UPS AND DOWNS

Unlike marsh ducks, which can spring into the air vertically or drop straight down, the scaups and other deep-water species rise gradually from the surface or descend gradually.

asked regarding every wild-fowl refuge created up to the present time. The answer implies that there must be a systematic planting of duck food in the immense barren areas before the problem of properly maintaining our wild fowl can be solved.

The experts of the Bureau of Biological Survey of the United States Department of Agriculture have listed the more important duck-food plants suitable to the climate or the character of the waters in many sections. That Bureau, however, does not have funds to collect and distribute these plants. In the last decade the Federal Government has spent many millions of dollars in reforesting areas, in helping the agriculturists in the selection and culture of their crops, and in aiding reclamation and irrigation projects. Why should not the Federal Government also provide funds each year to maintain an adequate growth of desirable wild-fowl plants in its growing series of great Federal wild-life refuges or in waters open to the public?

SHOOTING CLUBS ALONG THE ATLANTIC COAST

From Long Island to the Florida peninsula are many shooting-club properties of considerable acreage, some of which have been occupied for more than 75 years. This coastal area, with its marshes and wooded islands, has long been a favored region for hunting wild fowl in winter and for com-

HIS BAG FROM THE BLIND WAS GOOD

Such shelters for canvas-back shooting are made of the common kind of rushes growing in the marshes (*Juncus roemerianus*).

mercial fishing during most of the year. Membership in many of the clubs is limited to a few dozen persons, made up of groups of friends from some section of the country. As the older members retire, it is natural that their successors should be their younger relatives or intimates, and thus the close associations and friendships of their home region are continued.

A history of the more permanent hunting clubs throughout the country would be interesting, for it would present a picture of one phase of the social life of our sportsmen that is more representative in its character than any in most other gatherings. These close contacts for days at a time, year after year, have brought together those having common interests in sports under conditions of

A SUDDEN ALARM CAUSES COMMOTION

Swans have much difficulty in rising from the surface, their long wings beating the air with heavy strokes, while their broadly webbed feet, helping to give the body the necessary impetus, strike the water and dash it into clouds of spray.

CURRITUCK SOUND OFFERS FOOD FOR THOUSANDS

Mallards and black ducks gather on common feeding places in shallow water, where they are often joined by pintails and coots.

ALARM!

The contrast of the flight of mallards and black ducks with that of the coots when startled is well shown in this photograph.

MIXED COMPANY

Note the stately male pintail in the center. Beyond is a black duck, in front of it are two female pintails, and in foreground is a mudhen.

relaxation from business responsibilities that tend to create a congenial atmosphere.

I have met several sportsmen more than 80 years of age who, bereft of their contemporaries, have substituted the companionship of those of later generations at the club at a time of life when it is difficult to form such friendships in other places.

CLUBS ABOUT CURRITUCK SOUND

A membership in several clubs on the Atlantic coast, extending over more than 40 years, has given me an insight into the character and spirit of such organizations.

Currituck Sound is about 35 miles long, and from one to five miles wide. It is an important connecting link of the "inside passage" used by yachts and house boats on their way to and from southern Florida. In addition to this limited traffic are the numerous launches of the local fishermen and those belonging to ducking clubs that occupy different parts of the shooting ground.

The inhabitants of the region, almost to a man, favor club possession, for under State laws the nonresident members cannot own batteries or shoot from either fixed or floating blinds. Local hunters shooting from blinds placed at strategic points between club properties get many marsh ducks and the bulk of the geese and canvasbacks. Moreover, a large number of local citizens are employed as caretakers, guides, and wardens; and local merchants get considerable trade from the clubs.

In addition, the local taxes on clubhouses and on the adjoining marshes produce income from land that would otherwise be nonproductive. The hunting licenses of club members also mount to a large sum. All this revenue, available for local purposes, would be lost if these lands were not used in this manner. On the larger club properties there are at times as many as ten thousand ducks and geese at once; and, since the clubs often have a very small membership, it is doubtful that one bird out of ten of those wintering there is killed. This means that a large proportion of the birds go north again to breed and return in the fall with an increase.

In other areas it has been found that, when club properties are abandoned on account of restrictive laws or excessive taxation, the wild fowl are either killed or driven away through overhunting. In the case of Currituck Sound and adjoining waters, unlimited shooting would drive the surviving birds elsewhere.

SPORTSMEN AND BIRD CONSERVATION

My extended association with sportsmen and sportsmen's clubs, especially along the Atlantic coast, leads me to put on record here some ideas concerning the relation of sportsmen to bird conservation that I have long had in mind.

The sportsmen whose love of the out-of-doors leads them to seek out these birds in their remote congregating places, have the privilege of becoming more familiar with them than those lacking such opportunities. Although a strong believer in sane conservation, I have always felt strongly that no reasonable objection can be raised against the taking by sportsmen of a reasonable part of the surplus wild fowl, which, if conditions are right, should come to their wintering grounds each year. It is well known that feeding areas have become so reduced that if the surplus is not reduced each season the accumulation of birds would soon so exceed the available food supply that an appalling loss by starvation of both surplus and breeding stock would inevitably take place.

Prior to the 18th century the numbers and distribution of wild fowl on this continent were largely regulated by their food supply, which factor rather than predatory enemies, including man, held the species in check. So prolific are these game birds that until the comparatively recent increase in human population and the consequent settlement of the country, the spoliation of the haunts of the wild fowl, and the improvements in guns and methods of travel, the birds were easily able to maintain their numbers.

SPORTSMEN FAVOR CONSERVATION

From the time when it was first noted that wild fowl needed protection from excessive exploitation, intelligent, unselfish, and experienced sportsmen have been the foremost advocates of adequate laws and regulations to safeguard these birds. As individuals and as members of sportsmen's organizations they have been largely responsible for the legislative action that has been so helpful to both game and non-game birds.

Included here with the sportsmen's organizations are the sportsmen's magazines, which have so generally voiced the desires of their supporters. These are facts that can be verified by detailed inquiry into the real history of the enactment of all the most effective wild-life conservation measures.

That day has passed forever in which the intelligent hunter took a false pride in displaying a hundred or more ducks as the result of his skill during a day's hunt. This change in sentiment is evident from the preference of sportsmen's magazines for photographs illustrating living birds to those picturing rumpled heaps of dead ones.

The annual task of protecting the country's wild life gives employment to thousands of men and costs millions of dollars, and this fund is derived almost wholly from licenses taken out by hunters. The general public pays very little in taxes toward the enforcement of the law protecting game and other wild life and toward other costs of maintaining them in adequate numbers. Such expenditures are defrayed mainly from the income derived from the sportsmen.

It should be appreciated by the general public, interested especially in the insectivorous and other nongame birds, that the laws for their protection, in nearly every instance, have been passed by the active help

MALE LESSER SCAUPS

Their plain blue bills and light-gray backs, the white bars across their bills and the black middles of their backs distinguish the sex at a glance. The gray body and long sloping top of head and bill characterize the female mallard as does the white around the base of the bill of the female scaup.

of sportsmen, and that to a great extent the funds used for the enforcement of these laws are directly provided by those who take out hunting licenses. Should severely restrictive laws be passed depriving sportsmen of a reasonable opportunity for sport it is believed the resulting decrease of income from licenses would be an almost fatal handicap to effective bird protection.

The sportsman no longer hunts for a record kill. Similarly the bird lover who formerly was so much interested in checking up his lists of species observed in a day's outing is more and more turning to the careful observation of habits. Work by those who may be termed amateurs has added many interesting facts previously unknown to our store of knowledge of bird life. These data have been most acceptable to professional naturalists, who are too few in number and lack the funds to cover adequately such a great field of endeavor.

I have stressed the relationship between the two classes directly interested in bird protection because during recent years there has been a tendency in some directions to decry the sportsman and to ignore the vital part he plays in bird conservation as a whole.

It should be kept in mind that among sportsmen have been many outstanding figures in bird protection, among whom may be mentioned Dr. George Bird Grinnell,

AVIATORS MIGHT WELL STUDY THEM

Black ducks and mallards, unlike some of their cousins, get off the water quickly when alarmed.

ONE IS IN THE AIR, ONE IS TAKING OFF, THE OTHERS ARE MAKING READY

This picture of mallards and black ducks rising from the water should be compared with the one above and that at the bottom of page 117.

THERE IS MIGHTY SPLASHING ON FEEDING GROUNDS
Mallards, black ducks, pintails, and coots mingle in the shallows where food is available.

TAKE-OFFS DIFFER WITH SPECIES
This photograph illustrates some of the attitudes assumed by black ducks and mallards when they are
rising from the water in alarm.

A WINTER HAVEN FOR WILD FOWL

On the bays and marshes of Virginia, North Carolina, and Louisiana a great majority of our ducks, geese, and swans pass their winters. The above is a typical view of the first named rising from a Louisiana pond.

BLACK DUCKS TAKE WING

When marsh ducks spring from the water in alarm, their movements are too rapid to register in the human eye. The camera, however, requiring only a very small fraction of a second to make its record, shows the extraordinary attitudes taken as the birds spring into the air. Males and females of black ducks are indistinguishable, contrasting thus with other ducks the male of which has either a more conspicuous plumage, or differs in size or shape from the female.

SWANS MAKE SILHOUETTES AGAINST THE SKY

Among the stirring sights on Currituck Sound is the daily passage of flocks of these birds, which often make the air resound with their melodious notes. In this picture the swans are in full flight.

A PAIR OF CANADA GEESE VISIT CORE SOUND

On a good day many of these fine birds may be seen searching for coarse sand and bits of shell which they swallow to aid in the digestion of their food.

IT IS LUNCHEON TIME IN THE POND NEAR THE CLUBHOUSE

Learning quickly that the waters are safe, many kinds of waterfowl feed unconcernedly near the buildings on Currituck Sound (see text, page 97).

promoter of the original Audubon Society; Senator F. C. Walcott, Dr. John C. Phillips, John B. Burnham, the late Charles Sheldon, and William Dutcher—sportsmen-naturalists who with many others have done splendid work in helping to obtain the enactment of laws for the protection of all harmless birds.

Those whose sentiments are strong for bird protection should recognize the need for a practical consideration of the subject, since conservation, to be properly effective, must be practical.

Today the great problem confronting sportsmen is that of so limiting the annual kill that the breeding stock shall not be jeopardized and the annual surplus decreased. With this responsibility, the gunner must exercise his duty, or suffer if through indifference or selfishness he permits the supply of game to become dangerously reduced. The issue is that of conservation against improvidence, and the sportsmen seem to be awakening to this as never before.

With the growth of cities and the increasing tendency toward urban life it should be obvious that anything leading to a fuller participation in out-of-door life, amid invigorating and inspiring surroundings, such as those enjoyed by the sportsman, should be fostered as a matter of public policy in the development of the best type of citizenship.

ABUNDANCE OF WILD LIFE IN NORTH CAROLINA

Having given at some length an account of the hosts of wild fowl that frequent the coastal waters of North Carolina each winter, I consider it of interest to refer to the estimate of the various kinds of game taken in that State in the winter of 1927-28. These figures were based on the returns from the hunters who reported. The totals were as follows: Rabbits, 1,555,270; squirrels, 1,263,360; deer, 4,510; raccoons, 28,-260; opossums, 324,210; wildcats, 720; muskrats, 34,140; quail, 981,980; wild turkeys, 6,110; ruffed grouse, 500; pheasants, 2,820; snipe, 17,540; rails and coots, 1,220; doves, 170,070; geese, 5,280; ducks, 103,690. In this list no mention is made of black bears, mink, and otter, all of which occur in this State.

A TURKEY BUZZARD TAKES ITS OWN PICTURE

This was one of the raiders that tore the stuffed owl to pieces and ate the kitchen soap at the Hunting Lodge on Cumberland Island (see text, page 131).

A LITTLE GREEN HERON HAS A PRETTY HOME ON CUMBERLAND ISLAND

These birds are among the common residents. They devote much more care to building their nests than do many of the other species.

THE AMERICAN EGRET LOOKS HAUGHTY

This bird was photographed in a brackish pond on Cumberland Island, Georgia. Here the author had an exciting encounter with an alligator that had appropriated a jacksnipe dropped in the water by the gunner.

THIS IS A TYPICAL SCENE ON CUMBERLAND ISLAND

Marshes in low places and woodland on higher ground provide homes for many kinds of wild life. In the foreground are shown a little blue heron in normal color with one of the young birds in the white phase. To the right is a little scaup duck that is curiously out of place in this shallow water.

THIS LITTLE BLUE HERON IS IN THE WHITE OR IMMATURE STAGE

Note the yellowleg snipe in left-hand corner. It is not at all unusual in the author's experience to find unexpected subjects on negatives of birds and animals.

WHITE IBISES FLY OVER TAMIAHUA LAGOON, MEXICO (SEE TEXT, PAGE 245)

A LARGE WHITE EGRET WINGS OVER CUMBERLAND ISLAND OFF THE GEORGIA COAST

130

CHAPTER VI — PART II

On Cumberland Island, Georgia

CUMBERLAND ISLAND, which I first visited in the winter of 1885, is situated near the southern border of Georgia and just north of Fernandina, Florida. At that time this property had recently been acquired by Thomas M. Carnegie, a brother of Andrew Carnegie, and it has been occupied by members of the Carnegie family ever since. No more attractive island for a winter residence is to be found on the Atlantic coast. It is about 20 miles long, and several miles wide, and has fine hard beaches, is well forested, and contains fresh-water ponds and numerous lagoons which are frequented by ducks and many varieties of water birds.

ALLIGATORS MENACE BIRDS

The large and numerous alligators that occur here cause havoc among the larger swamp-breeding birds, as well as devour young pigs, deer, and hunting dogs when they cross the lagoons. In the woods are many deer and wild turkeys, but these are sparingly shot, so that the island is really a game refuge for animals and birds. By a coincidence my maternal grandfather had an option on this property in 1866, and for this reason I viewed the attractive surroundings with a special interest.

In 1901 I visited the island again while on a photographic trip, and passed a week in a comfortable cabin six miles up the beach and close to the principal lagoon.

On Cumberland Island were many turkey buzzards, with now and then a black vulture consorting with them amicably. These somber birds often proved a nuisance about the dwellings, but their most serious offense was the habit of plucking out the eyes of newly born fauns. After the lingering death of the victims, the birds patiently awaited until the bodies reached the proper degree of decomposition to suit their taste.

On my arrival at the hunting cabin I saw no buzzards, and thereupon I had John wire a large stuffed owl on the limb of a dead pine. It was my expectation that some of the more pugnacious birds of the neighborhood would attack their nocturnal foe and thus afford me a chance to take their picture while their attention was diverted.

When I returned from my first canoe trip on an adjoining lagoon, I observed several buzzards flying away. A glance at my lure showed that the legs of the owl, which had been wired to the limb, were all that remained. I searched among the scattered feathers on the ground for the large glass eyes of my dismantled lure, but without success. A large bar of soap left on the wooden bench near the kitchen door for use in washing the dishes had also disappeared.

It may seem strange to charge this larceny to an effort on the part of some buzzard to gratify its appetite, but when it is recalled how readily an alert trout will seize an artificial fly, or how the most cautious of wild fowl will settle down among their wooden counterfeits to be awakened from their sense of security by the booming of a gun, it is more easily understood how the most stolid and stupid of birds should be deceived by the glistening eyeballs, or by something that appears to be delectable food at the kitchen door. The next day I photographed one of these marauders as it released the shutter of the camera by a pull on a baited string.

Among the pictures taken on Cumberland Island is one of a cotton-mouthed moccasin that recalls a rather amusing adventure in connection with another reptile there. Close to the cabin was a small fresh-water pond, where I flushed a number of jacksnipe every time I passed by. I borrowed a gun in order to have game for the table. One snipe soon flew over the area, and when I shot, it fell into the middle of the pond.

WATER MOCCASIN AND ALLIGATOR

Taking off my shoes and stockings, I waded out after it. When I reached the place where the bird had fallen, I could not find it. Consequently I mounted what I took to be a sunken log in order to get a better view. Suddenly the head of an alligator appeared between my legs and I was drenched with water. I had stepped upon a submerged 'gator, which resented such familiarity! Deciding that the snipe must have disappeared down the capacious jaws of this saurian, I went ashore in some haste.

When I narrated this incident to one of my hosts, he declared that I had taken a great risk in wading about this pond. I

IT WAS LOOKING FOR FOOD IN THE SHALLOWS

Where plants grow above the surface of the water near the shore of Cumberland Island, wild fowl find good forage.

grew by itself in the middle of the lagoon. Previous to this time I had never seen this bird, and it made so interesting a picture with snow-white body, pink, curved bill, and black-tipped wings, that I was eager to photograph it. I placed the tripod with the camera in the shallow water about six feet from the nest, covered the outfit with green branches, and led a string to operate the shutter back to a neighboring group of mangroves. In order to give the somewhat distracted parents time to quiet down and to return to their nest, we continued along the lagoon in search of other subjects.

scoffed at the idea, saying that the alligator was too small to be feared. To this he replied that it was not the alligators, but the water moccasins he meant, for the pond was filled with them, and that I should always wear something on my feet. Thereupon I suggested that his wishes could easily be complied with, "for I could enter the water barefooted and come out with a 'gaiter' on one foot and a 'moccasin' on the other."

As we were paddling along the largest lagoon one morning, I discovered a pair of white ibises with their crude nest of sticks low down in the crotch of a mangrove that

Half an hour later we shoved the canoe into the thicket of mangroves within reach of the pulling string. I was surprised to find that the pair of ibises were still soaring uneasily about overhead. Neither of the birds consenting to return to the nest, I decided to take a picture of the four white eggs. But when I looked into the nest I found it empty. A large water snake coiled about the lower part of the mangrove trunk furnished the explanation.

CHAPTER VII

Florida—Its Woods, Waters, and Wild Life

THROUGHOUT the year Florida is an out-of-doors State. The seasons are only nominal, and gradations between them are almost imperceptible. When the last oranges are being picked from trees continuously green, fragrant blossoms are again whitening the branches.

Animals enjoy virtually unbroken holiday weather, and birds during the so-called winter months surpass in numbers those of the summer, for their ranks are increased by thousands of visitors from the North.

FLORIDA IS "DIFFERENT"

From the time of my first visit to the State, Florida has always appealed to me. Its wealth of wild life, its pleasing variety of vegetation, and its peculiar topography, so different from that of any other region in the United States, combine with its equable climate to form a paradise for nature lovers.

Mainly a fingerlike peninsula 100 miles wide, the State stretches for about 400 miles southeasterly from the continental land mass. The Gulf of Mexico on the west and the Atlantic Ocean on the east give it an extent of more than 1,100 miles of coast line, a length of shore greater than that of any other State.

Florida's mean annual temperature of 70 degrees Fahrenheit is due not only to the southern location of the peninsula but also to the warm oceanic currents on both coasts. Annual rainfall averages about 52 inches.

The land is mainly a limestone plain covered with sandy loam. Low along the coasts, especially in the southern third, it rises gradually to gently rolling elevations, varying at the highest from 300 to 400 feet above sea level and extending from near Lake Okeechobee northward to the border.

For long distances the shore has beautiful beaches of coral sand backed by sand dunes and broken by bays, inlets, and tidal lagoons—curious waterways, usually long and narrow, and paralleling the shore a short distance inland, as do Indian River and Halifax River, the most notable of the lagoons. There are no great rivers in Florida, but the St. Johns River, rising on the east slope in Lake Helen, Brevard County, and flowing northward for 400 miles into the Atlantic Ocean a few miles below Jacksonville, is navigable for small steamers for a distance of more than 300 miles above its mouth.

Florida's inland water surface, of approximately 3,905 square miles, is made up largely of small fresh-water lakes of various sizes, none of much depth. The largest, Lake Okeechobee, is about 30 miles wide and 40 miles long, and covers some 1,200 square miles, with an extreme depth of only about 15 feet. Few of these lakes have outlet streams.

Lake Okeechobee has an outlet through the Caloosahatchee River, flowing down to Charlotte Harbor on the west coast. This natural drainage is so inadequate that within recent years five large drainage canals have been cut from the lake to the Atlantic coast. This has lowered the water level and bared a great acreage of formerly flooded peat lands, now utilized for growing early vegetables and other crops.

Most of the lakes are drained by seepage or underground channels, and some are known to have subterranean connections. These pent-up underground waters from the interior furnish an abundant supply for shallow artesian wells, which are drilled along the coasts. In places the water bursts forth in gigantic springs.

GEOLOGICAL BASE OF THE PENINSULA

In 1931 a well was completed to the depth of 6,000 feet in Marion County in the central portion of the peninsula. For the first 4,000 feet it penetrated sedimentary formations consisting of limestone, sand, marl, clay, phosphates and recent deposits of varying character. Then it reached an underlying metamorphic formation, composed of mica, slate, and quartzite, the date of which has not been definitely determined.

Since the formation of these ancient deposits of more than three-quarters of a mile in depth the peninsula has gone through many changes, sometimes for many ages being dry land and then covered by the sea for other long periods, until it became the Florida of today.

South and southwest from Lake Okeechobee, extending to the coast, lie the famous Florida Everglades, a broad, very shallow, swampy basin covering about 8,000

PONCE DE LEON INLET LIGHTHOUSE ONCE MENACED
WILD FOWL

Until this light was changed a few years ago to the automatic flashing type, thousands of birds, from warblers to ducks, perished here during migrations by being blinded and dashing against the tower or the glass protecting the light.

In this same country lies the Great Cypress Swamp, containing the finest cypress timber in all this region. Along the coastal border of the Everglades is a belt of mangrove thickets, which become a veritable forest in the Shark River section north of Cape Sable; and the "Ten Thousand Islands" along the southwestern coast of the peninsula, north of Shark River, form a long, narrow group of keys overgrown with mangroves and separated by a maze of shallow little tide channels and lagoons paved with natural oyster beds.

Before going to the Bahama Islands in the spring of 1907, I paused at Miami for several days in order to make excursions into the eastern part of the Everglades. Miami at that time was a temporary terminal of the Florida East Coast Railway, then designed to be extended along the keys to Key West.

square miles. The land is covered for the most part with from one to twelve feet of fresh water, and a rank growth of sawgrass—a sedge with sharp edges that cut like knife blades—often extends away to the horizon with the appearance of a great prairie. Scattered here and there over the swampy surface of this sawgrass plain are small islands of rich humus soil, a few feet above the water level, overgrown with luxuriant tropical or semitropical vegetation, above which tower the stately royal palms. Along these "hammocks," as they are called, live the scanty remnants of the romantic and picturesque Seminole Indians.

In a small rowboat I went up a winding stream into a semitropical marshland and was able to visualize the more remote sections. I saw a few alligators and several species of herons, but the other wild creatures were farther inland.

About 18 years later and after the railway was completed, I left Miami with a friend to go over the unique highway to Key West. The superstructure lay close to the water, here and there resting on keys, big and little. Key Largo, one of the intermediate islets, was a popular fishing resort in summer and spring; it is graced with coconut palms and rimmed by white beaches

YELLOW PINES AND LIVE OAKS CONCEAL THE HOUSE

This is the water front of the author's winter home on the east bank of the Halifax River at Ormond Beach, Florida. Here he has pursued his fascinating hobby for portions of many winters.

FISH CROWS CONGREGATE ABOUT A FEEDING STAND AT ORMOND BEACH

From Revels Island, Virginia, to Florida these fellows have increased so greatly in recent years that they have become a serious menace to many other birds, whose eggs and young they destroy.

WHAT IS THE SAD SEA SAYING?

This lone heron was stalking majestically along the shore in March, 1935.

of marl. From the observation car we could look down upon waters tinted blue or yellow, where fish of various colors were outlined sharply against the beds of chalkwhite coral.

Naturally at the crowded end of the peninsula one could not expect to see much in the way of bird or mammal life. A short trip in the gulf, however, brings one to the Dry Tortugas Islands, long famed as the home of several large colonies of sea birds, such as noddy and scoter terns, not to be found on the main shore. There, formerly, my friend, Dr. A. G. Mayer, was at the head of the Carnegie Marine Laboratory; after the establishment of these historic islands as a Federal bird reservation his investigations were greatly facilitated.

THE EVERGLADES ATTRACT SPORTSMEN

Interesting and unique as is this chain of keys, separating the Gulf and the Atlantic and used as stepping stones of a highway leading to our southernmost city, the naturalist, sportsman, and bird lover must look largely to the Everglades, and northward, for study or sport. There marshlands and swamps, tidal beaches, and lagoons, thousands of lakes, and many streams winding in and out of pineries to the sea afford homes for the feathered, furred, and finned creatures of the Peninsula State.

The flora and fauna of the northern two-thirds of the State are similar to those of the adjacent region to the north; but from the latitude of Lake Okeechobee south,

especially on the hammocks in the Everglades and along the keys from Biscayne Bay to Key West, the trees and other vegetation are so tropical in character that one might readily believe oneself transported to the coast of Cuba or eastern Mexico.

The long southerly extension of Florida into the sea has made it a highway for many migrating birds, both in fall and spring. The extraordinary number of salt marshes and coastal lagoons, and of freshwater lakes, streams, and marshes in the interior has made it the home of multitudes of herons, ibises, pelicans, cormorants, snakebirds, skimmers, gulls, terns, and other water-loving birds without parallel on this continent. Quail and wild turkeys also abound, but the flamingo and parakeet now seem to be gone forever. In the southern keys and hammocks occur several tropical birds, such as the white-crowned pigeon and the Zenaida and Key West doves, while the cayman, or American crocodile, in part replaces the alligator.

As might be expected, the land mammals of the peninsula and adjacent keys appear to be derived entirely from the mainland to the north. When I first studied the region, mammals were plentiful, the main larger species being the white-tailed deer, black bear, puma, wildcat, gray wolf, raccoon, opossum, otter, and skunk. In the salt lagoons along shore were many manatees, a few of which still remain.

Within comparatively recent years, rapidly increasing occupation and development of the State have had their usual effect on wild life. Conservationists, however, have been active trying to save threatened birds and mammals from the local extermination that has overtaken the flamingo and parakeet; and a greater appreciation of the value of wild life appears to be developing among the residents. Improved game laws and this awakened public sentiment make the future appear more hopeful for the wild creatures.

VIEW ACROSS HALIFAX RIVER FROM THE AUTHOR'S WINTER HOME

Bonaparte gulls in winter plumage rest on the water, and an adult ring-billed gull is on the wing.
These graceful aviators add much to the attractiveness of the view from the windows.

RED-WINGED BLACKBIRDS IN WINTER DRESS

In winter they come daily in flocks to enjoy the contents of a feeding tray under a large palm tree about 25 feet from a veranda where people are usually gathered, at Ormond Beach, Florida.

A DOVE OF PEACE BECOMES BELLIGERENT

A male Florida ground dove assumes a threatening attitude to drive an approaching blue jay (not in the picture) from the feeding place it occupies.

EVEN A STUFFED OWL MAKES HIM SEE RED

One of the chief delights of a group of Florida blue jays is to locate some sleepy old owl and worry him. This one is attacking a stuffed owl and is a bit puzzled at the victim's docility.

A PAIR OF GROUND DOVES

These beautiful little birds, about half the size of the mourning doves, are common about the yard and orange grove at Ormond Beach, where they live throughout the year.

A FLORIDA GRAY SQUIRREL PULLS ON THE NUT BAIT AND TAKES HIS OWN
PICTURE IN THE DAYTIME

Several gray squirrels discovered this feeding place; so corn and nuts were substituted, the loose end of the string being just long enough to permit the squirrel to rise on its quarters—the most graceful and characteristic pose of this animal.

Those interested in preserving parts of the American wilderness have been making efforts to have set apart as a national park about 2,000 square miles in the southwestern part of the Everglades. If this plan succeeds, one of the wildest and least-known parts of the country will be perpetuated in a nearly natural state.

In beautiful hammocks with their tropical vegetation, and in the mangrove and other great swamps, herons, wood and white ibises, spoonbills, limpkins, and other interesting birds may then continue to rear their young in safety. When not nesting, they will still wander in picturesque hordes over the shallow waters of the vast neighboring sawgrass plains.

Without some such organized effort to preserve their haunts, however, the wild life of one of the strangest regions in America is confronted with a perilous future. Birds nesting in colonies, and such conspicuous species as deer and wild turkeys, are threatened with extinction.

I first visited Florida in 1885, and in subsequent years made frequent trips there. In 1906 I established a permanent winter home in a cottage at Ormond Beach, fronting the eastern shore of Halifax River, just below the Ormond Bridge, and since then I have returned with my family every year. Ormond Beach has been the headquarters of my excursions by boat and automobile to other parts of the State.

Halifax River, as previously stated, is a narrow tidal lagoon extending parallel to the coast. Its pass from the sea is at Ponce de Leon Inlet, 18 miles southward from my cottage, and it extends approximately seven miles farther northward. In recent years Ormond Beach, Daytona Beach, and several other small winter resorts have developed on the peninsula, and tourists swarm along the beaches to the inlet. The remainder of this narrow belt is in surprisingly primitive condition, despite the late lamented land boom.

The sandy peninsula, extending about 25 miles north of Ponce de Leon Inlet and lying between the river and the beach, three-quarters of a mile to more than a mile wide, had few visitors in the early days. Along the river, for about 300 yards back, was a forest of yellow pines and low live oaks with much undergrowth. Beyond that to the east, extending to the sea beach, was a much broader belt of sand dunes overgrown with low scrub palmetto and bushes, forming large, almost impenetrable, thickets. From the water the house is nearly concealed amid yellow pines and live oaks.

It was not long before I discovered that in the woods back of my cottage were numerous small animals, wildcats, raccoons, opossums, skunks, cotton-tail rabbits, and wood rats. Occasionally tracks of deer and bears were seen farther up the river.

Purple martins occupied bird houses on the dock. In the growth along the low shore of the river were red-winged blackbirds, marsh rabbits and cotton rats, with fish crows and little green herons perching on the pine trees over the edge of the water. Many different kinds of land birds loitered about the cottage or the orange grove in the rear.

THE AUTHOR SETS OUT HIS FLASHLIGHT APPARATUS

With my guide, John Hammer, I set out a number of cameras connected with a flashlight. At first, the glare of light and the heavy report that followed astonished the people in the neighborhood, but finally they became accustomed to it and would ask each morning what luck I had had the night before.

About the house we placed feeding boxes, and in the course of the season we were able to see nearly every species of bird that lived or wintered in the vicinity. The principal exception was the Florida jay, and this was to be found a quarter of a mile away in the sand-dune scrub nearer the ocean.

No matter how far one may travel by automobile, or how many miles one may walk along forested trails, one sees few of the more timid birds. One may notice crows, hawks, blackbirds, robins, meadowlarks, woodpeckers, and English sparrows, or witness the flight of gulls and other water birds along the beaches; but without a lure to attract and concentrate the smaller woodland inhabitants it is difficult to see or study

ON THE WINGS OF WIND

THE TAKE-OFF

CAUGHT IN THE AIR

The aviator at the top is a cardinal; the two below are blue jays snapped with a fast lens in the author's yard.

BLACK SKIMMERS MASS ON THE TIDE FLATS AT PONCE DE LEON INLET

This species winters from Florida and the Gulf Coast to South America, nesting as far north as New Jersey.

TWO GROUND DOVES PECK AT THE BAIT, WHILE A MALE CARDINAL LOOKS ON

those that in form, plumage, or song differ so much from the commoner types of the open country.

By placing different kinds of food within easy sight, people may attract birds about their homes virtually throughout the year. Many Florida residents have always been interested in bird life, and others have acquired the first knowledge of their feathered neighbors by thus coaxing them from the thickets or woods, where it is difficult to find them with any certainty or to study them carefully.

In the last 20 years I have had three feeding stations at different seasons in widely separated localities—one at my camp on Whitefish Lake, Michigan; another in the suburbs of Washington, D. C., and the third at Ormond Beach, Florida—the three representing a more than 1,800-mile diagonal section of country, in which may be found many kinds of feathered visitors. I

have had thus means of photographing most of the species of this continent.

Passing part of each winter and spring since 1906 on the narrow peninsula lying between the Halifax River and the ocean, I have become much impressed by the many species of small birds visiting or resident there. Some of these are native, others are winter visitors, and a great number loiter for only a day or two in their spring migration. I shall not attempt to list here the hundred or more species that may be seen in the several seasons, but shall confine my comments to the land birds that have been habitués of the feeding-stations placed on platforms or on the ground.

The bird most welcomed was the richhued southern blue jay, with its brilliant coat in contrast with the paler hues of its northern relative in Michigan. The cardinal with its bright red garb also had a strong appeal to all of us.

THE FLORIDA JAY IS A FRIENDLY CHAP

This plain, grayish-blue species is peculiar to Florida, where it occurs mainly in the Ormond Beach district, along the palmetto and brushy belt covering the sand-dune area. In the Halifax River country it stays in the shore belt and does not frequent the more wooded vicinity of the river, where the Florida blue jay occurs. The Florida jay has something of the same confidence in mankind as that shown by the Canada jay. The readiness with which it may be taught to come to hand for pieces of bread or other food is illustrated in this photograph, made at Ormond Beach.

The bait used at this southern station consisted of "scratch food," such as is carried by most feed stores; bread broken into small pieces, and suet. Two of the feeding platforms were only a few yards from the front porch, and a third was about 100 yards behind the house in a 40-foot clearing surrounded by bushes and trees, with a couple of orange trees in the center and an observation pavilion on one side, half surrounded by the bushes.

In addition to the jays and cardinals, red-bellied woodpeckers, flickers, myrtle warblers, mockingbirds, chipping sparrows, white-throated sparrows, catbirds, grackles, and red-winged blackbirds visited the front boxes daily. The last-named birds are most unusual visitors to feeding stations near a house, but the proximity of the reedy shore of the river and their observation of other birds feeding served to break down their reserve until they began to come regularly in small flocks.

The companies, which contained young and old of both sexes, congregated in the adjacent tops of small live oaks, or on the feeding stands for a large part of each day. They became so numerous that, like the starlings in Washington, they quickly consumed the feed put out.

One winter I saw a male grackle carry away a large piece of dry bread and soak it in a near-by bird bath. After a moment he pulled it out and ate it without difficulty. This act I attributed to a specially ingenious individual, but later I saw the same thing done by other blackbirds and decided it must be a characteristic habit.

The same species came to the feeding box in the thicket as to those in front of the house, excepting the red-winged blackbirds, but on the ground in the thicket station were several other birds that love to keep close to shelter. Among these were bobwhites, mourning doves, ground doves, brown thrashers, and numerous chewinks in their handsome black, white, and brown colors. The odd habit chewinks have of scratching the dirt vigorously made them appear like little barnyard fowls. These

BLACK SKIMMERS WHIR ALOFT AT PONCE DE LEON INLET

These birds are nearly white below and black above. Graceful on the wing, they make a charming picture against a gray sky above the desolate and barren sands.

AT LOW TIDE BLACK SKIMMERS GATHER IN LARGE NUMBERS ON THE BARE SAND AT THE INLET

WHEN ALARMED, BLACK SKIMMERS TAKE WING IN A COMPACT FLOCK

Their appearance is so different from that of the gulls and terns, with which they are neighbors, that they may be readily distinguished at a long distance.

BROWN PELICANS COME TO REST WITH FULL POUCHES

They are alighting on a sand bar exposed by the falling tide at Ponce de Leon Inlet. They have come from fishing for menhaden off the adjacent coast and remain in large groups digesting their prey until high tide starts them off again.

RUDDY TURNSTONES, OR CALICO-BACKS, SIT ON THE RAILING OF THE APPROACH TO PORT ORANGE BRIDGE, FLORIDA

They are waiting near an oyster-shucking house for the dumping of empty shells, among which they search for food. These little waders are more ornate than most members of the snipe family, to which they are related.

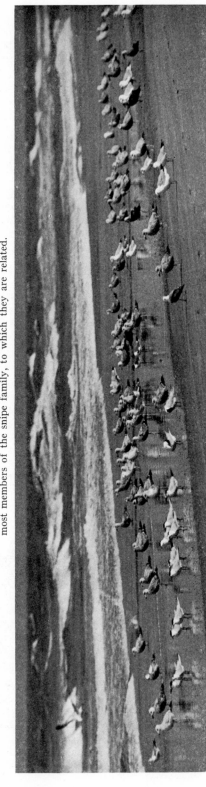

GULLS AND TERNS CONGREGATE IN LATE WINTER ON DAYTONA BEACH, NEAR PONCE DE LEON INLET

A stretch of 20 miles of flat, hard sand at low tide here has been the scene of many famous automobile speed trials and world records. The beach is also traveled by many waders and other birds during migrations. This photograph shows herring, ring-billed, and black-headed gulls and royal terns.

RUDDY TURNSTONES FLY ALONG THE MARGIN OF THE WATER

These handsome little waders, like their relatives of the snipe family, contribute much to the pleasure of the bird lover who strolls along Florida beaches. They come in early spring and give animation to the flat landscapes.

SANDERLINGS STRUT ALONG DAYTONA BEACH

During the late winter and early spring many shore birds appear along the shallow borders of lagoons and on the sands. They are interested not in what "the sad sea is saying," but in what bits of food the waves may bring to them.

A PAIR OF LONG-LEGGED, BLACK-NECKED STILTS REST IN MOSQUITO LAGOON

These fellows are admirably equipped for surf wading, for their spindly underpinning offers little resistance to the rushing water. They are famous travelers, journeying from the Middle West of the United States to the Canal Zone and Mexico. The author has photographed them throughout their rooks.

ALONG ORMUND BEACH THE AVIAN POPULATION IS COSMOPOLITAN

Almost every drive along the miles of smooth sand north of Ponce de Leon Inlet in winter will reveal a new combination of birds. They may be a businesslike troop mainly of young herring gulls on their way to a better feeding ground; or, as shown here, a small flock of willets.

SCAUP DUCKS RISE GRADUALLY FROM THE SURFACE

This photograph, taken at Halifax River, Florida, shows the manner in which these waterfowl make their take-off. They are not so quick and graceful as some of the other species, and there is considerable splashing and spray as they leave the water.

BONAPARTE GULLS AND LESSER SCAUP DUCKS FRATERNIZE NEAR DAYTONA
Birds of different species sometimes avoid each other, but these get along in friendly manner.

SANDERLINGS BRING CHEERY ACTIVITY TO DAYTONA BEACH
These nimble little sandpipers are common all winter along the shore sands of Florida. They nest
in the far north, half the world away from this sunny clime.

LESSER SCAUP DUCKS SHARE TIDBITS WITH BONAPARTE GULLS

There is nothing "upstage" about these waterfowl. So long as food is available they are unconcerned about their avian neighbors (see opposite page).

interesting occupants of the thickets are willing but not gifted vocalists.

Dr. Frank M. Chapman has written concerning the male: "When the desire to sing comes upon him, he leaves his lowly haunts and, taking a more or less exposed perch, 15 to 20 feet from the ground, sings with an earnestness which goes far to atone for his lack of striking musical ability."

Among the birds that fed on the grain scattered about in the rear lot was the beautiful little ground dove, which surprised me by its belligerent ways. Surely it was no emblem of peace, for it drove away every other bird in sight, attacking with equal vigor either its neighbors or those of its own kind; the duels between them on the ground or in midair showed the strong determination of each to be the sole guest at the banquet.

An essential in attracting birds is a supply of water placed either in a concrete basin elevated several feet, or in a galvanized pan sunk into the ground. They enjoy drinking or bathing every hour of the day.

In contrast to the many land birds seen almost daily about my winter home were those seen on voyages in my little house boat *Heron* on the Halifax River and connecting waters. The craft had accommodations for several passengers, the rear containing the engine, kitchen, and quarters for the guide. Its draft was about two feet, and the maximum speed around nine miles an hour. Large windows running the entire length of the cabin gave an unobstructed view of the surroundings.

We used the boat for visiting such places as the beautiful Tomoka River, where in the marshes alligators basked in the sunlight, and ospreys nested in solitary pines. Farther up the river there was good bass fishing in pools edged by moss-draped trees. In the other direction, near the Ponce de Leon Inlet, we could pass a day or two near the colonies of sea birds massed on the sand bars.

We made more extended trips southward, visiting in successive springs the lower end of Mosquito Lagoon, where the broad, shallow waters lie between the ocean beach and the head of Indian River. One large mangrove island was occupied by breeding pelicans and Ward herons, and the mud flats near by were dotted with active groups of sandpipers or the more stately willets and black-necked stilts.

RING-BILLED AND BONAPARTE GULLS ARE EAGER BEGGARS

These birds are contesting noisily and with much flapping of wings for scraps of bread thrown to them from the Daytona waterfront.

MOCKINGBIRDS ENJOY THE SUET

At Ormond Beach the pair that lived in the author's yard were regular guests at the piece of this delicacy which was attached to a tree trunk.

FLORIDA QUAIL TAKE THEIR OWN PICTURES AMONG THE PALMETTOS

This type of bob-white is a little darker colored than the familiar northern bird, but its habits and cheerful call notes are virtually the same as those of its better known cousin. The bait so tempts them that they are oblivious to the mechanism their pecking has set in motion.

153

A MYRTLE WARBLER WAS A FREQUENT CALLER

A MOCKINGBIRD TAKES HIS ORANGE JUICE

These little fellows were bolder than their neighbors; one of them even knocked over a stuffed screech owl placed on the author's lawn (see accompanying text).

I could always create an interesting diversion on my front lawn by placing a stuffed screech owl on a feeding box. In a few minutes a blue jay would utter harsh notes from the neighboring trees with an intonation indicating alarm or indignation, and open a chorus of its fellows. The jays, gathering like a clan on the warpath, would dart from the treetops down at their hated nocturnal enemy. Their assaults would become bolder and bolder until they would finally knock the little victim off its perch.

A STUFFED SCREECH OWL CREATES EXCITEMENT

Although many birds joined the jays in uttering cries of protest, a mockingbird proved the boldest of all; for, unsupported by any of its kind, it would often strike the little owl on the back of its head, and in one instance it knocked over even a great horned owl that had been wired loosely to the top of a fence post.

Blackbirds and similar species that were accustomed to move about in flocks fed more or less amicably side by side, but most of the others came singly and often appeared to be more tolerant of strangers than of their own kin. In many years of observation I never saw a Florida jay about the premises. In the bushes along

A BROWN THRASHER APPROACHES A FEAST

Common in winter along the Halifax River, these birds come freely about the author's premises to partake of halved oranges and other food provided.

THE CATBIRD ENJOYS A HALF ORANGE

Like the brown thrasher in the upper picture, this chap enjoys the author's hospitality. It looks around alertly, however, to make sure that no enemy is in sight.

FLORIDA QUAIL FIND SEEDS PUT OUT FOR SMALLER BIRDS

Six pictures of this flock the author took by pulling the string, and the quail recorded two others during his absence (see, also, illustration, page 153). In the above group are four cocks and two females. The cock in the center released the shutter by pecking at a seed attached to a string to the camera.

the ocean front half a mile to the east, however, they are numerous; and many cottagers living in the brushy sand-dune belt had them as daily visitors. At times these birds were so tame that they would eat readily from the hand (see page 143).

These jays afford a good illustration of the restricted distribution of certain birds. Unexpectedly, robins at Ormond Beach furnish somewhat similar evidence. Though millions of them move south from the northern States in winter, I have seen only one on the peninsula east of the Halifax River. On the main shore to the west they are often seen.

A CONGREGATING PLACE FOR SEA BIRDS

The mouth of Ponce de Leon inlet (formerly called Mosquito inlet), which forms the mouth of Halifax River, is a broad gap cut through the sand dunes that border the ocean front along most of eastern Florida. Flanking the channel just outside, and lying immediately inside this pass, are broad sand bars and flats that become exposed at

low tide and serve as favorite gathering places for thousands of birds belonging to the several species that glean their subsistence from the adjacent waters. Their main resting places are on the sandy flats inside the inlet, on the south side.

Sometimes 500 or more brown pelicans may be seen, all standing in groups in close array. These birds have been working up and down the coast offshore, fishing for menhaden, and now come with well-filled gullets to the broad flats to bask in the sun and doze away the hours while digesting their finny prey.

On other parts of the sand flats may be seen blackish patches formed by hundreds of skimmers gathered in groups; and elsewhere are similar but smaller congregations of royal terns, with scattered representatives of other kinds of terns close by. Near these or by themselves are groups of herring, ring-billed, Bonaparte, and laughing or black-headed gulls.

When these fish-eating birds are seeking food, they spread over the face of the

YOUNG PELICANS EXPRESS DISAPPROVAL OF THE CAMERA

Huddled against the far side of their nest of sticks, they registered disgusted protest. With these birds, the author had difficulty because of their tendency to panic (see text, page 167).

THIS FLASHLIGHT PICTURE CAUSED A PELICAN PANIC

The flash and report caused the birds to leave their nests in fright and fairly mob the occupants of the boat. They struck the jacklight, and some fell aboard. The alarm among the birds was so great that no further pictures were taken at night (see text, page 167).

BROWN PELICANS ARE BUSY ON PELICAN ISLAND, EASTERN FLORIDA, DURING THE NESTING SEASON

Long ago, when these and other birds occupied the island as a breeding place, it was heavily overgrown with mangroves. As the years passed the mangroves were killed by the excrements of the birds. All departed but the pelicans, which built nests on the ground. So many of them made their home here that they began to breed in December and continued to do so at intervals until May.

A FLIGHT OF PELICANS APPROACHES

This wingshot with the camera was even more difficult than a shot with a gun at waterfowl coming head on, and its success afforded the author far greater and more lasting satisfaction, for it gave him a trophy not of one bird but of a considerable flock.

NEST AND EGGS OF THE BROWN PELICAN

waters in wide array; but when they take their daily siestas they prefer the close companionship of their own kind and stand almost touching one another. The amicable relationships of the great groups are interesting, and I cannot recall ever having seen any sign of bickering among them. Another noticeable characteristic of all these birds is their habit, when standing in close formation, of heading toward the wind. Thus their array has somewhat the appearance of a military formation.

During the resting periods a few fish hawks may be seen hovering over the mouth of the inlet, with enough pelicans, gulls, and terns on the wing to give a sense of pleasant animation to a scene otherwise smacking of somnolence. The liveliness is enhanced by an occasional black-breasted plover, willet, or a group of sandpipers, on the beaches.

Whenever something alarming occurs, like the report of a shotgun or the passing of a large, noisy motor boat, all the birds take wing, and for a time the air is filled with a profusion of graceful forms. Even the clumsily built pelican has a wonderful mastery of the air. "The Inlet," as this locality is known by the people of the neighboring towns, is at low tide a favorite place for visitors wishing to study the birds with field glasses.

I have already expressed the opinion that there is no more convenient form of outdoor shelter than a motor-driven house boat of light draught. It may be anchored near the gathering or breeding places of aquatic

birds or may be taken to some fresh-water lake in a locality remote from settlements, where the animal life exists undisturbed.

One afternoon we anchored the house boat in mid-channel half a mile above the Halifax inlet, in order to study and photograph the morning and evening feeding flights of black skimmers, which have the habit of fishing throughout the night. Whenever we disturbed the skimmers in their midday resting places on sand bars, they filled the air with an almost solid mass of fluttering wings, flying in closer formation than any of the larger water birds I have ever seen (see page 145).

Late in the afternoon, the skimmers separate into small files of a dozen or more and, with open bills, fly rapidly along close to the water. They keep the bladelike lower mandibles below the surface, so that they literally "plow the main," scooping up the small aquatic animals and usually "uttering a sharp *yap, yap,* like a pack of hounds on the trail."

Being partly successful in our efforts that afternoon, we concluded to stay at the same anchorage until the following morning, when there would be another flight of the birds. Just after dark an unusually strong wind came out of the north, and, with a high tide running out, the boat was subjected to a heavy pressure from the combination of wind, waves, and ebbing tide.

Fearing that under such conditions the craft might drag its anchor, we kept watch on the shore line to detect any change in our position.

THE HOUSE BOAT GETS A BUMPING

About 10 o'clock, while John and I were contentedly listening to the tumult outside, there came a tremendous crash on the port side. The windows rattled, loose articles fell to the floor, and the little craft shivered from bow to stern.

John seized a large wind-proof lantern, which had been kept lighted for any possible emergency, and, hastening out on the stern deck, saw a 75-foot scow swing away in the darkness. We recalled that earlier the scow had been anchored half a mile above us.

Evidently the scow was slowly dragging its anchor, and unable to withstand the pressure exerted by the wind and tide, the long cable was permitting it to swing back and forth like the pendulum of a clock. The

"DIGNITY PERSONIFIED"

The young brown pelican in its downy stage is a proud fellow. The photograph was taken
at Indian River, Florida, where there are thousands of the species.

YOUNG PELICANS RETURN FROM FISHING

Although awkward and ungainly in appearance as they stand on shore, these birds have a marvelous mastery of the air (see text, page 160).

A GROUP OF FINE OLD PELICANS AND A FEW YOUNG FACE ONE WAY

ABOUT 1,000 YOUNG PELICANS BATHE AND PLAY AT THE WATER'S EDGE

These birds are most gregarious in their habits, often standing shoulder to shoulder in almost military array, as in the upper picture.

PELICANS HUDDLE IN THE SHADOW OF AN APPROACHING THUNDERSTORM

THE CAMERA RECORDS THE RISING FLIGHT OF A PELICAN

IN THIS POSE THE PELICAN RESEMBLES THE CANADA GOOSE

GROUPS OF YOUNG PELICANS ARE PHOTOGRAPHED AS THEY SLEEP AND AS THEY PREEN THEMSELVES

question now arose whether on its return swing the scow would strike our boat again.

Anxiously peering into the darkness, we soon saw it coming back, but fortunately it missed our stern by about 5 feet, striking the rowboat that was fastened behind, but apparently not injuring it.

When the danger had passed, we realized that had the scow struck the bow of the house boat it might have forced it under water. We should have sunk within a few minutes, or if our anchor chain had broken as a result of the pressure we should have gone whirling down on the swiftly running tide to the open sea, where the wind was driving huge waves into the mouth of the inlet.

Since our engine was often slow in getting into action, we might easily have been forced into rough water with little chance of keeping afloat. Next morning the scow lay high and dry on a sand bar a short distance below us. The falling tide had saved it from going out to sea.

For many readers of these chronicles big game hunting may lie beyond the horizon, but any who so desire may have delightful adventure in photographing the ordinary forms of wild life. Some of my pleasantest thrills have come from taking portraits of unexpected visitors to my country home, although I have gone far afield for nobler quarry.

SMALL GAME PLENTIFUL IN A FLORIDA ORANGE GROVE

Near my Florida home the scene of many interesting hours has been an orange grove which extends back to a wall of low forest and undergrowth thickets. There one winter I took advantage of a long dry period, when all wild things were eager to find water, to make some special observations.

I sank a small wooden pail level with the ground among the orange trees, filled it with water, and placed about it a supply of seeds, bread crumbs, and a cut orange. About 20 feet back from the drinking place I erected a small green canvas observation tent and partly covered it with palmetto leaves.

Many small visitors soon came to sample the fare provided, and each day I moved the tent a little nearer the bait and water, with no sign from the visitors that they distinguished it from the natural surroundings. On the fourth day, for the first time, I entered this blind and, using my 14-inch focus lens, proceeded to record the doings of the patrons of my small, out-of-doors restaurant.

In succeeding days I passed a total of about four hours in this blind, and photographed a mourning dove, a ground dove, a pair of quail, a pair of cardinals, a pair of chewinks, a brown thrasher, a mockingbird, gray squirrels, cotton-tail rabbits, and roof rats. Several of the species in the pictures were shown approaching or sampling split oranges, which appeared to be favored by several of them, although they had not learned to open the fruit. The quail excited my interest the most—their appearance was entirely unexpected, although for several days I had heard their melodious spring notes in the neighborhood. In later years several coveys of these birds made their homes about us.

BROWN PELICANS OF INDIAN RIVER

For many years I had been familiar with the pelican colony on Indian River, Florida. On April 21, 1903, I visited Pelican Island to take flashlight pictures of the breeding birds, but when I fired the first flash the whole colony took wing and passed so low over the boat with its glaring lantern that we were fairly overwhelmed by them, their flapping wings and large bodies banging into or over the boat. Crouching down in the bottom, with the cameras dashed from the bow, we waited until the avalanche was over.

My Virginia guide, a stranger to these waters, was somewhat outraged by this performance, and he remarked as he tossed a flapping bird overboard, "Darn these pell-mellicans." Through fear of further disturbing the birds in the midst of the nesting season, we quietly withdrew with a single much-prized picture to our credit, and decided to carry on our photographic activity only by day.

Another season, in company with Doctor Chapman, I revisited the island, he to take moving pictures of this wonderful colony, some by the new colored-plate process, and I to get photographs of these birds in flight and to find some suitable subject for the stereoscopic camera. On March 10 we found about 500 young birds ready for flight. Scattered about were the mummifying bodies of fully 800 more that had been killed in a midnight raid by local fishermen.

Disregarding the fact that the pelicans live almost wholly upon the nearly worthless menhaden, which they take in the open sea, the fishermen in recent years have shown unrelenting enmity toward these birds, because occasionally the young, in their early efforts, catch a few mullet in the Indian River and other coastal waters.

When going to or returning from the fishing grounds, the pelicans usually fly in flocks of from four to 10, in single file, sometimes abreast and sometimes in echelon, the leader setting the pace and the rest in slow measured strokes, flapping or sailing in unison.

COLOR OF ADULTS AND YOUNG

The adult, in the breeding season, has a seal-brown head and neck and a yellowish crown, the remainder of the body being silver-gray. The half-grown young are covered with a soft, white down, which later changes to dull-gray and brown plumage.

After Pelican Island was made a Federal reservation, the birds did not frequent it much, if at all, during the nonbreeding period. As the time approached for them to assume family duties, they did not straggle into the breeding place; but just in advance of the nest-building time, late in October or in November, they suddenly appeared in considerable numbers, as if by a general understanding.

Within a few weeks the nests were built, and in December many of the birds were occupied with their family cares, while others appeared to await their turn in this congested nursery. Because of the limitations of the area available, the pelicans nested on the island more or less continuously from November until May. On the Gulf Coast at Tampa Bay and Charlotte Harbor the nesting season does not begin until spring.

When Doctor Bryant visited the island late in the 1850s, the pelicans and thousands of other birds were nesting in the tops of a heavy growth of mangroves that covered it, as they still do the adjacent islands. In 1898 Doctor Chapman found some mangroves left in which a few pelicans had nests, but most of this growth was gone, and the majority of the birds were nesting on the bare ground.

Before Pelican Island was finally deserted, the mangroves had all disappeared, and the entire colony was forced to nest on the ground. Its attachment to the locality appeared greater than its desire to nest in the tops of mangroves, which were plentiful on adjacent and apparently equally suitable islands within about a half a mile. All the other birds mentioned by Doctor Bryant had long before left this island for more congenial haunts.

Brown pelicans, unlike the boobies, usually raise two or three young and so apparently have a better opportunity to survive. The continued abundance of the boobies about their favorite haunts seems to indicate that they are less subject to harmful vicissitudes than are the pelicans. Otherwise these last would increase to a far greater extent than they do.

One rather surprising cause of the decrease among brown pelicans on Pelican Island is the cannibalistic habit of the large or nearly full-grown young of catching newly hatched younger birds, left unguarded for a short time, and gulping them down as choice morsels. Fortunately for the future of their kind this is not a common practice.

THE FIRST FEDERAL BIRD RESERVATION

The brown pelicans of Florida owe much to the interest taken in their welfare by nature lovers outside the State. It was due mostly to their representations that on March 14, 1903, President Theodore Roosevelt set aside, under Federal guardianship, the Pelican Island Bird Reservation, the first refuge of this kind ever made in the United States. This splendid precedent has since been followed by the setting aside of more than 90 similar reservations scattered over the entire country and as far as Alaska, the Hawaiian Islands, and Porto Rico.

In 1906 Indian Key, a breeding place for brown pelicans on the coast just north of Tampa Bay, was made a reservation, and others have followed. Without these sanctuaries it is unlikely that these remarkable and picturesque birds could have survived the ill-founded but persistent enmity of Florida fishermen.

It has been a source of amazement to me that some of the fishermen of the State, so notoriously wasteful of fish life because of their plying such illegal practices as "stop netting," and seining in forbidden waters, should continue to blame the really innocent pelicans for the decrease of fish caused willfully by themselves. Some of

A PELICAN NESTS ALOFT IN ITS NEW HOME

When the brown pelican colony deserted a century-old gathering place near Sebastian, Florida, its members selected the large and partly wooded Brevard Island in the Mosquito Lagoon, east of the northern end of Indian River. There they built their nests in large mangroves, thus reverting to the normal habit of this bird in Florida.

them have frankly admitted the unjust character of the charges against the pelicans and have recognized the harmfulness of the methods of fishing so commonly in vogue.

PELICANS REPLACE OLD FAVORITES

As the direct result of Federal protection, now aided by much favorable local sentiment, brown pelicans may be seen every day flying along hundreds of miles of the Florida coast and about its bays and lagoons, where they are always objects of interest. In part they fill that vast hiatus left by the disappearance of enormous num-bers of herons and ibises, of the roseate spoonbill now nearly gone, and of the flamingo, which long since became extinct on these shores.

Soon after Pelican Island was made a Federal bird reservation, the National Association of Audubon Societies, which had been active in its establishment, cooperated with the Biological Survey in maintaining a local warden to guard it. As a means of notifying the public that the birds on the island were wards of the Government and were not to be disturbed, a great board sign with large letters warning off all trespassers was erected.

THE WARD HERON IS AN AVIAN ICHABOD CRANE

While visiting the brown pelicans at Brevard Island, the author had a fine opportunity to get records of these birds in numerous strange postures, worthy of places on Japanese screens.

about half a mile from Pelican Island. These houses and the disturbance caused by their occupants' small motor boats, which were continually going past one end of the island, so worried the birds that they set about moving to another home. In the fall of 1922, between 2,000 and 4,000 birds came to nest on Pelican Island, but a few dissatisfied pairs, instead of trying a new place in the district where they had lived so long, went north to Brevard Island, near the south end of Mosquito Lagoon.

THE HOUSE BOAT VISITS MOSQUITO LAGOON

After it was learned definitely that the brown pelicans had deserted their century-old home on the Indian River and had established farther north a new and apparently permanent one at the lower end of Mosquito Lagoon, we decided to go there in the house boat.

That this innovation on their breeding grounds was not appreciated by the birds soon became evident; for when Doctor Chapman visited the place in the spring of 1904, the next year after the reservation was established, he found not a single pelican on the island. More than 700 nests had been built on adjacent islands. The next fall the actions of the birds so plainly showed their objections to the sign that the warden removed it. At once the birds reoccupied the premises.

At the time of the general land development that began in Florida after the World War, two patches were cleared in the mangroves and two small frame houses were built on the eastern shore of Indian River

On April 14, 1924, in company with Doctor Nelson, I left for the lagoon. We paused overnight on Halifax River near the inlet, where many skimmers were in their usual haunts, even at this late date.

On the following morning we took on board the Federal game warden of the district, who was to be at the wheel in traversing a long stretch of tortuous or shallow waters, the navigation of which required expert knowledge of local conditions. John Hammer took charge of the engine and the frying pan, two items of great importance to the running of the boat and to the wellbeing of its passengers.

Soon after starting we passed New Smyrna, an attractive little tourist resort that had been greatly invigorated by the development there of the shrimp industry. When we reached the head of the lagoon, we were only a short distance east of the canal leading into the headwaters of the Indian River, a locality still known as the "Haulover" from the early days when boats were portaged on a tramway across a neck of land. This canal diverted all the traffic of launches and house boats on their way down the inland waterway to Miami.

With no such travel on the rest of the lagoon, visitors like ourselves could study bird life under favorable conditions. Every evening, however, a fleet of fishermen's motor boats spread out over the lagoon and drew their seines at night in the belief that it was easier to ensnare the fish after darkness. These visitors were regarded by us with some interest, for

THE WARD HERON AT REST IS COMELY

It is only when flying (see opposite page) that it seems grotesquely angular and awkward.

their glowing lanterns and gasoline torches gave a sort of Venetian touch to the calm surrounding waters. Their activities afforded a supply of fresh fish, in kind and size suitable for our requirements.

We arrived opposite one end of the new pelican home on Brevard Island about 7 p. m. and anchored some 300 yards to the north. A few belated pelicans were still returning from the ocean, indicating that a greater number would be found nesting in the long line of mangroves.

On landing the next morning, we were first attracted by several hundred feathered skeletons—mute evidence of a raid made a month before by local fishermen, and of the same merciless slaughter as that suf-

fered by the birds' ancestors at their Indian River home about 17 years before. As in the former case, the fishermen believed that the thousand or more pelicans meant that much competition in the fishing business.

Since learning that the pelicans get their food supply from the ocean, the fishermen have left the colony unmolested. This security, however, may be due in part to the fact that the island has been made a Federal bird refuge.

A more encouraging sight than the dead birds on the ground was the large number of pelicans nesting in the mangroves, where the big nests of sticks were built on the lower and stronger branches. The weight

"OLD BILL" GATHERED "TOLL" AT PORT ORANGE BRIDGE

The great blue heron is usually one of the shyest of birds, yet this member of the species has for years regularly frequented the bridge and taken his gleanings from the fishermen along its rail (see text, page 176).

sloping, sandy shores were lined with hundreds of dignified-looking pelicans quietly sunning themselves, while many others were splashing about in the water as if having an aquatic tournament.

Passing eastward, we came to a clump of high mangroves, and, to our gratification, found about 25 occupied nests of the Ward heron, a light-colored phase of the great blue heron. This was a bird I had never photographed, although occasionally I had seen one well out from shore in shallow water.

THE HERONS TAKE ALARM

No sooner had we come in sight of this rather rare breeding place than all the adult herons departed separately, alighting here and there in a foot of water 100 yards away from their deserted nests. I erected my little green umbrella blind close to a tree containing two nests in the upper branches. These structures were very light and frail compared with those of the pelicans, but they commanded an extended view and offered a striking example of the difference between gregarious birds and those that lead a more or less solitary life.

It would be hard to find a more stolid and tamer bird than the pelican, or one more watchful and alert than the great blue heron. This latter wader of the shallows is ever on the lookout for signs of danger and has developed a much higher degree of caution than one would expect in a bird that is neither sought for the table nor regarded as harmful in any way to other forms of wild life.

of the clumsy parents and the ever-increasing burden of the young require a well-supported nest. It was the first time I had seen the pelicans of eastern Florida occupying nests in trees. At their former home on Pelican Island, all mangroves had disappeared, and the hundreds of nests were built on the ground, where skill in construction was not required.

DIGNIFIED PELICANS ENJOY EASE

It was necessary only to select a site on the more elevated portion of the island to avoid inundation from flood waters. After easily obtaining pictures of the tree-nesting birds, we visited a little horseshoe bay a short distance from the nests, where the

After I had entered the blind, and the skiff had returned to the house boat as ostensible evidence that the party had gone, the herons began reconnoitering overhead, but were still suspicious of my blind. Consequently I cut some long branches from a mangrove and screened the green canvas covering.

The parent birds now began dropping lightly down upon their elevated nests, and I obtained a series of satisfactory pictures, some showing the herons passing overhead with their long legs stretched out behind like aerial rudders, others descending or ascending, and now and then one standing like a sentinel on the tree-top or bending over the nest in regurgitation. The size of the fish being fed appeared to depend upon the age of the young birds. A day later, entirely content with our first visit, we left these interesting scenes and headed for the Halifax River, determined to return the following spring.

CROP FULL, "OLD BILL" BECOMES ALOOF

When his appetite is satisfied, Bill leaves the bridge for a shallow bar immediately above it, where he stands for hours apparently in dignified consideration of such matters as occupy a heron's mind.

In the middle of April, 1925, I again went to the lagoon, accompanied this time by Doctor Chapman, whose special purpose was to obtain half a dozen pelicans for the American Museum in New York. These were to be shown later beneath a dome, the mounted specimens suspended high overhead by invisible wires, in a realistic representation of the birds in their columnar flight.

This time the house boat was anchored a little way to the east of the island, where, in the morning and late in the afternoon, the pelicans passed overhead. Chapman was able to select the birds he wanted.

We passed several days exploring the shores, where the slight fluctuations caused by the going and coming of the tide north of the lagoon temporarily flooded numerous sand bars and mud flats, thus furnishing the shore birds many forms of life not readily obtainable in stationary waters.

This was the only place in Florida where I found conditions so favorable for shore birds. Kinds noted included willets, yellow-legs, calico backs, black-breasted plovers, several species of sandpipers and some long-legged stilts, which, dressed in a striking combination of black and white, stalked about in unconcern. I had not seen this last-named southern wader since my trip to Mexico in 1910.

Early in the spring of 1927 Doctor Nelson, on his second trip to Brevard Island, in company with the local game warden, found 80 white pelicans resting with their brown relatives in the lagoon near one end of the reservation. They had come from the Gulf coast where they winter every season. Since then white pelicans making winter visits to this place have been observed repeatedly.

The differing methods of these two species in catching fish are interesting to observe. The brown pelican dives heavily with a loud splash from a height of 20 to 75 feet, sometimes disappearing below the surface, and capturing the fish in the distended pouch. The white species swims about in a dignified way and scoops up fish near the surface, as in a dip net.

Both on Yellowstone Lake and Henry Lake, Idaho, I have seen the white pelican capture fish as agile as the trout. This species might prove harmful if it became abundant on the lagoons along the east coast of Florida, but at present it is an uncommon visitor there and is the object of much interest. In 1926 white pelicans were found nesting in considerable numbers as far south as a small island off the Gulf coast of Texas.

OLD-TIME ABUNDANCE OF FLORIDA BIRDS RECORDED BY DOCTOR BRYANT

To illustrate the almost incredible abundance during the past of water birds in Florida, I quote the following from an account of Pelican Island as it was seen in 1858* by Dr. Henry Bryant, an early ornithologist:

The most extensive breeding place he visited "was on a small island, called Pelican Island, about 20 miles north of Fort Capron. The nests were here placed on the tops of mangrove trees, about the size and shape of large apple trees. Breeding in company with the pelicans were thousands of Herons, Peales, Egrets, the Rufus Egret, and Little White Egret, with a few of the Great Blue Herons (Ward Herons), and Roseate Spoonbills; and immense numbers of Man-of-War birds and White Ibises were congregated on the island."

The mangroves as reported here so plentiful in 1858 were killed by the birds nesting in them so abundantly. They completely disappeared years ago. With them

* Boston Society of Natural History, VII, 1859, p. 19.

went also the swarming bird life of other species that made this one of the most marvelous breeding places for large birds ever recorded. The brown pelican alone remained faithful to the ancient home until they were crowded out by man.

For many years after I began visiting the Halifax River country, more than 45 years ago, little blue and Louisiana herons were very abundant, and both the snowy and the large American egrets were numerous, not only in the river but everywhere in swampy ponds. They were an interesting part of the landscape wherever one went.

EGRETS GRACEFUL IN FLIGHT

Their morning and evening flights over the river were such notable sights that people made excursions to observe them and to admire the beautiful forms of the birds in the air. These flights were made northward up the river early in the morning and southward in the evening back to their roosting places on some mangrove-covered islets in the river a few miles above Ponce de Leon Inlet.

There the little blue and the Louisiana herons gathered each evening by thousands in the winter months, and in April or about the first of May many of them set up housekeeping and raised their young. At one place several miles above my cottage on the river was a strip of tall reeds about a quarter of a mile long, where hundreds of herons roosted each night.

For the same purpose others came in small parties to some small reed patches along the river bank within a few hundred yards above Ormond Bridge. These birds could be seen from the highway as they came down to the larger patch of reeds, and from the shelter of some small trees they could be observed at close range in the reeds near the bridge.

These herons gave a delightful animation to this area and served as an unusual attraction to northern visitors. They were regarded as permanent occupants of this district, where no one molested them. Since about 1920, however, they have steadily decreased, until during the winter of 1930-31 the appearance of a few of them was a cause of comment.

Since they have had protection under both State and Federal law, as well as the good will of the community, their disappearance is hard to explain. No signs have been noticed of any disease affecting the

AN AMERICAN EGRET STANDS BY ITS NEST AT ORANGE LAKE

Plume hunters threatened these birds with extinction, but Federal protection saved them, and they are now slowly increasing.

UNGAINLY, PERHAPS, BUT IT CAN FLY

This is one of several attitudes of the Ward heron recorded by the author's camera at Brevard Island.

A WARD HERON SAILED LIKE A KITE

IT LEFT ITS PERCH ON A MANGROVE

AT REST IT LOOKED HEAVY

The Florida form of this great blue heron, which the author photographed at Mosquito Lagoon, is a much paler bird than its relative of the Northern States in summer.

herons, and my observations have convinced me that the fish crow is responsible. At the time the decrease of the herons was noted a definite increase in the number of fish crows was also observed along the river and in the surrounding district.

In front of our cottage fish crows became daily visitors, usually occupying vantage points of the tops of several yellow pines growing there. Then, before the cottagers were astir in the morning, the crows would visit the feeding boxes for food intended for other birds.

For many years the crows came to the boxes in small numbers, but in more recent times as many as 40 or 50 would appear at a time, blackening the tops of the pines. Elsewhere along the river they increased from straggling small parties to flocks not uncommonly containing hundreds, all busily engaged in satisfying their hunger.

These black-garbed robbers have been known to be persistent enemies of breeding herons in Florida, as well as elsewhere in their range. In a preceding chapter I have recorded the depredations of these crows among the breeding herons, clapper rails, and other birds at Revels Island, Virginia.

That they destroyed the heron rookeries on the Halifax River is rendered certain also by the fact that the crows increased to a maximum in the period when the herons were most numerous. As they have gone, the crows have decreased greatly in number.

A FEATHERED TOLL GATHERER WAS "OLD BILL" THE HERON

A Florida great blue heron (*Ardea herodias wardi*), known personally as "Old Bill," has for many years passed most of each day on the roadway near the middle of the Port Orange toll bridge over the Halifax River. He is a fine, big, dignified bird, and his friendly confidence in his human neighbors is so appreciated that he is a well-known local character.

Old Bill always has an aristocratic air of aloofness and pays little attention to the public notice he attracts. Pedestrians may approach him slowly within a few yards without exciting his alarm, and when vehicles pass, he merely hops upon the bridge railing.

The increase of automobile traffic, however, is forcing him to avoid the roadway much more than formerly. When not on the bridge, he may usually be seen a few yards above it on a shallow bar.

LOUISIANA HERONS VISIT IN ANOTHER STATE

These birds are common residents throughout the year in eastern Florida, where they haunt retired shallow waters in which food is available.

IN FLORIDA THE LOUISIANA HERON IS BECOMING SCARCE

In the last 15 years these birds have decreased vastly in numbers because of the destructiveness of fish crows. The enemies are less numerous because of their absence (see text, page 176).

THE WING SPREAD IS IMMENSE

In flight the Ward heron presents some strange pictures with its long legs adangle and its huge wings outspread.

ITS FEET ARE LIKE KITE TAILS

With such enormous wings, the Ward heron need not worry about minor details of flying form, but it will never win renown for grace.

TWO ALERT BLUE JAYS MAKE A DISCOVERY IN FLORIDA

This pair, in searching for grain, discovered a partly concealed camera only a few yards away and
expressed their distrust by elevating their crests.

Old Bill's presence on the bridge is not from any desire for a place in the public eye, but for a much more prosaic purpose. During most of the daylight hours the railings of the bridge are occupied by scattered fishermen, their interest centered on the water below. Whenever one of them drops his catch on the bridge, Old Bill watches his opportunity to step silently forward.

With a flip of his big beak he seizes and casts the smaller-sized fish into the water. He then flies down, and, wading up to the floater, proceeds to send it down his long neck. Herons will not try to swallow a dry fish, but must have it wet so that it will go down easily. One fisherman complained that Old Bill had robbed him of eight fish in one day.

Old Bill's confidence in humanity, so unusual in birds ordinarily shy and suspicious, originated in the friendly advances of a bridge tender, who encouraged and winked at his protégé's flagrant violations of property rights.

In addition to the friendly little owls about our Florida home was another bird of the night which proved equally interesting to the members of our household. This

was the chuck-will's-widow, belonging to the goatsucker family and somewhat larger and browner than its northerly relative, the whip-poor-will. The difference in names "expresses the syllabic differences in their calls" (see illustrations, pp. 84 and 85).

The chuck-will's-widow comes from lower Florida in late March, immediately making its presence known by the tribal slogan. As the mating season approaches, its limited vocabulary finds expression in an almost uninterrupted serenade for man or mate, with a slight variation in intonation.

It is the one bird that, when casually observed, apparently has no feet, for it lies flat on the ground or crouches low on a limb until taking flight, when, doubtless, the concealed feet and legs help in the take-off.

"SHINING" THE CHUCK-WILL'S-WIDOW

One warm night in the middle of April, 1935, we had an interesting experience while motoring along a well-wooded road near the Halifax River. We had gone only a short distance when we saw, some 200 feet ahead, a chuck-will's-widow. Coming nearer, we could see this bird plainly. It was crouching on the roadway, its bright eyes glittering until it was flushed a few yards away. Its eyes were in marked contrast to the eyes of certain animals, which fade away when the bodies become plain.

Before returning late in the evening, we saw about a dozen of these birds. Secluded roads seemed to serve as flightways for the chuck-will's-widow, where betwixt the bordering trees the broad-mouthed hunters of the night had little trouble in catching the different species of winged insects.

More than twenty years before, I had discovered that both the large and the small species of the goatsucker in the Panama Canal Zone had eyes that readily reflected the rays of electric lamps strung along the edge of the barracks in which we stayed. Doubtless these lights attracted insects and gave the southern relatives of the chuck-will's-widow an equally favorable feeding place. But it was not until the present writing that I personally noticed in Florida or any of our other States a nocturnal bird that had glowing eyes.

A recent inquiry shows that many auto drivers had occasionally seen eyes shining along rural roadways but attributed the same to such animals as the raccoon and the rabbit. I have little doubt that in a majority of these cases the eyes seen were those of the chuck-will's-widow, for there are few persons, even among ornithologists, who know that there is any species of bird having eyes that shine at night under suitable conditions (see Volume I, Chapter XXIII).

These little trips recalled the earlier times, when, in a canoe, I went out after dark to "shine" deer with a gun at my side, and the later period when the camera and flashlight afforded a less destructive pastime in studying wild animals in their midnight rambles.

FLORIDA SCENERY ENTICES TRAVEL UP THE HALIFAX RIVER—EASTERN SIDE

The heavy draping of Spanish moss on the oak trees along the river gives a singular charm to woodland vistas there as well as in many other parts of the State.

CHAPTER VIII — PART I

Further Experiences Among the Wild Life of Florida

LATE in April, 1903, while on an expedition to the great Green Swamp to photograph sandhill cranes, I visited the town of Taveras, a little south of Sanford. In the midst of the place was a large, nearly completed opera house, which had been built just before a disastrous winter when the surrounding orange groves were destroyed by a hard freeze.

For some years the building had stood with gaping doors and windows. It had become the resort of thousands of bats, which secreted themselves by day under the roof and in the unplastered walls. Every evening at dusk the bats, undoubtedly the free-tailed species of this region (*Tadarida cynocephala*), poured forth from the upper windows and chimneys like a cloud of smoke, and dispersed over the surrounding country on their nightly hunt for insects. They always returned before daybreak.

BATS MAKE AN OPERA HOUSE PAY

So great were the numbers of these bats that the owners found it profitable to gather and sell the droppings, which are valuable as a fertilizer. From this source they obtained some hundreds of dollars each year, the only income from the opera house.

These bats are close relatives of the Mexican free-tailed bat, a species that is abundant in southern Texas and that has been exploited about San Antonio as a supposed controller of malarial mosquitoes. There a number of especially constructed bat roosts have been built, but so far as I have learned only one of them has been occupied by the bats.

Microscopic examinations of the stomach contents and droppings of these bats have failed to show that mosquitoes form any considerable part of their food. Furthermore, it is well known that malaria is prevalent in many localities in Texas and Mexico that are frequented by tens of thousands of these animals, another fact that puts into question their efficacy as mosquito destroyers. The free-tailed bats of our southern border and the tropics gather to roost in enormous numbers in great limestone caves, especially in Texas and in the Carlsbad Cavern, New Mexico.

The swamp rabbit of Florida and the coastal swamps and marshes of adjacent States swims nearly as well as a mink or a muskrat. Though similar in general appearance to the cottontail of the North, it is a heavier-bodied, shorter-legged, darker-brown animal, with slender, long-clawed feet and a much smaller tail. It lives in grassy marshes or in wooded and brush-grown swamps.

When small vegetation, such as grass or reeds, forms a dense growth, these curious rabbits make well-worn runways, which they use constantly. They habitually leave the roads and voluntarily take to the water or, when frightened, cross waterways with the utmost facility. The partial webbing between the hind toes helps make them expert in the water.

For several hundred yards up and down the shore of Halifax River in front of my winter home, a fringe of reeds, swamp grass, and water-loving brush grew both in and out of the water. On the bank were palmettos. The rabbits constantly frequented this cover. When pursued by stray dogs, they swam out among the reeds and quietly lay totally submerged, except for their noses, until the enemy had departed.

For years I had seen the runways of the rabbits in this nearby growth, but because of the abundance of their native food in these haunts, it was doubtful for a long time whether they would invade our garden. One evening at dusk, however, I saw a pair at the foot of the little slope near the river. Encouraged by this evidence of their neighborliness, I placed some celery and carrots near the water.

PHOTOGRAPHING SWAMP RABBITS

The next morning, I was delighted to find that these offerings had vanished; for it indicated that swamp rabbits, like cottontails, have a taste for garden truck. I set a camera and flashlight, with a baited pull string. Early the following night the flashlight suddenly illuminated our living room and the loud report of the explosion caused much excitement in the nearby cottages. The photograph that resulted showed a swamp rabbit feasting on the bait at the end of the string. On subsequent nights I

A YOUNG NIGHT HERON DISPLAYED TEMPER

This protesting youngster provided one of the few photographs that rewarded the author's visit to middle Florida.

platform to keep the squirrels from climbing it. This plan worked very well for a while, but the animals soon learned that they could reach the feeding box by dropping upon it from overhanging limbs. Then I tried the device of hanging the platform suspended from two guy wires midway between the porch railing and the trunk of an oak tree, but the squirrels promptly overcame this difficulty. The wires were too small for them to use for a "tight rope," but soon they were descending from the tree trunk, using all four feet hand over hand along the wires, their bodies hanging below.

TAKING A WILDCAT PICTURE

Besides the bears, there was another animal that foiled me. It was the wildcat, a southern cousin of the Canada lynx. I had once succeeded in getting a flashlight picture of the lynx in western Ontario (see Volume I, page 150), but the wildcat had eluded my every effort to photograph it.

For putting out bait around the edges of swamps and thickets near the Florida coast, where wildcats were abundant, the only rewards I got were pictures of raccoons, skunks, opossums, and roof rats. Finally I heard of a raid made on a chicken coop at a plantation up the Halifax River, where 40 out of 45 chickens had been killed by wildcats.

Visiting this place, I borrowed one of the surviving fowls and placed it in a box, well guarded on the open side by a strong wire mesh, with enough food and water to last several days. I nailed the box to a

had no difficulty in taking, all practically in my front yard, a series of pictures of these nocturnal animals in several different attitudes.

GRAY SQUIRRELS BECOME NUISANCES AT THE BIRD FEEDING PLACES

The gray squirrels, too, were regular boarders. Although we did not begrudge them the food, they became a great nuisance and drove away other visitors. They had the habit of sitting frequently on a feeding platform for half an hour. When one retired another would take its place to the exclusion of all birds during this time.

To prevent this monopoly, I covered with smooth tin the wooden stake supporting the

A YOUNG SANDHILL CRANE GOES WADING

These birds are resident in large marshy plains in middle and northern Florida. They were once
very numerous there but now exist in only a few localities.

FLOWERS SURROUND THE NEST OF A LOGGERHEAD SHRIKE NEAR SANFORD, FLORIDA

FLORIDA SWAMP RABBITS TOOK THEIR OWN PICTURES FREELY BY FLASHLIGHT

When pursued, these rabbits take to the water and swim as freely as muskrats. The Florida form is dark reddish-brown. The tail is very short, with only a little white on the underside.

FLORIDA SWAMP RABBITS ARE SELDOM SEEN IN DAYLIGHT

IT APPRECIATES A LITTLE ASSISTANCE

Gray squirrels are common residents about the author's winter home at Ormond Beach. They enjoy
orange juice when the fruit has been cut, but apparently do not open the skin themselves.

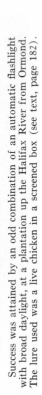

"THE SAME OLD COON"—ONLY A LITTLE WILIER

Disturbed by an explosion on a former night, this animal on the next visit came to the bait from behind with the idea, perhaps, of being screened from the dazzling flash.

THE AUTHOR PHOTOGRAPHED ONLY ONE WILDCAT

Success was attained by an odd combination of an automatic flashlight with broad daylight, at a plantation up the Halifax River from Ormond. The lure used was a live chicken in a screened box (see text, page 182).

THE FLORIDA RACCOON IS AT HOME AMONG THE PALMETTOS AND TRAILING SPANISH MOSS

Near the author's winter home, at Ormond Beach, a number of raccoons have taken their own pictures by the automatic flashlight camera. When young, this animal makes an interesting but inquisitive pet. It is practically omnivorous, eating frogs, fish, small mammals, birds, eggs, insects, fruit, young corn, etc.

A LITTLE GRAY SQUIRREL SITS FOR HIS PICTURE

A FLORIDA RACCOON TAKES HIS OWN PHOTOGRAPH

These animals feared neither the flashlight nor slumbering people when they were seeking a meal within an orange grove at Ormond Beach.

FOURTEEN SKUNK FLASHLIGHTS WERE OBTAINED IN TEN DAYS

VISITORS WERE OF MANY SORTS

An almost black skunk took his own picture at the same place where the raccoons, the opossum,
and the cat were also photographed.

A VIRGINIAN THRIVES IN FLORIDA

Opossums are the only American marsupial. Their young are born in an embryonic condition and are attached to teats in a pouch on the mother's abdomen.

THE COTTON RAT IS A SLY CREATURE

Like the swamp rabbit, this little rodent makes its runways in the damp ground covered with heavy grass and reeds along the Halifax River.

ANOTHER FLORIDA OPOSSUM TAKES ITS OWN PORTRAIT

These animals were common about Ormond, along the Halifax River, though because of their nocturnal habits few visitors know of their presence.

magnolia tree in an abandoned orange grove near the thicket where the slaughtered chickens had been dragged.

Every few days I went to the place to care for my "decoy" chicken and to see whether the flash had been fired. After ten days I returned again to the plantation to get the camera.

The owner of the place met me with an apology, saying that on the day before he had let his big boar out of the pen for an airing. It had been shut up all the time I had been trying for a picture. The boar had gone unseen to the rear grove and evi-

dently had fired the flash, for there had been a loud explosion.

On looking up the trail, he had seen the boar return at full speed with head and tail up to the shelter of its pen. It seemed to have had all the fresh air it desired. I told the gentleman that I should be glad to develop the plate.

It was some time after I returned before the plate was developed. In it, instead of the big hog, appeared the crouching form of a wildcat! Most amazing is the fact that the picture was taken in bright daylight, so that it represents a combination of

NIGHT CUSTOMERS TAKE GRAIN INTENDED FOR OTHERS

Roof rats, usually house frequenters, occur wild in great numbers throughout most of Florida. At Ormond Beach these agile climbers, old and young, nightly eat the food placed for birds.

A TOMCAT ON A HUNT FIRES FLASH SET FOR RABBITS

No animals more destructive to birds and small game exist than stray cats, for they possess all the cunning of their wild ancestors and much more, acquired through domestication. This fellow caused the author some annoyance by firing flashlights set for other creatures.

daylight and flashlight exposure (see page 186).

Among the many interesting animals in Florida is the cayman, sometimes called the American crocodile. It was first recorded in Florida by Rafinesque in 1822. The next time it was observed by a naturalist in the State was in 1869 at Biscayne Bay, when Dr. Jeffries Wyman collected specimens which are now in the Museum of Comparative Zoology, Cambridge. Since then it has been found to inhabit the salt lagoons and marshes of extreme southern Florida and the adjacent keys, to which section it is restricted because of the absence of frost, to which it is very sensitive.

THE CAYMAN AND THE ALLIGATOR

The cayman is the largest of the lizards in North America, sometimes exceeding 15 feet in length. It occurs also in the tropical lowlands of the West Indies, Mexico, and Central America. In recent years its numbers in Florida have greatly decreased, although it appears to be harmless there so far as human beings are concerned. This American relative of the dreaded Old World crocodile is readily distinguished from the well-known alligator by its long narrow snout, as contrasted with the broad, rounded, shovel-shaped nose of the alligator.

When I first went to Florida, the alligator was abundant in most parts of the State, frequenting the fresh-water streams, shallow lakes, and marshes and tidal lagoons. The increasing demand for its hide, from which ornamental leather goods are made, has greatly reduced its numbers. This decrease has been hastened by the fact that very young ones find a ready sale to tourists. The man with a gun also has helped to lessen the numbers of alligators by thoughtlessly killing them just because they serve as large living targets.

The mouth of the Tomoka River, a tributary of the Halifax, is about 6 miles above my winter home. This stream is navigable by large power boats for about 10 miles above its mouth, which is in the midst of broad, grass-grown marshes, with stately groups of tree palmettos here and there along the adjacent higher ground. Narrow, winding, and sluggish, the river is a favorite resort for picnic parties in launches and other excursion boats.

Farther up, the marshes are more broken by wooded areas, where palmettos, pines, and live oaks are intermingled in picturesque array. The upper reaches of the Tomoka are narrow and heavily fringed with trees, including the live oaks, which are beautifully draped with Spanish-moss, its hanging strands sometimes 12 to 15 feet long. The marshy borders of this river have long been a favored haunt of alligators; and by common consent, because of their interest to visitors, they have had there a certain degree of protection.

During my first trip up the Tomoka, in an excursion boat with many other passengers, I saw many alligators large and small lying in the sun near the water's edge. Whenever an unusually large one was seen, the boat would swing over and pass close to the apparently sleeping animal without causing any sign of alarm from it, even when the excited passengers made loud cries and rushed across the deck of the boat to get a better view.

This indifference on the part of the alligators made me feel sure that a brief visit to the river in a rowboat would afford many opportunities to take photographs of them. In a small boat with John at the oars, I made a 20-mile round trip, which recalled our long hunting and fishing excursions along the shores of Lake Superior.

As we carefully rounded the first point in the marsh, we saw about half a dozen alligators lying on the muddy shore. They saw us at once, too; and as the boat came into the line of their vision, they all promptly slid into the water, some splashing a little. This unexpected wariness continued among them all the way up the river, and we were unable to take any photographs.

TOMOKA RIVER ALLIGATORS WERE WARY OF SMALL BOATS

It was plain that the alligators had learned that the passing of the large boats with many passengers was of no concern, but that the appearance of small craft meant possible danger. Afterward I invited a party to accompany me up the river on the large boat, and from its deck had no difficulty in obtaining a good series of pictures. Every time the boat was backed up to try for a second picture, the alligators became suspicious and disappeared.

Many years ago when I went to the Big Green Swamp, south of Mohawk, Florida, to take pictures of the rapidly decreasing Florida sandhill crane, a local trapper took me to a marsh where he said these birds

PORPOISES DISPORT THEMSELVES IN PONCE DE LEON INLET

These mammals range freely into the inlet after fish. They sometimes show curiosity in regard to a person along shore and raise their heads high enough to get a free view with one eye. The one to the right is gazing at the photographer.

ALLIGATORS BASK LAZILY ON THE TOMOKA RIVER

These reptiles may be at once distinguished from their relative, the cayman, found farther south in Florida, by their broad, rounded, shovel-shaped snouts (see text, page 193).

TOMOKA RIVER WAS ALLIGATOR TERRITORY

Sailing along this stream, the author saw many of the huge reptiles sunning themselves. When approached for camera "close-ups," however, they slid into the stream (see text, page 193).

IT WENT OUT OF SIGHT IN THE WATER A MOMENT LATER

On a trip along Tomoka River the author had indifferent success in attempts to photograph alligators. This reptile was caught by a snapshot just as he was taking to the water.

IT LOLLS ON A LOG IN THE TOMOKA RIVER

Alligator mississippiensis is a sluggish fellow ordinarily, but he can cause havoc when aroused.
Strange as it may seem, his most dangerous weapon is his tail, not the teeth in his huge jaws.

were nesting. On arriving, we found all the nests empty. The guide said this condition might be due to his collecting the eggs and sending them north at the rate of a dollar apiece. His explanation, indeed, threw some light on the rapid disappearance of the bird in this locality.

Desiring to mollify me, he told of a little pond nearby, where I could get a picture of "the biggest alligator in Florida." Approaching the place cautiously, I saw what seemed to be a small alligator wriggling its way through the tall grass to the pond. Reaching down, I seized it in the middle and held it aloft.

To the horror of the guide and me, it proved to be an extraordinarily large water moccasin!

Meanwhile the snake was trying to swing its head up so that it could strike my wrist, the nearest part of my body, and a spot where the poison would be particularly dangerous. Of course, I dropped it at once, and was glad that this reptile had lived up to its reputation for sluggishness. Few persons are killed or injured by the many thousands of moccasins occupying the southern swamps.

The Everglades and Kissimmee Prairie, north and west of Lake Okeechobee, and the surrounding region have long been noted for the huge size of the rattlesnakes living among the grasses and other low vegetation of these open plains. Formerly, specimens more than six feet long were not uncommon, but in recent years with the coming of many people their numbers have so decreased that even a naturalist would have difficulty in finding one so large.

FLORIDA RATTLESNAKES

The ordinary visitor to the State is not likely even to get a glimpse of the moccasin or of the rattlesnake. While we were camping at the edge of the swamp, I took photographs of two half-grown night herons, the first pictures I had obtained of this bird. Another trophy obtained here was the skin of a rattlesnake more than six feet long, with 12 rattles. It long adorned the living room of my hunting cottage at Revels Island.

In my many years in the southeast, I never saw more than half a dozen rattlesnakes, or until lately heard of one that measured more than 8 feet 2 inches. The

THIS SPECIES IS KNOWN LOCALLY AS THE FLORIDA GOPHER

The large land tortoise (*Gopherus polyphemus*) occurs in most of the dryer parts of the State. It lives in burrows which it digs in sandy soil. There it hibernates during most of the winter.

experience of my old hunting companion, Prescott Ely, had been similar during the nearly 40 winters he had passed in Florida and adjoining States. He has recently sent me a photograph of a diamond-back rattler killed south of Palm Beach. It is said to measure more than 8 feet 6 inches, though there seems to be no authentic case of a rattler exceeding 8 feet 4 inches, according to Dr. Ditmars of the New York Zoo.

Many timid persons hesitate to venture on foot into wild places, whatever the character of the snakes. Very few of our land snakes in North America are poisonous, and the rattler, most numerous of the venomous few, usually coils before striking, first giving a distinct warning with its rattle.

It is generally believed that most of the snakes in the South have been killed by razor-back hogs and deer, or by the increasing number of hunters. The drivers of automobiles that now travel most roads are alert in running down most snakes, especially the rattler. Many of these reptiles are harmless and work a practical benefit to man by destroying field mice and other small rodents. They should,

therefore, be regarded with greater toleration.

James A. Groover, of Ormond, an old and lifelong resident of the Halifax River section, gave me in May, 1931, some reminiscences of conditions there between 1850 and 1870, when this region was a wilderness. The last vestiges of earlier English plantations had disappeared, and the cutting of live-oak logs along the river and shipping them through the inlet were the only occupations.

EARLY DAYS ON THE TOMOKA

The few settlers led extremely primitive lives. They occupied rude log houses, and depended for their subsistence almost wholly upon game and the products of little farms. Their clothing was made from cotton raised, spun, and woven by hand. The few necessities that could not be produced on the farms were obtained at the nearest trading station, 35 miles away, on the St. Johns River.

Deer, plentiful in the Tomoka woods, gunners shot at night by shining their eyes with the light from a fire of pitch pine in a frying pan, a device I found in use among

HAVING FUN WITH A LOGGERHEAD (*Caretta caretta*)

Every spring both this species and the green turtle come ashore and, scooping holes in the sand above high tide, deposit large clutches of eggs, which they bury by using their front flippers. Then the mothers depart. In due course the little turtles appear, enter the sea, and swim away.

DRIVEN FROM SHELTER, HE GLARES AT THE WORLD

Routed from its retreat among leaves and Spanish moss, this little screech owl sits blinking in the sun. Many persons formerly believed his species harmless to other birds, but investigation proved that it is destructive to several small kinds.

THE SLUGGISH LAND TURTLE, OR FLORIDA "GOPHER," PROVED NERVOUS

As this fellow emerged from his winter hibernation he pressed against the set string and photographed himself. He was so alarmed by the explosion of the flashlight that he retired into his den and remained there for days afterward (see Volume I, page 73).

THIS WEB-FOOTED AVIATOR IS AN AMPHIBIAN

The snake bird was once abundant in Florida and may now be found in many places, but it appears to be steadily decreasing in numbers.

THE GREEN SEA TURTLE IS A GOOD NATATOR

These famous providers of the material for soup are common in Florida waters. When the young hatch, they dig up through the sand in which the eggs are buried and with unerring instinct proceed to the water and swim away.

ONE WOULD HARDLY VENTURE TO TOUCH IT ALIVE

This extraordinarily large diamond-back rattlesnake, killed south of Palm Beach, Florida, about
1923, was estimated to measure more than 8 feet 6 inches (see page 196).

the Ojibway Indians during my boyhood days in northern Michigan. Wild turkeys were all about and gobbled in reply to the crowing roosters around the house. At night black bears sometimes tried to capture one of the hogs under the house, which was built well above the ground, and panthers, or mountain lions, as they are called in the West, wandered fearlessly about the vicinity.

AUDUBON VISITS THE HALIFAX RIVER COUNTRY

Several winters ago there was brought to me at Ormond Beach a copy of a little-known letter by the famous artist-naturalist, John James Audubon. It describes a visit he made long ago to this river and the adjacent country, and gives an account of several days of his experiences. It affords such a good picture of the primitive conditions prevailing there a hundred years ago that parts of it are here included. It was written to the editor of the *American Monthly Journal of Geology* at Philadelphia. Audubon, of course, was interested in the bird life, especially the brown pelican, which then as now was a conspicuous inhabitant of this coast.

"Bulowville, Florida,
"Dec. 31st, 1831.
"My dear F.:

"I have just returned from an expedition down the Halifax River, about 40 miles from this place and 80 miles south of St. Augustine. I feel confident that an account of it will be interesting and I therefore set to:—

"Mr. J. J. Bulow, a rich planter, at whose house myself and party have been for a whole week under the most hospitable and welcome treatment that could possibly be expected, proposed three days since that we should proceed down the river in search of new and valuable birds, and accordingly the boat, six hands, and three white men with some provisions put off with fair wind and pure sky.

"We meandered down a creek for about 11 miles, the water nearly torpid, yet clear, the shore lined with thousands of acres, covered by tall grasses, marshes, and high palm trees rendering the shore quite novel to my anxious eye. Some birds were shot and brought back for the skinning operation. Before long we entered the Halifax River, an inland arm of the sea measuring in breadth from a quarter to nearly a mile. * * *

"We passed several plantations on the western bank, and at last reached a schooner from New York, anchored at what is called a live oak landing. Kindly received by the master and his men, we passed the night very agreeably and comfortably as circumstances would permit.

"At sunrise the next morning I and four negro servants proceeded in search of birds and adventure. The fact is, I was anxious to kill some 25 brown pelicans to enable me to make a new drawing of an adult male bird, and to preserve the dresses of the others. * * *

"My generous host proposed to turn toward home again. Preparations were made accordingly, and we left the schooner again with the tide and wind in our teeth, and with prospects of a severe cold night. Our hands pulled well and our bark was as light as our hearts. All went on merrily until dark night came on. The wind freshening, the cold augmenting, the waters lowering, all depreciating except our enter-

THE FLORIDA CORMORANT ADAPTS ITSELF
TO CHANGE

These birds commonly use channel markers along
the Halifax and Indian rivers as perches.

WHITE GANNETS VISIT DAYTONA BEACH

They winter in considerable numbers off the
coast of Florida, and breed on rocky islands from
near the mouth of the St. Lawrence River to the
coast of Great Britain.

prising dispositions, we found ourselves
fast in the mud about 300 yards from a
marshy shore, without the least hope of
being able to raise a fire, for no trees except palm trees were near, and the Grand
Diable himself could not burn one of
them. * * *

"Our only resort was to leap into the
mire waist deep and push the bark to a
point some 500 or 600 yards distant where
a few scrubby trees seemed to have grown
to save our lives on this occasion.

" 'Push boys, push for your lives,' cried
the generous Bulow and the poor Audubon,
'all hands push.'

"Aye, and well might we push, the mire
was up to our breasts, our limbs becoming
stiffened and almost useless at every step
we took. * * * It took us two and a
half hours to reach the point where the few
trees of which I have spoken were, but we
did get there.

"We landed, and it was well that we did,
for on reaching the margin of the marsh
two of the negroes fell down in the mud as
senseless as torpidity ever rendered an alligator or a snake, and had we white men
not been there they certainly would have
died. We had them carried to the grove,
to which I believe all owe our lives.

"I struck a fire and in a few minutes I
saw with indescribable pleasure the bright,
warming blaze of the log pile in the center
of our shivering party. We wrapped the
negroes in their blankets, boiled some
water, and soon had some tea. We made
them swallow the tea and with care revived them.

EARLY HARDSHIPS IN FLORIDA

"May God preserve you from ever being
in the condition of our party at this moment, scarcely a man able to stand, and the
wind blowing as keenly as ever. Our men,
however, gradually revived, the trees one
after another fell under the hatchet and
increased our fire, and in two hours I had
the pleasure of seeing cheerful faces again.

"All hands returned alive; refreshments
and good care have made us all well again,
except for the stiffness occasioned in my
left leg by nearly six weeks' wading through
the vilest thickets of scrubby live oaks and
palmettos that appear to be created for no
purpose but to punish us for our sins,
thickets that can be matched only in the
cantos of your favorite, Dante.

"To give you an account of the little I
have seen of East Florida would fill a volume, and therefore I will not attempt it
just now, but I will draw a slight sketch of
part of it. The land, if land it can be
called, is generally so sandy that nothing
can be raised upon it. The swamps are
the only spots that afford a fair chance for
cultivation; the swamps, then, are the only
places where plantations can be found.

"These plantations are even few in number. Along the East Coast from St. Augustine to Cape Canaveral there are about

a dozen, and these, with the exception of two or three, are still young plantations. Gen. Hernandez', J. J. Bulow's, and Mr. Durham's (Dummitt's probably) are the strongest and perhaps the best. Sugar cane will prosper and perhaps do well, but the labor necessary to produce a good crop is great, great, great.

"Between the swamps of which I speak and which are found along the margin lying west of the sea inlet that divides the mainland from the Atlantic to the river St. John, of the interior of the peninsula, nothing exists but barren pine lands, poor timber and immense savannahs, mostly overflowed and all unfit for cultivation. That growth which in any other country is called undergrowth scarcely exists, the land being covered with low palmettos or very low, thickly branched oaks, almost impenetrable to man.

"The climate is of a most unsettled nature, at least at this season. The thermometer has made leaps of from 30 to 90 degrees in 24 hours; cold, warm, sandy, muddy, watery, all these varieties may be felt and seen in one day's traveling.

AUDUBON MISJUDGED POSSIBILITIES IN EASTERN FLORIDA

"I am extremely disappointed in this portion of Florida and would not advise anyone to visit it, because he may have read the flowery accounts of preceding travelers. The climate is much more unsteady than that of Louisiana, in the same latitude, or anywhere along the Mexican Gulf to the Sabine River, which is our boundary line. Game and fish, it is true, are abundant, but the body of valuable, tillable land is too small to enable the peninsula ever to become a rich State. * * *

"And now, my dear F., adieu. In my next I hope to give you some account of St. John's river and of the interior of the peninsula of East Florida, to the exploring of which I mean to devote some time.

"Very faithfully yours,
"JOHN JAMES AUDUBON."

This letter is particularly interesting today in view of Audubon's gloomy view of the future of eastern Florida, especially his prediction that it would never invite settlement except on a few plantations near the swamps. If he could return now, he would be confronted by many modern miracles. There in that very region his hope-

A SCREECH OWL IS AT HOME IN A NESTING BOX

This comical looking little bird has a voice out of proportion to its size.

SCREECH OWLS LIKE THIS TIDBIT

Unlike its neighbor, the chameleon, this thin, dark, long-tailed lizard, is unable to change its color. The birds at first dismember it for their young and later teach the fledglings to eat it alive.

less wilderness has given way to many thriving towns, beautiful winter homes, great hotels, vast areas of citrus groves, and even greater stretches of farms supplying all kinds of winter vegetables to northern cities.

I have already recorded the intense interest that primitive islands, with their natural beauties and varied wild life, have always held for me. When in later years

TURKEY BUZZARDS TAKE WING

Note the large fish placed on shore. It served effectively as bait to lure the voracious birds into range of the camera.

THE GRAY KINGBIRD

In the Bermudas and many of the West Indies our common flycatcher is replaced by this species which ranges in summer to southern States.

I visited a long succession of islands ranging from the subarctics of both coasts down to Panama, I became enthralled by the attractiveness of these little worlds in the midst of broad waters.

Early in 1910 I was invited by Dr. R. V. Pierce, of Buffalo, N. Y., to visit him at his winter home on St. Vincent Island, near Appalachicola, northwestern Florida. Doctor Pierce did not use a gun on his little domain, and he not only fostered the native wild life but also had introduced the European red deer, the English pheasant, and some other game birds.

A PRIVATE GAME SANCTUARY

The native wild life included the white-tailed deer and the smaller mammals, as well as the birds of that region. Also, occasional wild hogs and cattle could be seen. The guardianship of the wild things on the island had been so successful that many of Doctor Pierce's friends visited him there in winter for the pleasure of seeing them.

In the middle of the island was a large lake with the outlet deepened to form a canal which passed Doctor Pierce's home.

This lake facilitated the study of the waterfowl by boat and the observation of the hundreds of alligators that sunned themselves along the stream and shores.

My host occupied a large, comfortable dwelling on the eastern end of the island, facing the Gulf, where a long dock provided shelter and accommodations for craft both large and small. In view of my projected trip to Mexico a few weeks later, my stay on St. Vincent was necessarily short.

The first afternoon, John Hammer and I set a mile or so from the house, several flashlight cameras fronting trails apparently used by deer, wild cattle, and other large and small creatures of the forest. From each camera a black thread led across the trail where it might be tripped by any passing large animal. On the ground other threads were left, baited to suit the taste of either meat eaters or vegetarians among the smaller species.

The first evening, sitting by an open fire in the living room, the Doctor and I talked on matters of mutual interest, especially concerning his efforts to naturalize here the red deer and several species of foreign

THE DRAKE IS A HANDSOME BUT UNGALLANT MATE

With some exceptions, these ducks are all male scaups, as indicated by the light backs and sides, and brilliantly black heads, compared with the drab coloring of the females. The drake's habit of consorting in flocks is even more marked in the early summer than in winter, for after incubation begins the males of most species permanently desert their mates, leaving to the latter the exacting duties of hatching and rearing the young.

game birds. Finally our talk was interrupted by the distant boom of the flashlight. The Doctor remarked that the explosion made a good deal of noise and wondered what effect it had on the animals firing it.

Continuing, he asked if a still heavier flash could be used. To this I replied that to do so would merely require the use of more powder, confined in a stronger receptacle to produce a report equal to that of a small-sized cannon. This information seemed to give him much satisfaction.

He told me that for some years he had been annoyed by poachers crossing to the island from the mainland and, by the use of headlights, killing many of his deer. Hoping to discourage this, he asked me to leave with him two of my flashlight machines arranged to fire a shotgun shell filled with flashlight powder, instead of the smaller charge for photographing.

He pictured vividly the surprise and terror of a poacher suddenly walking unconsciously into a string across the trail and firing a flashlight within a few feet. The dazzling light and a noise would almost stun the victim, and thus would probably end this man's invasion of the island.

THE AUTHOR'S FLASHLIGHT DEVICE A BURGLAR ALARM

My host was surprised when informed that many years before I had suggested this plan for frightening away unwanted intruders. Among the specifications submitted in the application for the patent granted me for the flashlight apparatus was the averment that immunity from theft and robbery might be secured by placing the device where it would be exploded by trespassers. They would be frightened into retreating before accomplishing their purpose. At the same time a concealed

A RED-BELLIED WOODPECKER EATS SUET ON A CABBAGE-
PALM TRUNK

This, one of our common birds, heralds the approach of the mating
season by hammering loud tattoos on tin roofs, metal tanks, wooden
copings, and other sonorous objects. The author photographed it near
his home at Ormond Beach.

negatives taken here on the preceding and following nights showed that the visitors had been limited to raccoons, opossums, and razor-backed hogs.

This was the only locality where I have ever seen raccoons wandering about during the day. They had been unmolested here for so long that they were often seen patrolling the beaches in search of crabs or shellfish within easy reach.

RED DEER COULD NOT WITHSTAND THE ENVIRONMENT

The second afternoon I found the freshly shed antlers of a red deer—proof that some still survived. They finally all succumbed, however, not being able to withstand an unfavorable environment.

One day I had a talk with an old trapper who was camping by the lake. He confirmed the information I had previously received that the white-tailed deer on this island do not drop their fawns until the middle of July, probably because of the better food supply at that time.

camera would photograph the men and aid in their identification.

Although I left with Doctor Pierce the two flashlight mechanisms he requested, I never learned whether he succeeded in using them against his undesired visitors. Another guest, however, who visited the island a year later reported that he had heard the Doctor say he had finally got rid of the poachers.

The next morning a visit to the set cameras showed that their flashlights had been exploded. When developed, the

This trapper was employed to reduce the numbers of the alligators that were destroying both domestic and wild water birds, and the occupation was much to his liking. He passed part of the nights killing the alligators, using a jacklight to shine their eyes, and occupied much of the days in taking off their hides. These of course found a ready market among manufacturers of fancy leather goods. Thus the trapper realized double profit from his efforts.

CHAPTER VIII — PART II

Caught in a Hurricane—A Visit to the Bahama Islands

IN the spring of 1907 I had a welcome opportunity to go on the yacht *Physalia* of the Carnegie Institution, Washington, to visit the breeding colonies of boobies and man-o'-war birds of the Bahamas. The expedition was made doubly enjoyable by the companionship of Dr. A. G. Mayer, Director of the Dry Tortugas Marine Laboratory, in command, and Dr. Frank M. Chapman, of the American Museum of Natural History.

We sailed from Miami on March 28. The *Physalia* was a 56-foot ketch, with a 20-horse-power auxiliary engine, which had been generously placed at the disposal of Chapman and me for this voyage. At first our boat appeared small and low in the water for a thousand-mile trip among the Bahamas, but it proved seaworthy under most trying conditions.

It was a trim little craft with a graceful overhang in the bow and stern that reduced the keel measurement to only 25 feet. The draft was 5 feet and the main deck 3 feet above the waterline. The masts were disproportionately long and heavy, later proving a source of danger. The gasoline engine was for use in making difficult harbor entrances or to fight the treacherous tides of the Bahama Banks.

We made a smooth run to Cat Island, where we anchored for the night. The following morning we sailed for Nassau and arrived there about midnight. The next day the local officials of this little British colony received us cordially and granted the permits necessary to enable us to visit the breeding places of the birds. We wished to take not only photographs, but specimens needed by Doctor Chapman.

It pleases me to record that the authorities of the Bahamas take real interest in the perpetuation of the local bird life, especially species such as the flamingoes, boobies, and man-o'-war birds that nest in colonies.

THE WIND SHIFTS

On the second night the *Physalia* anchored behind a small but sheltering reef, but at dusk the wind changed to an opposite direction, exposing the party to the fury of an ever-increasing gale (see text, page 209).

A FEMALE LESSER SCAUP SPURNS THE WATER IN A QUICK TAKE-OFF

This is the author's first flight picture of a duck. It was made on Mosquito Lagoon, Florida, in the winter of 1902. The difficulty in obtaining such photographs is due not so much to lack of lens speed as to the problem of focus.

The Bahama Islands form a broad chain, or rather belt, of islands, cays, rocky points, and reefs extending in a generally southeasterly to northwesterly direction. They lie to the southeast, and across the Gulf Stream, from southern Florida. The climate is mildly tropical, temperatures ranging from 66° to 88° Fahrenheit. The rainfall at Nassau is more than 60 inches.

Many of the smaller islands are barren, supporting a scanty growth of cactus, brush, or low trees and small plants, but some of the larger ones have luxuriant forests. The birds which we were intent on finding gain their subsistence from the sea and breed on the bare ground or bushy growth of rather sterile islets.

ANCHORED OFF NORMAN CAY

We left Nassau for Cay Verde, 230 miles away, on March 31. The day being perfectly calm, we used the gasoline engine and made about 40 miles, anchoring for the night off Norman Cay. Here a visit to the shore made us acquainted with several birds peculiar to these islands, including the beautiful honey creeper.

The next day, April 1, conditions changed, and a heavy head wind from the south hit us, displacing the customary easterly trade winds. For hours we tacked back and forth in a futile contest with the wind, but traveling to the windward was not the *Physalia's* strong point. At 4 p. m. we dropped anchor on the north side of Elbers Cay, a short, narrow reef which gave us excellent shelter from the thundering surf breaking on its windward side.

While we were enjoying our apparently safe berth for the night, a destructive hurricane struck Nassau to the north, and came roaring toward us. The barometer, however, had begun to fall and ominous thunder clouds were gathering overhead. Not liking the looks of the weather, we dropped a second anchor.

Within half an hour the wind abruptly changed to the north and, covering the sea with foaming white caps, threatened to cast us on the reef, which from a sheltering friend had become a threatening enemy. We hurriedly pulled up the anchors, the tumultuous waves nearly swamping us before the bow could be freed. For a time we were in deadly peril, but as the second anchor came aboard the yacht responded quickly to the helm.

As we passed clear of the cay we struck a hidden sand bar, however, and hung there long enough for a huge wave to sweep the decks and flood the engine room. It stopped the motor upon which we were relying to hold our course until a small sail could be raised.

The next wave carried us clear, and in a few minutes the engine was again running. Then began a struggle to clear some long, low coral-rimmed islands ahead which could be dimly seen in the gathering darkness. This required us to run at right angles to the gale, in the trough of the sea. Here it was that the big masts laid us over again and again, causing the lifeboats to be torn from the davits and wrecking things generally.

Darkness, accentuated by flashes of lightning, now came on. After a run of half an hour we hoped we had cleared the islands to the left, and turned the rapidly foundering yacht to run free before the wind. There followed an all-night's run through a network of coral reefs and shallow bars which for 600 miles form the easterly fringe of the Bahama Banks.

The night being impenetrably black no outlook was placed at the bow, but every minute or two the lead was thrown. When occasionally the Swede mate called out "Vun faddom," we knew that only a single foot of water lay between the keel and some jagged reef.

WITHOUT LIGHT IN A HOWLING GALE

At midnight the gasoline tank began leaking, and the little cabin was flooded with gallons of volatile oil. With a rush we extinguished all the lamps, including the binnacle light that illuminated the deck compass, just in time to prevent our sudden annihilation. The possession of a little electric pocket-lamp made it possible to see the wheelman's compass until, after an hour's effort, with a barricade of canned goods carried from the hold to the deck, we succeeded, despite the howling gale, in lighting a marine lantern.

At 4:30 a. m., in the first gleam of the coming light, the pilot made out a high, rocky island a quarter of a mile to the east, and in a few minutes he skillfully guided us into the narrow entrance of a shelter at Upper Gold Ring Cay, 91 miles from the anchorage of the night before, traveling under bare poles except a small jib to keep our steerage way.

CEDAR BIRDS HOLD CONCLAVE IN FLORIDA

During the spring migration they sometimes appeared in close flocks in the tops of low trees in the author's yard at Ormond Beach. After a short rest they would go on their way.

A FEMALE CARDINAL FINDS DISAPPOINTMENT IN FLORIDA

All the sunflower seed having been eaten by previous visitors, this one seems crestfallen, for the usual perkily erected topknot is not visible.

THE CRUSOE LIFE PROVED NOT SO BAD

After an experience with a hurricane the party landed on Gold Ring Cay, where an abandoned thatched hut gave welcome shelter (see text, page 209).

CURLY-TAILED LIZARDS ARE COMMON ON THE BAHAMAS

The twisty caudal appendages and quick movements of *Leiocephalus virescens* give these little animals an amusingly jaunty air.

A ROBIN VISITOR FROM THE NORTH COMES
TO A WATER HOLE IN THE BAHAMAS

THE LITTLE GROUND DOVE IS A PERMA-
NENT RESIDENT OF THE BAHAMAS

A CAROLINA RAIL (ABOVE) AND A MYRTLE WARBLER MEET IN BAHAMA

The warm climate and abundance of food attract these visitors from the north. They are quenching
their thirst at a water hole. The author found many species in the course of his sojourn here.

Here, in a spirit of thankfulness for our almost miraculous escape, we remained for two days, until the gale passed away, repairing the broken lifeboats and pumping out the gasoline from the bilge. We cooked our meals on shore, for the yacht was still filled with the sickening and dangerous fumes of gasoline.

How bright and lovely those scarred rocks and tangled thickets seemed! On board everything was thoroughly drenched, except our precious photographic plates, which fortunately had been put up in watertight tin cans.

It may be remarked that this was the first hurricane at such an early date for nearly 20 years, and, with the wind blowing more than 80 miles an hour, it beached, sank, or dismantled many vessels at Nassau and in our vicinity, principally the small craft of negro spongers.

Let no inexperienced one suppose, however, that this adventure of the *Physalia* is typical of life on the sea, or that he who seeks the remote forests or the open waters is necessarily leading a life of excessive danger and hardship. The dangers of the crowded city far exceed in number and variety those of the former.

"The perils of the deep" is a most misleading phrase. It is the peril of the shallows, of the reefs, of the fog-bedimmed coast, that makes navigation sometimes dangerous and uncertain. Not too much

THEY WERE CAUGHT AWING BY DAYLIGHT

As these ring-billed gulls, an adult and a youngster, were dropping to some floating food, the author snapped his camera.

FLORIDA WOODPECKERS LIKE FRUIT

They were welcome to the oranges the author put out, but that did not suffice them and they stripped a Japanese plum tree near the porch. In the robbery they were assisted by some cousins of the downy species.

wind, however great, but too little water, is the cause of most disasters upon the sea.

The loss of all the gasoline except a few gallons remaining in the bottom of the ruptured tank delayed the expedition for many days, and instead of returning to Nassau within a week, we saw nearly a month elapse before the trip was over.

On April 4, well rested and with our confidence somewhat restored, we set sail

BOOBY AND MAN-O'-WAR COLONIES ARE USUALLY CLOSE TOGETHER

The latter are in the dark cactus thicket in the left foreground. They are pirates, obtaining much of their food from their stupid neighbors, without whom they probably could not live on this island of the Bahama group. The *Physalia* is at the edge of the surf.

THE WESTERN PART OF THE BOOBY COLONY WAS ON THE ELEVATED PORTION OF THE ISLAND

This strictly maritime bird is known as the white-bellied booby, a member of the gannet family, the ten species of which, with one exception, are tropical and subtropical. The white bird is the young and the black the adult.

BOOBIES IN FLIGHT SPREAD THEIR FAN-TAILS

THIS NESTING BOOBY DOES NOT HEED HER DISPLACED YOUNG

THE YOUNG BOOBY AT THE LEFT WEARS ITS FINAL GRAY

THE PARENT BOOBIES STAND GUARD, EXCEPT WHEN SEARCHING FOR FOOD

PARENT BOOBIES COVER THEIR YOUNG FROM THE DIRECT SUN

With the thermometer registering 130 degrees, such protection becomes necessary. This front view of the birds' faces presents convincing argument that the rather contemptuous name has some justification.

THESE WERE THE ONLY YOUNG TWIN BOOBIES NOTICED IN 700 NESTS

They are in their snowy vestments, only a bit of the darker color appearing in their wings and tails. The parent turns its head as if to listen to the conversation they seem to be carrying on in whispers.

MALE AND FEMALE MAN-O'-WAR BIRDS FLY OVER A SEA-GRAPE THICKET

Note their wing action and forked tails. The stroke of the one in front reminds the observer of the motion of a swimmer performing the Australian crawl. The female can be distinguished by its white breast.

A MAN-O'-WAR BIRD'S NEST ON CAY VERDE HOLDS ONE EGG

Woe to the boobies in their colony near by when the pirate is hatched from this egg. Its parents will feed it at sad cost to their stupid and defenseless neighbors; and as soon as it is large enough, it will steal for itself.

BOOBIES PERCH ON A CORAL CLIFF, 75 FEET ABOVE THE SEA, ONE OF THE HIGHEST IN THE BAHAMAS

The black gannet is a maritime bird found on both oceans, with a range on the Atlantic coast confined to tropical and subtropical America. It inhabits lonely islets and in flight resembles both the cormorant and the gull, but in fishing strikes the water at a low angle, emerging against the wind. The adult has a white breast, and the rest of the body is a soft, dark brown. The young are white at first, shading gradually into gray and the final brown of the parents. The feet are webbed, of yellowish hue; and the odd wedge-shaped bill is a green-yellow or a pink-yellow, according to sex.

for Ragged Island, about 100 miles farther south, the nearest inhabited place to our destination at Cay Verde, but out of sight of it. The yacht continued so permeated with gasoline fumes that those who wished to smoke were towed behind in our only serviceable boat. Being a confirmed smoker, I traveled for many miles in this fashion.

While at Ragged Island, we knew it would be difficult to make a landing on such an unsheltered place as Cay Verde. When the wind blew, the waves were too rough to risk landing in a small boat; and during a calm the lack of gasoline made it impracticable to travel much in search of good places on the beach. It was necessary for us to remain here until light winds prevailed, for our gasoline was about gone.

MANY BIRDS ON LITTLE RAGGED

In the course of our enforced delay we went ashore on Little Ragged Island, where we found some interesting birds, especially at a small pool of fresh water in a thicket where such different species as the myrtle warbler, Bahama ground dove, and Carolina rail gathered (see page 212).

Finally, on April 8, with a light head wind, the *Physalia* slowly tacked its way toward our goal, and late in the afternoon, when we were within three miles of this little island, the wind died out and it became necessary to use several gallons of the scanty remaining gasoline in order to make a landing before dark. A fortunate move it was, for the next day there prevailed a heavy wind that would have prevented our landing upon, or departing from, the cay.

Miles away and long before the small boat was launched and loaded we had been anxiously eyeing the reef for signs of bird life. Our information was not at all encouraging, since such as we had only established the existence of bird colonies there in 1857 and 1896. Whether the birds were there this season or, if so, had their nesting been broken up by an unusual visit from some becalmed ship, we did not know.

Schooners carrying 15 or 20 dories and a crew of 20 or more negroes are continuously searching the shallow waters of the Bahamas for sponges, and, as might be expected, have made a practice of landing upon islands for birds' eggs and their young and, when possible, taking the breeding birds themselves. The result has been in recent years bird life in the Bahamas has been threatened with extinction.

Some of the readers may recall Doctor Chapman's efforts, covering three seasons, to locate on these islands a breeding colony of the pink flamingo, and how at last he succeeded, discovering a breeding place many miles in the interior of a large marshy island, so remote as to have escaped the vigilant eyes of the natives.

The extreme isolation of Cay Verde and the absence of protecting land in the neighborhood make the landing too uncertain to warrant a trip by the natives in search of eggs or young birds. As the yacht approached a little nearer we saw high over the island the graceful, soaring flight of several man-o'-war birds, and later could see, coming from all directions, wisps of boobies, bringing in their pouches the evening meal for their hungry offspring.

At times they were intercepted in midair and compelled to disgorge for the benefit of the man-o'-war bird. The diet of that hawk of the sea consists wholly of flying fish or the toll collected from the good-natured boobies, the presence of which makes certain a supply of fish for the young of its piratical neighbor.

Just as the tropical sun was sinking the *Physalia,* sailing through a crimson sheen, dropped anchor off a pretty little sand beach mortised in between black and jagged battlements of æolian rock, which in broken masses circled the rest of the island. We had a large cask of water and a box of provisions sent ashore for use in case we should be marooned by the forced withdrawal of the yacht under stress of weather.

AT CAY VERDE—AMONG BOOBIES AND MAN-O'-WAR BIRDS

Disembarking with our cameras, we landed for a three days' stay. A shelter for the night was made from an old sail supported by an oar and our tripods; and then Doctor Mayer returned to the rolling vessel with a calm and satisfied demeanor. We secretly rejoiced at having beneath our blankets solid ground, hard as it was.

In the fading light Doctor Chapman and I stood by the little tent, gazing with curiosity and pleasure upon thousands of dark-colored boobies, which stood in solid silence upright on either side of their single white-plumaged young. Some of them were not 10 feet away from the tent. Far-

MAN-O'-WAR BIRDS SOAR OVER THEIR NESTS ON CAY VERDE

The long narrow wings, having a spread of between six and eight feet, and the long forked tails, sometimes open and sometimes closed in flight, gave these birds a strikingly characteristic appearance as they fly high. Although very large, man-o'-war birds are extraordinarily agile on the wing and gain much of their food by pursuing flying boobies or other sea birds and making them disgorge fish. They then swoop down, and on a graceful upturn seize the food in their beaks as it falls. Flying fish, too, are taken.

ther away we could see the circling man-o'-war birds descending for the night to their nests, scattered throughout a low thicket composed of sea-grape bushes and spiny cactus. Later the lantern showed the boobies near us sleeping with their heads tucked under the feathers on their backs. They had the appearance of headless parents beside headless chicks.

At sunrise we were up, and before attempting breakfast made a hasty trip to the higher part of the island. There with field glasses we carefully studied the birds, mapping out our plan of action.

Our investigation then and later showed the island to be about 30 acres in extent and to contain more than 3,000 ground-nesting boobies and 500 to 600 man-o'-war birds. Each colony was at the time in the midst of its nesting season.

Some of Doctor Chapman's comments on the birds of these colonies are quoted:

"As the most abundant and easily observed of the two birds nesting on the cay, the booby first commanded our attention.

"A partial census of eggs and young led to the conclusion that about 1,500 pairs of boobies were nesting on Cay Verde. They were distributed in several groups, where the comparatively level surface and sandy soil furnished favorable nesting conditions. In most instances the young were covered with down, with the brown second plumage more or less evident in wings and tail. For the greater number of birds, the nesting season, as Bryant has stated, evidently begins in February. One or both of the adults remain, as a rule, with the young.

"The young booby is born naked, and since exposure to the sun before the downy

A BREEDING COLONY OF MAN-O'-WAR BIRDS

An old black parent is on the nest and young white birds are scattered through the thicket. The nests are built on sea-grape bushes surrounded by impenetrable cactus.

FIVE NESTS OF MAN-O'-WAR BIRDS WERE IN A RADIUS OF SIX FEET

They build their homes close together, their colonies reminding one of the hangouts of the human pirates who once made headquarters in these islands. In habits, too, they resemble the old-time marauders of the sea.

THE YOUNG MAN-O'-WAR BIRD ALWAYS STANDS ERECT IN THE NEST

When it grows up it will have a greater expansion of wing in proportion to the weight of its body than any other bird, and in power of flight will be unsurpassed. It will soar for hours at a great height, often far out at sea. The long, narrow, powerful bill has at the end a horny hook, in appearance and substance like a talon, while the feet, from lack of use, are small and atrophied.

plumage is developed would result fatally, it is constantly brooded, the parents taking turns at the brooding. Brooding continues even when the white down is well developed; the young bird is then too large to be wholly covered by the parent, and lies flat on the ground, the head exposed, the eyes closed, apparently dead. The young feed on squids and fishes, which in a more or less digested condition they obtain by thrusting their heads and necks down their parents' throats.

"The luxuriant growth of cactus among the sea grapes, in which the man-o'-war birds nested, increased the difficulty of penetrating the thickly branched, shrubby trees, and we did not attempt to make a census of the number of birds of this species breeding on Cay Verde. We estimated, however, that there were between 200 and 300 pairs.

"Occasionally they chased the adult boobies and made them disgorge in the air, but evidently, in the main, they did their own purveying, flying fish being taken from one bird that was shot."

The adults were not heard to utter a sound. The nests were frail, slightly hollowed platforms of open-work, composed of small sticks and twigs, placed in the tops of the sea grapes, at a height of six or seven feet, or among the cactuses within two feet of the ground. Several nests are often placed in one bush within reaching distance of one another.

WRECKERS EYED THE "PHYSALIA" WITH INTEREST

After the craft had survived the hurricane which drove it all over the seascape, it went aground on a reef in calm weather (see text, page 226).

BOOBIES AND MAN-O'-WAR BIRDS ARE POWERFUL FLYERS

Both the boobies and the man-o'-war birds interested me by their powers of flight. The boobies are rather heavy-bodied birds, but go far to sea in search of fish and have the power to soar or glide long distances on set wings. Boobies usually fish against the wind, flying low over the water and entering it in full flight at an acute angle and coming out at a similar angle still in full flight against the wind, some 30 or 40 yards beyond. While submerged, they appear to fly as they do in the air.

The man-o'-war birds have an extraordinary mastery of the air. They are lighter bodied than the boobies, with a much greater supporting expanse of outspread wing and tail. Although their wing strokes appear deliberate, they can easily overtake boobies or sea gulls in full chase and force them to disgorge their newly-captured prey. As the food falls, these great birds swoop down and catch it dextrously in midair. They sometimes soar for hours far up in the blue, like buzzards, and descend in splendid diving flight on set wings.

After Chapman and Mayer had made a careful count of the booby colony, they came to me, as their only auditor, to tell of the remarkable discovery that, while every booby's nest contained two eggs, no nest contained more than one young. Thereupon I went forth to make some discoveries on my own behalf, and soon returned with the news that while the man-o'-war bird laid only one egg, it hatched out two young, and that, therefore, my discovery, from an economic standpoint, was more important than theirs about the boobies.

This frivolity was received in silence by my two scientific friends, for joking on such a serious matter could not be approved. The mystery of the missing young of the boobies was solved when we discovered the peculiar fact that there appeared to be a difference of 10 days between the eggs, so that the first hatched became the sole survivor.

A DIFFICULT RETURN

Several times in the course of our stay on the Cay the *Physalia* changed its anchorage as heavy winds came on, and on one night in particular we were much alarmed when in the midst of a violent thunderstorm the lights upon the boat disappeared. The trouble was occasioned,

THIS FEMALE MAN-O'-WAR BIRD MEASURED EIGHT FEET FROM TIP TO TIP OF HER WING

In the background may be seen the expectantly raised heads of the down-white young on the platformlike nests. The mother has doubtless preyed on boobies, forcing them to disgorge the fish they have caught, and she is now returning to her offspring, which will thrust their beaks down her throat and obtain a part of the stolen meal.

we discovered the next day, by the violent rocking of the vessel. At the end of the third day our work was done, and then began the journey back to Nassau.

Delays were numerous, but none was serious until April 16, when, for the only time, aside from the night of the hurricane, we attempted a several-hours' night run with the advantage this time of a fair wind and full moon. We wished to reach Nassau next day if possible, when the last steamer of the season left for Miami. At 11 p. m. the yacht suddenly stopped, the masts shook violently, the sails flapped, and behold—we were upon a reef, at high tide, a

mile out of our course through the treacherous currents of these broken waters.

At daybreak, when the tide was low, we found ourselves perched on a sand bar in six inches of water, with a deep channel on either side. The wind remained light and with a large island a mile to the east the boat alone was in danger should the wind increase.

LABOR TO GET OFF THE REEF

Here we remained for three days, working like beavers at the windlass in an effort to drag the yacht into deep water, but not until it was stripped of all its ballast, pro-

A MAN-O'-WAR BIRD DESCENDS ON THE NEST

Note the remarkable forward wing movement. Perhaps this is a sort of brake to check speed. Certain it is that these birds are capable of amazing feats in the air. They can swoop down on a flying booby, force it to drop the fish it is carrying, and catch the food before it reaches the water.

visions, anchors, and other weights did we succeed in getting it off. Success came to us with high tide at midnight of the third day.

While we were stranded on the reef, we were the object of more than casually interested attention from native wreckers in a small boat. They evidently expected that we should be obliged to abandon our craft to their tender mercies (see illustration, page 225).

The bar we had struck lay just 10 miles south of where we had begun the all-night run of April 1. The next day we reached Nassau, too late, of course, for the Miami boat. Chapman returned to Miami on the

yacht and I to New York on a Ward Line steamer. Neither of us was any the worse for our exciting experiences; and though we naturally felt thankful to be safe home again, we should not have hesitated at taking the same risks a second time.

CHAPMAN OBTAINED MATERIAL FOR A FINE HABITAT GROUP

The tangible results of this unexpectedly adventurous voyage were the material from which, under Doctor Chapman's direction, were built two of those wonderful habitat groups of American birds for which the American Museum of Natural History has become famous; and a series of photo-

THE "PHYSALIA" WENT ON A REEF (SEE TEXT, PAGE 226)

In navigating the treacherous channels among the Bahamas, one must be constantly vigilant. The masts of this yacht were over tall for the hull and trouble resulted.

graphs by Doctor Chapman and me of two interesting sea birds at home.

The journey was one that I look back upon with genuine satisfaction; for in its course I experienced the thrill of shipwreck and a sort of Robinson Crusoe life on a lonely island, at the same time finding unusual opportunities for camera hunting. Both my pictures and Doctor Chapman's specimens form a lasting record of the lives of the booby and the man-o'-war bird in a remote breeding place where they are virtually undisturbed. There is a supreme thrill of discovery in coming upon such creatures of the wild in their natural state and in knowing how they live when they have not the softening, often demoralizing bounty of "crumbs from the rich man's table."

CHAPTER IX — Part I

Wild Fowl and Animal Life of the Louisiana Marshes

THE winter home of millions of the wild fowl that go down the Mississippi Valley flyway when the coming of winter in the North drives them southward, is in the vast marshes bordering the Gulf in Louisiana.

In February, 1920, with such congenial companions as Frederic C. Walcott, conservationist and later United States Senator, Lord William Percy, and Charles Sheldon, sportsman-naturalist, I realized a long-cherished ambition to visit the McIlhenny property and other parts of the Gulf coast marshes.

A MECCA FOR NATURALISTS

To have Edward A. McIlhenny as our host, both on shore and on his house boat, meant the height of hospitality and a pleasant and a profitable outing. Close by his residence were ponds that harbored several species of ducks; and when these migrated north, the snowy egret, the Louisiana heron, the purple gallinule, and other water birds took their places. We passed most of the time on the house boat, well out on the marshes, where the canvasbacks and ringnecked ducks were numerous. Specimens of the latter were especially desired by Lord Percy.

At our first breakfast on board, John Hammer, who usually accompanied me on such trips, came in with a heaping platter of corndodgers. Lord Percy eyed them suspiciously and said he would not touch such "blasted things." We induced him to try one, however; and after a dozen had followed, whatever umbrage John had taken at the insult to his cooking vanished.

A discussion arose one evening between McIlhenny and Percy as to whether ducks can smell a hunter in the blind when the wind is offshore. Our host took the affirmative and the rest of us silently backed Percy in the negative.

In the following two days I had experiences that weakened my belief. When I entered the blind the first day, a heavy wind was blowing from the water side and the ringnecks were being buffeted about and were almost thrown into the blind in searching for corn. It was almost possible to reach out and touch them; and photographing them was therefore difficult, since it was often impossible to get a proper focus at such close range.

On the next day conditions were reversed, and the wind blew from the blind across the water. After I had secreted myself, the birds began approaching, swimming in a solid mass from one side of the blind toward the other. But no sooner did the leading ducks cross the line of my scent than they turned back. This continued for two hours, and not one of the ducks went to its customary feeding place. I gave up the attempt to photograph them, for neither day had been successful from a photographer's point of view. What was the explanation?

In the course of our stay on the Gulf coast I made an effort to photograph the famous blue geese, and went to a sand beach where these birds came daily to pick up small gravel as an aid to digestion. The newly constructed and conspicuous blind kept them at a distance, and I finally left, somewhat disappointed at my failure to get pictures, although pleased at the opportunity of seeing these handsome birds. Several years later, and in the same neighborhood, I was more successful.

WHITE PELICANS

While on the Gulf coast, I saw large flocks of white pelicans resting on sand bars. The last time I had seen these birds, they had been nesting in large numbers on a Rocky Mountain lake. For a long time it was rumored that white pelicans breed on the coast of Texas, and in recent years it has been learned definitely that they nest in considerable numbers, with many other water birds, on Bird Island, in Maria Madre Lagoon, south of Corpus Christi.

Later in our visit, Colonel Alexander, head of the Louisiana State Game Commission, arrived in his comfortable yacht and showed us the Sage and Rockefeller wild-fowl refuges. After going as far as the Texas coast, where we saw many water birds, we returned on the commissioner's boat to New Orleans by canal. Here we had a good view of the French fishing

THEY ARE SAFE AT AVERY ISLAND, LOUISIANA

These blue-winged teal, lesser scaup, and coots are feeding in shallow water. At dusk the teal leave
for the rice fields, where the planters cannot shoot them legally after sunset.

villages and admired the gracefully constructed dugouts, known as pirogues, which
far surpassed in beauty those of the Ojibway Indians of the Lake Superior region.

Considering its brevity, one of my most
informative and interesting camera trips
was a visit to a 26,000-acre tract of marshland on the western side of Vermilion Bay,
near the southern coast of Louisiana. This
property was the former hunting grounds
of Paul J. Rainey, whose sister, Mrs. Rog-
ers, generously presented it to the National
Association of Audubon Societies as a perpetual memorial bird refuge in his honor.
Situated in the center of the winter home
of many kinds of ducks, it is winter quarters
of the blue goose, whose distant summer
home is on Baffin Island, within the Arctic
Circle.

In the first week in February, 1927, I
left Florida with Mr. J. P. Holman, an
official of the Association. We passed
through New Orleans, and then crossed the
Mississippi and beyond to Abbeville, where
we found awaiting us a large cabin launch
in charge of the Association's efficient and
agreeable superintendent, Richard Gordon.

The trip down the Vermilion River and
lagoon was interesting, for buzzards occupied every dead treetop and hundreds of
turtles of several kinds were disturbed
from their sunning places by the surge
caused by the passing launch. In Vermilion Bay, however, only the winds and
the waves showed activity, for the salt
waters permitted the growth on the submerged marshes of rank grasses only. In
the absence of duck foods few birds were
about.

THE RAINEY WILD-LIFE SANCTUARY

Near the reservation headquarters the
launch entered a small canal, and soon we
were quartered in a most comfortable habitation. A stone's throw away was a circular body of fresh water a mile in diameter, known as Belle Isle Lake. Here the
marshes, which were above most of the
higher tides, permitted the growth of
aquatic plants absent in saline waters.

Only a week before our visit it had been
estimated that more than 50,000 canvasback and broadbilled ducks frequented
this lake daily. During the previous fall
the surface had been entirely covered with
thick green leaves of the banana water lily;
but now, aside from a few uprooted plants,
all had been eaten, and naturally most of

the open-water ducks had departed. Only one flock of canvasbacks swam by my blind.

The quantity of food required by great gatherings of wild fowl is amazing. When the supply gives out on protected waters the birds must necessarily go to other marshes, which may be unprotected. Before the coming of the white man an excessive increase in bird and animal life must have been checked by the exhaustion of the food supply or by disease.

In the present day the problem of the conservationist is how to prevent starvation of the birds as well as the excessive shooting of them. To this end refuges are necessary, and few are proving more successful than the one we visited. We found marsh ducks, such as the mallard, black duck, pintail, widgeon, and teal, abundant on the smaller ponds, but wing pictures were hard to get because of several days of dark, cloudy weather.

THE BLUE GOOSE

The Rainey refuge is one of the principal winter homes of the blue goose, although this bird is found in many of the neighboring marshes. Local observers have recently estimated its total numbers at more than 400,000.

Mr. Holman recorded the incidents of the first afternoon as follows:

"Before supper we sped down the main canal, in the speedboat *Whistler,* to Belle Isle Ridge. As we shut off the engine and neared the bank, a loud cackling greeted our ears, and in a moment we were surrounded by thousands of blue and lesser snow geese, rising like a pillar of light against a blue-gray sky.

"It was truly a wonderful sight. As we gazed, new groups of birds rose and added to the sweeping tide of life and din of voice, until the whole heavens seemed to be filled with beating wings and soaring bodies, weaving in and out, etching a pattern of silver on a background of blue canvas."

The blue goose seems to spend most of each day on parts of marshes covered with only a few inches of water, and at night it sleeps on the open water of ponds and small lakes. It feeds largely on the roots of Scirpus and other marsh plants, which grow luxuriantly in water supplied by frequent rains. A flock of sometimes 5,000 or more blue geese, feeding on the marsh, is a stirring sight. In a solid phalanx they uproot all in front of them and trample down the rejected portions, so that the areas cleared each day become shallow, open water.

In the middle of the last century flocks of wild pigeons would work through a field of buckwheat and cause great havoc. Since they were more active than the geese, the ones in the rear would rise and alight ahead, so that they appeared like a wave rolling over the field. The general turmoil at the feeding places of both species are sights long to be remembered.

I passed several days in a blind baited with corn, trying to get photographs of blue geese; but they evidently knew nothing about grain, and numerous grackles were the main beneficiaries. One lone goose, however, was encouraged by the eagerness of the small birds to try the corn (see page 239).

After using my last plate on it, for I had taken many wing pictures of passing flocks, I noticed marching toward the blind a regiment of blue geese containing a few white ones, which looked like officers in their light uniforms. Rather than have the exasperation of this parade taking place in front of me when I was out of ammunition, I arose and frightened them away.

These geese come south in November from their island home within the Arctic Circle, and most of them depart between the last of March and the first of May. Considering the great size of the present flocks and the distance they travel, one wonders at the small proportion killed on the way. They must have little interest in the rest of the country when traveling between their two homes, although since spring shooting has been prohibited, they have been seen on some northerly waters, both in the East and in the West, awaiting the opening of the Arctic.

BREEDING PLACE OF THE GEESE

Within the last few seasons the mystery of the breeding place of these geese has been solved. Their nests have been discovered on Baffin and Southampton islands north of Hudson Bay.

On the canal we went several mornings after the sun was well up to a large circular pond, where we got into a flat-bottomed skiff for the other end of the pond. There a blind had been built and some grain scattered about. On our arrival all the

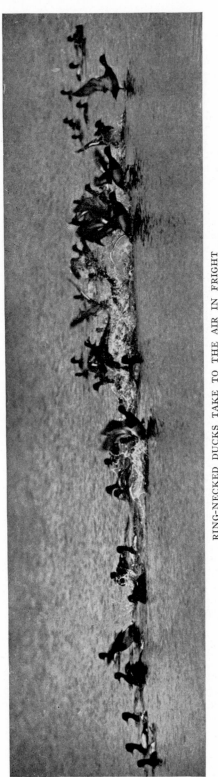

RING-NECKED DUCKS TAKE TO THE AIR IN FRIGHT

CAN DUCKS SMELL THE HUNTER?

The flock in the upper picture was photographed at Avery Island as it turned and flew away in alarm, just at the point where the slight offshore breeze carried the human scent to it. The phenomenon occurred repeatedly, and no other cause for the alarm could be noted. When the wind blew inshore, the birds shown below came within a few feet of the blind. Were they alarmed by the scent? (See text, page 229.)

Photograph by Shiras and McClintock

A LITTLE GREEN HERON STANDS BY ITS EGGS

Perched on its nest near Vermilion Bay, Louisiana, it keeps its eyes open for chance disturbers.

Photograph by Shiras and McClintock

A PURPLE GALLINULE COMES TO HER NEST

Many of these birds breed in the Louisiana marshes, where this picture was taken. They are semitropical birds found in summer on our Gulf Coast.

CANALS OPEN THE LOUISIANA MARSHES

Thousands of miles of these waterways and smaller tributaries for trappers' pirogues now render all parts of the area accessible. Such places once were natural wild-fowl sanctuaries.

A SNOWY EGRET STANDS WATCH OVER ITS YOUNG, NEAR VERMILION BAY

Like its larger relative, this bird was much reduced by plume hunters, but is now less persecuted and is again becoming common in some places.

THEY ARE AMONG THE BEST TALKERS

This pair of double yellow-headed parrots perch near their nesting hole in a tree trunk at the head-waters of the Tamesi River, Mexico.

PARROTS ABOUND ON THE TAMESI

This red-capped fellow, perched on a treetop, eyes the photographer with distrust, but remains quiet long enough for the picture.

larger ducks took wing, but no sooner were we in the blind than small flocks of coots came out of concealment in the reeds, determined to be the first at the banquet. They were followed by several dozen blue-wing teal.

In a few minutes the mallards, black ducks, and pintails would return, driving away the smaller waterfowl. It was an entrancing sight to see the mixed patterns and different colors of the marsh ducks at such close range; and then, after they had finished their repast, to see them climb up on little tussocks to sun and preen themselves.

In the afternoon, when the sun was in a favorable direction, I would sometimes go to a blind on Belle Isle Lake in hopes of getting a few pictures of canvasbacks and scaups that still lingered there after the lake had been depleted of the banana water lilies. In these efforts I was fairly successful. On our few days' visit there was plenty to do, and if I had an odd hour or so I would take flight pictures of the blue geese, high overhead, as in long files or platoons they circled over the vast marshes in the neighborhood.

The blue geese have a competitor for the Scirpus roots in the Louisiana marshes—the muskrat. Because of the scarcity of surface water in this section, muskrats build their dome-shaped houses, which resemble small haycocks, of coarse grass on top of the muddy soil. From the houses little canals filled with water, extend through the marshes in many directions.

THE LOUISIANA MUSKRAT PROLIFIC

Breeding throughout the year and having neither ice nor severe weather to contend with, the Louisiana muskrats are very prolific. This makes possible the harvesting of an annual catch that in some seasons runs into the millions, exceeding that of all the rest of the country combined. The total annual return to the trappers during several years of good prices is estimated to have exceeded $5,000,000.

I was surprised at the high grade of the pelts, for in such a southern range heavy fur would not be expected. The Rainey sanctuary income from the muskrat pelts is useful in the purchase of grain and other food for the feathered tenants. The food put out induces the birds to stay in the safety zone

BLUE GEESE THRONG THE RAINEY WILD-LIFE REFUGE NEAR VERMILION BAY

Most North American waterfowl are widely distributed, but practically all the blue geese in existence winter in the Louisiana marshes and breed on Baffin Island. The 26,000 acres of the Rainey Wild Life Refuge constitute one of their favorite haunts. There they find marsh grass roots in abundance.

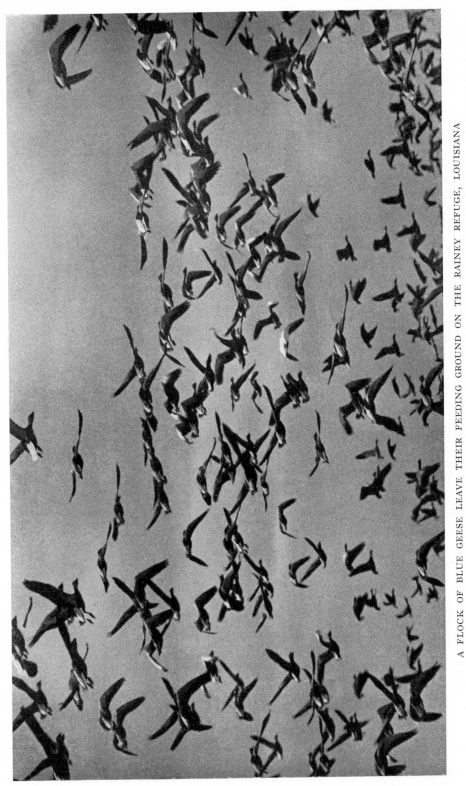

A FLOCK OF BLUE GEESE LEAVE THEIR FEEDING GROUND ON THE RAINEY REFUGE, LOUISIANA

Usually about one in eight or ten birds in these groups is a lesser snow goose, some of which appear in this picture. In the summer of 1929 the nesting place of the blue geese was definitely located in southern Baffin Island.

SUCH AN ANIMATED SIGHT IS COMMON ON THE LOUISIANA DUCK MARSHES

Unlike the deep-water ducks, those of the sloughs, such as the mallard, black duck, and pintail, rise perpendicularly from the surface when alarmed, whereas the diving ducks ascend gradually. In the Gulf region the wild fowl escape the rigors of the northern winter, and many find a safe retreat on the Rockefeller, Sage, and Rainey refuges.

A BLUE GOOSE IS ATTRACTED BY CORN BAIT IN THE LOUISIANA MARSHLAND

The author passed long hours in a blind waiting for blue geese to come to scattered corn bait. Boat-tailed grackles promptly came to the feast, and their presence may have attracted the solitary blue goose that came in to investigate this strange food (see text, page 231).

CANVASBACK DUCKS LIKE RAINEY REFUGE

Before the author visited this sanctuary, in February, 1927, a fresh-water lake adjoining the clubhouse was entirely covered with the banana water lily, which attracted more than 50,000 canvasbacks and scaups. But when he arrived, these plants had all been eaten, and only a single flock of canvasbacks remained to be pictured.

BOATING HAS ITS DEVOTEES ON THE TAMESI RIVER, MEXICO

Large cayucos, or dugout canoes, manned by natives in broad-brimmed straw hats, were often seen on the river before the camp.

HE WAS THE FAMILY PET ON THE PLANTATION ON TAMESI RIVER

This small form of the white-tailed deer is common in eastern Mexico, where the author passed some time photographing wild life.

THE END OF A SUCCESSFUL DAY BRINGS A SMILE

Toward sunset Superintendent Gordon in his ducking boat crossed over this pretty little fresh-water pond to the blind to get the author, who had bagged several hundred ducks with his long-focus camera.

instead of visiting nearby marshes where gunning is permitted.

The marshland of Louisiana is the main southern home of the muskrat, though a few of the species are found in Texas. Shortly after we left occurred the great Mississippi flood of 1927, which drowned or dispersed millions of muskrats on the lowlands nearer the delta. The flood waters, however, spread out rapidly on reaching the Gulf, and caused no damage in the vicinity of the Rainey sanctuary.

FUR PRODUCTION IN LOUISIANA

The Louisiana muskrat is a separate sub-species (*Ondatrazibethicha rivalicia*) and, like the other forms, is found naturally only in North America.

Even the beaver, generally regarded as a northern species, has several colonies in northern Louisiana, where they are protected throughout the year.

A recent tabulation for one year shows the variety and value of Louisiana fur-bearers, and clearly indicates the importance of fostering an industry on lands otherwise nearly worthless and exceeding 2,000,000 acres in extent:

Species	Pelts taken	Value to trapper
Muskrat	6,196,165	$5,142,896
Opossum	287,180	258,462
Raccoon	145,810	583,240
Mink	84,301	421,505
Skunk	14,752	18,440
Otter	2,110	31,650
Miscellaneous	947	947
	6,731,263	$6,457,140

In addition to its wealth of fur bearers, Louisiana is a wonderful State for game birds and animals with its deer, bear, wild turkey and quail, and its multitude of geese, ducks, snipe, and shore birds, which make it a paradise for the man with the gun or for him who prefers the camera.

Additional laws and better enforcement are needed, however, if the game animals and birds are to continue abundant. This criticism applies to many parts of the South, which, in general, underestimates the value of its wild life, not only to its inhabitants, but to visitors.

Florida, Georgia, Alabama, Louisiana, and Mississippi have immense areas that

MAIN CAMP WAS ON AN ISLAND IN THE TAMIAHUA LAGOON

There the author and his friends were in the midst of swarming breeding colonies of birds. The roseate spoonbill was the nearest, not more than 75 yards away.

COOTS SWARM ON THE TAMESI RIVER

Great numbers of these waterfowl frequented the lower river at the time of the author's visit. This group was photographed at a gathering place near shore.

THE BLACK ANI LOOKS LIKE A MOURNER

This southern and somber-garbed member of the cuckoo family is called a "tick hunter" by the natives living near the Tamesi River, Mexico.

furnish a congenial habitat to the white-tailed deer, and yet these States combined contain fewer of these animals than a single one of them should.

The South's long freedom from the necessary restrictions of game conservation has blinded it to the urgent demand of the present and future.

A notable feature in the recent development of the Louisiana marshes is the many canals, costing millions of dollars and extending hundreds of miles, many of them through sections heretofore inaccessible to the hunter or trapper (see page 234). This construction has been largely brought about by the muskrat industry and to a lesser extent by ducking clubs. Naturally, such development endangers the wild fowl in marshes where they have never before been disturbed.

I noticed that, unlike the northern muskrats, those of Louisiana do not build any of their homes in the many miles of banks formed by dredging canals, except in the large canal banks in some rice fields where their nests and young have been found.

CHAPTER IX — PART II

Bird Hunting With a Camera in Eastern Mexico

IN 1908 I found Doctor Chapman anxious to visit the great Tamiahua Lagoon, near Tampico, Mexico. One of the reasons for his desire was the declaration by our friend, Charles Sheldon, that a large colony of roseate spoonbills was breeding on an island in the vicinity. At that time this interesting bird had become nearly extinct in Florida. It has since increased, I am happy to learn, in a few localities there.

We planned to make the trip the following year, but became discouraged by a report that one of the largest oil wells on the shore of the lagoon had taken fire, got beyond control, and covered the surface of the lagoon with oil, besides forming a mass of sticky tar around its shores. All waterfowl had thus been destroyed or driven away.

A year later the floating oil had disappeared, and the tar on the shores had hardened. With this improvement of conditions many of the birds had returned and we undertook the trip. A third member of our party was Louis A. Fuertes, the famous artist-naturalist, whose congenial companionship contributed much toward our pleasure. His death a few years ago in an automobile accident caused great sorrow not only among nature lovers and scientists, but especially among the students and faculty of Cornell University, where, as an alumnus and preceptor, he was much beloved and honored.

At Tampico, before visiting the lagoon, we gladly accepted the invitation of a fellow American to visit his sugar plantation, 75 miles up the Tamesi River, where he assured us we should see many birds and animals not found along the coast.

Instead of taking a slowly moving dugout, such as is used by the natives, we were transported in a comfortable launch and reached our destination the first day. After passing through some duck marshes, we entered the river, which here flows between high banks, and resembles a canal. It was bordered on either side by tall banana

THEY ARE ROBBERS WHEREVER THEY GO

A mischievous small species of crow living in flocks occupies parts of both coasts of middle Mexico.

ROSEATE SPOONBILLS IN FLIGHT MAY EASILY BE RECOGNIZED

The peculiar silhouette of these birds distinguishes them sharply from the white ibises and herons which frequent the same locality.

GRACKLES AND RED-EYED COWBIRDS APPEAR TOGETHER

Mexican great-tailed grackles are numerous about towns and plantations of middle Mexico. Their courting and other antics are most amusing. With them commonly occur the red-eyed cow-birds which have a curious ruff of long feathers about their necks.

WHITE IBISES ARE APARTMENT DWELLERS

Among the mangroves bordering Tamiahua Lagoon the author found great breeding colonies of these birds. Many nests were built in the tops of single trees, where usually they were hidden by the outer foliage. Several of the slate-gray young in the nests are visible in the photograph.

plants that waved a friendly greeting in the breeze.

In the country back from the river aridity limits agriculture and tree growth. It was not until we had nearly reached the plantation that we came in sight of a dense, primeval forest above which muscovy ducks were flying back and forth.

These large, handsome birds, like the brilliantly colored wood ducks of the north, nest in hollow trees. Thus they escape the hordes of small prowlers that, in this region, jeopardize ground-breeding birds when they are rearing their young.

From Doctor Chapman's notebook I quote the account of our arrival and the first impressions we received:

"Soon the Tamesi narrowed to a width between 100 and 200 feet, which it kept with little variation throughout the day.

"When we arrived at 5:30 there was just enough light left to enable us to pitch our tents in the ranch-house clearing on the bank of the river. The brown stream flowed silently by some 20 feet below us, with no hint of the loss of life and property it had caused only the preceding season, when it had flooded the country for miles.

"It is commonly believed that to see tropical birds in abundance one must go at least to South America; but I have yet to find, in a somewhat extended experience, any place where certain eminently characteristic tropical species are more abundant

A ROSEATE SPOONBILL TAKES FLIGHT FROM A TREETOP

Because the bird turned its head to one side to watch the photographer, its bill appears narrow.

A ROSEATE SPOONBILL GUARDS ITS NEST

The dark band extending back from the bend of the wing is rich deep scarlet. The rest of the bird's plumage is a bright pink.

Photograph by Frank M. Chapman

FEEDING WENT ON UNDER DIFFICULTIES

Doctor Chapman wrote, "We could see dozens of delicately colored pink forms, while in nearly every tree one or more nests held young nearly as large and as pink as the parents which had just left them. We had at last reached the home of the spoonbill."

than we found them at this camp on the Tamesi River, distant less than four days from Chicago!

A BIRDLAND BABEL

"We were awakened by the loud calls of flying parrots, not passing over at a great height, en route to some distant feeding ground, as one usually sees them, but stopping, with much conversational chatter, to join scores which were breakfasting in the trees overhanging our tents.

"At once we recognized the 'double yellow-head' (*Amazona oratrix*) of the bird stores, rated by dealers as second only to the gray, red-tailed African parrot in its

power of speech, and second to none as a whistler. With it was a slightly smaller, red-capped parrot (*Amazona viridiginalis*), which, whatever it may be in a cage, is vocal enough in nature.

"Parakeets of two species, with darting, dovelike flight, shot through the clearing, uttering their sharp, rolling cries, or, entering a treetop, disappeared with incomprehensible completeness until, assured of the safety of their surroundings, they began slowly to move about in search of food.

"Red-billed pigeons (*Colomba flavirostris*) nearly as large as our domestic bird shouted their emphatic hurrah, and the dainty little scaled doves filled in the gaps

A FLIGHT OF WHITE IBISES WHEEL AND TURN IN SPECTACULAR MANEUVERS

When the author approached the closely occupied nesting place of these birds at Tamiahua Lagoon, south of Tampico, Mexico, they would rise in a cloud of white flecked with their jet-black wing tips. They soared about in a maze, almost dazzling the eyes in the brilliant sunlight.

with their quaint *put-a-coo, put-a-coo;* ground doves mourned gently, if inconsolably, and the pygmy owl (*Glaucidium*) whistled with clocklike regularity from the top of a leafless tree—a perch which this diurnal, light-loving midget prefers.

"Great-tailed grackles creaked, sniffled, whistled, choked, and rattled; queer little Mexican crows, looking not much larger than blackbirds, perched in flocks in the leafless trees, snoring and grunting; flycatchers (*Myiozetetes texensis* and *Tyrannus melancholicus*) twitted excitedly; Derby flycatchers (*Pitangus*) cried *hip, hip, hurray;* gold and black orioles whistled like schoolboys homeward bound; anis whined; golden-fronted woodpeckers coughed; and ever and again the big Mexican pileated woodpecker sprang his trumpeting, reverberating rattle with astonishing effect.

WALKING WAS NOT A PLEASURE

"Three factors accounted for the abundance and familiarity of the birds about our camp in the ranch-house clearing: First, the larger forest trees had been left standing and only the undergrowth cut out; second, many of these trees, locally known at 'otatheite,' were bearing fruit of which parrots and some other birds were particularly fond; third, the birds were not molested.

"To see the species which required either undergrowth or wholly primeval conditions, one needed only to climb the corral fence 200 yards away and enter the forest on its farther side. The trees were not high, but the growth was dense, and in places the ground was covered with wild pines having leaves bordered by a series of strong hooks, which, set in both directions, were more productive of pain than pleasure to the unwary walker.

"No one lacked for occupation at Paso del Haba. Shiras hunted with camera by sunlight and flashlight, obtaining photographs of birds by day and of beasts by night, and left, no doubt, a more vivid and lasting impression on the minds of two natives who unwittingly sprang one of his flashlight camera traps than even his dry plates recorded."

Of the 88 species of birds we saw in the week of our stay, no less than 36 are tropical forms that in this latitude are at or near the northern limit of their ranges.

In addition to the many birds mentioned

ROSEATE SPOONBILLS STAND ALOFT

by Doctor Chapman, there was one that forced its attention on me by its rattling, raucous calls, that sounded like "chach-al-acca." This rendering of the call has been adopted as the name of the bird. It is a member of the pheasant family, and of course is classed as a game bird.

I had never before heard a bird of an edible character announce its presence in such loud tones. In the North a game bird that so noisily and carelessly proclaimed its whereabouts all day would not last long.

After taking pictures of several kinds of parrots and small birds, I tried to get flashlight pictures of the several members of the cat family; but, as so often has been the case when I have been photographing in tropical America, the opossums and other small animals usually fired the flashlight soon after dusk.

Alas, the only large creatures taking their own pictures were roving cattle and, in one instance, two native girls, who, on the explosion, fled to their thatched hut in terror, believing they were the intended victims of the visiting Americanos. I got several pictures, however, of a white-tailed doe, which, being accustomed to our host and his family, permitted me to approach it closely as it was quietly feeding at the edge of the forest.

After our return to Tampico we made preparations for our long-deferred visit to Tamiahua Lagoon, and learned that the journey was to be much easier than we had anticipated because of the recent

MEXICAN CORMORANTS HAVE HEADQUARTERS ON THE TAMIAHUA LAGOON

These powerful swimming and diving birds live upon fish they pursue and capture under water, but they habitually perch on the tops of trees, where they also make their nests.

A FEMALE MAN-O'-WAR BIRD SITS ON ITS NEST

Note the white breast which distinguishes this sex from the uniformly black male. The picture was taken near Tamiahua Lagoon.

HIS THROAT SWELLS WITH AFFECTION

The male man-o'-war bird in the mating season inflates a large bright red sack on its neck, like a toy balloon. This amazing nuptial adornment may be seen at a long distance, as indicated here.

construction of a canal from the Panuco River to the north end of the lagoon.

With two local guides, we departed in a launch, on the afternoon of April 11, and at the coming of sunset were still in the canal. While we were preparing the evening meal on shore, we saw two teal ducks flying swiftly down the canal in our direction. Fuertes, always alert to whatever was happening, deftly brought down one of them almost into the frying pan. The following day we reached the southern end of the lagoon. We passed great numbers of coots, besides some canvasbacks, gadwalls, and shovelers, but most of the ducks had gone North.

On reaching the island supposed to harbor the colony of spoonbills, we were all expectant. Disappointment seemed in store, however, for none of the birds were to be seen. We ran the launch into a narrow cove well shaded overhead by dense trees, and while the rest of us busied ourselves in getting out the camp equipment, Chapman made a reconnaissance to canvass the situation. He soon returned with the good news that hundreds of spoonbills were nesting within a hundred yards, and

that a little farther away were flocks of white ibises also in attendance on their nests, which were built on the low bushes (see page 247).

For the next few days we were busily employed among these colonies. Taking an afternoon off, we visited a colony of man-o'-war birds that were breeding on a small island a mile away (see page 252). In addition to taking motion pictures of spoonbills, Doctor Chapman obtained a number of specimens of the birds for his habitat group, which may now be seen in the American Museum of Natural History.

SAFETY FIRST

It should be noted that on this trip I was accompanied by my old Norwegian camp companion, John Hammer, whose announcement that a meal was ready always found us nearby.

One morning I noticed that John, famous for his corndodgers, was not eating them. "Are you sick?" I asked. "No," he replied, "but I don't want to be." Then he spoke about Doctor Chapman's taking a lot of our corn meal and mixing it with arsenic to preserve the skins of his

A NEIGHBORLY GROUP OCCUPY A MANGROVE TREE

Here we have, at the top, a great American egret; below, on the right, a roseate spoonbill, showing the beak that gives it its name; and on the left a Louisiana heron.

PORTRAITS OF TWO MEXICAN CORMORANTS

These birds were abundant in the country around Tamiahua Lagoon, where this photograph was taken. The author found here a remarkable number of species.

A BLACK MAN-O'-WAR BIRD GUARDS HIS WHITE YOUNG

They look alike despite their color difference. Note the hooks on the bills.

A BLACK-NECKED STILT VISITS TAMIAHUA LAGOON

Many breed in the western United States, but go south in winter.

THE COMMON IGUANAS ARE TABLE DELICACIES

These great lizards, three to five feet long, live among trees and on rough ground in tropical Mexico. In many places they are much prized as food, their flesh resembling that of a chicken. The photograph was taken near the Tamiahua Lagoon.

specimens. John said that he preferred being a live but hungry guide to becoming a well-preserved specimen.

Each evening I went forth to set out the flashlights, while my two companions were busily engaged in taxidermy or drawing. It was here that I learned of the infinite care with which Fuertes insured the accuracy of his subsequent paintings.

After making a rough outline of one of his specimens, showing its dimensions, he colored in only those parts of the drawing where the tints were perishable, such as the bill, eyes, iris, and the iridescence of the head and neck, if any, and the feet and legs if these parts were unfeathered. Since such careful methods guaranteed that his pictures were true to life, they can often be studied by ornithologists to better advantage than can the skins of specimens in museums or private collections, for in the latter many of the colors fade or darken as time goes on.

Swarms of mosquitoes appeared at sunset one evening when we were on our way back to Tampico, and continued active until morning. The tent John and I occu-

pied had no mosquito netting; and, after fighting the pests until midnight, I sought relief in the Chapman tent, which with its floor cloth, netting and two collapsible cots, was much more luxurious than those I usually had in my one-night camps.

A NEW TROPICAL FEVER

Lifting Chapman's mosquito net, I quietly crawled in, and found a good place on the floor cloth between the two cots. I had to move a tin plate holding a smoldering pile of insect powder. This I quietly shoved under Fuertes' cot.

Soon the sleeping artist became restless and finally sat up, calling to Chapman that he did not feel well, and that he feared he had contracted some strange fever, his hips especially being affected. This was a new disease to Chapman. Telling them that I had "a prompt and infallible remedy," I pulled the now blazing fire from under the cot.

The belated trip to Mexico had been made none too soon, for shortly after our departure insurrections broke out in most parts of the country.

CHAPTER X

Days and Nights on Gatun Lake, Canal Zone

WHEN information was received from Panama that the great basin for holding the waters of the proposed Gatun Lake had been completed by the construction of the long embankment at the north end, which closed the only gap in the rim of hills left open by nature, it seemed to me that the time had come to study and record the effect this disruption had produced on the wild life.

Month after month the gathering waters of tributary streams slowly covered the lowlands, crept up the wild, tangled valleys, drowned the mighty forests and the rank tropical jungles, flooded out native villages and destroyed scattered plantations, marooned such wild creatures as the monkey, ocelot, jaguar, peccary, armadillo, and sloth on hilltops unexpectedly converted into permanent islands, submerged the mud flats on which dwelt the herons and the ibises, drove the deer, tapirs, iguanas, and monster snakes through the rising water to less hampered retreats, and opened up a new and larger home for the cayman, or American crocodile, and the stream-confined fish.

Although all this necessarily represented a transitional condition, in which organic decay and the dispersal of wild life marked a definite break between the past and the present, yet in the very processes of transition there would be much of present interest and possibly of future value.

TWO HELPFUL OFFICIALS

On February 23, 1914, accompanied by C. J. Anderson, of northern Michigan, who had been my guide and camp assistant on many former expeditions, I landed at Colon. I remained in the Canal Zone until April 3. H. E. Anthony, of the American Museum of Natural History, New York, and later curator of mammals of that institution, met us on the dock and accompanied me as my guest while he was engaged in collecting specimens of mammals for the museum. My two companions proved to be congenial for such an expedition, and their cooperation added greatly to the enjoyment of what constituted the most novel and interesting of my wilderness experiences.

Promptly after my arrival I presented a letter of introduction from the Secretary of War to Colonel Goethals, then Governor of the Canal Zone. He received me cordially and displayed his usual keen interest in the promotion of scientific investigations in that region.

Since he was soon to go to Washington, he introduced me to Colonel Gorgas, notable for his success in controlling yellow fever and malaria, an achievement that changed the Canal Zone from one of the most unhealthful to one of the safest tropical districts in the world. The Colonel allotted me quarters at Gatun and in other ways materially facilitated my work.

ADVANTAGES OF A HOUSE BOAT IN COLLECTING AND EXPLORING

Many years' use of a house boat in the wilderness about Lake Superior had demonstrated to me the great convenience of such a movable habitation and its superiority over tent or cabin in most places accessible by water. In the tropics such advantages, I felt sure, would be tenfold greater.

Before we started for Panama we had planned to convert a small scow or flatboat into a house boat by merely erecting on it a frame that would support a canvas roof and wire netting along the sides—a simple structure that would exclude the sun and rain, and prevent visits from troublesome insects. This house boat we would tow from place to place with a swift and powerful launch, and we could use the launch for extended daylight excursions.

On arriving at Gatun on the lake, however, we found that all suitable scows were in continuous service by the Government, and only some that were too bulky for our use were available. Fortunately, we were able to convert a floating boathouse, in which a launch had been berthed, into a comfortable craft.

It was 9 feet wide by 30 feet long, and had a zinc roof and a covered tool house at one end, excellent for storage purposes. The sides and front were open. By putting in a floor, building a V-shaped prow at the towing end, and tacking on screening between the roof and the floor, we had a boat that was superior to the kind we

FAIRY GARDENS DRIFTED BY

Floating logs were a mass of long-leaved plants and slender reeds, surrounded by an exquisite display of blue-tinted and fragrant water hyacinths.

had originally sought, except for its heavy draft and a deck so low that it would be awash when the boat ran into a head sea.

While our improvised house boat was being made habitable, we made several excursions by motor boat, mainly up the Gatun and Chagres valleys. One of the canal employees at Gatun could take a launch at full speed through densely timbered districts, swerving here and there with wonderful skill, and he was seldom in doubt about direction.

Gatun Lake, with a surface elevation of 85 feet above sea level, is estimated to cover 164 square miles. It extends not merely over the previously existing swampy ground of the Chagres Valley, but so far above the floor of the lowlands as to penetrate for miles between the hills, forming estuaries, lagoons, and ponds. Rapid, unnavigable streams have been changed into deep, sluggish rivers, and hilltops con-

verted into beautiful islands, some of them miles in length. The thousands of acres of flooded and fallen timber into which stretch or circle narrow necks of land virtually preclude any accurate estimate of the actual shore line of the new lake.

SHORES UNSURVEYED

Apparently no one in 1914 knew the size, shape, or location of much of the partly submerged lands; nor can satisfactory surveys now be made at the water line without clearing a hundred-mile line of dying trees and bushes. Even a five-foot fluctuation in the level of the lake's surface, which may be expected between the dry and the wet periods, will necessarily change to a considerable degree the superficial area of the lake and the lines of the shore.

Some day, however, the warm and ever-present waters will destroy the obstructing forests, and then the half-shrouded lake will glisten, near and far, in the tropic lights; while the surrounding shores, each bay and promontory, and the islands, big and little, will be defined by a new and permanent border of bamboo and other semi-aquatic growths.

At the time of our arrival the lake had risen to its full height; island after island and point after point had sunk out of sight; and the steady diurnal winds of the Caribbean Sea, whirling across the narrow, low crest of the embankment, lashed into life within a few yards waves that ever increased in size in the long course down the lake.

LIKE A WORK OF NATURE

As one gazed across the broad expanse of water, with its ruffled surface, it was difficult to realize that the lake was the recent creation of man and was responding for the first time to the action of the tropic winds.

Once when we were going after gasoline, the launch encountered a heavy head sea in mid-lake, and because the small pump was insufficient to take care of water shipped from the breaking waves, the boat nearly filled, and the engine went out of service. In consequence we drifted in peril of being wrecked by a collision with some tottering tree or buried beneath a falling top brought down by the impact.

Like most natives of the Southern Hemisphere, the Indians of Panama, when using the interior waterways for travel, employ the dugout, or *cayuca*, which they are expert in poling or paddling through the swiftest streams. On the first flooding of the lake it was easy for them to reach the construction towns along the shore in boats heavily laden with fruits and other products, but as the waters rose and the wind and the waves began to exert their full force, it was discovered that not one among them all knew how to handle a canoe safely under such conditions. Now the Indians paddle the lake in the stillness of the night or dodge by day in and out through the flooded forests near the shore.

Eventually skilled canoemen, perhaps with canoes of more seaworthy construction, will be able to buffet the waves; and these picturesque craft will be seen from the great steamers, gliding across the white-capped surface through waters that are insignificant to ships just from the turbulent waters of the adjacent ocean.

Probably in no other country in the world is there such an interesting area of original timber covered with deep, still water. Here are slowly dying trees, containing great pendant nests of termites isolated and doomed to slow starvation.

Here are trees that died when the area was first flooded, and others that are still green and apparently vigorous, with roots and trunks that have been under water for several years. On the decaying branches grow many beautifully colored orchids, tillandsias, ferns, vines, and mosses, replacing for a time the lost foliage and tropic blooms. Upright stumps and floating logs are green with long-leaved plants, and in the intervening pools are purple clumps of drifting water hyacinths (see page 258).

MAROONED BY FLOOD

The termites in this nest in the inundated district were still active, but doomed to slow starvation (see accompanying text).

ISLANDS IN THE MAKING GO FLOATING BY

Here, too, are floating islands, with waving grasses and slender reeds, seemingly destined to live forever, which, when anchored by projecting snags or hemmed in between tree trunks, will gradually become wide, tremulous bogs, unsafe alike for man and all sharp-hoofed animals. They will be places of sunshine and of comfort, however, for the coming cayman, and refuges and feeding places for the herons, ibises, and other water birds, long exiled by the shoreless forests. These birds will spear numberless little frogs and lift many a fish from along the ragged edges.

Day after day we explored these unknown wastes, ever alert to avoid the sudden fall of treetops and massive limbs, weakened by inward decay or by heavily burdened masses of parasitic plants. Twice we were nearly overwhelmed, and

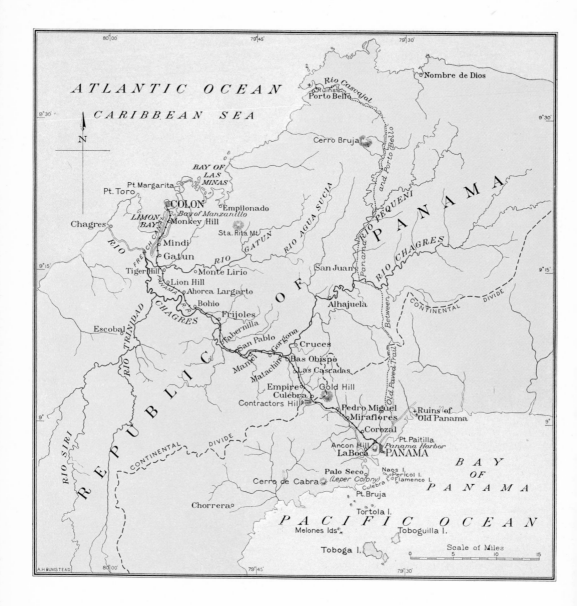

THE ISTHMUS OF PANAMA BEFORE ESTABLISHMENT OF THE CANAL ZONE

This map shows the former route of the Panama Railroad, the several watercourses, and the valley basins later occupied by Gatun Lake, with the location of the larger native villages therein. Comparison with the map on the opposite page will reveal the extent of the changes wrought by the impounding of the water. Inhabitants of the towns in the flooded area, once able to navigate their crude craft everywhere, were baffled by the winding channels among half-submerged trees. The author and his companions found them useless as guides.

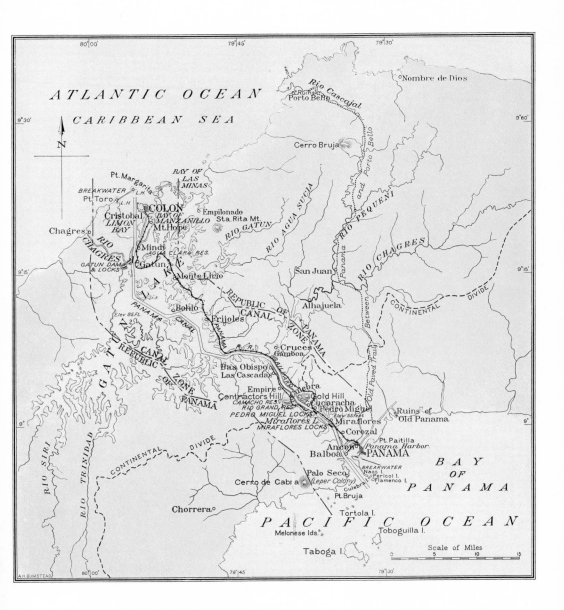

THE CANAL ZONE AND SURROUNDING TERRITORY OF THE PANAMA REPUBLIC

This map shows the relocated railroad; the canal route; Gatun Lake, covering 164 square miles; and the portion of the impounded water extending beyond the zone, with the watershed and tributary streams still under the exclusive jurisdiction of Panama. At the time of the author's visit one-third of the lake and all the flooded valleys contained much standing timber living and dead. Navigation through half-submerged forests was difficult but the house boat proved seaworthy under trying conditions.

IN THIS FLOODED FOREST OF THE TRINIDAD AN IGUANA CLINGS TO AN UPRIGHT STUMP AND A WHITE EGRET SITS ON A LOG

The new lake of this region has now an extent of 164 square miles and a depth in places of 70 to 90 feet. At the time the photograph was taken the inundation had not driven away or destroyed animal life.

once the camera and flashlight at the edge of the shore were buried out of sight.

Because of the anticipated encroachments of the lake, the Panama Railroad along the Chagres Valley (as shown on the maps) was relocated, but most of the foot trails were obliterated, and the narrow, well-defined canoe routes were lost in a maze of flooded forests, the tortuous channels being no longer indicated by wooded banks or rapid currents.

A SWIFT RIVER WAS LOST IN THE FLOODED FORESTS

In the estuary formed by the flooded valley of the Trinidad there was no suggestion of the swift stream of former years, once navigable for many miles in a canoe; for now the broad, stagnant, forested waters were covered here and there with floating vegetation and driftwood that often blocked the old route and made travel uncertain. One had to resort to the compass, for here no land was visible, no blazed trails or flowing waters indicated the direction. One might be lost for hours while trying to locate the temporary anchorage of a launch or house boat.

The timidity of the natives in exploring these flooded forests was in keeping with their fear of the open lake, and as guides we found them quite useless for reaching hunting grounds by boat. They were accustomed to following the ancestral trails and streams, and knew nothing about a compass or the direction indicated by the prevailing winds or the position of the sun.

Late in the afternoon of March 6 our improvised house boat was ready; and, towed by the launch, it drew up to the wharf for our outfit. Such a strange-looking craft, the first of its kind on Gatun Lake, excited considerable interest among the natives and the canal employees, who half an hour later watched us depart with the launch owner, Captain Brown, at the wheel. Our destination was the Trinidad River, several miles up the flooded valley. We were to enter a *trocha* leading to a new plantation, three miles within the flooded forests, through a narrow lane that had been made by felling the larger timber before the coming of the lake.

Of the thousands of employees about the locks none except our pilot had ever visited the plantation, for this particular region was regarded as a most likely place

in which to get lost, a fact of which we were warned by the resident engineer. A heavy but favorable sea was running, and as the waves surged harmlessly along the low deck we wondered what would be the rate of speed or the condition of the boat were we obliged to head into it.

We now had all the comforts of a commodious yacht, much freer ventilation, and a continuous opportunity to view the landscape or wild life from the open sides. There was plenty of room to store the bulky outfit, as well as pleasant quarters for identifying and preserving the material collected.

Cots and hammocks for beds, a large oil stove, a 30-gallon tank for pure water, a long table hinged to the side of the boat for the serving of meals and for use as a work-bench completed the equipment.

On a house boat one escapes the cumulative annoyances connected with breaking camp every few days. There is no repacking of fragile or loose articles or selection and clearing out of new sites in the ever-present brush, where giant vine-tangled trees, too formidable for the ax, exclude the light, air, and every outlook, and convert the jungle camp into a gloomy hot-house, surrounded by prickly plants and subject to raiding ants in daytime, fever-bearing mosquitos at night, and vicious red bugs and ticks at all times.

NAVIGATION IS BY BOATHOOK ON SHORT CUTS

Before dark the interior of the house boat was put in order, an operation that was interrupted now and then as the wheelsman took a short cut through the dead timber and all hands with boathooks and oars assisted in keeping the boat clear of the trees and floating logs. Several hours after sunset and under the light of a half moon, we reached the nearly submerged point that marked the entrance to the valley of the Trinidad.

Here had once flourished the native village of Escobal, now covered except for several huts on top of the ridge (see page 264). In one of the huts lived an enterprising Chinese, who made a poor living selling groceries and a better one dispensing intoxicants. He was safely located a few yards beyond the zonal line of Federal prohibition.

By previous arrangement the Chinese

MANY A NATIVE VILLAGE ON GATUN LAKE IN 1914 HAD TO BE ABANDONED

Flooding of the basin wrought havoc with wild life, too, cutting off the food supply (see text, page 259).

THE HOUSE BOAT ON GATUN LAKE WAS COMFORTABLE

This view shows the use of the living quarters by day for the preparation of specimens of birds and mammals and the other indoor work. The explorers were protected from insects.

had engaged two native guides for us; and with these aboard we promptly continued on our way in order to reach the plantation before the setting of the moon. Seated within the house boat and facing the open side, we could watch the course of the boat through the tops of the tallest trees of the dead forest. The deep waters had destroyed or covered many of the smaller trees.

Running at low speed, we were several hours crossing. By a combination of good luck and skill Captain Brown found the entrance of the *trocha* just ahead, although he was guided only by the knowledge he had of trees near the mouth. How the house boat ever traversed this narrow and more or less blocked passageway will always be a mystery to me, for later, when running in daylight with the launch, we often went astray or fouled on snags a foot or two below the surface.

JUNGLE TOO HUMID TO BURN

At midnight, in rounding a turn, we heard the barking of dogs and saw the glowing embers of scattered fires, where cut timber had been stacked and then burned continuously during the dry season. This condition, which I had not expected, I feared would alarm

THE HOUSE BOAT WAS ANCHORED OVER THE FLOODED VILLAGE OF ESCOBAL

Note the floating islands near shore. These become of great size when permanently held stationary by snags and dead trees.

the wild animals of the neighborhood. Unlike northern animals that are partial to "burnings" and tender new-growth vegetation, these creatures seemed likely to abandon a region unexpectedly covered with smoke and disturbed by crackling flames. In the dense and humid jungles fires are rare and seldom progress very far, even with the aid of man.

After our house boat had been tied up to a large tree a few yards from shore, we were visited by the native superintendent and given a generous welcome. Because Captain Brown was anxious to return to Gatun before the morning wind had roughened the lake, he left at once in the launch with Anderson, who was to bring the boat back the next day. Less than a mile away he encountered a mass of floating logs, and the moon being below the horizon he was compelled to stop until daylight.

At sunrise the next day flocks of chattering parrots flew over us, and occasionally a pair or two alighted on the higher trees and peered down on the half-screened house boat. Frequent shots from the cabin in the clearing proclaimed doubtful additions to the larder. Nothing was spared by the native hunters. There were no game laws outside the Zone, and no effort was made to preserve even the ornamental birds of the country.

RESCUED FROM A FLOODED FOREST

The author took a flashlight of this nocturnal
monkey which he had saved.

The well-earned outings of the canal employees were too often signalized by their
using the harmless, nongame animals and
birds as targets, until Colonel Goethals
took measures to prevent such thoughtless
destruction.

While we were breakfasting on the house
boat, a strange sound, rising and falling
in a torrent of guttural notes, came from
the hills to the westward. It was our first
greeting from the "black howler," the largest of the South American monkeys, a species whose uproarious conduct, whether
in tribal conversation or in protestation
against man or the weather, was always a
source of astonishment to us thereafter.

THE "BLACK HOWLER" MONKEY MAKES THE WELKIN RING

My friend Fuertes, the bird artist and naturalist, whose realistic mimicry of bird notes
was on a par with the fidelity to nature
of his brush, declared that the noise of the
"howler" is by far the most striking sound
to be heard in the American tropics. It
is "a deep, throaty, bass roar, with something of the quality of pig grunts or of the
barking bellow of a bull alligator or an
ostrich. The noise is as loud as the full-
throated roaring of lions, and its marvelous
carrying power was frequently attested
when we heard it from the far side of some
great Andean valley."

It is a popular belief on the Isthmus that
the "black howler" is an infallible weather
prophet. So far as we could discover, it
was only when the clouds blackened overhead and the first preliminary drops began
to fall that this prognosticator considered
it safe to commit himself to a definite forecast of approaching storm.

About 10 o'clock Mr. Anthony, carrying
a gun and accompanied by his guide with

a pack of steel traps, left for the only
open trail in the neighborhood, one leading
to an older plantation bordering the lake
on the far side of the promontory. I went
in another direction, following a dry creek
bottom, to select places suitable for the
taking of flashlight pictures. The bait for
luring the animals to the chosen localities
was to be the freshly skinned carcasses of
animals trapped for specimens.

It may be noted here that the only natural foot-trails available during the dry
season are the creek bottoms, which have
been cleared of all underbrush and fallen
trees as a result of the torrential rains that
fall during eight months of the year.

WILD LIFE SEEKS CREEK BEDS

It is in these creek bottoms, also, that
many of the wild animals, large and small,
seek easy routes of travel; and here they
come to quench their thirst at the small
pools and pot-holes scooped out of the soft
sandstone formation of all the creeks. The
predatory species naturally come to prey
upon the smaller animals that seek this
favorable ground.

On returning at noon, the trapping party
discovered a band of "black howlers" passing overhead, with a result described in the
collector's notebook as follows:

"I felt a pang of regret at silencing one
of the 'howlers,' but since a specimen was
needed, I shot the foremost and heard him
crash through the limbs to the ground.
Pangs of a more effective source were experienced when my native boy and I attempted to retrieve the monkey, for he had
fallen through the nest the size of a
bushel basket and we found the nest too
late to avoid the consequences."

After the coming of darkness the specimen, a fine large male, was recovered, with
the aid of a lantern, and brought to the
house boat (see page 265).

The following morning the traps yielded
only some small rodents, while the runways, formerly used by larger game,
showed scarcely a track—plain evidence
that the heavy smoke from the clearing had
frightened them away.

This circumstance compelled us to make
long and hard trips into the more-distant
forests, in which trails had to be cut with
a machete, foot by foot. The process resulted in our amassing a wonderful collection of ticks and red bugs and other insect
pests, which bothered us until the trails

IT KNOWS WHEN A STORM IS APPROACHING

The black howler, the largest of the Panaman monkeys, is looked upon by the natives as a weather prophet, its loud, long, and reverberating howl being most frequently heard just preceding a heavy rain, but too late to give useful warning (see text, opposite page).

THE MARMOSET MONKEY HAS HAIR LIKE SILK IN SHADES OF BROWN AND GRAY

It makes a beautiful and attractive pet. There are five species of monkeys in the zone, from the black howler, the size of a small ape, down to the little squirrel monkey.

SHE WAS RESCUED FROM A FLOATING ISLAND WHEN A FAWN

This female white-tailed deer might have perished, as did many of her kind, had not a Good Samaritan brought her in from the flooded area.

had been cleared for a day or two. It was our later experience here and elsewhere that the jungles of Panama are abundantly supplied with a great variety of wild life.

The explorations of Major E. A. Goldman and others in Panama, the Canal Zone included, have shown the existence in that region of about 50 kinds of bats and more than 100 species of other mammals, among which are nine species of monkeys.

As in most tropical areas, fur bearers are scarce in Panama, the continuously warm climate not causing the growth of the warm coat of fur so usual among northern animals. Only the otter and the rare water opossum in this region seem to develop a coat that can be classed as fur.

A WAIF ON GATUN LAKE

For centuries the valleys now occupied by Gatun Lake had been the home or feeding places of many wild animals, especially noteworthy among the larger ones being the tapir and the deer. In the fall of 1911

the rising waters began to drive the two species of deer from the bottom lands, where the thickets and more tender vegetation had afforded the best of shelter and of food. Some sought the ridges and other elevations near by, unaware that within a few months these refuges would become isolated as islands or would be wholly submerged by the rising lake.

About this time Captain Brown had made a trip in his launch exploring the new avenues for motor boats in a territory in which he had hunted for years afoot. In passing some matted drift composed of dead vegetation, which under the force of the wind had just been pushed from a recently flooded island, he noticed lying fast asleep thereon a beautiful little fawn. It was only a few days old, and the debris had been its cradle within the flooded timber.

Now, separated forever from its mother and drifting in the open lake, it was likely to starve, drown, or become the prey of an

THE HOUSE BOAT CRUISES IN THE FLOODED FOREST OF GATUN LAKE

It was because of the flooding of the Gatun and Chagres valleys by the huge dam at the Gatun locks, thus causing abrupt changes in the faunal conditions, that an expedition was undertaken (see text, page 257).

eagle or the cayman. The captain took it aboard and added it to his collection of native animals at Gatun. Raised by hand and kindly treated, it reached maturity and became the favorite pet of the canal village (see illustration, opposite page).

A few months later, while on another expedition in the same region, the captain kept a good lookout for other marooned animals. One day, in an upper crotch of a large tree surrounded by water and situated a considerable distance from dry land, he observed a round, furry object. As the launch approached, the ball unrolled itself and disclosed a small monkeylike creature, with bulging eyes that suggested a lemur. Captain Brown felt sure that this was the rarely seen nocturnal species known as the owl monkey.

Since this was a rare find and afforded another opportunity to save an animal in distress, the captain tied the launch to the tree and made an effort to slip a noose over the animal's head by means of a boat-hook.

His effort proved unsuccessful. He then placed a ripe banana invitingly on the bow, and retired to the stern to await results.

In a few minutes the little animal came down the tree, leaped on deck, and eagerly began devouring the fruit. It was evidently on the verge of starvation, for it permitted the rope to be cast off without showing any desire to leave its food and seek its former retreat. An hour later the little monkey was placed without difficulty in the same pen with the fawn.

SHOOTING A BOA CONSTRICTOR

Afterward it sought a shelf on the rear porch, where during the daytime it was concealed by boxes and coils of rope. True to its nature, it was never seen in the daytime, except when purposely disturbed, but after dark it was very active (see page 257). On chilly nights it would seek the sleeping fawn and curl up on its back for warmth. My introduction to this interesting animal occurred later, when I tested its

NATIVE PANAMANS GO TO SEA IN CAYUCAS, OR DUGOUTS

These craft vary in length from 8 to 35 feet, and each is cut from a single tree. They bring produce to market, often being loaded with sugar cane cut in sections 8 to 10 feet long.

A GATUN LAKE IGUANA TAKES A SUN BATH

This species, the giant lizard of the South, is considered by the natives a real prize, for its flesh, when properly cooked, is said to taste like chicken.

HERON FISH AT A HEADWATER STREAM

As the shores of Gatun Lake open up, they will be a favorite resort for all wading birds. Floating
islands will become stationary and wild life of many sorts will occupy them.

A FEMALE OPOSSUM OF PANAMA NURSES HER BABES

These relatives of the well-known Virginia species have the same habit of carrying the naked and
undeveloped young attached to their teats within a pocketlike pouch on the abdomen.

TWO NOCTURNAL RAILS USED THE DRY CREEK BOTTOM WHERE THE FLASH WAS SET

Like the opossums, they fired it repeatedly, pulling on the string whether it was baited with fruit or meat (see text, page 274).

HIS SORT FIRED MOST OF THE FLASHES

This particular opossum is the commonest of several varieties encountered in the Canal Zone. It proved a serious obstacle to night photography (see text, page 274).

AT FIRST GLANCE IT LOOKS LIKE A PIG

The long, naked tail, however, shows the subject of this flashlight picture to be a member of a common species of Panama opossum.

ANOTHER OPOSSUM FINDS THE BAIT

After these ubiquitous animals had fired most of the author's powder set to flashlight more important subjects, the statement which heads this legend was uttered in disgust (see text, page 274).

HERE THE AUTHOR ALMOST ACHIEVED A TRIUMPH

In this creek bottom, arbored over with giant ferns and swaying vines, the flashlight was fired by a jaguar. However, the camera outfit (marked X, lower left center) was so far from headquarters that the plate was ruined by moisture before it could be developed (see text, below).

eyes to see whether they would shine under an artificial light.

Most of the process of the dispersal and isolation of wild life had gone on before our arrival. Through the assistance of hounds we obtained some fine specimens of the larger animals on several islands where deer and peccaries were still abundant, though more or less preyed upon by jaguars and ocelots. One afternoon when cruising through a forest of gaunt, dead trees, in an area in which the water was fully 20 feet deep, we were surprised to see a large boa constrictor sunning itself on a limb not much above the surface of the water.

A BOA CONSTRICTOR CAUSES SOME COMMOTION

Since this snake was regarded as a good museum specimen, we put a rifle ball just back of its head. With a convulsive movement the snake hurled itself toward the bow of the launch, but fortunately it slid into the water. Only a crimson circle on the surface and a string of bubbles marked its way to the bottom where it was beyond recovery. Whether it had sought a dead tree in the open water as being the only available basking place in this deluged district or had found some form of prey unknown to us was hard to determine.

Although I had previously been successful with flashlight photography in southern climes, this method proved to be difficult of application in Panama. The country was alive with opossums, ranging in size from that of the Virginia opossum to that of a mouse (see pages 271, 272, and 273). The moment darkness fell I could hear the reports from the scattered flashlight machines and always there was the probability of their having been fired by marsupials. As if this annoyance was not enough, many a flash was sprung by a species of night rail, by large rats or flying bats (see page 272), and even by decaying vegetation dropping from the forest tops.

In the daytime, the ever-present buzzard soon associated with a feast the green tin boxes covering the cameras, and whenever meat was used as bait, it became necessary to delay setting the flash until dusk was beginning to gather.

But the worst obstacle of all was the extreme humidity. Plates left exposed in the camera for more than two nights and developed at irregular periods became so mildewed as to be worthless.

A PACA BITES A MANGO AND TAKES ITS OWN PICTURE

One of the largest of the existing rodents, this creature is exceeded in size by the closely related capybara alone. It is an animal of nocturnal habits, and therefore can be photographed only by means of flashlight apparatus set at night.

Once when the flash was fired by a jaguar at a considerable distance from the house boat, the locality was visited too late for the plate to be saved, and all I had for the effort was the sight of the clawed bank caused by the big animal as it sprang away in terror when the dazzling, booming flash greeted its effort to carry off the skinned body of an opossum. Much the same thing occurred in the case of a tapir that was passing along a runway to the water.

Moisture-absorbing chemicals in the camera would have overcome this difficulty, but none was at hand. Undoubtedly flashlight photography is the ideal way of getting pictures of the larger-sized and mostly nocturnal animals of South America, where the dense brush prevents any possibility of daylight pictures unless the subjects can be cornered or treed by hounds.

On several nights I tried to get flashlight pictures of animals on the shore of Barro Colorado Island. We occasionally caught glimpses of glowing eyes back from the water's edge, but floating logs and tottering trees made the approach so difficult that before we could come within range the mysterious beast we were eager to photograph had always disappeared.

That the obstacles to flashlight photography with a set camera in the jungle can be overcome and admirable results obtained was demonstrated by Doctor Chapman on Barro Colorado Island several years after my visit there. In 1926 he built a winter cottage at the Biological Station established on the island, and devoted much time to studying the habits of the rich bird life of that delightful sanctuary. At the same time he observed the mammal life about him, and the tracks of some large species in trails cut through the forest excited his interest.

DOCTOR CHAPMAN SUCCESSFUL WITH FLASHLIGHT DEVICE

For many years he had been my close friend and a frequent guest, and had become familiar in a general way with the technique of flashlight photography. The conditions about him on Barro Colorado Island were so tempting that he procured the necessary equipment and used it skillfully enough to obtain a fine series of photographs of tropical animals that had never before been pictured at large in their native haunts.

Among these were such small game as agoutis and coatis, besides the collared and

Photograph by Dr. F. M. Chapman

IN MANY RESPECTS THE PUMA IS AN OVERGROWN KITTEN

These animals will frolic together or alone, fight sham battles, chase butterflies, or play hide and seek. This one is not full grown. The picture is one of Doctor Chapman's masterpieces with the automatic flashlight camera on Barro Colorado Island.

larger white-lipped peccaries and the tapir. The most remarkable of the collection were the pictures of the ocelots and the mountain lion journeying stealthily along the trails (see illustration, above).

Doctor Chapman's account in the NATIONAL GEOGRAPHIC MAGAZINE for September, 1927, of his experiences in getting these photographs should inspire others to make similar records of the rarely seen beasts that haunt the jungles of the American tropics. There is in these virtually unknown fastnesses a wealth of material for study by naturalists, and a photographer who could obtain satisfactory pictures there would contribute a valuable service.

CHAPTER XI

Further Observations in the Canal Zone

ON OUR Panama trip we devoted considerable time to studying the reactions of the eyes of mammals, birds, and other animals to bright light at night. Naturally, many of the species tested were those available only in the tropics.

Up to this time I had not found a member of the primates with eyes that reflected light, for all tested were diurnal species, like man. In several countries there are species of monkeys that are nocturnal, but I could never find one in zoological collections. Therefore, it was with great interest that I tested the eyes of the little owl monkey, whose rescue from a flooded forest has already been mentioned.

Turning the lantern toward the monkey as it sat on the upper edge of the porch one dark night, I saw its eyes glisten like two brilliant diamonds. After I had taken a flashlight picture of it, it became so wild that I could not approach it for further study. Since this particular species of monkey has not a prehensile tail, and since its eyes and general features resemble those of the lemur, a strictly nocturnal animal, it may represent a connecting link between the monkeys and the lemurs.

In the North I had discovered that the eyes of one species of nighthawk, belonging to the goatsucker family, would shine brightly under the light. While at Gatun, I at once noticed that the nighthawks circling about the electric lights after insects had brilliant eyes.

A LIGHT CAUSES A BIRD TO BE MISTAKEN FOR A CAT

Mr. Anthony, "headlighting" in the forest for specimens of the cat family, saw a large pair of brilliant red eyes glowing from the top of a tree. He fired with the expectation of getting an ocelot or a similar animal. Instead of a heavy body crashing through the branches there was only a slight swish. Looking under the tree, he found that he had killed a large goatsucker, one of the largest of all the nighthawk family. He was disappointed in his failure to bag the large quadruped he had expected, but the result of the shot showed that at least certain other members of the group of nocturnal birds possess a *tapetum* (p. 179).

We discovered, also, that the eyes of the larger species of southern rodents, such as the agouti and paca, could be easily shined at night. Since the northern rodents, with the exception of the rabbit (which is not a rodent although popularly classified as such), do not have shining eyes, it is possible that this physical characteristic might be used to some extent as a basis for distinguishing a suborder of rodents.

On the Upper Chagres we found one species of fish that apparently fed mostly at night. Under the light its eyes would glow with the same brilliant red as in those of the cayman, another night feeder.

THE AUTHOR'S THEORY OF THE TAPETUM CONFIRMED

While the results of our experiments in Panama enlarged our list of the number of species having reflecting eyes, they confirmed my opinion that the possession of the *tapetum* is directly associated with night vision, and that the brilliancy of the reflection corresponds to the animal's need of such a faculty in defense or aggression.

One day Mr. Anthony, scanning the treetops for a shot at a squirrel, was nearly knocked over by a big boar peccary. He fired at it with small shot, and it rolled over dead a few feet away.

At the same instant his Indian guide at his elbow uttered a cry of terror. A big jaguar had sprung up and roared in his face. So intent had this beast been on following the peccary's trail that it had ventured close to the hunting party. It sprang away in a line with the guide, so that a shot could not be fired at it without endangering his life.

This adventure provided us with fresh meat and a good museum specimen. That night Anderson, whose bed was on the floor between our cots, was restless, the usual indication that his daily supply of ticks had not been removed before he retired. When he held up several objects and inquired sarcastically whether they were "young turtles," his knowledge of entomology was enlarged. We told him that they represented a very large species of tick from the peccary he had skinned on the floor of the boat some hours before.

THEY ENTERED AN EERIE CAVERN

The low entrance to the bat cave on the Chilibrillo River opens into a series of long corridors and chambers more or less intercommunicating.

TRIPS WERE MADE UP THE RIO CHILIBRILLO TO VISIT THE BAT CAVES

Since palms never grow in water, something of the extent of the flooding of this region can be judged.

BLACK VULTURES CONSORT WITH TURKEY BUZZARDS

This is a common scene on the beach at Panama City. The tireless scavenger birds are of inestimable value to communities in tropical America.

Many years ago some large limestone caves were discovered near the Upper Chagres. They were the haunt of numerous bats, ranging in size from a small species only about 3 inches in length to the huge, so-called vampire, whose wing-spread may be two feet or more (see page 285).

Formerly it had been impossible to visit this section otherwise than by an uncertain trail that ran through the evercrowding jungle. After the main stream and its tributaries had been deepened by the back waters from the lake, however, the caves could be reached by launch in a few hours. Under the guidance of a former canal employee, an erstwhile trapper and market hunter, we made a trip to the caves on March 1.

After ascending the broad, inundated valley of the Chagres for some miles, we entered a branch called the Chilibrillo—narrow, deep, and tortuous and with no perceptible current. As the boat glided smoothly through the straight courses and swerved violently at the numerous turns, the overhanging shrubbery and the flooded palm trees on each side marking the bed of a stream formerly unnavigable for any kind of craft, we realized more fully how the new lake had opened up these canal-like avenues of travel into the very heart of the jungle (see page 278).

We had made a run of five or six miles when a current became noticeable. In a few minutes we came to a transverse ledge of rock with a slight flow of water rippling over it. This indicated the end of the trip by boat. While we continued our way by walking up the nearly dry bed of the

stream, it became plain to us that many animals had sought the higher ground as a refuge; for trails to the scattered pools came in from all directions, bearing the fresh imprint of tapir, deer, peccary, and agouti, and the occasional claw marks of the jaguar and ocelot. The frequent roaring of the black howler showed that this big tenant of the treetops was also abundant.

The grotesque toucans vied vocally with the noisy parrots, and the notes of the parrakeets and the peculiar choruslike calls of the chachalacas produced an impression that I shall ever associate with the memories of the jungle. Turning to the right and ascending a creek bottom, we soon came in sight of the low entrance to the caves, encircled with ferns, vines, and flowering plants.

CLUSTERS OF BATS FESTOON WALLS

Lighting the lantern and stooping low, we entered a corridor leading to a series of interconnecting rooms with high ceilings and dark and grimy walls, relieved here and there by light-colored stalactites, the tapering ends of which dripped with limestone waters. In the central room, both on the walls and on the ceiling, were great clusters of bats segregated by species and, as later examination showed, according to sex (see illustration, pages 284 and 285).

A bunch some 10 feet square and containing hundreds of small bats was discovered on an end wall. The bats were only 6 feet from the ground and were particularly well situated for a flashlight picture. Our guide, filled with the enthusiasm of the occasion, unbuckled his leather belt,

A STREAM BED THROUGH THE FOREST HELPED THE HUNTERS

The visit being during dry weather, the party took advantage of this open route to set traps for mammals and cameras with flashlights.

noiselessly overhead, creating a perceptible current of air as they flew continuously back and forth through the connecting caverns. Finally, they attached themselves to the roof and we were able to obtain a sufficient number for our purpose. I took a series of flashlight pictures.

FEW EXPLORE CAVES

Upon the large detached rocks were dozens of big black beetles, either nocturnal in their haunts or accustomed to feed on the vermin or excrement of the bats. A careful examination of these caves indicated that they did not belong to the group formerly discovered by visiting Americans. They contain a vast deposit of bat guano, and since they are near water transportation this supply may become of considerable value as a fertilizer.

The animal in which I was particularly interested on this trip was the white-tailed deer of the Canal Zone, a distant relative of the Virginia deer. The several species of the whitetails with their geographic races form by far the most wide-ranging group of the American deer, extending as they do from coast to coast and from Canada southward to Brazil and Peru.

and before we could anticipate his action, began lashing them. In a moment a surplus of specimens lay at his feet. The rest took wing and in bewilderment circled about the lantern.

Our next efforts were directed toward getting specimens of the larger bats, which hung from the highest domes and could be obtained only by throwing missiles at them. While picking up some loose pieces of rock for this purpose, we were startled by a flash and the reverberating report of a heavy rifle discharged by the guide in another misdirected attempt to aid us in our specimen gathering.

A few mangled and useless bodies fell, and then a black stream of bats circled

In the Canal Zone as well as elsewhere in the tropics the whitetails frequent the borders of the forests and the edges of open savannahs and clearings. They come into the open usually at night, but sometimes they venture out about sundown or very early in the morning.

In the North the mating season of the whitetail covers about 30 days in the fall, and the bucks shed their antlers a month or so later. The fawns are born within a correspondingly 30-day period late in the spring. Such periodic and seasonable habits are undoubtedly caused and controlled in part by the rigorous winters and the supply of nourishing food which is obtainable at the period of fawning.

BREEDING SEASON OF DEER IN THE TROPICS

Even in the Gulf States the mating and fawning seasons correspond approximately with those farther north, for even there the winters are too severe to permit any material change. South of the Mexican border, however, especially from Vera Cruz southward, the breeding season is much extended and more irregular. In those regions there is virtually always a sufficient food supply.

On the Isthmus of Panama, which has a

OUT OF THE FRYING PAN INTO THE FIRE

This boar peccary was shot when he was fleeing before a jaguar at Gatun Lake. Whether he ran on or stopped, he was doomed.

mean annual temperature of about 80 degrees Fahrenheit, and a variation of only about five degrees between the so-called summer and winter months, the periods of the rut, the shedding of the antlers, and of fawning are very irregular. There are at least nine months when fawns may be born; and antlerless bucks and those with antlers in different stages of growth may be found throughout the year.

It is an interesting and unanswered question whether this prolonged breeding season in the tropics does not result in many bucks carrying their antlers much beyond what would be the normal period in the North. I believe that the growth of antlers is purely a sexual manifestation, which

incidentally provides a weapon for battling with rivals; for in the North the antlers are shed long before the time when they would be of the greatest use against wolves and other predatory animals. Among the tapirs and many other large animals a prolonged breeding season is also usual, but among birds it is less marked.

The dense forests of the Canal Zone are inhabited by a little reddish-brown species of deer known as the brocket. It keeps so much secluded in the dense jungle, in which it makes its home, that comparatively few white men have seen it. The brockets form a group of tropical American deer that live in the heavy forests from Mexico to Brazil. Because of their retiring habits little is

BARRO COLORADO IS ONE OF THE MANY ISLANDS STUDDING GATUN LAKE   Official Photograph U. S. Army Air Corps

From the air one can best appreciate the primitive state in which Barro Colorado has remained. This island, in the foreground, has an area of about six square miles, and rises to an extreme height of 452 feet above the lake. As shown by the unbroken sea of treetops, it is densely forested and has been set aside by the Government as a sanctuary wherein the wild life of tropical America may be conserved and studied. The arrow points to the laboratory.

known concerning the characteristics and the life histories of these animals.

During and since the construction of the Canal many Americans as well as other people in the Canal Zone have hunted deer with dogs and by still hunting. Hunting clubs have been organized and considerable game is available to those skillful and persistent enough to find it.

Anyone who tries hunting in tropical jungles soon realizes that the hardships and difficulties are greater there than they are in the temperate regions of the North. Many of the game animals and the beasts of prey in the Zone present a strange appearance to a hunter new to the tropics.

No fully organized game laws are in force in the Canal Zone, but under its police powers the government of the Zone controls hunting through executive orders and by the requirement that every one wishing to hunt shall first obtain a hunting license. Shooting is forbidden within 100 yards of town sites and roads and within certain localities, and there are several other restrictions. Hunting by the use of artificial light at night is prohibited.

In general, birds with their nests and eggs, except the birds of prey, are protected; but there is an open season on ducks and waders, and on pigeons, quail, currasows, and guans. The last named are large, dark-colored birds of the pheasant family. They resemble hen turkeys both in size and proportions, and are often called wild turkeys by uninformed hunters. As a matter of fact, the guan has no near kinship to those familiar birds of the North, which do not range south of Mexico.

MOST NORTHERN WILD FOWL ABSENT

The southern range of the majority of the migratory wild fowl of the North does not extend to Panama. With the exception of three varieties of ducks—the pintail, the blue-winged teal, and the lesser scaup—no geese, brant, swans, or any of the other numerous species so common in the United States were seen by us or noted by careful resident observers.

This fact indicates that the Federal Migratory Bird Treaty with Great Britain, which has so effectively prohibited spring shooting in the United States and Canada during the northern flight, need only be supplemented by a similar treaty with Mexico in order to cover the main part of the range of these valuable and rapidly vanishing birds.

For some reason tropical fresh-water lakes do not appear to favor the growth of the food plants necessary to support an abundance of wild fowl. In addition to the visiting ducks from the North, black-bellied plovers and a number of northern shore birds visit the Canal Zone during their migratory flights. A great blue heron wearing a band placed on one of its legs in Wisconsin has been shot there.

FISH AND FISHING

The waters of Gatun Lake in the vicinity of our house boat were plentifully supplied with a good-sized, coarse fish resembling the black mullet. We put into service a large line and our single rusty hook, and soon landed a dozen of these fish, averaging a pound or more apiece. They were only fairly edible, but served excellently for baiting the traps set to catch mammals and to lure animals to the neighborhood of the flashlight cameras.

These fish, though everywhere abundant in the lake, are not fitted to become a game species or to be a favorite on the table. There were also smaller fish that annoyed bathers by nipping them severely. These could be frightened away only by creating a vigorous commotion.

I was impressed by the lack of desirable native food fishes and the apparent opportunity to stock this great body of fresh water with some of our well-known species that would add greatly to the recreational opportunities of the Zone and make a welcome addition to the larder. This idea evidently occurred to others, for in 1916 and 1917 the United States Bureau of Fisheries planted in Gatun Lake young black bass, rock bass, sunfish, and catfish. In 1924 some additional black bass, together with crappies and bream, were placed there.

Little definite information is available concerning the outcome of these experiments, but in June, 1931, I was informed that the black bass introduced into a small lake on the Stilson plantation had greatly increased in numbers, and that large crappies had been caught in Gatun Lake. This indicates that to a certain extent at least some of our game fish might prove successful in Panama.

Thus far anglers in Gatun Lake have had poor returns from their efforts, but below

A FLASHLIGHT PHOTOGRAPH RECORDS LIKENESSES OF SMALL BATS

They were isolated by species and sexes, each species confined to a particular grotto, where it was found in hundreds. The bats of each mass were all of the same sex (see text, page 279).

the spillway of Gatun Dam there is good tarpon fishing, and about the submerged banks and around the islands on both coasts the sea fishing is excellent.

Our refusal to accept the proposals of European nations for an unfortified or neutralized canal, and the erection of the heaviest possible armament on the seaboard at both ends of the canal, become vain if it is possible to suspend the operation of the canal for months by the use of a few sticks of dynamite on the spillway, or if the Pedro Miguel locks can be destroyed by projectiles fired from slopes beyond the boundary of the Zone.

To protect the entrances to the canal by fortifications and warships while trusting to the supposedly enduring friendship of Panama or to the inviolability of the neutrality of the Canal Zone by other nations is much like locking the front and back doors

while leaving those on the sides open. In short the canal is far from impregnable unless fortifications or other means of protection are provided to guard the sides.

Fortunately, the terms of the treaty with Panama permit the safeguarding of the Canal Zone by the necessary extension of its borders. This has been done already about Gatun Lake and elsewhere in places that may be overflowed by waters raised by the creation of other reservoirs.

TREATY WITH PANAMA SAFEGUARDS THE CANAL ZONE

The danger that might arise within a zone extending only 5 miles on each side of the canal was so well recognized that on February 26, 1904, President Roosevelt proclaimed a treaty with Panama containing broad stipulations to cover possible future requirements.

THIS GREAT TROPICAL BAT SPREADS 26 INCHES FROM TIP TO TIP OF ITS WINGS

It is a giant of the largest species found by the author and his companions in their explorations of the caves near the Chagres River (see text, page 279).

HANGING BATS WERE FLASHLIGHTED BEFORE THEY WERE ALARMED

Clusters of these creatures ordinarily contain a great number of individuals, several hundred in some instances. The kind shown here is one of the larger of tropical American bats. The bats are strong and muscular and always ready to bite. The masses of them bear a close resemblance in form to the stalactites with which the walls and domed ceilings of the cave are covered (see text, page 280).

THE FLARE BANISHED THE PITCH DARKNESS

This was the method of photographing bats by flashlight in the Stygian caves on the Chilibrillo (see text, page 279). Since the powder used is exceedingly explosive, the expression on the face of the operator is not to be wondered at.

Some development has taken place about David, in the province of Chiriqui, from which fruit and other products are shipped to Panama by boat. The paved motor highway extending from Panama City to David will no doubt aid in the growth of such businesses. This road forms a link in the great Pan-American Highway that is gradually being built to make possible motor traffic from the United States and Canada to the countries of South America.

U. S. MUST OWN ALL LAKE SITES

In the course of my explorations about the shores of Gatun Lake, a considerable part of which lies far beyond the five-mile limit to the southwest and to the northeast of the canal, I was deeply impressed by the necessity for the United States to have absolute control of it, and so expressed myself in the NATIONAL GEOGRAPHIC MAGAZINE for August, 1915. Fortunately, the treaty with Panama permits necessary readjustments of the Canal Zone boundaries as required for purposes of its proper administration, control, and defense.

The drainage basin of Gatun Lake has an area of about 1,300 square miles. No high mountains exist there to send cool water into the lake; consequently its temperature is always warm, although, like the air above, it varies somewhat with the season. The temperature at the surface in July is about 87 degrees, and in January about 84 degrees. Near the bottom, at 44 feet, in July it is 76.5 degrees, and at 48 feet in January, 75 degrees.

The canal is dependent for its continued operation on the precipitation on the

Because of the peculiar administrative requirements of the Canal Zone, and in order to avoid needless friction, the Government promptly proceeded to buy up every private holding within its limits. Since then private occupation of land within the Zone has been prohibited except under permit revocable at will.

A few necessary semipublic businesses, such as the Cable Company, have such permits and canal employees enjoy the use of little tracts for residences and gardens. However, it is not feasible to permit any considerable private development.

Early in the history of our connection with the canal much publicity was given to the potential development of agriculture on neighboring land in Panama. Up to 1931 this had failed to materialize.

Gatun Lake drainage and what water may be collected in the Chagres River basin above Alajuela. This makes it essential to observe the greatest care in noting and recording the rainfall on these watersheds and to provide for guarding any part of the lake basins subject to dangerous overflow or pressure.

WEATHER IN THE CANAL ZONE

In more northern latitudes we are always concerned about the weather and its numerous daily and seasonal changes; for these have a direct bearing on the welfare and comfort of practically everyone. Variations between daylight and darkness, and between heat and cold, the growth and decline of vegetation, and the slumbering of nature beneath a mantle of snow, all are factors that must be recognized in any program of human endeavor.

As was expected, in the tropics at Panama I found a much greater uniformity of weather conditions than in the North. The periods of daylight and darkness were nearly uniform in length. On February 25 the sun rose at 6.35 a. m., and set at 6.30 p. m.; exactly a month later it rose at 6.20 a. m., and set at 6.30 p. m. The average annual temperature of the Canal Zone is about 80 degrees Fahrenheit; in the two months I was there the temperature ranged from 72 to 74 degrees in the early morning, and from 84 to 88 degrees at

CABLELIKE ROOTS CARRY NOURISHMENT ALOFT

Many plants live on the upper surface of large branches of trees in tropical American forests, and some of them, lacking sufficient food in the humus there for their proper growth, send down long, threadlike rootlets, which finally touch the ground and firmly take hold there.

3 p. m. The highest recorded there is 98 degrees, and the lowest, 59 degrees.

Based on the relative amounts of rainfall, the year on the Isthmus is divided into two parts—a dry season of about four months (from January to April), and a wet, or rainy, season of eight months (from May to December). Although these sea-

NATURE PLAYS TRICKS WITH TREE TRUNKS

The author made a study of these queer formations at
the north end of Gatun Lake (see opposite page).

air and clouds such as I had
learned in the North to associate
with electrical displays. Continued
official observations have disclosed,
however, that such storms are more
numerous there than in any part
of the United States. They are
rare in the dry season, but average
about 15 a month in the rainy season, a total of 100 to 140 annually.
They are most numerous over
the continental divide, and fewest
along the Atlantic coast. These
storms usually travel across the
Zone from southwest to northeast
as elsewhere on the continent, and
seldom exceed 45 miles per hour.

THE CANAL ZONE FORMS A CROSS-
SECTION OF TROPICAL LIFE

Although the several insular
possessions of the United States
contain many strange forms of
plant and animal life, most of these
are beyond the current of our domestic intercourse and are little
visited by travelers from other
lands. Wonderful as are our national parks, they can be seen by
slight diversion from the customary lines of travel, and most of
them are within the temperate regions with which we are familiar.

The Canal Zone, however, constitutes a cross-section of the tropical land bridge joining North and
South America. It is the only
portion of our tropical domain that
is traversed by boat and rail on a
main traveled route. It is a unique
part of our public domain, and
every citizen should have a feeling of personal pride and proprietorship in it and
favor its improvement and beautification,
even though few can see it.

The terminal cities of the canal—Colon
and Panama—will continue to be objects of
interest, but how refreshing and entertaining to all will be the trans-Isthmian trip,
if along the way may be seen tropic growths
in all their luxuriant beauty of foliage and
bloom. There, too, efforts should be made
to attract and show so far as possible an
adequate representation of the local mammal, bird, and reptile life.

Since the settlement and the agricultural
development of the Canal Zone are forbid-

sons are fairly well defined, there are some
rains in the dry season and some fair-
weather days in the wet season. The average daily period of rainfall during the wet
season is said to be only an hour and a
quarter.

The amount of rainfall varies locally,
the heaviest occurring at Colon, on the Atlantic side, at which place it averages 129
inches annually, and the least at Ancon, on
the Pacific side, where the average is only
71 inches. The heaviest rainfall recorded in
24 hours amounted to 12.25 inches.

I was surprised by the absence of thunder-
storms while I was in the Canal Zone, for
I noted often a feeling of humidity in the

den, the 10-mile belt across the Isthmus and its great extension about the shores of Gatun and Alajuela Lakes should take on the aspect of a great international park.

The rich tropical vegetation of the forest shelters deer, peccaries, tapirs, pacas, agoutis, jaguars, ocelots, mountain lions, opossums, spider and howling monkeys, marmosets, and a multitude of bats, together with many reptiles, including the boa and the cayman in the swamps.

Colonies of egrets might occupy the trees on secluded islands in the lakes. In places the noisy cries of macaws and parrots would break the silence, and the brilliant hues of trogons, toucans, tanagers, and other tropical birds would add their charm to the orchid-laden trees. An epitome of nearly all this already exists on Barro Colorado Island in Gatun Lake.

THE CANAL ZONE AN IDEAL SITE FOR A BOTANIC GARDEN

The Canal Zone is ideally situated for the development of a great botanic garden, such as the world-famous examples in Ceylon and Java. There, with the aid of an authority on tropical botany as resident director, it would be possible to bring together for scientific study and exhibition not only the useful and interesting plant life of the tropical Americas, but that of the entire world. Such an establishment would not only attract botanists from many countries, but would hold a fascinating interest for the growing number of travelers who are now passing through the canal each year.

I was so impressed by the richness of the flora and fauna about the shores of Gatun Lake, especially the mammals, birds, and reptiles, that it appeared to me to be an ideal place for a center of research by scientists. What my companions and I had seen in the course of our house boat trips would be negligible compared to what detailed study could discover.

In an article which was published in the NATIONAL GEOGRAPHIC MAGAZINE for August, 1915, I voiced this idea and suggested some governmental action to bring this about. Whether or not this suggestion had any weight, it gave me the utmost satis-

THIS ONE HOLDS THE TREE ALOFT ON STILTS

Queer tree trunks in the forest at the north end of Gatun Lake fascinated the author (see opposite page).

faction when the following Executive Order was issued by the Governor of the Canal Zone and a copy of it was sent to me.

THE PANAMA CANAL, CANAL ZONE

EXECUTIVE OFFICE

Balboa Heights, C. Z.,

April 17, 1923

To All Concerned:

Barro Colorado Island in the Gatun Lake area of the Canal Zone is hereby reserved for use as a Natural Park, subject to later arrangements for its development. This island is also known as West Island.

Hunting of game of all kinds is prohibited on this island except for strictly scientific

THOUSANDS OF TREES FESTOONED WITH GROUPS OF BRILLIANT ORCHIDS WERE
DYING IN GATUN LAKE (SEE TEXT, PAGE 259)

THE HOUSE BOAT WAS TIED TO DEAD TREE MANY MILES FROM DRY LAND

The open space gave sunlight, cooling breezes, and freedom from insects, and the deep, clear water invited the morning and evening swim. Fish of several species were very numerous, but were of little value. Since then bass and several other desirable fishes have been introduced, and some, at least, appear to be thriving.

purposes, for which a special permit shall be issued by the Governor or by his direction.

JAY J. MORROW,
Governor.

———

This action was taken on the recommendation of Dr. Thomas Barbour and others interested in tropical natural history, for the purpose of establishing a Biological Research Laboratory on the island. Doctor Barbour succeeded in interesting the National Research Council in the project; the first laboratory buildings were erected in 1924, and the station has ever since been conducted under its auspices. Undoubtedly the station owes more of its success to Doctor Barbour's tireless interest and financial assistance than to the efforts of any other individual.

This station is used every year by a group of scientific men who desire to study the mammals, birds, reptiles, insects, and other forms of life in their native environment. More than 100 papers, many of them of great scientific value, have been published by well-known scientific men, including Barbour, Chapman, Fairchild, Gross, Van Tyne, Standley, and many others. Dr. F. M. Chapman's book, "My Tropical Air Castle," dealing with some of his studies there, gives a beautiful picture of what nature in the tropics may mean to a devoted student. Barro Colorado Island promises to become a world-famous center of scientific inspiration and research.

A LAST-MINUTE ADDITION

In the many consecutive seasons that Dr. Chapman has occupied his comfortable little cottage on Barro Colorado Island, I have received from him interesting letters, giving an account of his hermitlike life in that temporary abiding place. By a coincidence, he sent me under date of January 24, 1935, a letter that reached me the very day this manuscript was to be sent to the printers. I take the opportunity of quoting a paragraph in concluding my narrative relating to our most southerly possession.

Photograph by Dr. Frank R. Chapman

AN OCELOT FOLLOWS A TRAIL THROUGH THE JUNGLE

This most beautiful of the medium-sized cats is a nocturnal forest dweller that subsists largely on birds and monkeys. Although a few have been tamed, ocelots are not usually dependable in captivity. This is another one of Doctor Chapman's triumphs on Barro Colorado (see NATIONAL GEOGRAPHIC MAGAZINE, September, 1927). It illustrates once more the value of the automatic flashlight in picturing nocturnal animals too elusive to be photographed in the daytime.

"A letter from you always recalls the many good times we have had together. Would that we could repeat them, but you can't have your cake and eat it, too. I am much better though I can't go very far, but you don't have to do that to see things here. Tonight, more than 20 howling monkeys are sleeping in the trees over my house. They have been there since noon and are an unending source of interest. A neighboring Almendro tree has had half-a-dozen coatis in it, and the one that I call Jose greets me daily and has revealed a sur-prising degree of intelligence. I have made almost 500 feet of motion films of him."

This brief quotation terminates an account of a great accomplishment in Central America—where, by reason of skill and persistence, the western hemisphere has been severed into two nearly equal parts by the building and maintenance of a continuous waterway between the two oceans. By the creation of Gatun Lake, it is now possible to circumnavigate the northern continent without putting a foot on shore.

CHAPTER XII

In the Yellowstone National Park Region

IN 1904, while a member of the Committee on Public Lands of the Fifty-eighth Congress, I went West to look into the advisability of recommending that Congress extend Yellowstone Park to include possibly Jackson Lake and the Teton Mountains in northern Wyoming, these areas then being parts of a national forest. Inclusion of the Tetons would not only add a region of singular beauty and grandeur to the park area, but enlarge both the summer and the winter ranges for the increasing bands of big-game animals.

When I entered the park at Gardiner, I called on my old friend, the military superintendent, Colonel (afterward General) S. B. M. Young, who was quartered near the Mammoth Hot Springs Hotel. He was favorably disposed toward the proposed southern extension of the park, and many others interested in the park's development took a similar attitude.

On my return to Washington, Congressman Mondell, of Wyoming, who was also a member of the Public Lands Committee, vigorously objected to my project on the grounds that most of Yellowstone Park had been created out of public lands in Wyoming when it was a territory, and that after it became a State considerable parts of it had been set aside as national forests. His constituents had become rebellious at the idea of any further encroachments on the State lands.

STATE GAME REFUGE ESTABLISHED

The affair resulted in a compromise by which the Wyoming Representative agreed to recommend that the State Legislature should establish a State game refuge on the national forest just south of the park, in which the game would have the same protection as was contemplated in the proposed legislation by Congress. The year following this agreement the Wyoming Legislature created a large game reservation which covered much of the area in question. Thus was consummated my plan to give needed protection to big-game animals south of the park boundary.

Meanwhile I had become interested in the reports that a few moose could be found throughout the year in the Upper Yellowstone Valley and about Bridger Lake in northern Wyoming. They were said to have lived long there in seclusion at an elevation of some 8,000 feet. Seton had recorded seeing moose in the park in 1897. Colonel Young told me that some of his rangers had reported seeing several at the southwestern end of the park, and he hoped I would return the following year to learn something more about an animal that had generally been regarded as extinct in the Rocky Mountains south of Canada. The project appealed to me and I determined to return when a propitious time arrived.

THE GRAND TETON NATIONAL PARK

In 1928 Congress established the Grand Teton National Park, thus carrying out a part of the recommendations I made after visiting that region in 1904. In 1929 President Hoover appointed a commission to examine the area lying south of the southeastern part of Yellowstone National Park and known as the Thoroughfare Country, including Bridger Lake, to determine the desirability of adding it to the park. The committee visited the area in the summer of 1929 and unanimously recommended that it be taken into the park.

A bill to accomplish this result was introduced in Congress but was not acted upon. Public sentiment, however, is so favorable generally to the project that little doubt exists that the extension will be made. With this accomplishment the recommendations I made after a personal examination of all that region will have been carried out after a lapse of more than 25 years.

These additions to the national park system will be of the greatest value not only in preserving some of the finest scenery of that region, but also in helping to perpetuate the Rocky Mountain moose, the elk, and other large and small game.

After concluding in the autumn of 1904 the inquiry regarding the park extension, I set out with my guide, John Hammer, for a 10 days' shooting and photographing trip to Henry Lake in northeastern Idaho, intending to fill in the odd hours with the excellent trout fishing. On the way down the Madison River from Yellowstone Park we stopped at a tourist camp for lunch.

A MOUNTAIN WOODCHUCK WAS MET

This stockily built little animal, common in the Yellowstone region, looms up in the photograph almost like a small bear.

I saw two brown bears, one very large, leaving the woods and coming toward us.

A camp attendant said that these animals came daily for their lunch, and were particularly fond of crackers covered with jam. They appeared to be very friendly, and before leaving I asked John to pose for a picture with a big bear standing erect and eating from his hand.

He demurred at this, saying that he "didn't want to make any nearer acquaintance with such brutes."

POSING WITH A BIG BEAR

I promptly offered to be a substitute. With John handling the camera I held aloft a choice morsel, and the larger bear stood up on its hind legs beside me. At that moment the sun was covered by a passing cloud, and I asked John to wait for better light. As he replied, "All right," the bear dropped to its front feet and made for him with a rush. He quickly picked up an imaginary stone and made a threatening gesture; whereupon the bear growled and departed for the woods. When I asked the substitute photographer how he had the presence of mind to make such a demon-stration, he replied that he had been watching these animals for an hour, and had noticed that whenever one of them came too close to the kitchen tent the cook would chase it away by threatening to throw something at it.

The only explanation of the bear's rush seemed to be that he regarded John's answer to me as an order not to give it anything. This is a question for an animal psychologist to decide. Had John started to run, he would probably have been pulled down and given a cuff or two or something worse.

JOHN WAS SUSPICIOUS OF BEARS

Two weeks later we read in the press of two brown bears that had broken into a hotel cache in Yellowstone Park and badly injured the caretaker when he tried to drive them away. John's comment was, "So you see that your two brownies were not such nice companions after all."

Such occurrences are extremely rare in any of the national parks; for whenever one of the bears loses its fear of man and threatens serious injury to property or visitors, it is promptly killed by park rangers.

A drive of 18 miles brought us within sight of Henry Lake, nestling in an amphitheater among the hills at an altitude of 6,500 feet. Among the early pioneers located there were Vic Smith and Dick Rock, noted big-game hunters and guides. About 1888 my uncle, Major Kennedy, while on a hunting trip, had made his headquarters with Dick Rock. He was so impressed with the solitude, the beautiful scenery, the exhilarating climate, and the great variety of game, that in 1890 he organized a small club composed of friends from the East. Among these were Col. W. R. Howe, Col. John Pitcher, Emerson Hough, Doctor Penrose, my classmate Carter Harrison, and my brother.

Soon after the clubhouse was built, Dick Rock met a tragic death by being impaled on the horns of one of the supposedly tame buffaloes in the corral near his cabin. This affords another link in the chain of evidence that male deer, elks, or buffaloes, if kept long enough in confinement to lose their fear of man, are much more dangerous than the carnivorous beasts such as the wolf, bear, or puma at large in the wilderness.

Henry Lake, three miles long and more than two miles wide, is shallow and fringed with marshes. It is much frequented by

THE BEAUTIFUL TERRACE AT MAMMOTH HOT SPRINGS WAS THE FIRST
PHENOMENON PHOTOGRAPHED

After leaving Gardiner, at the northern entrance to Yellowstone Park, the author and his
companions soon reached the Mammoth Hot Springs Hotel, opposite which was the residence
of the military superintendent.

wild fowl, and contains an abundance of
brown mountain trout. In its inlet streams
are speckled trout. In the south fork of the
Madison River, a short distance away,
grayling afforded me excellent sport, but in
recent years this species has become much
reduced by excessive fishing. The ducks
breeding at the lake were canvasbacks, mallards, blue-winged teals, and lesser scaups.

At the time of our visit several pairs of
trumpeter swans rearing their young on the
lake were rigidly protected in an endeavor
to help restore this stately bird in its former
western range. Sometimes an early freeze
in the beginning of September, and before

the opening of the shooting season, would
compel the locally reared birds to take wing
for the South, but soon the waters would
open again and ducks from lower altitudes
to the northward would continue to come
until well into November.

GROUSE AND SAGE HENS ABUNDANT

On the foothills about the lake were
grouse of several species, including the blue,
sharp-tailed, and ruffed, and on the plains
a short distance to the south were great
numbers of sage hens. The upland birds
afforded a pleasing diversion in shooting and
a chance to stretch one's legs after a day or

A COYOTE PAUSED ON AN IDAHO HILLSIDE

This industrious rover was so intent on his hunt for small game in the low vegetation that he was
unaware of the author's presence until the click of the camera drew his attention.

two in the duck blind, and besides made a welcome addition to the table.

After hunting a few days with the gun, I tried the camera for photographing waterfowl in flight, for I had just begun to take an interest in this method of wing shooting (see page 299). The most successful of these efforts were pictures of avocets on the wing with the mountains in the background.

One night John and I skirted the shore in search of muskrats and found them plentiful, for their pelts had not then advanced sufficiently in value to interest the western trapper. Whenever the flashlight was fired, these little animals plunged squeaking into the water, believing perhaps that the guns that boomed in the daytime had now been turned on them. When we took these night trips, the bushes at the edge of the water were sparkling with frost; for at this elevation there is a great contrast between the temperatures of day and night.

With the completion of the railroad to the western entrance to the park, many of the larger game animals about Henry Lake moved into safer regions. The overflow of elk and deer each fall from the park, how-

ever, still continues to afford the settler or visiting sportsman excellent shooting.

This is a good example of what these great game reservoirs may mean. When only the surplus stags are killed, the main herd remains intact. It can be sustained indefinitely except when severe winters or other harmful conditions cause such a loss, that the surrounding States must modify their open seasons in order to maintain a proper breeding stock.

JAKE BROWN'S FOXGLOVES STILL GREW AT HENRY LAKE

In front of the clubhouse I noticed a thrifty row of foxgloves raised from seed brought there 10 years before by my old guide, Jake Brown. These were a sad reminder of what we, at that time, considered his desperate and ill-fated trip overland toward Alaska. Before leaving for the East, I collected some of the ripening seeds, and later planted them about the Michigan camp, from which their ancestors had made a trip to the Rockies nearly a decade before.

The information gathered concerning the moose in the Upper Yellowstone and Bridger Lake country during my brief trip

MOUNTAIN MUSKRATS WERE WILLING NIGHT SITTERS

The author hesitated about taking flashlight pictures here and risking alarming the wild ducks on the lake, but the muskrats were too bold and inviting to resist.

to that region in 1904 lingered with me. It always seemed to carry an element of mystery. Many inquiries about these animals and the character of their antlers elicited little information from naturalists and sportsmen in Washington and elsewhere.

The only specimen from the region that I found was a fine mounted head belonging to Carl Rungius. It now is a part of the collection of heads at the New York Zoological Park. Probably other heads from the same region existed in private possession or in museums, but most of them no doubt had passed beyond the possibility of positive identification.

Scientific institutions, such as the National Museum, had few specimens and no data bearing on the detailed distribution or on the number existing in the Rocky Mountains south of Canada. Information came to me that in 1906 moose had been seen about Bridger Lake, Wyoming, a few miles south of the southeastern corner of Yellowstone National Park, and I determined to try to learn the facts about them.

An examination of the map indicated several possible routes to the district in question—one by the way of eastern Wyoming

and Thoroughfare Creek; another from Jackson Hole through Two Ocean Pass; and a third by way of the park and up the Upper Yellowstone River by pack train or possibly by canoe. The last-named route I selected as being the most feasible for carrying the heavy outfit I needed.

Wishing to avoid dependence upon a pack train in the mountains, and believing from information received that the Upper Yellowstone was navigable for a light boat early in the summer, I took with me a large collapsible canvas canoe capable of carrying three persons and more than a thousand pounds of outfit.

A REVOLVER IN THE PACK

At that time Yellowstone National Park was under military supervision, with headquarters at the Mammoth Hot Springs. Upon our arrival there late in July, 1908, our party was registered for Wyoming via the park. It then developed that somewhere in my outfit there was a little 32-caliber revolver. To the request that it be produced and sealed I demurred, simply because I had no idea where it was and to search for it might mean the removal of everything from the wagon. A few minutes later I looked up Colonel Young, the superintendent, and after making the proper stipulations, he directed that the outfit be passed just as it was. What later effect the carrying of this unsealed revolver had must be judged by the readers.

The second morning out, as our team was laboriously traveling up a long hill between the Grand Canyon and Yellowstone Lake, we met two persons on horseback approaching at a rapid gait. As they were passing I recognized them as Nicholas Longworth, a colleague in the 58th Congress, and his wife, the former Alice Roosevelt. I touched my hat and shouted a greeting. Very soon afterward I heard behind me the sound of approaching hoofs, and turning saw Longworth returning.

SPEAKER LONGWORTH GUESSES RIGHT

We checked our team, and he rode alongside while we had a friendly visit. Before he left us, he said he had guessed who had given the greeting and had come back to verify his guess.

That afternoon we arrived at the lake, where we received a hearty greeting from Billy Hofer, the well-known guide. He was opening a package of Roman candles to be used in firing at the bears, whose ever-increasing depredations made the running of an outfitting store an unprofitable undertaking.

That night I slept in one corner of a canvas-covered storehouse. Noticing a large ragged hole in the wall, I told Hofer that there seemed to be no trouble about ventilation.

He replied, "I think not, and you may have more air before morning, because that hole was made by a black bear night before last, when he butted in and went off with one of my biggest hams."

My Michigan guide thought we ought to sleep on an upper shelf, but John never did have much use for bears on the hoof.

In the morning I arranged with Billy Hofer, who was the controlling spirit in a boat company recently granted privileges for public transportation on the lake, to use one of his larger launches to convey me to the southeast corner of this beautiful body of water. Thence I planned to ascend the Upper Yellowstone to Bridger Lake in Wyoming.

Before leaving for the West I had made inquiry through the appropriate department in Washington for information regarding the navigable character of the Upper Yellowstone and had received assurances there, as well as from the authorities at the park headquarters, that the upper river was without falls or rapids and carried sufficient water for a heavily laden canoe. Whether the current was swift or not, no one seemed to know, for so far as had been reported, no boat or canoe had ever ascended it.

Besides my Lake Superior guide, I took with me George Farrell, of Gardiner, who for 25 years had been a hunter, guide, and park attaché. He was believed to have more knowledge of the country north of the Tetons than any one else then available.

On July 23 we left the north end of Yellowstone Lake with Mr. Sargent, one of Hofer's right-hand men, at the wheel. When we were midway in the lake, a heavy southwester came up and thoroughly tested the seaworthy character of the launch. Just before the storm broke I had a momentary sight of the Tetons in the southwest, and recalled that four years previously I had obtained a view of these pinnacles from the opposite side at Henry Lake in northeastern Idaho.

To keep out of the trough of the sea, we were compelled to bear several points west of our destination, and after reaching the lee of the shore, we turned and ran into the southeast bay near the delta of the Upper Yellowstone. There we planned to camp for a couple of days before attempting to ascend the river.

VAST PELICAN FLOCKS LOOK LIKE SNOW FIELDS

As we entered this bay, I noticed the two small reeflike Molly Islands were covered with what looked like windrows of snow. The glass disclosed these patches to be hundreds of great white pelicans standing erect in solid columns or scattered here and there on their nests. The island lying nearer to us was almost wholly occupied by a colony of gulls and terns. We hurried by, intent on making camp before dark, hoping at a later opportunity to examine these birds at closer range.

As we tossed our equipment ashore, I was surprised to hear Sargent say that so far as he knew we were the first in 14 years to come by boat into this end of the lake, and that the only times this part of the lake came under the eyes of man was when park scouts or hunting parties bound for

AVOCETS FLY OVER HENRY LAKE, IDAHO

Jackson's Hole were traveling along the trail that skirts the eastern shore of the lake and follows the hills bounding the eastern valley of the river to Two Ocean Pass.

On the following days I discovered that his description of a perfect wilderness was true. In our explorations along shore, into the various lagoons, and up the smaller streams, we found no trace of a camp or other evidences of man except a few signs of Government survey camps occupied many years before.

THE BULL ELK KEPT ALOOF

The first night we camped by a bay on a small promontory facing the broad delta of the Yellowstone. The canvas boat was set up and strengthened by hardwood strips cut for the purpose. As the sun descended and the wind fell, hundreds of elks, cows, and calves sauntered down from the lower hills to feed on the swamp grass of the valley; but not an adult bull was seen then or later on the trip. During the midsummer period of antler growth they remain secluded among the highest timber.

The wild fowl had nearly completed their nesting, and many species were beginning to gather along the sand bars, mud flats, and grassy islands, which largely occupy the shore line of that part of the bay lying between the great ridges forming the barriers of Yellowstone River. I saw fully a hundred families of wild geese, the young of which were then in the stage known as flappers. It would have been no trick at all to have tender goslings on our bill of fare had we wished to violate the rules of the park and the ethics of sportsmanship.

We made several pleasant trips to the pelican and gull islands to obtain photographs of the breeding colonies. Although these birds had long been familiar to those who follow the great driveway along the Lower Yellowstone at the north end of the lake, I had been unable to find anyone who knew where they bred. It was assumed that they occupied an island somewhere in the southerly end of Yellowstone Lake.

Yellowstone Lake is one of the largest bodies of fresh water for its altitude (7,741 feet) in the world; and while its northwestern shore is traversed each summer by probably more tourists than any other mountain lake, it is less frequented at the upper end than any of the others.

Such a condition is due to the park's having been established so long ago, and to the scarcity of big-game hunters coming over the mountains to the southern boundary.

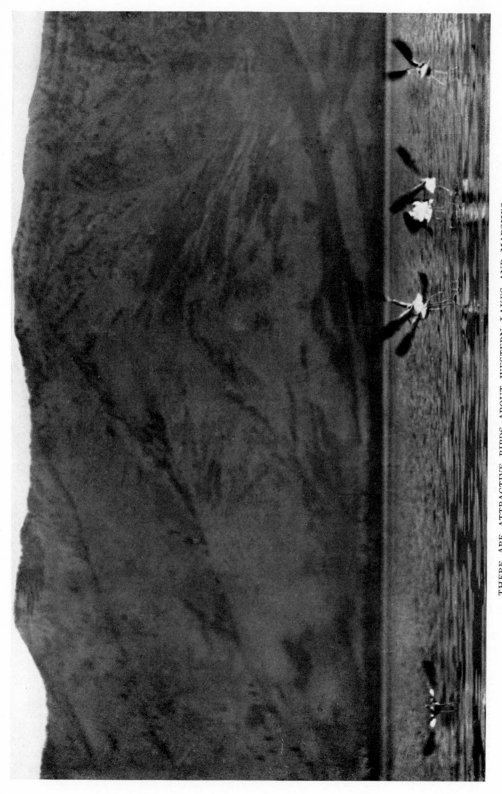

THERE ARE ATTRACTIVE BIRDS ABOUT WESTERN LAKES AND MARSHES

About the lakes of Idaho and Utah, avocets are numerous. Their long necks and legs, contrasting black and white plumage, and shrill cries attract attention.

DELTA OF THE UPPER YELLOWSTONE RIVER

To the right is a bit of shore line of Yellowstone Lake, and in the middle are some ponds in which several small black objects indicate feeding moose.

A GOLDEN-MANTLED MARMOT FEELS AT HOME IN A LOG PILE

This western woodchuck, which abounds everywhere along mountain trails, is similar in general appearance and habits to the familiar animal of the Eastern States.

The same game can be found lower down, and the State of Wyoming has made the adjoining national forests into a State game refuge. With no hunters passing either way through the valley, this area has lapsed into an almost untrodden wilderness.

Occasionally a Government scout follows a blazed pony trail on the eastern foothills of the valley, but such persons remain mostly out of sight of the timbered bottom lands teeming with unseen and uncounted game. Since there are here none of the more spectacular manifestations of nature, so abundant elsewhere in the park, inducement has been lacking to divert into this distant corner the great flood of tourists that annually sweep along a circular journey in and out of the park.

THE MOUTH OF THE YELLOWSTONE

On the morning of July 26 we loaded our canvas canoe for the start, but lost some time trying to find the real mouth of the Yellowstone River, which lies well under the eastern chain of mountains and has several side channels and deep bays. Two other small streams that enter the bay near it added to our difficulty. While we were paddling about, we saw thousands of geese and ducks, mostly females with their broods, and all as wild and unapproachable is if they were in a less secure retreat.

Migrating wild fowl shot at during eight or nine months of each year do not lose their dread of man in the short nesting period unless they are brought into continuous contact with those who do not kill, as is the case in the many ponds alongside the park highways, where the birds sit preening themselves as the heavily laden coaches rattle by. The same is true of game animals, for those about the tourist hotels are frequently tamer than domestic stock, whereas those in the more secluded parts of the park are the wildest of the wild.

After entering the river, we soon found the current much swifter than we had expected. Looked at casually from a distant trail on the mountain side, the river appears to be a sluggish stream, but in the entire trip we found not one foot of slack water, although by those voyaging in a trim cedar canoe the stream would by no means be considered a swift one.

We used a pair of very light pine oars and two paddles, rather frail because of their being jointed with brass ferrules. One could not apply more than half strength to the work. By 11 o'clock we had gone several miles up the river, at an estimated speed of about a mile and a half an hour, and since Bridger Lake was about 35 miles distant the outlook was rather discouraging.

By an oversight I had neglected to bring my long tracking line, which I had so often (page 417) used in the swift waters of Canada, Newfoundland, and elsewhere. Our short line, about 20 feet long, however, helped us work around dangerous log jams.

Since neither of my two guides had ever handled a long pole while standing erect in a canoe, I knew it was useless with the poor material available to attempt to pole the heavily laden canoe up the river. Although I had had some experience in handling a pole, I hardly felt like undertaking the task in this case. A large and cumbrous canvas canoe, laden as this one was, makes difficult work for even the strongest and most experienced canoeman.

CHARGED BY A SILVER-TIP GRIZZLY

While I was taking advantage of the opportunity when we were stranded on a sand bar to look at a favorite crossing place for elk, I suddenly saw a large animal leap out of the bushes at the head of the bar and come down toward us. It proved to be an immense silver-tip grizzly. Since he was fully 100 yards away, none of us thought other than that he was badly frightened, probably by our scent circling in behind him. This belief was but momentary, for with his head up and eyes on us, he obviously intended visiting the stranded boat.

Aside from my exclamation, "Look ahead," we were silent and motionless. When the bear was 40 yards away, I managed to get hold of the small revolver in a bag at my feet, and in desperation fired two shots over his head; but on he came, probably not having heard the slight crack of the smokeless powder. I fired the third shot at his exposed chest when he was only a dozen yards away, and saw by a swirl of the heavy hair to the right that the misdirected bullet had creased his side.

At the same instant the Montana guide, Farrell, gave one of his mountain war whoops and brandished an oar as threateningly as possible. The bear stopped, swung his head from side to side, with his small eyes fixed for the first time intently on the boat, and then with a quick whirl, which

sent the loose gravel in every direction, he put for the bank and into the heavy bushes at a gait that did our hearts good.

Although relieved by the sudden change in the situation, we lost no time in shoving out into the deeper water and were soon on the way again. Undoubtedly, there are many, either in good faith or under the stress of temptation to magnify the perils of the wilderness, who would attribute to this bear a deliberate attempt to kill us, and say that he was deterred only by the apparently courageous reception he met.

Such, in my opinion, was not the case at all. Both sides were equally frightened and both labored under a misapprehension.

The animal had been waiting to catch calf elk when they were swimming the swift waters at the crossing. From his ambush on the bank he had heard a commotion down the river, and, hampered by the notoriously poor eyesight of all bears, he had mistaken our brown canvas coats and the splashing paddles for the game he sought.

Had he meant to harm us, the sting of the pistol bullet, and the accompanying demonstration would have had no effect beyond aggravating his rage. That he had run into an unexpected gathering, and that it was purely "a case of mistaken identity," his hasty retreat sufficiently proved. The day has gone when any bear in any part of the United States will wantonly attack a man when it is unmolested.

At the next bend, however, as a matter of precaution, we took the axes out from under the outfit and cut a heavy pole for use in "a crack on the nose," which, according to Farrell, an old-time bear hunter, is worth a dozen random rifle shots.

THE AUTHOR ON THE TOW LINE

We continued to struggle against the swift current, but our progress was slow. It seemed now that the only way that we could make more speed was for me to get out of the canoe and thus lighten the bow to a material degree, and with the 20-foot rope occasionally pull the boat against the swift water at some of the bends. Since the rest of the crew had their axes and the club, I, of course, took the revolver ashore with me, Farrell remarking, I thought with a little sarcasm, "You might have occasion to use it in another case of 'mistaken identity.'"

At one place, while walking in thick brush a hundred yards ahead of the canoe, I heard a heavy animal crashing toward me

IT BELONGS TO THE TIN-CAN BRIGADE

Grizzly, brown, and black bears daily sort over the garbage piles back of the park hotels, where thousands of pictures are taken of them. When these animals are en route along wooded trails to the garbage field, they are not infrequently described as "wild bears in their natural habitat." Such statements are very misleading.

through the bushes on my immediate left. My theory of a few minutes before somehow vanished, and, jumping to the edge of the bank, I drew the revolver and faced the approaching animal. I intended in case it was a grizzly to fire a couple of bullets into him and then take the revolver between my teeth, jump into the swift current, and swim down to the canoe below me.

As I stood with the revolver pointed at the quivering bushes, out came the head of a large cow elk, which appeared as ill pleased as I was gratified at the encounter. She turned and rushed along the bank, jumped into the stream, and swam across, much to the amusement of my two guides, who had been watching the pantomime from below.

Almost at once I saw some moose tracks, and as I continued on hardly a mud flat was without them. At the time this came as a surprise, for, according to the park authorities, there were not supposed to be more than a dozen moose in the entire park. An opening in a wood near by suggested a pond, with water probably warm enough for aquatic vegetation. I approached cautiously and found just such a place, with a big, black-colored bull moose in the midst of a feast.

Heretofore I had made a rule not to photograph animals in public parks or game reservations of any kind, because the lack of skill needed to take these half-tame creatures makes such a pastime as unattractive with the camera as with the gun, and because many of these animals have lost their wild characteristics.

NO PARK "WILD ANIMAL" PICTURES

This wary and uncontaminated creature suggested, of course, an exception; but since it is always difficult to draw the line, I decided that the park line should still be the one to go by. After noting the color and size of the animal and the shape of the antlers, I returned to the river, hoping that after we crossed the boundary we might have another chance at an animal supposedly rare in the mountain States.

The next afternoon I walked within 50 feet of a large bull moose that, lying half

A BROWN BEAR EYES HOFER'S STORE AT THE LAKE

Roman candles were used to deter these marauders during their night raids (see text, page 298).

asleep at the lower end of a small island, did not rise until the canoe came in sight. Then another bull got up farther back, and as they ran off they were joined by a cow— one of the few instances in which I have seen the female consorting with bulls in midsummer.

Before reaching the lake on the return trip several days later, I saw six more bulls and another cow. This made a total of 11 seen along the swift, cold waters of the Yellowstone. Doubtless a visit to some of the small ponds and lakes in the valley, where summer food abounded, would have shown many more. This area was not more than eight miles in extent in a direct line, although because of its circuitous course it was probably 16 miles by the river.

BOTH OARS BROKEN

On the third day our ascent of the river was definitely ended when both oars broke. Although mended and wound with copper wire, they became useless in combating the heavy currents we had to conquer at every turn of the river. At this season the warm weather was melting the last of the snow drifts on the higher summits, and although the high water was favorable for reaching

Bridger Lake, the current proved too strong to be surmounted by our outfit. In my visits of succeeding years, all of which occurred later in the season, low water became an equal impediment.

The comparative abundance of moose in this isolated valley was now no longer a matter of speculation. If I was able to return the following year, it would be for the purpose of estimating their numbers and of studying their peculiarities.

When on our return we passed the sand bar where the bear had greeted us silence was the order of the day, and we glided by with all the armament within easy reach. At the next bend the canoe nearly ran into a band of 50 elks, lying drowsily in the sun on a small, sandy island, with two or three old cows standing guard. Evidently the big silver-tip had left the neighborhood.

The night of August 4 we made camp under a high mountain at the southeast corner of the lake. I had previously arranged that the canoe should go down the shore a distance of 10 or 12 miles to Signal Point, where a big fire was to be built after dark at an elevation sufficiently high to be seen 20 miles diagonally across the lake. On the following afternoon the launch was

THERE IS A BREEDING PLACE FOR WHITE PELICANS ON YELLOWSTONE LAKE

Molly Island is marked by the white line of birds on it. The high, forested mountains in the background make an impressive setting for their nursery.

WHITE PELICANS ON YELLOWSTONE LAKE TAKE REFUGE FROM INVADERS OF THEIR BREEDING PLACE

In 1920 and 1927 the author saw hundreds of these birds wintering along the Gulf coast. In 1928 and subsequent springs a colony of them has been found nesting on a small island off the Texas coast, far to the southward of their usual breeding grounds.

to come for us, for it was not considered safe to cross this deep, wind-raked lake in a canvas canoe.

Now occurred the second episode in bear antics, which is best detailed from the camp notebook.

"Last night we had a surprise. I was awakened at 9 o'clock by loud yells from the guides' tent, followed by cries of 'Bear! bear! bear!' Seizing the little revolver and hurrying out of the tent, I looked about in the moonlight, but saw nothing. Approaching the guides' tent, I asked what was wrong. Hammer, who had not yet succeeded in crawling out of his sleeping bag, replied that a big bear had just seized the sack containing all our salt meat and canned goods and had made off with it. An investigation showed this to be true.

"Farrell, perhaps irritated at the idea of going on short rations for two days, declared that my habit of placing bait close to the camp to coax coyotes and other prowlers of the night was responsible for the bear's intrusion. Although, of course, the robber was a black bear, Farrell was of the opinion that it had not developed its thieving habits about any of the tourist hotels. We were more than 30 miles from the nearest one by any land route. He was certain it was not a grizzly, since he had never known one to enter an occupied tent.

A BEAR CHEWED A TIN CAN OF JAM

"The next morning, about 75 yards away from the camp, we found the empty bag, as well as a can that had contained raspberry jam. The contents of the latter had been extracted through perforations made by the animal's large teeth and, though pressed nearly flat, the can was otherwise unbroken.

"On thinking the matter over, I now felt entitled to make one exception to the rule of not photographing animals in the park, and thought that I ought to remain that night for the purpose of taking the bear's picture by flashlight. It was quite certain that the marauder would return in search of another feast.

"The guides, viewing the matter as fun lovers and not as photographers, thought it would be a good joke on the bear. We therefore agreed that the two guides should take one tent and paddle down the shore to Lookout Point, where the signal fire would be built. On the following morning they could return for me in plenty of time to be picked up by the launch.

"After the men had passed out of sight, I began preparations for the coming bombardment. The little table, made of driftwood, in front of the guides' tent, had been left standing, and on this I placed two cameras facing down the elk trail. To a stake 30 feet away I hung some trout, with a string running to the flashlight apparatus. Impatiently I awaited the coming of twilight, sitting for a time on the edge of a hill and watching some moose feeding in ponds a few hundred yards from the river.

PREPARING FOR THE FLASHLIGHT BATTLE

"As the day declined, the light of the nearly full moon became so brilliant that I could see plainly 75 yards down the trail. I was surprised, as time passed, that there had been no signs of the bear, and at half-past 9 decided to lie down in the sleeping bag. I had not been there more than five minutes when a metallic click indicated that a bear or some other animal had pulled the string of the flashlight machine and that it had missed fire. Hastily looking out of the tent, I saw a large, dark animal leisurely devouring the fish, and knew it had already thrown open the shutters of the cameras; but, in the absence of an illuminating flash, the effort was a failure.

"For a minute this was disconcerting, until I recollected that I had a hand-flashlight apparatus, loaded for any emergency, and that by crawling to the cameras I could fire this and get precisely the result that would have been obtained had the other one gone off.

"This plan I attempted to put into execution, but just as my finger was pressing the trigger there came a deep 'waugh' and then the sound of a heavy animal running away. Looking over the cameras, I saw the bear galloping down the elk trail and disappearing around a bend.

"Examining the apparatus, I found that the safety catch had not been withdrawn, and that the firing pin, in striking an intervening piece of steel, had made the click mentioned.

"For several minutes I worked away resetting the shutters and adjusting the string, when I became aware of heavy breathing close by, and in some trepidation looked about, but could see nothing. I raised myself slightly, so that I could see over the stand, and there within five feet of me, standing on its hind feet, was a huge silver-tip grizzly. The bright rays of the moon fell directly upon its head and breast. The little, beady eyes stared at me steadily, the half-open mouth showing a fine set of teeth. This was Farrell's 'black' bear, and my guides were sitting by a glowing fire a dozen miles away!

"To run to the tent to get my revolver and ax seemed a dangerous proceeding, for visible evidence of fear might invite attack from any dangerous animal, wild or domestic.

"An instant later I realized that safety was at hand, for, reaching out, I cautiously picked up the hand flashlight. By shoving this close toward the bear's face and firing it, closing my eyes at the same time, I should blind the animal for several minutes, and in the interim I could reach the tent, even were he disposed to be ill-tempered after such a greeting.

A HISS DIVERTED A BIG GRIZZLY

"Realizing this, I looked at the bear with more composure, trying to figure out the best way of making him depart without alarming him too much. Finally I gave a low, steady hiss. He came down on all fours and, descending the bank, passed through some thick bushes. I heard him walking along the gravelly beach.

"By this time I had made up my mind to give the silver-tip a surprise the next time he came. Removing all the flashlight powder from the hand flash, I added this and some I had in a box to the original load. I placed on top of the powder a large flat stone to increase the speed of the flash and to awaken me by the noise were I asleep, as well as to let the bear know that something was happening.

"Hurrying back to the tent, I reloaded the hand flash, and put the ax and pistol within easy reach. An hour passed. It was 11:30, but no bear appeared. Worn out with continual watching, I once more thought it best to get into the sleeping bag.

"Warned by some presentiment after I had taken off my clothes, I went once more to the front of the tent, and stuck my head out through the narrow opening. I had just got my right eye around far enough to see the cameras when a large shadow appeared to flit across the camera stand, as if the flight of an owl had cut off the direct light of the moon.

"Before this impression had more than suggested itself, there came from the table a dazzling burst of light such as I had never

seen equaled by any bolt of lightning. It shot high into the air and extended on both sides for many feet. Several whirling missiles cut through the pine branches above the tent, and a roar like that of a cannon added to the excitement. An instant later the flat stone came down, striking the edge of the tent.

"My right eye was, for the time, useless; but twisting my head around, I saw with my left eye a large gray object roll down the bank from the camera stand and land in the bushes, where there was a great thrashing about for a moment, and then up the bank came the big silver-tip, headed almost directly for the cameras, and missing them by only a foot or two.

"A yard farther on the bear struck a tall poplar tree with his left shoulder, and the slender tree came to the ground with a crack and a crash. It had been broken off at the base without being uprooted. The animal, tripped and thrown to one side by the collision, rolled over on his back and for a second lay there motionless, with four big feet sticking rigidly up into the air. Then he scrambled up again, and I saw that he was headed in the opposite direction from that in which he had been going. He had turned a complete somersault—something of a feat for an 800-pound animal.

"The bear had now lost all sense of direction, and with another rush he passed the cameras and shot out over the bank, catching with his feet a large bowlder. Bear and rock together went in a heap to the bottom.

THE BEAR TORE UP THE SCENERY

"By this time I was beginning to chuckle. The next move the bear made was a plunge through the fringe of bushes between the elk trail and the lake shore, and 75 yards away I saw him cross into a small gulley. By the rolling of the loose stones and shale I could trace his going up this gulley and, later, his ascent of the mountain slope. Finally all was still.

"Examining the seat of war, I found that the huge flash, placed entirely too near the cameras, had burned most of the leather off the boxes, and little was left of the flashlight machine except the bedplate. The leaves on the overhanging poplars were burned or whitened for a distance of 30 feet. Altogether the place presented a scene of devastation.

"Looking the ground over in front of the cameras, I saw where the bear had made

THE FLASH FAILED PHOTOGRAPHICALLY, BUT PROVED A GOOD BURGLAR ALARM

The nearest tree on the right was knocked down by this silver-tip grizzly when the animal was blinded by the flash (see text, page 308).

the first whirl as the flash exploded, when he was not more than two feet away. While I was gazing from the tent, the bear evidently had been standing erect, possibly wondering whether the bright barrels of the lenses contained raspberry jam like the can he had bitten the night before. As he dropped upon all fours his body had struck the string running from the flashlight to the bait. When the explosion occurred, his head and shoulders must have been within the radius of the flame and fumes.

"Is it, therefore, any wonder that he was surprised at the demonstration? Possibly in his cubhood days he had become aware of the danger of putting his feet in boiling geyser springs, and possibly he had had some sad experiences sniffing into vent holes filled with sulphurous steam. He had never dreamed of anything like this.

"Toward noon I saw the canoe approaching with my two men in it. No sooner had they got within greeting distance than they made inquiries about the bear. As Farrell stepped ashore he asked me if 'Old Blackie' had returned.

"Not answering the question directly, I pointed to the fallen poplar and asked him

whether he had cut down that tree. Replying that that was not the kind of a tree he used for firewood, he walked up to look at it.

"Suddenly bending over the trunk of the tree, he seized a bunch of hair and exclaimed, 'My God! It was a grizzly.'

"I cheerfully assented, and then proceeded to tell the adventures of the night.

"After I had finished, Farrell said: 'I am mighty glad you stayed over, now that you are uninjured, and for one reason. That old devil got just what was coming to him, and even if we do not have much to eat for the next two days, I will never fast with better grace.'"

THE GRIZZLY LEARNED A LESSON

A week later the negative was carefully developed, although I felt certain that it would be a failure because of the close proximity of the bear and the heavy charge. The reproduction of this photograph appears on this page. Although the flash failed photographically, it was a success as a burglar alarm. No one need have fear of camps being invaded again by the singed grizzly of the Upper Yellowstone.

NAVIGATION PRESENTS DIFFICULTIES ON THE UPPER YELLOWSTONE RIVER

While high water made the trip difficult in July, 1908, low water in September, 1909 and 1910, was worse. The canvas canoe had to be pulled up hundreds of such shallows. The author can find no record of a boat's getting up to Bridger Lake, though, doubtless, Indians and trappers got there before 1870.

The great snowy-white pelicans, with broad jet-black wing tips, are among the beautiful and interesting sights about Yellowstone Lake and the neighboring waters. It was our good fortune to find these birds during the last of July on their breeding place upon Molly Island at the southern end of Yellowstone Lake. Most of the young birds were hatched and partly grown at the time we saw them.

THE WHITE PELICAN AND THE YELLOW-
STONE TROUT

These youngsters had a curious habit of gathering into a sheeplike flock when their home was invaded. The old birds presented a magnificent spectacle as they flew away on heavily flapping wings, and were even more impressive as they soared about on outstretched pinions, their gleaming white bodies and black-tipped wings sharply marked against the brilliant blue of the cloudless sky.

The pelicans subsist almost wholly upon the cut-throat trout, known scientifically as *Salmo lewisi*. This is abundant in Yel-

lowstone Lake, where since time immemorial it has been the only fish. Unfortunately, most of the trout are infested with a species of tapeworm, both in the flesh and in the viscera, but those from Pelican Creek are reported to be free from this parasite. Most of the trout in the lake are healthy looking and active, and afford much sport for transient fishermen, many of whom make a catch on the afternoon of their arrival at the lake and have them served that night at the hotel in blissful ignorance of their true condition.

When the trout are cooked there is, of course, no danger in eating them, for the heat destroys the parasite, but our party, like most others staying there any length of time, rarely used them, although now and then we would catch one showing no evidence of infection.

Occasionally we noticed that certain fish had become very gaunt and yellow, looking more like pickerel than trout. It seemed to be the impression among the old-timers that the absence of minnows, crustaceans, and other forms of fish food accounted for the

THEY ARE COMMON ABOUT YELLOWSTONE LAKE

The California gull (*Larus californicus*), in considerable numbers, comes from the Pacific coast to make its summer home about the Yellowstone and other high interior lakes. It is a beautiful bird, adding charm to all places it frequents. Many breed on one of the Molly Islands, near the island occupied by the pelican colony.

condition of such trout, and that continual cannibalism accounted for the general distribution of the tapeworm.

Later investigations, however, indicated that white pelicans were hosts of this worm during one stage of its existence, and it was recommended that all these birds should be killed in order to protect the trout. This announcement caused great concern to the visitors and park officials, for the sight of hundreds of these great white birds soaring overhead or swimming about scooping up the fish in their pouches, was one of the great attractions about these waters.

It was found that none of the fish below the falls were infested, and that in the neighboring lakes, both within the park and beyond the boundaries, the fish were healthy, although they were visited almost daily by pelicans from Yellowstone Lake. This evidence put an end to the proposed slaughter.

One quiet, warm night we visited the white pelican colony on Molly Island, north of the long promontory dividing the south end of Yellowstone Lake. We had already taken a series of daylight pictures of these large and handsome birds, in which

the nearly grown young were shown congregated like flocks of small sheep while the older ones soared overhead.

A NIGHT VISIT TO THE WHITE PELICANS

As we approached the island, the swinging jacklight gave a view of many white forms standing erect like military guards. Before we were close enough to take their photographs the old pelicans were on the wing, but their young remained detached in the vicinity of their nests. Because the young remain close to their birthplace when undisturbed, it is easier for the parents to single them out amid large gatherings and feed them.

After taking several flashlights of the young pelicans we paddled over to a smaller island occupied by breeding gulls and terns, but these birds were even more wary than the adult pelicans. We gave up any further efforts to get photographs and returned to camp, quite satisfied with probably being the first to navigate this wilderness lake under the cover of the night and to witness from a darkened boat the shores unfolding before the jacklight.

THIS BREEDING COLONY OF WHITE PELICANS WAS PHOTOGRAPHED IN YELLOWSTONE LAKE

Until the author entered the southeast arm of Yellowstone Lake in 1908, it was not known whether the pelican nested on the lake or not. From 800 to 1,000 adult birds were there each season. On an adjoining island were gulls and terns.

YOUNG WHITE PELICANS STICK TOGETHER WHEN ALARMED

When a white pelican breeding place is invaded by men, the partly grown young have a sheeplike desire to mass as if for mutual protection, although they are exceedingly helpless.

WHITE PELICANS FLY OVER THEIR BREEDING GROUND

Although a close view of these birds on the ground or water gives the impression of a clumsy, ungainly form; yet on the wing, especially when soaring high with all the ease of an albatross, they present a magnificent spectacle. The jet black wing tips contrast strongly with the uniform snowy white of the remainder of their plumage.

CHAPTER XIII

The Wilderness of the Upper Yellowstone

ALTHOUGH I failed to reach the extreme headwaters of Yellowstone River and Bridger Lake in 1908, I saw so much of interest that I returned to Yellowstone Park late in August, 1909, and again in September, 1910.

When I arrived at Mammoth Hot Springs in 1909, I found that Colonel Young had been replaced by Major Benson, who was greatly interested in the wild life of the park. Colonel Young had urged me to photograph the moose within the park if I failed to get satisfactory results outside its limits. Major Benson also suggested this course as a means of presenting to the public tangible evidence of the existence and abundance of these animals in the area.

MOOSE NOT IN RANGE OF TOURISTS

So far as I could ascertain, not one of the 200,000 people who had visited the park in the preceding 15 years had seen a moose within its boundaries. However numerous moose might become in their chosen haunts, they were beyond the range of the tourists' kodaks.

My guide, John Hammer, and Tom Pearson, one of Billy Hofer's most experienced men, accompanied me on this second trip into the moose country.

On August 30, 1909, smoke curled up from our camp fire on the spot where the year before the robber bear had investigated the flashlight camera on the provision box. The new guide examined the quaking aspen that had been laid low by the bear in his flight from the explosion. A tuft of grizzled hair still adhered to the bark. The guide remarked that this animal might claim to have discovered the fifty-eighth variety of canned goods.

It is significant that on this trip we saw no bears in the wilderness, and that we caught a distant glimpse of just one in the wilds the following year. At the same time dozens of brown, black, and grizzly bears were daily visitors to the garbage dumps behind the park hotels. It was estimated that more than 5,000 photographs were taken of them each season by tourists, at distances varying from 5 to 100 feet.

Ordinarily bears are so wary and secretive that photographing them is an exceedingly difficult task, and I could recall only two good pictures actually taken of them in the wilderness. No sportsman photographer could be interested in big game tamer than domestic stock.

Near the Hofer place two big-game photographers, one of whom had tried with little success to photograph bears in the State of Washington, were bombarding bears, big and little, by daylight and flashlight, with every prospect of exposing several hundred plates within a few days. Such a collection, if truthfully labeled, ought to be valuable and interesting to the general public, and even to sportsmen; for it would illustrate the varying personalities of the animals and their psychological response when their ancient enemy, man, declares a truce and feeds them.

However, photographing bears under such conditions is mere picture taking; it is not *hunting* them with the camera. "A photograph of a Wild Grizzly in His Native Habitat in the Rocky Mountains of Wyoming" may be only a picture of a park mollycoddle bear, and the retoucher's pencil may have been invoked to remove the tin cans from the background.

I once saw seven silver-tip grizzlies within a circle of 20 feet, and the limbs of several adjoining trees were fairly breaking under the weight of black and brown bears and their cubs that had sought the treetops with alacrity upon the coming to the feast of their large and more contentious brethren.

A PHOTOGRAPHER'S DILEMMA

After taking a satisfactory series of pictures in a breeding colony of white pelicans on Molly Island, I decided to use my last roll of films to illustrate the harmlessness of the bears at the garbage pile behind a hotel at the other end of Yellowstone Lake. I gave one of the guards some food that would appeal to the bears, and several of them soon gathered around him, standing on their hind legs and reaching for morsels held aloft.

While I was grinding away on the crank of the camera, one large bear ambled toward me, and I slowly retreated, picturing

Photograph by A. M. Lindsay, Jr.

BRIDGER LAKE LIES IN MOOSE COUNTRY

This little body of water, a few miles south of the park boundary, at the time of the author's visit was the objective of his first expedition to verify that moose had been seen here in 1905.

BEAVERS HAVE BEEN BUSY EVERYWHERE IN UPPER YELLOWSTONE VALLEY

All the small streams entering the upper river were dammed at short intervals by these animals. The plants growing in the beaver ponds were often visited by the moose.

A WIDELY PALMATED ANTLER PROJECTED FROM A SAND BAR

On removal it showed that some of the mountain moose had broad antlers. The author had doubted
that such was the case before he found and examined this specimen (see text, below).

its approach. Alas, I backed into a log,
and came down with a thump, my feet in
the air. The bear evidently regarded the
camera as a lunch box, for he reached
over and tried to take it away from me.
Had not the guard come to my rescue, he
would have succeeded. Another moving-
picture camera should have been in use
recording my dilemma.

ON THE UPPER YELLOWSTONE

On September 1 our party started up
the river in a rowboat and a large canvas
canoe. A mile up the stream we left the
rowboat for use on our return to the lake
in case the canvas canoe should be irrep-
arably damaged by snags in the deeper
places or by the sharp rocks in the shallow
parts of the upper courses of the stream.
From the first our progress was slow, and
even with the aid of a long tracking line we
never exceeded two miles an hour.

We devoted considerable time, of course,
to a careful examination of the surrounding
country to locate moose. The first six
moose that we saw were all bulls, and each
carried the long, narrow antlers of the kind
noted the year before. I had now little

doubt that the moose of this region were
unique in this particular.

On the third day, however, my hasty
judgment was completely reversed. As we
were slowly passing a long stretch of beach,
I noticed projecting several inches above
the sand the broad and well-serrated tip of
what must necessarily be a moose antler of
unusual size. With some effort we finally
drew it out of the packed sand.

The trophy proved to be the right antler
of a big bull. It measured nearly 30 inches
in length, and had a palmation exceeding
15 inches in breadth. In every respect it
resembled a normal antler growth of one
of the larger bulls of lower Canada, Maine,
or Minnesota. With seven inches allowed
for the breadth of the skull between the
burrs, this pair of antlers would have measured more than 50 inches in spread.

The injuries to some of the points were
not the work of rodents, but plainly frac-
tures that had resulted from contests with
other bulls. Since I had never before found
well-preserved antlers in a wooded country,
where rodents were abundant, I assumed
that the intactness of this find was due to
its having been buried in the sand.

THE BULL, COW, AND CALF MOOSE WERE PHOTOGRAPHED WHERE NO ONE HAD BELIEVED THEY EXISTED

There are dozens of ponds and beaver dams in the valley of the Yellowstone, where the warm waters are favorable to the aquatic vegetation which the moose devours. About 1,500 moose were probably living in this, the most populous moose country in America, until they began migrating into the Jackson Hole country, Wyoming.

Late the next afternoon, while fishing in the shadow of a heavy cedar, I noticed two big bulls making their way to the water at the opposite bank. The larger of the two bore wide-spreading antlers of some 30 points. Here again the palmation was extremely broad, and particularly noticeable, since the velvet was nearly gone and the newly exposed surface shone like ivory in the afternoon sun.

The smaller bull also had large and well-formed antlers, but still wholly in the velvet. Later in the same evening we saw, just above our camp, a cow and a four-year-old bull, the latter bearing antlers similar to those we had seen a few hours before. I was now certain that the long, narrow antlers borne by the 15 bulls seen before represented only one type of antlers of the Rocky Mountain moose. This conclusion led to the opinion that a further inspection might disclose other types and intermediate forms.

SHALLOW WATER CAUSES DIFFICULTY

On the fourth day, after passing the last camp of the year before, we began to lose hope of reaching Bridger Lake; for now the water at the widest parts of the river channel was shallow in many places and ran swiftly over gravel bars, causing the canvas canoe to drag heavily on the pebbles and broken rocks. Frequent unloading and repairs were necessary.

At sunset we struck a long, swift stretch of water divided into several channels by temporary islands, and here, in our haste to reach a camping place before dark, we put too much power on the tracking line. To our consternation, we saw the canvas canoe shiver from stem to stern, as an upturned piece of shaly rock cut a two-foot slit in the middle of it.

Hastening into the shallow water, we dragged the half-sinking boat ashore. Our second effort to reach the headwaters of this stream by water was ended. We determined to camp for several days on this part of the river and explore on foot the valley to the southward. Since we had plenty of strong thread and needles, extra canvas, and pitch, John was sure that while we were exploring the valley he could put the canoe into condition for our return.

Next morning, in the midst of a heavy thunderstorm, I walked some miles up the valley and I saw several moose and a great many elk. I walked to within a hundred feet of a large bull moose and a smaller companion. These animals stood looking fixedly at me as I approached them in an open meadow. After I had taken several pictures, the large bull turned and walked off slowly, followed by the younger one. They walked for perhaps a hundred yards and then broke into a run. I ascended a hill near by and traced their course for three miles across the valley without observing any slackening in their speed.

The next afternoon I found this same pair 12 miles to the south. The two animals were so stolid that they could have been shot without any difficulty, and yet when finally alarmed they left for an entirely new range. Such habits distinguish the moose from all our other antlered animals.

Their disposition, however, to keep away from civilization and to live apart from one another except when yarding in the winter, together with the fact that the female moose, unlike the elk and the caribou, usually bears two young at a time, favors the long-continued existence of these strange animals. The immense forest areas that are now covered with second growth because of lumbering or fire provide much better food and shelter for the animals than ever before. With good laws properly enforced, there is no reason why these animals cannot be preserved indefinitely in suitable ranges.

Ascending the higher peaks from time to time, I examined and mapped the river bottom to a point several miles beyond Bridger Lake, which I could see glistening in the deceptive atmosphere of this region, apparently only a few miles away. The trip verified my impressions of the preceding year that the country lying between the south end of the lake and the source of the Yellowstone River was the wildest area of its size in the United States, and that it probably contained the greatest abundance and number of species of animal life wholly uninfluenced by man.

AT THE HEAD OF YELLOWSTONE LAKE

The river delta at the lake is 7,741 feet above sea level and the gradual rise of the river to its headwaters is only about 160 feet in some 20 miles. The valley, walled in on both sides by abruptly sloping mountains, ranging from 1,000 to 3,000 feet in height, is marked here and there on the borders by the entrance of tributary streams. The width of the bottom lands

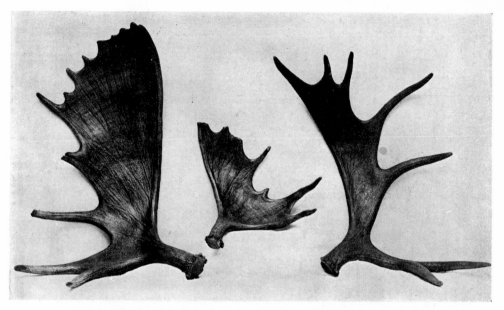

YELLOWSTONE MOOSE ANTLERS ARE OF THREE TYPES

The generally smaller but more varied antlers of this moose may be attributed, in part, to interbreeding, high altitude, the deep snow, and the absence of a dependable supply of nourishing winter forage. Subsequent investigations by Dr. E. W. Nelson, of the Biological Survey, found this segregated animal to be a geographic race of the well-known eastern moose, and it was named *Alces americana shirasi*.

COW AND CALF MOOSE WADE IN A LAGOON

The mother shows a small tassel, or a "bell," under her throat. All the moose on the author's trips to the Yellowstone country were unusually dark in color.

COW MOOSE AND CALF APPEARED UNCONCERNED

These animals, found in a pond back of the south arm, in a richly wooded district of the Upper Yellowstone, stood calmly while the author photographed them.

along the river varies from one to five miles, being greatest at the lower delta and near the park boundary at Thorofare Creek.

The river, extremely sinuous, is double the length of the valley and, like most large mountain streams, at the immediate base of a watershed and adjoining lake basin, it has filled up its valley to a depth of from 25 to 50 feet with silt, so that on a cross-section measurement the bottom land between the foothills is practically on a dead level. The stream is, therefore, now free from falls or any pronounced rapids, although these doubtless occurred prior to the leveling of the river bottom.

THE LAKE ONCE MUCH LONGER

It is quite likely also that in remote years the lake extended much farther up the valley, for the gradual filling in of the southeast arm of the lake with the soil from the mountain sides still continues. It is possible to estimate, from the age of the growing timber, how far this deposition has advanced in the last 50 years or so.

During midsummer and early fall the surface of the river lies from two to six feet below the top of the bank, but a careful examination of the driftwood and of the water marks shows beyond question that during a part of each June the bottom lands, except for a few scattered hummocks, are all under water. The result of this annual overflow had an important bearing upon the results of the expedition.

Yellowstone Lake collects and holds the detritus carried down by the river. The course of the river for a number of miles below the lake is broken by a series of large falls and rapids until it again reaches a country of broad, open valleys.

For several reasons it is important to compare, with special reference to its influence on the different game animals, the vegetation along the valley of the upper river with that of the foothills and higher ranges. The bottom lands of the valley consist in part of numerous meadows covered with luxuriant grass, interspersed among which are hundreds of willow groves and forests of lodge-pole pine. Small lakes and ponds provide many aquatic plants.

THE ROCKY MOUNTAIN JAY IS AS SAUCY AS HIS COUSIN
These relatives of the whiskey-jack of Canada have the same confident ways and soon become familiar about camps high up in the forest.

The confluent branches of the Yellowstone are converted by beaver dams every few hundred yards into slack-water pools, which likewise afford green food and the muddy bottoms sought by the moose in the summer months. However much these animals may loiter about the ponds in midsummer, pulling up tiny sprays of moose grass and other small forms of vegetation, the leaves and twigs of the willow form their staple food during the winter months.

MOOSE STAY IN LOWLANDS

From the foothills to above the timberline grows a great abundance of grasses and many-hued flowers, and lower down forests of pine, red cedar, and the quaking aspens afford a fine summer shelter for the elk and mule deer. The elk may be seen daily descending the slopes to graze on the more tender grasses of the humid bottom lands; but the moose seldom, if ever, leave the bottom land in search of food or cover on the mountain side.

The moose is by nature not a migrant or a wanderer, and unless disturbed by man or forced by shortage of food to change its location, it is content to live throughout its life in any locality where it finds ready subsistence, and where the cover is sufficiently dense to conceal it from its enemies and to protect it from the wintry blasts. This characteristic tendency to contentment is intensified to an extreme degree in the Yellowstone Valley, where, walled in on three sides by high mountains and on the fourth by a large and deep lake, the moose apparently selects a limited area, and travels neither up nor down the river, nor ascends the foothills far above the valley.

With these animals scattered everywhere in the low country we examined fully 20 miles of plateaus and benches just above the river without seeing a moose, a moose track, any droppings, a hair, or a discarded antler of this species. This limitation of the moose mainly to a valley never traveled by canoe and well concealed from the scout trail that follows the wooded slopes to the eastward explains why these animals were then practically unknown to the guides and to sportsmen from the adjoining States.

In the 10 days we devoted more particularly to moose we saw 68 of these animals. Since on my expeditions in other regions I had usually seen five moose at night under the jacklight to one observed in the day-time, it is probable that we should have seen fully 400 in this valley had we traveled about the lakes and ponds at night. Even this large number would have been only a fraction of the total number actually in the moose territory.

Another noteworthy fact was the late-ness of the rutting season of the moose at this high altitude, as indicated by the con-dition of the antlers. Only four bulls out of 35 had their antlers free of velvet at the end of September, whereas the elk, of which I saw some 200 bulls, often had lost their velvet by September 10. When we were leaving the valley, the elk, preparing to migrate, were rapidly assembling in small bands under the charge of individual bulls, but I saw no evidence of mating on the part of the moose, and only a few times did I hear a bull calling. Two weeks later I saw bulls with velvet still on their antlers, but evidently mated—an unusual sight.

MOOSE ANTLERS FOUND INTACT

In the first trip up the valley of the Yellowstone I had found no shed antlers, and my conclusions had been drawn wholly from observations of moose seen along the banks of this river as we endeavored to force our way toward the headwaters. On the second trip, after we had picked up the big antler already referred to, it seemed well to look for additional ones, although I hardly expected to find any others in equally good condition.

Going one afternoon into a part of the valley in which moose were frequently seen, I instructed both guides to keep a sharp lookout for shed antlers. In less than half an hour we found three. Two were of the long, narrow type already mentioned, but the third was entirely different in form, being small and almost as broad as it was long, and shaped somewhat like an open fan. To our delight, each specimen was perfect, and in no wise injured by rodents or exposure.

An hour later we came across four more, one of them almost as large and broad as the one found on the first day, another narrow and long, the third of the fan-shaped type, and the fourth of an inter-mediate form. Two days later we picked up two more. We thus found 10 in all, each one belonging to a different bull. The fact that none of these antlers had been injured by squirrels, porcupines, or mice,

seemed at first very strange, until it finally dawned on us that in these willow bottoms all mice are repelled or destroyed by the annual overflow, and the larger rodents are seldom seen outside the pine thickets.

Loaded down with these heavy trophies, which we would have to transport 100 miles by canoes and wagon and nearly 3,000 miles by rail, we reluctantly gave up the search for more. But since these particular specimens included the three prevailing types represented by the living animals we had already observed, there was perhaps no reason for adding further to the collection.

I had to keep one guide in camp nearly all the time to prevent the antlers from being injured or destroyed by the numerous red squirrels, which, on several occasions, when we were not watching, entered camp and gnawed at the points.

When, on our return trip in the last week of September, we reached the southeast arm of the lake, the two guides climbed to the top of the high ridge behind camp to pre-pare a rousing fire as a signal for Hofer, 25 miles away at the outlet of the lake. He would thus be notified to come with his launch on the day following.

I had intended to join the guides just before the fire was started, but when I was part way up the mountain I saw a cow and a calf moose feeding in a pond a little way below me. While watching them with the aid of a powerful glass, I saw three dark animals on their way to the lake shore. These were followed in five minutes by four more. Even without the aid of the glass, it was easy to see that they were moose, for they appeared to be ebony-black in comparison with the light-colored elk that surrounded them.

SEVENTEEN MOOSE IN SIGHT!

These moose waded out into the shallow waters near the mouth of the Yellowstone and evidently began feeding on water plants. To add to the excitement, three more moose appeared, and almost imme-diately afterward five others, and all these soon ranged themselves along the shore with the first, so that within a radius of less than half a mile I had 17 moose in sight at one time—a picture never before equaled in my 20 years' trips to regions where moose were considered most abundant.

Since I had already added to my list ten animals seen within the area in which these were now feeding, I struck these ten from

THE MAIN CAMP ON PEALE ISLAND WAS IN MOOSE COUNTRY

This beautiful camping place on Southwest Bay, near the head of Yellowstone Lake, was ideal. The animals were all about it by day and by night and often appeared in front of the tents. In the adjoining bay the author saw more cow and calf moose than during two seasons of looking for them on the Upper Yellowstone River.

A BIG SHIRAS MOOSE AND TWO CALVES VISIT A BEAVER POND IN THE UPPER YELLOWSTONE VALLEY

In the background is one of the heavy pine forests which harbor the animals during the winter. The adjacent willow thickets provide nourishing bark after the coming of the deep snows, just as the numerous beaver ponds afford choice summer food. One bull has two of the three prevailing types of antlers, the left being round and long, like that of an elk, while the right one is heavy and broadly palmated.

THE UPPER YELLOWSTONE VALLEY WAS THE HOME OF PROBABLY 1,500 MOOSE

Beneath the ridge, on the opposite side, flow the swift, cold waters of the Yellowstone, and in the foreground is Trail Creek, with two young bull moose feeding close to a beaver house (left foreground). This valley, situated at an elevation of 8,000 feet, is hemmed in by steep ridges varying from 600 to 1,500 feet in height, except where drainage ravines cut back short distances.

my count in order to eliminate any possibility of duplication. Only in the last three days had I seen at close range any bulls with the short, wide antlers of the type mentioned. A comparison of the long, narrow type with the equally long, but broadly palmated type affords no greater contrast, marked as it is, than is seen when either of these forms is compared with the short, broad-antlered type.

Instead, therefore, of the moose of the Rocky Mountains showing characters of unusual uniformity representing a single unique type, as I was at first inclined to believe, it can safely be concluded that they may show greater variations in formation than other members of the species anywhere else in its great range. In other words, extreme isolation and residence in a high altitude may be factors that are working toward a diversity rather than uniformity of antlers.

From the mouth of the St. Lawrence River westward, on both sides of the boundary waters, through Minnesota and Ontario, and in Alaska, I have seen hundreds of moose antlers, but they showed much less divergence in form than was shown by those of the moose of the Upper Yellowstone.

I brought out a dozen of the best antlers, and the residents of Gardiner expressed astonishment at the sight of antlers they had never before seen in Montana, although the animals that had borne them lived barely 50 miles away. This collection, now in the possession of the Biological Survey, represents the three distinct types mentioned, with several intermediate variations.

PREDATORY ANIMALS AND GAME

The third day up the river I ran across the carcass of a cow moose that had been killed some months before by a mountain lion, or by wolves. When we remember that every deer and every elk leaves this high altitude before November, and that the larger predaceous animals must either live upon the young moose or get out of the country, may it not be, with the great increase in the numbers of the moose, that the wolves and mountain lions have found a sufficient food supply to maintain themselves during the winter without now being compelled as formerly to seek the lowlands? Twice we heard coyotes and, on another occasion, timber wolves. Just back of camp

we found the carcasses of two elk, but could not tell by what animal they had been killed.

With the snow more than five feet deep on the level and all the moose segregated into yards each winter far away from the nearest military post or station, the conditions favor destructive raids by the cougar and the wolf. The same peril existed at the head of the valley in Wyoming, where the hunters and trappers were excluded from the forest reserve under a closed season, and no one was in a position to hold in check a class of predaceous animals capable of thriving even under adverse conditions.

WHITE-TAILED DEER

I saw on this trip to the Upper Yellowstone just one white-tailed deer. The whitetail was always uncommon at such elevations, being more at home in the lower, or what might be called the foothill country, where they found food and shelter among the cedars, or among the alders, aspens, willows, and other deciduous growths.

Since the time of my visits it has been reported that they have disappeared from the park. In my opinion this was caused by the invasion of their feeding ground each fall and winter by great bands of elk and smaller numbers of mule deer and moose. This not only deprived them of food but created conditions so unpleasant that they had to seek other haunts.

Our camp on the Upper Yellowstone was enlivened by visits from Rocky Mountain jays. These pale-colored relatives of the whiskey-jack we had become acquainted with in Newfoundland are equally entertaining camp companions, with boldly inquisitive ways. Their habit of helping themselves to any food left unprotected has earned them the common name of "camp robber," and it is true that their performances are often exasperating, even to the most friendly inclined camper.

Here we learned, also, that these birds, like their more northern relatives, nest in February or March, at a time when the winter cold is so intense that the eggs and young in the thick, warm nests must be brooded continuously. The birds' choice of this strange nesting time is difficult to account for, since it occurs not only at the coldest period of the year, but also when the food supply for all wild things is scarcest.

On one trip out from our camp at the southeast corner of the lake I walked along

A BULL ELK APPEARS WITH HIS HAREM OPPOSITE PEALE ISLAND

During the mating season in the fall, the old bulls gather little groups of cows, which they hold together and guard jealously. The master of this herd goes alertly ahead of his consorts.

ELK ABOUND AT THE SOUTH END OF YELLOWSTONE LAKE

Throughout the river valley they occupied the hills above the moose, coming down often to feed in the valley meadows. They ate some willows, almost the sole dependence of the moose in winter. By October 1 they began migrating to lower ground.

INTERCEPTED, IT WONDERED WHAT TO DO

This large bull elk, crossing a narrow inlet leading into Yellowstone Lake, sighted the author awaiting it with his camera; hence its hesitation and look of suspicion.

A COW MOOSE WITH TWIN CALVES WAS A VISITOR AT SOUTHWEST BAY

These animals were not easily frightened, for their presence had never been suspected by the legion of hunters that pursued their kind in the East. It was not until the author penetrated their range and photographed them that the public realized that they were not elk or caribou.

A BIG BULL ELK WALKS HEAD FIRST INTO A FLASHLIGHT STRING

Here the camera and flashlight apparatus faced the opening between the stake and the tree on the right. The animal probably caught the string in his antlers.

the foothills for nearly half a mile to a place where there was an unobstructed view of the river delta below. Near the edge of a steep bank a spring had formed in the clay a small basin that was rimmed with bright-colored moss.

Its clear purity and coolness tempted me to try it. I was surprised to find it a highly charged effervescent water that seemed to surpass in quality any I had tasted before. This little spring proved so attractive that other members of the party visited it daily, and became firm in the belief that there were few if any equaling it in this country.

Its resemblance to Apollinaris water was most striking, and it was far superior in quality to the much exploited spring of that name situated on one of the main highways of the park. This water might be piped and bottled at the spring for the use of the tourists, who would doubtless prize it,

not only on account of its high quality, but because of its origin in one of the subterranean natural laboratories of the park.

A LAST TRIP TO THE UPPER YELLOWSTONE CAMP ON PEALE ISLAND

My last trip to study the Yellowstone moose was made during September and October, 1910. We camped for two weeks on Peale Island, in the long south arm of the lake. This locality proved to be as little frequented by man as that on the other side of the dividing promontory. The island, beautified by a fine growth of trees, made a splendid camping place, from which we could watch moose and elk day after day.

This area seemed to be the nursery of the cow moose, for fully 80 per cent of the 400 moose seen here were cows and calves.

A MOOSE CALF STOOD QUIET FOR A CLOSE-UP

Finding it feeding some distance from its mother, the author approached to within 15 feet in a canvas canoe covered with pine brush. Note its splendid condition and the reflection in the water.

On the second afternoon 21 moose, including two bulls, appeared at one time in the shallow water of the bay, a sight rarely witnessed even in districts where this animal is deemed most abundant.

I think it can be safely said that at that time 1,500 moose were living throughout the year in the valley of the Upper Yellowstone, an area only 20 miles long (see map, page 363). Until a visit is made in midwinter on snowshoes, when the animals have yarded, it will be impossible to estimate the number accurately.

MOOSE ENJOY WINTER SOLITUDE

When the first flurries of snow come in the Upper Yellowstone Valley, and the frost nips the meadow grass, the elk depart for the lower ranges, leaving the moose in their home, where amid snow, ice, and zero weather they live in contented seclusion under the towering crest of the Rockies.

In our ascent of Yellowstone River on the first trip, and in that of 1908, we saw

a total of about 30 cow moose. The total number of calves observed was only three, a number so amazingly small, considering the fact that we were there both in August and September when the calves usually accompany their mothers, that I made a special effort to find one whenever a cow was located. I also examined the runways and beaches for tracks of the young. But all this was to no purpose. What was equally significant, we saw only four yearling moose.

This scarcity of calves caused me to fear that through the depredations of predatory animals or some other cause the young animals were being destroyed to an extent that might have serious consequences to the species here. Fortunately, on the last trip, in 1910, these misgivings were allayed by my discovering many calves concentrated in another locality.

From my first sight of a Rocky Mountain moose to my last trip three years later I was impressed by the darkness of their

A COW ELK TAKES ITS PICTURE AT NIGHT

During the rutting season of the elk, in September, 1910, these animals moved about somewhat at the full of the moon. The camera had been set for moose, but got the best female elk in the author's collection.

pelage. Frequently in bright sunlight I got within less than 100 feet of these animals, and in each case the fur, excepting on the legs, was a dark brown verging on black, in contrast to those I had seen in Minnesota, western Ontario, and New Brunswick. A few years later I was equally surprised by the light reddish-brown color of the moose on the Kenai Peninsula, Alaska, this color so blending with the red soil that it was often hard to distinguish the animals.

NO FOOD PLANTS IN COLD STREAMS

On my first trip up the Yellowstone River I received the impression that in contrast to the moose in most other parts of the country the moose of this region did not rely upon water plants for their summer diet. This impression was doubtless based upon the absence of aquatic plants in the swift, cold waters of the upper river, along the banks of which I saw most of the animals at that time.

On my subsequent visits it became apparent that the moose depended largely upon water plants instead of eating the willows growing along the bottoms, which remained for winter use. To the warm, sluggish pools on tributary streams made by beaver dams, or the large shallow bays at the south end of the lake, moose came throughout much of the day as well as at night. The series of accompanying pictures is practically limited to moose searching for water plants.

One morning I went up the little stream flowing into the lake close under the western hills, where I knew there were many ponds above beaver dams. At the first one I found a large bull moose, a cow, and two vigorous looking calves. Since it was late in September, the mating season had just begun. Most of the time the bull was motionless, not deigning to partake of any food, but uttering low grunts expressive of his courtship.

Concealing myself behind a clump of bushes, I took a seat on the fiber camera box and prepared to get some pictures of the group. The calves were feeding within a few yards of the bull, the cow standing farther away, so that all could not be included in a picture.

After getting several views of the bull and calves, I endeavored to drive the cow into closer contact with the others. This I tried by standing and clapping my hands.

For a moment all the animals looked across the pond and then one calf ran to its mother. With her head up, ears turned forward, and nose twitching to get the scent, she suddenly started for the woods beyond, the calf at her heels. Meanwhile the bull was looking at me stolidly and seemed not to take alarm until he noticed the flight of his partner. Then he swung about, and in a deliberate way moved toward the woods with the other calf in his wake.

As is so often the case under such circumstances, the bull finally broke into a run after making up his mind that this was the safe course. Meanwhile the mother and her detached twin had entered the woods. The other two took a course farther to the south and went into a jack-pine forest a quarter of a mile beyond. I had no means of determining whether the group came together again.

This bull showed a combination of the two prevailing types of antlers, the left antler being long, narrow, and forked something like that of an elk, while the other antler was large and broadly palmated with many points. I saw this eccentricity in antlers further illustrated a week later when I found what looked like a three-year-old bull wading about in a large pond. This animal had a narrow, solitary antler nearly three feet long extending from the center of the head. It resembled the mythological unicorn. Of course, it is possible that one antler had been detached by some sort of an accident; yet the central position of the one the bull bore indicated very strongly that the usual pair had not been present at the beginning of the season.

A MASTER OF AN ELK HAREM

The rut of the elk occurs chiefly in October, and the period of gestation is approximately eight months, the young generally being born in June. On the approach of the rutting season, the clear buglelike call of the bull elk rang from the beautiful parks on the mountain sides as a challenge to his rivals and as a notice to the females that their lord and master was preparing to round up his harem. It was now the mating season of the elk. No more exciting scene can be imagined than the great bulls fighting for supremacy, while the cows and calves stand by with apparent indifference.

I passed the later afternoons studying elk in meadows half a mile to the south of our camp on Peale Island, bringing the animals within easy vision with a powerful pair of binoculars. It was the beginning of the rutting season, and each of the large bulls presided over a herd of docile cows, that with their calves fed unconcernedly, while the bull saw that none wandered too far away and that no rivals interfered.

The elk are the only branch of the deer family in America in which the cows are herded by a master bull during the mating season. One day the largest bull I had yet seen had rounded up about two dozen cows. While the latter grazed, the antlered monarch strode about, never lowering his head for a moment to partake of the tender meadow grass. Finally two cows strayed off, and the bull started to bring them back, but they took to their heels and a chase began across the meadows.

A BULL ELK'S STRATEGY

Soon it was easy to see that the runaways were increasing the distance between themselves and their bulky pursuer. The bull stopped and began nibbling at the grass. The ruse was successful, for the two cows also stopped and began to feed. Gradually the bull made a semicircle until he got beyond them, and drove them back.

A little later there was another getaway, but this time the pursuit led to a heavy forest, where the bull gave up in disgust. At this moment a second large bull came on with a rush, in evident surprise at seeing a ready-made harem without a master.

It now looked as if a battle royal was imminent; I could see the first bull returning to recapture his flock. The interloper, however, was satisfied after detaching half a dozen cows, and departed with his prizes. On reaching the now depleted herd, the old bull evidently decided that it was better to keep what he had than to enter on a chase that might result in the loss of all his family.

Just as darkness was descending an amusing encounter occurred. I had been watching an immature bull taking a mud bath in a wallow near the lake. Rising, covered with a coating of mud, very much as if he had donned a suit of mail, he made for the big bull. The two met head on, and the smaller one was thrown back on his haunches. Then began a pushing match in which the intrepid rival was forced steadily backward until he reached the water. He disengaged his antlers and ran out into the shallow bay, while the victor shook his great head threateningly.

Finally, apparently impressed with the idea that he had put up a pretty good fight, the little bull boldly waded ashore. Then came the knockout, for the big stag made a terrific lunge at him, and down he went full length, remaining motionless and apparently dead. Satisfied with the outcome, the big bull returned to his neglected family as darkness closed on the scene.

That night we argued over the legality, as well as the ethics, of having an elk roast on the following day, for such feasts were proscribed in the park. The next morning, however, there was nothing to be seen of the little bull. We concluded that his motionless form had been only an indication that he was discreetly taking the count in the final round.

Like the caribou, the elk feed mostly during the day, but in the mating season, especially on moonlight nights, they wander about, the bulls bugling as they go. Two automatic flashlights set out for moose one night revealed a big bull elk following the scent and a fine cow, apparently motionless, as her foreleg pressed against the string that ran to the camera (pp. 330 and 332).

Another interesting sight on the meadows opposite the island camp was the rubbing of trees or bushes by the bull elk. The antlers at this time had been entirely free of velvet for more than three weeks, and this "horning," therefore, was not for the purpose of removing the velvet, as so many suppose, but was a masculine demonstration at the beginning of the mating season when dexterity in the use of the antlers would determine which contender should be master of the harem.

BULL ELK FIGHTS AN IMAGINARY FOE

Late one afternoon an unusually large bull elk approached a solitary yellow pine, the lower limbs of which extended nearly to the ground. When within 10 yards, the animal, with head erect, and the massive antlers glistening in the sunlight, eyed the tree carefully, uttering a buglelike note as if challenging an imaginary foe. Then lowering his head he advanced, shoved his antlers among the branches of a lower limb, and twisted them about in a leisurely way. In a few minutes he withdrew a short distance and returned at a more rapid pace. After warming up by several bouts of the imaginary battle, he renewed the attack each time with more vigor. Finally he pushed back a large limb so that it became

A COW MOOSE SPRINGS THE FLASH FOR ITS OWN PICTURE

Unlike the elk and caribou, these animals are confirmed night feeders. This photograph
was taken where a moose trail led from the forest to a number of ponds.

momentarily engaged with one beyond.
This limb snapped back into place and
struck him a severe blow on the nose.

The blow seemed to indicate a foe worthy
of more serious attention. Backing off a
few yards, the bull came on again with a
rush. He pushed the offending limb back
farther and farther, his hind legs sinking
deep into the sand. Suddenly the limb
broke with a crash that I heard across the
bay. Satisfied with having brought to the
ground its erstwhile opponent, the elk
marched off trumpeting its success.

Later in the week another bull approached a clump of willows and shoved
his long, sharply pointed antlers among
them, twisting them to the right and left,
or up and down in a regular movement, but
displaying none of the pugnacity of the previous bull. An examination of the willows
showed much of the bark stripped from the
branches. In this instance the animal may
have been polishing its antlers for future
use rather than testing their strength in a
mock battle.

This sparring and fencing is common to
all our antlered animals at the mating period. Horned animals, too, such as rams,
goats, and domestic cattle often do it. The
males undoubtedly regard their head gear
as armament to settle individual disputes
rather than as purely ornamental appendages.

In the summer months I passed in the
Upper Yellowstone Valley I heard no calling by bull elk. With the coming of the
first frosts in fall, however, their clarion
calls could be heard well up on the mountain side, where they passed the season
while their antlers were in the velvet. It
was a majestic sight to see one of these
great stags standing on some small elevation on the general slope with its noble
crown of antlers glistening in the sun. From
such vantage points with slightly lowered
heads they would send forth their challenge
call to any possible rival.

THE BULL'S BUGLE CALL

These calls begin as low tones and rise
until they reach high, clear buglelike notes,
which quickly end in a series of grunts.
These notes are quite different from the
whistle or snort of the white-tailed deer, or
the bleating of their fawns. It is equally
different from the loud wail of the cow
moose and the guttural response of the bull.

Mr. O. J. Murie, who has made a study
of the elk in the Rocky Mountains, sum-
marizes the notes of young and old thus:

"Elk calves give voice to a squealing call, to which the mother replies in a deeper voice. Adult elk express alarm, concern or curiosity by a sharp bark. Adult bulls in the rutting season, and cows in the spring during the period of parturition, give emotional expression by bugling, most highly specialized in the bulls. Elk calls, for the most part, are an expression of individual feeling and do not appear to be in the nature of direct, conscious communication."

AN ISLAND HAVEN FOR MICE

Our little island was densely populated with mice. Never before had I seen or heard of such a popular gathering place for them. The absence of foxes, coyotes, skunks, and weasels probably accounted for some of the abundance.

Late the first afternoon, just as the sun was setting, I noticed several little red-backed mice feeding on green ground vegetation. They resembled, in shape and color, miniature muskrats. After darkness had descended and the campfire cast a cheerful glow about our tent, there came an ever-increasing number of white-footed mice. These scampered about just like their relatives, whose graceful forms, long ears, and slender tails I had admired in Michigan.

After we had gone to bed the mice indulged in some strange pranks. The tent in use was supported by a pole in front and sloped steeply back to a two-foot wall. There was ample ground space for the three of us, but one could stand erect only at the front of the tent. The covering was thin canvas thoroughly saturated with paraffine. In the daytime the canvas was soft and pliant, but during the chill of a mountain night the surface became stiff and smooth.

We had been in bed only a little while when we heard some odd sounds on the steep slope of the tent. The moon, being nearly full, disclosed small dark forms climbing up to the apex of the tent, turning there, and sliding down the full length of the canvas. They slid as straight as boys on a toboggan slide, and seemed to enjoy the sport quite as much as an otter enjoys its slide on the clay bank of a stream.

This unexpected form of entertainment finally interfered with our rest, so we procured short sticks, and whenever a mouse became visible on the white canvas we would catapult it away. Thus we soon put an end to the evening performance.

At dark each evening we had noticed owls crossing over from the main shore. The presence of the mice suggested the reason. At times there must have been a dozen of these night marauders in the large pine trees back of the tent, but being on a hunt they were unusually silent, and only once did they indulge in vocal expression. On this occasion there seems to have been a family row, or more likely an inter-racial battle, for birds of prey are disposed to maintain exclusive hunting privileges in particular areas.

I became confirmed in this opinion when I found a dead screech owl with a crushed skull. I think it had fallen a victim of the great horned owl, which seemed to be the principal visitor to the island. I had never before found a dead owl except where man would account for it. Undoubtedly, these owls helped to a certain extent to reduce the great annual surplus of mice. Perhaps many of the mice went ashore each winter over the ice, but more probably perished. Otherwise there would have been insufficient food to maintain many of them.

MUSKRATS BUILD RAPIDLY

One morning at Peale Island, I found a pair of muskrats asleep in a newly made nest of grass built in the sheltered space beneath the bottom of the bow of a flat-bottomed rowboat pulled up on shore. On two succeeding nights the boat was pulled up in different places near by, and each following morning a similar new nest had been built under the bow as before.

The material was abundant and handy, and the nests were easily made. These occurrences convinced me that the muskrats in this locality must have the habit of building nests under the shelter of fallen tree trunks or other similar refuge along shore.

CHAPTER XIV

General Notes on the Yellowstone National Park

THE publication in the NATIONAL GEOGRAPHIC MAGAZINE, in July, 1913, and later in *Forest and Stream,* of an account of my experiences with the Yellowstone moose resulted in an unexpected and gratifying sequel. The articles aroused the scientific interest of Dr. E. W. Nelson, and at his suggestion, and with the consent of Governor Joseph M. Carey, of Wyoming, I cooperated in the collecting on the Snake River, a few miles south of the park, of a fine adult bull and cow for the Biological Survey collection in the National Museum at Washington.

Comparison of these with moose from Maine, Nova Scotia, and New Brunswick confirmed Doctor Nelson's idea that the Rocky Mountain animal differs from the typical eastern one and represents a geographic form previously unknown to science. He considerately named the new type for me, *Alces americana shirasi.* The fact that this new race is peculiar to the Yellowstone National Park region gives it special interest to both naturalists and lay visitors to the park and makes its perpetuation highly desirable.

SHORT OPEN SEASON GRANTED ON BULL MOOSE IN WYOMING

During the years that have passed since I first drew the attention of the public to the presence of many moose in the Upper Yellowstone Valley, these animals appear to have increased in numbers. They are now known to occur in much of the southern part of Yellowstone National Park and in the adjacent territory in Wyoming. In winter some descend regularly to Buffalo Fork Valley, and occasionally even wander southward across the Snake River Valley above the Elk Refuge, near Jackson.

They became so numerous in this area south of the park that the Wyoming Legislature in 1921 passed a law authorizing the State Game Commission to declare an open season on them, and under a limited license system to issue up to 100 licenses to kill one bull each season. In later years the number of licenses has been reduced to 50, with one bull allowed to each.

Previously these moose had been under protection for many years, and this protection should continue within the Yellowstone National Park, in which most of them have their homes. Placing an open season on these animals, even in the limited way stated, alarmed many conservationists who were not personally familiar with conditions in the country affected. Among inquiries came a letter, dated November 22, 1927, from Mr. Madison Grant, president of the Boone and Crockett Club. I replied:

OPEN SEASON BENEFICIAL

"The three seasons I devoted to the moose in the Yellowstone region and my familiarity with subsequent events lead me to think that a short season and a kill of 100 bulls will not prove disastrous to the restoration of this fine animal to the adjoining States. There is a limit to the summer and winter food supply for the moose in the Upper Yellowstone, and this I think may have been reached some years ago.

"Unlike the deer on the Kaibab Plateau, Arizona, where all suffered starvation when the food was exhausted and the surrounding desert prevented migration elsewhere, the moose of the Upper Yellowstone have a chance to migrate when gradual starvation threatens. A hundred-dollar license for each bull and the expense of a registered guide mean that practically all of the limited number of bulls permitted to be killed will be from among the big old ones—thus allowing the three and four year old bulls to escape the gun. Consequently the breeding stocks of bulls is ample, probably averaging one for each cow. The death of a bull reduces the herd by only one the next year, whereas the death of one cow with its successive offspring of 10 years means the loss of 65 bulls and 65 cows, as shown by the calculation made by Dr. A. K. Fisher of the Biological Survey at my instance.

"The moose, like the whitetail, averages one and one-half offspring after the second year. This is one of the reasons why moose and deer can be restored more quickly than elk or caribou, which bear only one young annually. Therefore, in view of the fact that hundreds of adult bull moose must be dying each year of old age, it seems only proper that some of these should be killed

PEALE ISLAND IS A PRETTY SPOT IN YELLOWSTONE LAKE

This heavily wooded island, like many others. would be obliterated if the waters should be dammed
at the outlets for commercial purposes.

in those localities where the males are abundant.

"If these views are accepted as reasonable, shooting can be stopped any season when the facts seem to justify it. If, in 1908, there were more than 1,500 moose in the Upper Yellowstone Valley, a very moderate annual increase would be beyond the summer and winter food supply.

THE FOOD SUPPLY A PROBLEM

"These animals stay on the floor of the upper valley throughout the year and do not move to lowlands in fall, as do the elk. I fear that the food shortage is likely to take place in the winter months, for the main supply consists of willows and aspens (much sought by the beaver), and the conifers. When these latter are trimmed beyond reach of the animals and the seedlings are destroyed each year, dangerous conditions must inevitably result.

"It should be borne in mind that there are probably 2,500 moose in the Yellowstone-Wyoming area. This means an annual birth of bulls that should exceed 700. The killing each year of 50, most of which are past their prime, would prove negligible so far as their effect on the maintenance or the continual increase of the rest of the herd is concerned.

"Each year I have become more and more reluctant to favor the killing of any of our game animals in numbers that might endanger their future, but in the present instance sound conservation, together with a fair regard for the interests of sportsmen, seems to warrant a very restricted kill under the Wyoming law. The great game refuges of this country must be largely justified by allowing the taking in the adjoining areas of some of the surplus animals, especially when such killing is limited to males, and above all, when the increasing number of animals threatens the continuance of an adequate food supply."

One of the advantages of Yellowstone National Park, in addition to its size, beauty, and accessibility, is its inclusion of two kinds of country. One section contains the geysers and other strange natural phenomena, well-constructed highways, hotels, and prepared camp sites where the multitude of visitors congregate. The other, mainly in the southern part of the park, is accessible only by launch, canoe, and pack train, by way of the streams, lakes, and borders of valleys, or through rough mountains. The existence of these primitive and unspoiled wilderness areas affords a most interesting contrast in the general utilization of the park.

PERPETUATION OF BIG GAME AND THE YELLOWSTONE PARK

The continued existence of from 25,000 to 40,000 elk within the Yellowstone National Park and adjacent territory is unquestionably due primarily to the protection that has been given them through the establishment and maintenance of the park as a wild-life sanctuary. This is obvious to any one familiar with the fate of big game elsewhere in most parts of the Rocky Mountain region. The same circumstance has enabled the Yellowstone moose to survive and has also perpetuated herds of mountain sheep.

The Yellowstone is the last stand of the rapidly vanishing grizzly bear within the

A PLEASANT VISTA OPENS ACROSS BIG MEADOWS AT THE HEAD OF YELLOWSTONE LAKE

The lower end of this scenic valley would be destroyed if Yellowstone Lake were raised. Thus wild life would suffer hardship, and a fine recreation area would be inundated.

United States. This noble member of our fauna has already gone from most of its former range and is rapidly approaching extinction south of Canada except in this park, where it now outnumbers in population its kind in the rest of the entire country.

To have exerted such a powerful influence is a most interesting and notable accomplishment, for which the park management is to be congratulated. Other national parks and national monuments also are doing their part in the conservation of wild things. In this connection special mention should be made of the favorable effect the establishment of the Olympic National Monument has had in the salvation of the splendid Olympic elk from the destruction that has befallen its kind in most other parts of the Pacific coast region.

With the establishment of refuges for big game it must be kept in mind always that unless such refuges are so situated that the animals have free passage into the surrounding country or the surplus is otherwise controlled, the natural increase will inevitably overstock the area and destroy the limited forage produced. The result

will be starvation just as would be the case if domestic animals were involved.

In many instances even the forage in the areas surrounding the refuges may be too limited to care for the surplus safely. To meet such situations, State laws should authorize the conservation authorities to control surplus game animals in a practical manner.

OUR NATIONAL PARKS—OUT-OF-DOOR UNIVERSITIES

The establishment of national parks in the United States and Canada has received general commendation. Through personal visits to some of the parks and through information gained otherwise, I have been deeply impressed by the growing appreciation by the public of these wild and picturesque places. They are filling a place in the life of this country far beyond anything dreamed of by their originators. In 1934 more than three and three-quarters millions of people visited our national parks, and the number is increasing yearly at a rate that is causing some concern to those in charge.

As a trustee for many years of the National Parks Association, I have seen this organization, with the support of the public, successfully defend national parks from commercial exploitation and aid in establishing and maintaining proper standards to govern the selection of areas for national park purposes. At the same time active and friendly cooperation has been built up with the rapidly developing State park systems. One of the greatest and most difficult problems has been to restrict the national parks to areas commanding nation-wide interest, and thus avoid interference with the proper field in which the States can develop their own park systems.

"BOOKS IN THE RUNNING BROOKS"

In an article in the *National Parks Bulletin* for July, 1927, Dr. John C. Merriam admirably voiced the public educational value of these areas. He wrote in part:

"For many purposes the purely educational value of our national parks is far beyond that of any regularly established formal educational institutions. Among the most important features are those which concern the nature of the earth—the manner of its building—the forces which have come into play—the meaning of the almost limitless history of earth-making as it is pictured before us. The work of the Creator's hand presents itself here in such a way that all may comprehend.

"Here is much that represents the unmodified primitive life of the world, both plant and animal, remaining just as it was moulded over the mountains and valleys. Nature is said to be an open book to those who really wish to read it, but there are grades and shades of meaning which may be hard to understand. There is certainly no place where the leaves are more widely spread or the print more clear than in these portions of the book."

To make available to the public these advantages, which have a high inspirational as well as educational value, museums have been or are being established in some of the more important parks, and the services of scientifically trained biologists and nature guides are made available each season for the benefit of all interested. Furthermore, at the Grand Canyon National Park, a real out-of-doors university is being established that seems destined to give the public a practical knowledge of Nature's varied forces as they have operated in the past and as they are carrying on today.

Under the cooperative auspices of the Na-

tional Academy of Sciences, the National Research Council, the American Association of Museums, the Geological Society of America, and other organizations, under the leadership of Doctor Merriam, there has been inaugurated at the rim of the canyon a series of what may be called research lectures given by highly qualified scientists on the many phases of Nature's activities in that vicinity. The lectures cover the geology, the fossil records of past geological ages, and the existing animal and plant life, with special reference to ways its development has been affected by varying climatic conditions, from the hot, arid bottoms of the canyon up to the cold, treeless, subarctic summit of San Francisco Peak only a few miles away.

Besides its other features of wide interest, the surrounding region is probably the best in this country for the study of notable existing Indian tribes, and it is the richest field known within our borders for its prehistoric records of man. I am convinced that the educational work undertaken here will have an important and far-reaching influence, even beyond the expectations of its pioneers. Certainly no better service can be given the people of this country than to make them more familiar with Nature and its operations in places where they are inspired and awed by the magnificence of its manifestations.

NO DAM SHOULD BE PERMITTED HERE

Some ten years after my visits to the Yellowstone Lake region a bill was introduced in Congress that, if passed, would have permitted the damming of Yellowstone Lake at its outlet for the benefit of private interests. Although the measure failed in that and in succeeding Congresses, its sponsors are still active and may revive the attempt.

In view of the havoc that would be caused by the contemplated raising and lowering of the lake's surface, a process that has caused inestimable damage to many other beautiful inland lakes, I presented to the Committee on Public Lands at a hearing May 25, 1920, the following statement:

"In many years of exploration in the wilder portions of the northern continent, I have become familiar with the scenic value and the varied uses of many inland lakes, from both a recreational and an economic standpoint. Few, if any, of these lakes can be compared with Yellowstone in beauty, as a resort for wild life, or with greater possibilities for popular use. With one exception, Lake Titicaca, Yellowstone is the largest lake above an altitude of 7,000 feet, and it is surrounded by high mountains.

A FEMALE GOLDEN-EYE TAKES THE YOUNG FOR A SWIM

These handsome ducks are common summer birds about Yellowstone Lake. Here the author first saw them on their breeding ground.

"I have witnessed on many occasions the direct and collateral effect of the raising of lake levels for irrigation, for water power, and for logging on outlet streams, and am, therefore, familiar with the effect such increased levels have upon the adjacent shores, and with the disturbances caused thereby among the fauna and flora. Many of the observations and conclusions that follow are based upon trips I took in 1904, 1908, 1909, and 1910 to Yellowstone Lake and the valley of the upper river.

MANY ARROWHEADS ARE FOUND ON YELLOWSTONE LAKE

Early Indian lore asserted that the red man had avoided the Yellowstone Lake region on account of the weird manifestations of nature found therein. The author found on an island in this lake many finely wrought arrowheads and spear points, ranging from one to three inches in length. They were white, gray, yellow, and streaked. Some were of flint and some of glossy black from the obsidian cliffs of volcanic rock not far away.

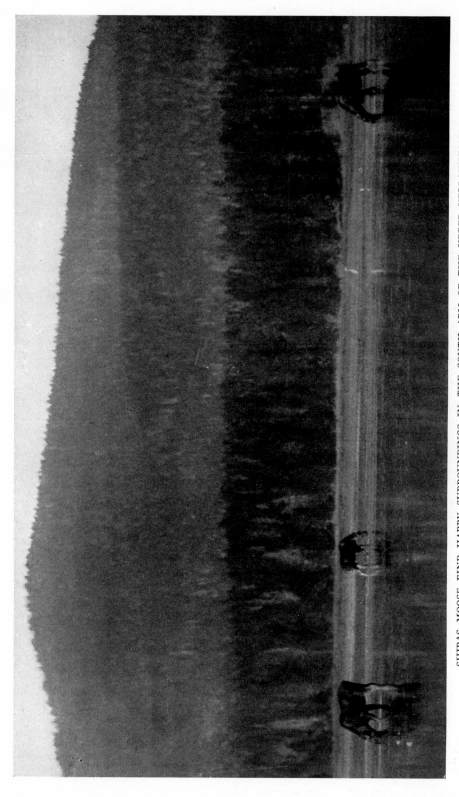

SHIRAS MOOSE FIND HAPPY SURROUNDINGS IN THE SOUTH ARM OF THE UPPER YELLOWSTONE

On the third trip to the Yellowstone Valley, the author found the south arm of the lake to be the nursery of the calf moose. Twenty-one moose were seen in the shallow water at one time. The picture shows a cow moose and twin calves.

"In my opinion, the proposed irrigation dam on Yellowstone River just below the lake would cause more widespread and irreparable damage to Yellowstone Lake than the public at present has any conception of. In the first place, one notion that has been sedulously cultivated is the erroneous one that raising the level of a lake, such as the Yellowstone, some five or ten feet is a matter of only temporary injury or inconvenience, and that in the course of a short time conditions would adjust themselves to this change without any particular damage.

"It has taken thousands of years for Nature to create Yellowstone Lake in its present form, and it would take hundreds of years, at least, to overcome the damage caused by such a proposed dam. Much of it would never be overcome if the level were intermittently raised and lowered to permit economic use.

THE LAKE A WILD-LIFE MECCA

"This lake has a shore line of approximately 150 miles, much of it sand beaches, with attractive coves, some seven islands, and at the south end two large bays formed by a promontory four miles wide that extends northerly out into the lake for 10 miles. In the southeast bay is the delta of the Upper Yellowstone River, three and a half miles wide. It contains many small lakes and ponds, and the lake waters are equally shallow for several hundred yards. These warm, shallow waters are filled with aquatic vegetation much used by the moose in the summer and early fall. They are equally essential to myriad wild fowl as breeding and feeding places, for the river water is too cold to produce abundant vegetation.

"Furthermore, in this bay is Molly Island, the only local breeding ground of hundreds of white pelicans. Immediately to the west of this and separated from it by a narrow peninsula lies Southwest Bay, very similar in character, in which lies Peale Island, suitable for camping and especially for observing the dozens of moose feeding in the shallow waters in the vicinity, and the hundreds of elk on the meadows near the shore and on the hillsides.

"By the raising of the lake to the proposed level, all the sand beaches, coves, and all the islands with the exception of one, which would still be marked by a sand dune, would be obliterated, and the water would cover the lower delta of the Yellowstone for a number of miles. Also access of moose and elk to the western bay would be prevented if the shore approach under the precipitous rocks were cut off.

"This increased amount of water would also prevent the wild fowl from feeding in the south end of the lake, or elsewhere, since many of them are of the non-diving, or marsh-feeding kinds, and would wipe out the breeding islands of the white pelicans, gulls, and terns. Furthermore, this higher level would kill thousands of trees growing along the shores and in the coves, and now affording the only suitable places for camping. Within a short time these dead trees, deprived of the support of their roots, would be blown over and would form an almost impassable barrier to the higher ground beyond. In this dry and rarified atmosphere, they would remain undecayed for 20 or 30 years.

"With the waters rising and falling at different periods, all bushes and ground vegetation near the shore would be destroyed, leaving only unsightly and ill-smelling mud flats, and the now beautifully weathered gray rocks at the present water level would be bleached or banded with the discolored lines of a fluctuating surface.

"It must be remembered that the formation of the present shore line and shallow bays has been caused by the gradual disintegration of the shores of a lake that formerly was rock-rimmed. This detritus, together with the sand washed up by the waves, has in the course of time made permanent beaches, at the outer edge of which grow many varieties of trees, shrubs, and flowers, while the delta of the Yellowstone and the shallowing of the adjacent waters are due to the deposition of silt from the river.

OBVIOUS POINTS OMITTED

"The low banks are now clothed with willow, the winter food of the moose, and by dense clumps of pine into which the moose retreat during severe weather. The injury that would result to the driveway along the western shore and the submerging of the peculiar geyser cone near the shore need not be discussed in detail, since the purpose of this article is to describe features of the lake not generally known.

"The Bill introduced in Congress by Senator Walsh, of Montana, in December,

NORTHERN PHALAROPES LIKE A SMALL LAKE NEAR UPPER YELLOWSTONE RIVER

These graceful little waders, unlike the rest of the snipe family, are expert swimmers, passing most of the time feeding upon minute animal life on the surface. Another oddity is that the male is smaller than the female and performs all the duties of incubation.

1920, provides for the erection of a dam on the river several miles below the outlet. The increased water level would flood the lower banks of the river, and cover more than 150 miles of shore line. In many places the width of this overflow would extend back from the present shore for a mile or more. The bill grants to the State of Montana, or to the organizations to which it may delegate its authority (representing purely commercial interests), the perpetual use of the dam site and overflowed territory. This would amount to thousands of acres in the center of the park.

"The public is using Yellowstone Park more each year, and at present the customary routes and camping places are overcrowded. Many miles of new roads should be opened in the southern and southwestern portions, the localities most seriously threatened by several irrigation projects now under consideration.

Any action that will circumscribe for present and future generations the largest and most popular of our parks should meet with the energetic resistance of the public, and should be vigorously opposed, as it doubtless will be, by all broad-minded and provident members of our National Congress. No plainer test of vested public rights against selfish private privileges could be imagined than this threatening project."

CHAPTER XV

Mule Deer on Kaibab Plateau, Arizona

OF THE several species of deer in the United States, the whitetail, or Virginia deer, is the most numerous and widely distributed, since it thrives under many varying conditions of climate and surroundings. The blacktail inhabits the heavy Pacific coast forests, one small race ranging north to the islands of southeastern Alaska. The mule deer frequents the foothills and pine forests of the higher altitudes and more open spaces of the West, ranging from the Canadian Rockies, in British Columbia, to central Mexico.

The mule deer is the finest and largest of the three species. It somewhat resembles the elk in habits and in the size and uniformity of the antlers. It is usually miscalled the "blacktail" by local hunters throughout the Rocky Mountain region. This animal is much larger than the true blacktail, and has a stubby white tail tipped with black, enormous ears, a white patch on the rump, and much larger antlers than those of the real blacktail on the Pacific coast.

At one time the mule deer was found in abundance in most of our Rocky Mountain region. Large in size, migrating each fall to lower elevations, sometimes in herds along well-defined trails leading from the mountains to the foothills, and lacking the cunning of the whitetail, this animal, like the elk, has rapidly become reduced over much of its original range.

WHERE THE MULE DEER INCREASED

One notable exception to this statement may be cited, for in one part of their range in the South, which formerly was only sparsely inhabited by these animals, the mule deer in late years have increased until they outnumber their population in any other section of the same size anywhere in the Rocky Mountain region. This area lies within the Kaibab National Forest of northern Arizona, a large part of which President Roosevelt set aside in 1906 as a game refuge. This National Forest and game refuge crowns a great plateau, which is almost surrounded by a desert except in the south side, where the Grand Canyon of the Colorado presents a barrier to free movement.

The plateau has an elevation of from 5,000 to 9,000 feet. It is about 50 miles long and 40 miles wide, a strip about 10 miles wide to the south being included in the Grand Canyon National Park. The area in the national forest, however, does not include the foothills at the base of the plateau, the winter home of the deer.

The summit of this plateau, although heavily forested, has scattered here and there open glades and parklike meadows that produce considerable grass and other food for grazing animals, including cattle.

INACCESSIBILITY A BOON

Such a tract was ideal for the gradual building up of the stock of native deer, for they could not wander forth freely into unfriendly territory, since the arid plains and the precipitous Grand Canyon form the boundary of their native range, nor could poachers take much toll, for few settlers lived in the neighborhood. Furthermore, the means of conveyance were unsuitable for the encouragement of unlawful traffic in large game, the nearest accessible railroad being 160 miles away to the north.

Under the efficient supervision of the National Forest Service and the Biological Survey, such predatory animals as the cougar and the coyote were quickly reduced in numbers, and this islandlike retreat was permitted to foster an annual increase of deer probably unparalleled in any other part of the country.

During October and November, when the ground is covered with snow, which by midwinter sometimes reaches a depth of more than eight feet on the higher elevations, the deer migrate to the foothills bordering the desert country, where the scrubby growth of juniper and cedar and several kinds of deciduous shrubs have in the past furnished them shelter and food for the winter.

The decrease of forage on the Kaibab Plateau, owing to the increasing numbers of deer, has been evident for some years. It has resulted in a gradual reduction in the number of livestock permitted by the Forest Service to be grazed there.

Within the last few years the problem of the perpetuation of the increasing numbers of deer on the Kaibab has become so serious

TREES SHOW INFALLIBLE SIGNS OF TOO MANY DEER

The well-marked, light-colored band along the base of the aspen grove shows how the deer have destroyed all the small branches and offshoots up as high as they can reach. Such a denuded line on trees in a range always means that the game is too numerous and must be promptly reduced.

that the Forest Service requested the Biological Survey to investigate conditions and make recommendations for the future management of the herds.

Without now considering in detail what others saw and what they reported, I shall confine myself to my own investigation in that locality. Previous to visiting the Kaibab Forest early in the fall of 1923, and at the request of the Biological Survey, I prepared a summary of my experiences in protected areas in which deer, moose, elk, and other animals by unchecked increase had been reduced to acute starvation. This paper was entitled "The Increase of Game on Limited Areas." The opening paragraphs will be substantially quoted as pertinent to the present discussion.

"A refuge for large game animals, whenever fenced or limited by natural barriers, sooner or later develops a state of acute starvation among its habitants. The loss in one or two seasons may amount to 50 per cent, and ultimately may include the entire herd, unless food is supplied regularly thereafter or the number of animals is reduced by shooting, by transportation from the area, or by such natural agencies as dis-

ease or the free range of predatory animals.

"This condition applies to all game reserves, however well situated, and whether the initial herd be 5 animals on 500 acres or 25,000 animals with the range of a million acres (unless the area is bordered by territory easy of access and suitable for the needs of the growing surplus). With the deer particularly this is true, for they are the most prolific of our antlered game.

BIRTH RATE AND FOOD SUPPLY

"It has been scientifically determined that one female white-tailed deer and her offspring in a 10-year period will produce 130 animals, and that one dozen does will have 1,560 descendants in the same period. Therefore, however large the confined area, the animal inmates are doomed to starvation unless man steps in or allows Nature's drastic methods of controlling a species to have their way.

"The time to act in any given case should be several years in advance of the starvation period; for, with the protected animals rapidly increasing and the food supply on a proportionate decline, thousands may die in a single season, where only a few may

OVERBROWSING BY MULE DEER CAUSED SUCH CONDITIONS ON KAIBAB PLATEAU

The picture gives an example of the animals' work on a pinyon tree. Under pressure of hunger among the deer even the small pines suffer. These trees were defoliated on the winter range. At one time there were about 40,000 deer on the Kaibab, at least twice as many as the area will feed.

have died the previous year. The cause of such a sudden tragedy may be accounted for in the case of the deer family because of their feeding habits, since they are primarily browsers.

"When the herd is not excessive for a given area, each season's growth of annual and perennial vegetation will suffice; but when the numbers become too large, a disastrous change takes place. Ground vegetation is permanently destroyed; sapling trees, denuded of their leaves, buds, and bark, die; and the larger trees, both coniferous and deciduous, are stripped of their limbs as far as the animals can reach. Though these trees may appear large and thrifty to the casual observer, thereafter they provide no food."

Many cases were cited, showing that, as with domestic cattle, there necessarily must be a limit to increasing numbers of large game on a restricted range, especially where the vegetation is permanently destroyed by overgrazing or browsing.

Impressed with the seriousness of the deer problem on the Kaibab Plateau, and willing to help solve the difficulty, I visited northern Arizona in the fall of 1923.

With my old guide, John Hammer, I left Marquette, Michigan, early in September. During the concluding part of the trip south

of Salt Lake City I gave the desert country closer examination than had been possible on my former visits. Two hundred and fifty miles of travel through this arid region brought us to Lund Station, on the Union Pacific, where a recently opened branch of 32 miles took us to Cedar City, in southern Utah. From this point automobiles are taken for the Zion National Park, or to the northern part of the Grand Canyon National Park.

A GARDEN SPOT IN THE DESERT

Under the guidance of an assistant predatory animal inspector of the Biological Survey, we left Cedar City in a light touring car and paused for the night at the village of Hurricane, where the waters of a small stream, coming from the nearby mountains, are drawn upon before they sink into the thirsty desert a few hundred yards away.

Through the use of this water, shade and fruit trees have made an oasis for the hot and dusty traveler, and afford an abundance of peaches, pears, grapes, melons, figs, and almonds, evidence of what the surrounding fertile soil would produce if given the needed moisture. Interesting, too, were the climatic conditions of this region. Late in the afternoon the thermometer at Hurricane registered 95 degrees; and at midnight

MULE DEER DID NOT WAIT TILL DARK TO SPRING THE FLASHLIGHT

Aspen branches were cut and placed with set flashlight cameras at the edge of the forest bordering a natural meadow.   By the lighted sky it is evident this picture was taken before dark.

descended to 80 degrees. The following night on the more elevated Kaibab Plateau we suffered from cold, the temperature dropping to 28 degrees.

Some time before we reached the Kaibab Plateau our attention was directed toward a long, dark elevation apparently mortised into the desert, which, because of the covering forest of evergreen, differed materially in color from the ruddy and almost barren hills we had been passing over or alongside all the morning. This was our destination.

WINTER RANGE OF MULE DEER

On the first slope the scanty vegetation of the desert gave way to scattered cedars, which increased in number until as we ascended, they intermingled with buck-brush and scrub oak. This was a portion of the winter range of the mule deer, a broad belt that circled the entire tract north of the Grand Canyon.

The road from the base of the plateau is constructed and maintained by the Forest Service. For many miles it was of low grade and well surfaced, in striking contrast to the narrow, rough roads leading up to the forest border. Later on the road narrowed, swinging up and down over small ridges, but it was still of good character all the way to the canyon.

About two-thirds of the way up the main slope began an encircling forest of yellow pine (*Pinus ponderosa*)—straight, large, and nearly limbless to the spreading tops. The ground beneath was barren and covered throughout with the brown needles of the great pines. It afforded neither shelter nor food for ruminant life. At the summit, at an elevation of more than 8,000 feet, the pines disappear and are replaced by dense forests of spruce and fir, with here and there open glades or meadows, bordered with a beautiful edging of aspen, whose white trunks and fluttering leaves relieve the otherwise somber background.

Here we were told to look out for deer, this point being within their summer range and also that of cattle belonging to local ranchmen. Not, however, until we passed beyond the northern drift fence of the Grand Canyon Cattle Company, which controls the remainder of the range, did we see any.

Although intent on watching occasional deer grazing as we passed, I was equally interested in the character of the ground

THIS BUCK ENJOYED AN UNINTERRUPTED FEAST

So hungry were the mule deer on the Kaibab Plateau in Arizona that after the flashlight exploded they would retreat only momentarily from the aspen bough bait put out for them.

vegetation, which was sparse and seemed to consist mainly of young fir and spruce, unsuitable food for any member of the deer family. If other growths existed in earlier years, not a trace was left.

Finally, descending in a graceful spiral, we came into a long, narrow meadow, the largest on the plateau, and known as V. T. Ranch, near the end of which was a large cabin and a group of cottages for tourists. This was a convenient stop for those visiting the canyon, one of the inducements being the opportunity of seeing hundreds of deer coming out of the forest and feeding in the meadow late in the summer afternoons or early mornings.

AN IDEAL SPOT FOR STUDY

The locality was to be our headquarters; for it was considered the most suitable place for examining the deer and their food supply and for visiting the rest of the range.

We reached this lodging place an hour before dark and just in time to join an assembly of tourists who were watching the deer streaming out of the forest on either side and mingling in ever-growing numbers on the lower portion of the meadow, where were several pools of water at which they quenched their thirst. These pools gave a greener tinge to the closely cropped vegetation.

As I was finishing dinner, I was surprised to see Maj. E. A. Goldman, who had just come from the south rim of the Grand Canyon on mule back, crossing over the swinging footbridge that gave a limited access to the southern end of the Kaibab Forest. This was his third trip to the region. Like the previous ones, it had been made in behalf of the Biological Survey for the purpose of estimating the number of deer, their annual increase, and the character and extent of the remaining food supply.

We found that after 7 o'clock in the morning the deer returned to the woods for the remainder of the day, a few being seen along the borders or sometimes hurriedly crossing from one side to the other.

Although not wild, these animals are timid. They allow a man to approach no nearer than a few hundred yards, and then hurry off in single file. Daylight photography, therefore, must be from a blind. Since the deer usually remain in the shadows until sunset, it is only by chance that

TWO MAGNIFICENT BUCKS SHOW ANTLERS IN THE VELVET

The deer in the rear is chasing the other to make him drop the aspen bough he is holding in his mouth. These large animals of the Kaibab herds had driven the smaller ones from the branches that had been cut and placed there for bait.

properly exposed negatives can be made. The habit of the deer of keeping under cover in the daytime proved to me that I had done well in bringing a number of small cameras and several flashlight machines in case bad weather or the seclusion of the deer interfered with daylight photography.

The program for the first day was to pick out the best places for setting the cameras along the edge of the forest. The remainder of the day was given over to studying the character and extent of the food in and around the park.

On examining the narrow fringe of aspens surrounding the meadows, I found that all the lower limbs within reach of the deer had been trimmed. These trees ranged in height from 12 to 30 feet, and not a single one seen was less than six years old. This indicated that during recent years the numerous seedlings had all been destroyed.

No intermediate growth could be found, a circumstance which showed that for at least five years the aspens, which previously had furnished the bulk of the summer food, had not been available. Later, examination of millions of aspens growing along the borders of this forest for more than a hundred miles disclosed the same conditions.

The condition of the meadows was almost as bad. They looked as if a lawn mower had been in daily use, the grass and clover being cropped to less than half an inch in length. Not a weed or bramble could be seen, excepting a flat, grayish plant, apparently not eaten by deer or livestock, that was encroaching upon and replacing the grass and clover.

GRAZING REPLACES BROWSING

The changed forage conditions here had forced the deer to become grazers instead of browsers. They fed with heads continually held down, just like a flock of sheep, and so closely did they crop this vegetation that it never came to seed. All pasture lands must at times have periods of reseeding, for drought, extreme cold, or overgrazing will sooner or later require the natural replacement of the plants.

As an aid to picture-taking, I had expected to put rock salt near the set camera to lure the deer to take their own photographs. However, since several hundred head of horses and cattle were feeding in the neighborhood, it seemed quite likely that most of my negatives would picture domestic livestock. I changed my plans, cut

down a few aspen trees, and used the small limbs for bait. These provided the deer with a long-missing item on their bill of fare, and at the same time did not offer anything that appealed to the cattle.

Late in the afternoon, when the last camera was in place, we looked back and saw four or five deer headed for the bait. On reaching the first branches some distance from the camera the deer acted like a pack of hungry dogs. Each seized a branch, ran a short distance, ate the leaves and tender twigs, and returned for more.

PHOTOGRAPHING MULE DEER

At that moment four big bucks appeared, and each seemed to divine that an unexpected feast was at hand. Hurrying up, they drove away the does and fawns. When the remaining branches had been much reduced, they began chasing each other about. Realizing that we were soon to witness the taking of the first flashlight picture, we turned the field glasses in that direction.

When only one branch remained, the one to which the thread was attached, the largest of the four bucks tried to drive off the others. One in the endeavor to escape took a flying leap over the bait, and its rear foot touched the thread. A blaze of light and a great puff of white smoke were followed an instant later by the heavy boom of the flashlight powder (see page 352).

The deer, instead of rushing to cover in alarm as we expected, ran only a short distance in the stiff-legged jumps characteristic of their kind. Then they faced the scene of the explosion and looked wonderingly at the cloud of white smoke drifting out on the meadow. In a few minutes they walked slowly back toward the cameras. Another picture could be taken if the apparatus was reset. Cautiously driving the deer away, we accomplished this. Before we reached camp, there was another explosion. We could picture in our minds the scene taken by the first flash, but just what happened on the second was learned only after a journey of more than 2,000 miles.

Before the evening meal was prepared, two more heavy explosions were heard farther down the park. It then became certain that the supply of flashlight powder would soon be exhausted, for we had brought only 12 cartridges. On the fourth night the last of these was fired. In all, 13 large bucks, four adult does, and two fawns were photographed. Only one negative had

THE FLASHLIGHT RECORDED A GRACEFUL LEAP

The author had been gone only a short time after cutting and putting out aspen branches for bait when large bucks came forward eagerly to get them (see text, page 351).

THEY FIRED A FLASHLIGHT AT SUNSET

The bright sky shows that this picture was taken before dark. Through field glasses the author saw both this pair and the buck above as they fired the flashes.

ONE COUPLE SEEMED INCOMPATIBLE

When the deer discovered that a ready-set meal of aspen branches awaited them, all gallantry disappeared. The large bucks chased away all the others, and does chased does and young ones.

SHE WAS CAUGHT IN THE OPEN

This young doe was found in the daytime hunting for grass on the meadow near the V. T. Ranch. The entire area of pasture land was closely grazed.

A REAL CHIPMUNK (EUTAMIAS) PERCHED ON A LOG

Seeds and berries were so scarce in the devastated Kaibab that even these friendly little creatures, whose food needs are almost negligible, had a hard struggle to live.

fewer than two deer, a most unusual happening with the automatic flashlight.

Another unusual feature of these night pictures was the action displayed in most of them. With a few exceptions, the contest over the food caused the deer to run continually back and forth, the largest buck usually being the one that furnished the picture. This proved beyond question that the deer, driven in recent years to depend upon scanty grass, were eager to get a taste of the leaves and limbs which formerly had been their mainstay and which had again been unexpectedly placed within reach.

DIMINISHING FOOD SUPPLY

In appraising the diminishing food supply of the deer on the Kaibab Plateau, three factors were involved: first, the present condition; second, the character and extent of the vegetation before any marked depletion; and, third, the feeding habits of the animals during the two periods of abundance and scarcity.

The conditions described at V. T. Ranch were found to exist in all the other glades in which the deer and cattle had largely ex-

hausted the pasturage. In addition to examining the forests bordering the meadows, we made a trip along a recently opened road to the edge of the Marble Canyon of the Colorado River, some five miles to the southeast. Here all the leaves and twigs of bushes and deciduous trees had been eaten by the deer as fast as they were cut by the road builders.

At the edge of the canyon I found several tall bushes covered with tender, green leaves, and wondered why they had not been eaten. The forest ranger accompanying me said that if I would turn up one of the branches I would see the reason. There, beneath each branch, an inch or so apart, was a row of long, sharp thorns, which, if swallowed by the deer, would so lacerate the tongue, throat, and entrails as to cause death. A more careful inspection of these bushes, however, showed that the annual growth of about three inches had been snipped off, there being no thorns under the terminal part.

The hungry deer in accomplishing this difficult feat were unable to see the thorns, and thus must have measured the nearest one by the tongue. These thorn-guarded

THE GOLDEN-MANTLED GROUND SQUIRREL RESEMBLES THE CHIPMUNK

This little fellow and the one shown on the opposite page came one day to share the author's luncheon in Kaibab Forest. Both animals were ravenously hungry.

bushes were the only signs of deer food I saw on the day's trip.

Of one summer resident I asked what the deer had to eat in any portion of this large forest, and he answered cheerfully, "Oh, they get lots of mushrooms." Twice only did I see such fungi—once within a small windfall, where three species were growing in surroundings inaccessible to any large animal; and again, close to the edge of our cabin, where the squirrels were coming daily for them.

EVEN FUNGI FAIL IN DROUTH

Doubtless in August and September there is a considerable crop of edible fungi (for deer can eat many kinds poisonous to man), but this supply is only temporary at the best and most often fail during dry seasons. Moreover, such destruction of nearly all the fungus growth before the spores have ripened, largely prevents reproduction. Upon the meadows I noticed a few scattered puff-balls, but none more than 48 hours old.

Probably the most significant observation made on my trip was during an excursion some 15 miles southward to the northern rim of the Grand Canyon. Several hundred yards back from the edge a wire fence had been erected to prevent the deer and cattle from straying into a small area set aside for the summer camps of tourists staying overnight. Within this narrow strip I was able to make a good inventory of the many kinds of vegetation that had been destroyed on the rest of the Kaibab Plateau.

Scattered about were scrub oaks filled with an abundance of acorns, a delicacy most eagerly sought by many animals; also buckbrush, cedar, and fully matured grass and clover, besides a variety of flowering weeds and brambles. This told the story of the former richness of the deer range on the Kaibab, now so greatly denuded of its normal plant life by overbrowsing.

Several days before we left camp 15 or 20 cowboys arrived and began herding hundreds of cattle for the fall drive. One of these told me that the pasturage had become so poor that the removal of the stock was necessary before the animals deteriorated too much to be desirable for the winter market. The drive was being made more than a month in advance of the usual time; and yet the number of cattle has been reduced nearly every year under Government orders. One of the oldest of the herders said that 15 years before these now bare upland meadows had produced grass "stirrup high" and many weeds and bushes suitable for livestock.

When, in 1906, the Kaibab Plateau was made a game refuge, the deer on it numbered only a few thousand; but when I was there in 1923, Forest Service and other officials and local residents estimated the number to be from 30,000 to 50,000. A normal fawn crop for a herd of 30,000 deer would be 10,000 or more.

A DANGEROUS SITUATION

My observations convinced me that this game refuge was dangerously overstocked, and that unless there was a prompt reduction in the number of deer a progressive deterioration in the forage production would be followed by the starvation of the animals on a large scale. I refer here to a reduction in the number of deer only, for the livestock is being gradually eliminated to make way for the purposes of the reservation.

A significant light was thrown on the situation by my observation of a great number of spotted fawns, but only three yearlings and five two-year-olds among about a thousand animals. This meant that out of the large fawn crops of several years only a few were surviving their first winter. A checking of the annual increase by starvation had already begun. My photographs point to the same conclusion, for out of 18 deer pictured not one was under four years of age except a single spotted fawn. That one probably perished the following winter.

If the deer have been starving in large numbers during recent years, then it may be asked why their remains have not been seen. It is on the winter range that the greatest mortality would naturally occur. Reports indicate that 80 per cent of the deer winter on the eastern and western lower slopes and the remainder at the north and south ends of the plateau. This extensive winter range, up to the time of my visit, had seldom been visited.

Thousands of deer might have died from starvation in this large area every winter. Their flesh would have been disposed of quickly by coyotes. The scattered bones would be pretty well destroyed by disintegrating climatic influences and by rodents.

To me the idea of leaving surplus deer to become the prey of predatory animals or victims of starvation seems an unworthy means of solving such a problem as has developed on the Kaibab. To capture and remove animals for restocking other places would be impracticable, for such action would not decrease the surplus sufficiently.

The sensible way of handling the matter and of bringing the numbers within limits that will permit the forage production to be restored is by hunting. The herd could be permitted to increase gradually as the food supply warrants. The surplus killing should be by means of an open season under cooperative control of the Arizona State Game Commission and the United States Forest Service. If necessary, large numbers could be killed by official orders and sent to charitable institutions. The developments on the Kaibab should be a lesson for those who oppose any killing of wild life, for here this means inevitable slow starvation on an appalling scale.

Largely as the result of my report to the Biological Survey, Henry C. Wallace, Secretary of Agriculture in 1924, appointed a committee of sportsmen and conservationists to investigate the conditions on the Kaibab and report with recommendations for effective control of the situation. The committee consisted of John B. Burnham, of the American Game Protective Association; Heywood Cutting, of the Boone and Crockett Club; T. Gilbert Pearson, of the National Association of Audubon Societies, and T. W. Tomlinson, of the American Livestock Breeders Association.

ATTEMPT TO CONTROL SURPLUS DEER

In accordance with my suggestion, two deer were killed in the morning and two in the evening to determine the food they had eaten. The stomachs of the two that had passed the day in the forest contained nothing but the stomach juices, and those killed in the morning, after they had passed the night in the meadows about V. T. Park, contained a little grass.

After studying the problem on the ground, this committee recommended that in view of the excessive number of deer on the Kaibab and the danger of heavy loss by starvation the reduction of the deer should be accomplished in three ways: first, by capturing and shipping animals alive to other localities; second, by hunting, under careful regulation; and third, as a last resort, by official killing of surplus deer by Government hunters.

CHAPTER XVI

The Author's First Alaska Trip in Search of the Giant Moose

ALTHOUGH my father was a hardworking lawyer whose life was mainly within walls, he had a keen love for the out-of-doors, and for 65 successive years passed much of his summer vacations under canvas on the south shore of Lake Superior. He showed further evidence of his love for outdoor adventure by purchasing and reading all books on polar exploration as soon as they appeared. Through these books my youthful mind was fired with a desire to see the Land of the Midnight Sun.

A WISH DEFERRED FOR 19 YEARS

In 1891 the long awaited opportunity seemed to be at hand when President Harrison took my name under consideration for appointment as Governor of Alaska. This position appealed to me very much, since the duties of the office consisted mainly of tours of inspection, which would give me opportunity to observe closely the rather primitive natives, and especially the wonderful and little-known wild life of the North.

My dreams of life in the northern wilds were abruptly ended, however, when in October, 1892, my father was appointed an Associate Justice of the United States Supreme Court, and it became necessary for me to assume the care of private legal work that he relinquished. I never abandoned my intention to visit that remote wonderland, however, and 19 years later the opportunity came for me to go there to study the big-game animals and some of the strange birds for which Alaska is notable. On this expedition I was to capture permanent trophies of the hunt with the camera rather than with the gun.

Experience had long before shown me that success in the pursuit of wild life does not depend on how far one travels away from home, or on how extensive and primitive the country is. In the virgin forests and the burnt-over, second-growth country immediately north of Lake Huron and Lake Superior, a country now largely deserted by fur traders, Indians, and trappers, one may find a greater variety and abundance of big game in a week, and sometimes in a single day, than one might encounter during an arduous canoe journey of several months on any of the many open streams leading from the lake country to Hudson Bay.

All these waterways have been traveled for centuries and the large game along their courses has been so reduced that little is seen. Because of the inhospitable winter climate and the lack of proper food conditions and shelter, most of the big game in Ontario, except the caribou, is found on the southern watersheds draining into the Great Lakes.

So it is in Alaska. The reports of miners, trappers, Government explorers, and sportsmen, covering many years of persistent travel and exploration, have shown clearly that the mere distance traversed in this vast country often means little in regard to the numbers of big-game animals observed. Persons often travel a thousand or more miles on the Yukon and some of its tributaries without seeing a single individual of the larger animals.

The caribou is a wandering animal, difficult to find in such a limitless country. In summer the moose frequently remain concealed for months in thickets of alder and willow at the edge of timber line. The bears, besides being largely nocturnal in habits, hide most of the time in the densest jungle or feed high up on the slopes on the tender grasses and wild berries until the coming of the salmon. As for mountain sheep and goats, they habitually occupy the higher ranges beyond the valleys of the larger streams.

MOOSE AND SHEEP THE OBJECTIVE

Of the two big-game animals I sought particularly on my trip in 1911, one, the moose, was to furnish, if I was successful, a valedictory chapter of my many years' observations of this great game animal in the most westerly and northerly of the five districts of its range. The other was the beautiful white sheep of the subarctic mountains, a species with which I had no personal acquaintance, but which I now desired to cultivate in a friendly way.

To stalk, study, and photograph in these remote haunts the largest and most impressive of our antlered animals and then, when this was accomplished, to seek out on

A TRAIN LEAVES SEWARD FOR KENAI LAKE

From these steamship docks at Resurrection Bay the author set out for his Alaskan adventures (see text, opposite page).

the rough mountain summits the snow-white descendants of the latest migrant big-game animal from Asia, constituted a program seemingly sufficient in itself. However, a plentiful stock of sensitive plates was in reserve for any other animals or birds that might be considered worthy of portraiture.

If one obtains satisfactory results from a first and rather hasty exploration of a new and unsettled country, I think it is due as much to the comparatively easy accessibility of the game field as to abundance of the game itself.

THE KENAI PENINSULA—A MINIATURE ALASKA

I selected the Kenai Peninsula, lying between Cook Inlet on the west and Prince William Sound on the east, and within 1,500 miles of Seattle, not only because it was the most accessible territory with an abundance of game, but because in this favored region the moose and mountain sheep reached their highest perfection in physical development and, what was of equal importance, were to be found with certainty in well-defined ranges.

Were all of Alaska blotted from existence except the Kenai Peninsula and its

immediately adjacent waters, there would yet remain a tract that typifies the whole of this wonderful country.

On Kenai Peninsula the remaining few of the original tribal race enjoy nearly all the advantages of modern civilization, yet all about them lies an almost unspoiled wilderness of forests, mountains, glaciers, streams, lakes, and sea.

Here and there snow-capped mountains drop to plateaus, rough and shaggy in coats of moss or yellow-barked willows, and farther down the green coniferous forests border and enclose areas of tundra dotted with glistening ponds, the feeding places for moose and the home of the black fly and the mosquito.

Here in summer occur weeks of brilliant weather and periods of wet and fogs, and here the frequent seismic disturbances show how superficial are the ice fields and the blizzards in a country possessed of great volcanic energy.

Here occurs a midyear season when the calendar days are separated by only an hour of twilight, and another when for weeks the trapper in his sheltered winter cabin cannot see the sluggard sun above the horizon of the surrounding mountains. Here are the tidal waves and ripraps of

AT THE HEAD OF RESURRECTION BAY LIES THE TOWN OF SEWARD

The cross to the north indicates the position of Upper Kenai Lake. Forty miles to the westward was the hunting ground of the author.

Turnagain Arm, similar to those of the Bay of Fundy, and here so rare is the atmosphere that at times Mount McKinley, distant 200 miles to the north, can be seen from the higher mountain tops.

Almost at the last moment of preparation for my trip I was obliged to get a substitute for my old Michigan guide, John Hammer, who for 25 years had accompanied me on such excursions. Sickness in his family kept him at home. Charles Anderson, another tried employee, who possessed a fair knowledge of the woods and waters, took his place.

On July 8 we left Seattle for Seward, and had pleasant weather throughout most of the voyage. Toward sunset on the evening of July 14 the steamer entered Resurrection Bay, which penetrates deeply into the Kenai Peninsula and forms the most wonderful harbor on the whole Alaskan coast. It is open throughout the winter, when the Great Lakes and connecting rivers are closed for many months.

After a run of 10 miles between two snow-covered ranges that paralleled the bay, we reached the town of Seward. First to respond to the shrill and echoing whistle of our boat were a hundred or more dogs of every breed and color, which amicably ranged themselves in several compact rows along the edge of the dock, each hoping that some of the garbage saved by the kindly steward would fall to his lot (see page 361).

On their home grounds or street fronts these shaggy beasts maintained a deadline against all canine intruders, but at the wharf there was no distinction based upon race, size, sex, or relationship. Whenever a steamer whistled at night, or any unusual noise aroused them, they would voice wolf-like howls in rising and falling chorus that told plainly of their near kinship to the gaunt and ravenous creatures of the wilds.

TRANSPORTATION ARRANGED

On disembarking, we were met by an obliging innkeeper and soon were in earnest confab with our local guide, Thomas B. Towle, who had just come in from his mining camp on the Upper Kenai River. His launch, he said, would meet us at Kenai Lake two days later, on the arrival of the motor train.

So varied and reasonable in price were camping supplies at Seward that little need be brought in from the outside. The courteous and reliable character of the inhabitants, private and official, made the entry

SEEN FROM THE CAMP, SKILAK LAKE WAS LOVELY

and return to this little town a source of pleasure and kindly recollection.

On the morning of July 17 we boarded a gasoline car of the Alaskan Northern Railroad, en route to the Upper Kenai Lake, 23 miles to the north. The canoe and the bulk of the provisions were to be forwarded by freight several days later. The railroad extended to the end of Turnagain Arm, halfway to the Matanuska coal fields; but because of the lack of sufficient capital and the withdrawal of the coal lands it was in financial straits. It was a most convenient highway for hunters and miners, however, and if anyone lacked cash to pay the fare of 20 cents a mile, or was of an economical turn of mind, the road bed afforded a fine trail to the interior.

ON TO THE GAME COUNTRY

The car stopped close to the lake shore, and it took but a few minutes to transfer our baggage to a comfortable launch. Soon we were traversing a part of the longest watercourse of the peninsula, which from the head of Snow River to Cook Inlet is 117 miles. The Upper Kenai Lake is 23 miles long. It has a maximum width of 1.5 miles, and is 460 feet above sea level. The Upper Kenai River, its outlet, is 16 miles long. The lower lake, usually called Skilak, is 15 miles long, four or five miles wide, and 150 feet above the sea, and its waters reach Cook Inlet after a tortuous run of 53 miles.

At the outlet of Upper Kenai Lake we transferred the outfit to Tom's big flat-bottom skiff, and, dropping down the river several miles, went into camp at the mouth of Cooper Creek to await the arrival of the canoe and provisions. The maximum temperature was 80 degrees at noon. The next day it rose to 87 degrees, a most unusual record.

A GOOD WEATHER GUESS

Seeing that the half-embedded boulders were sweating vigorously along the river trail, I predicted a big thunderstorm, and elicited the information that such storms were very rare in this region. Soon, however, the rain came down in torrents and thunder echoed for hours throughout the valley. Thus I gained that distinction which comes when one makes a lucky hit. The storm proved to be the only heavy rain of the entire trip. Thereafter clear days and a high temperature surprised and pleased us all.

As usual on expeditions when supplies can be carried by water, my outfit was varied and heavy. It is the height of bad management, when one is visiting a remote and unsettled country, to economize in money, time, or labor at the expense of a proper equipment or an ample supply of provisions, provided it is practicable to transport the outfit reasonably. We devoted several hours to the loading of the boat and

WINTER SLEDGE DOGS LOITERED AROUND THE STEWARD'S PANTRY

canoe, putting in each an outfit complete enough to fill temporary needs if either craft capsized on the run to the lower lake.

The clear, warm weather had melted from the mountain range an unusual amount of the last winter's snow and caused the river to overflow its banks. The rapid current that had balked upstream traffic for weeks made it possible to cover the 16 miles down to the lake in a few hours. The hot weather continued until the first week in September, and on our return trip we toiled for four days on the tracking line to bring up the skiff.

The canoe we had abandoned in order that the three men might devote all their energies to the navigation of the larger boat. Even at that late date we were the first to get up the river, a feat that was due to Tom's skill and the energy of all.

STERN FIRST DOWN THE KENAI RIVER

On the short trip downstream from the outlet of the upper lake to our first camp at the junction of Cooper Creek and the Kenai River, I found that it was the invariable practice for all boats, big or little, to go down this stream stern first. To me this was a new method of navigating.

Heretofore I had boated bow first on many such northern streams, originally in the frail and buoyant birch-bark canoe, then in dugouts, and, later, in modern canvas-covered cedar canoes or those of the knock-down type. Occasionally I had used the big, strong, sharp-pointed bateaux of the Hudson Bay and Newfoundland kind, which could plunge with impunity into the roughest water or, if sufficiently manned, could be lined up any stream, irrespective of inshore rocks and snags.

To load down a small, frail, flat-bottom, square-stern skiff with 1,000 pounds of outfit and two occupants, and then start down the river wrong end foremost, where every 100 yards or so the combers in the narrow channels or the cross currents throw the waves a foot or two higher than the stern of the boat, seemed to be inviting catastrophe. My misgivings were lessened, however, by the knowledge that Tom had the reputation of being the most capable and experienced riverman in the Kenai Valley.

The others expressed grave concern, however, over the safety of our canoe; and thus the feeling of distrust was mutual. Tom said he would rather take his chances on a sawlog, "because it never took in water, and the part above the surface was always the top, no matter how often it rolled over." Here was a chance to compare the efficiency and safety of the two boats running virtually side by side.

The explanation for Tom's method of handling a skiff soon became plain. No ordinary boat can safely run a swift and

BREEDING ROOKERY OF THE BLACK CORMORANT

There were two rocky islets near the eastern end of Skilak Lake, this one occupied by cormorants exclusively, and the other by gulls and terns. Note that the cormorants, unlike the gulls, on skyline or rock background, are not protected by their coloration.

TO ALASKA THE AUTHOR MADE TWO CAMERA-HUNTING TRIPS

It was in this territory represented by this map that he photographed the white sheep of the Kenai Peninsula and discovered the new species of bear later named *Ursus shirasi*.

NESTS OF CORMORANTS TOPPED A PINNACLE OF THE ISLAND
On the mainland mountain in the background are the snowfields close to the shore of Skilak Lake.

tumultuous stream when floating at the same speed as the current. It must go either faster or slower, in order to respond readily to the rudder or paddle when one is steering. In a canoe the occupants, of course, face ahead. By letting the skiff run down stern first the oarsman and the steersman also faced down the river, the advantages of which I learned later.

SERVING AS COXSWAIN

Since the river was unknown to my Michigan guide, who was to manage the canoe, it was arranged that I should sit in the stern of the skiff, facing upstream, with the canoe keeping 50 yards or more in the rear, so that I could note the character of the water at each bend, and by signals tell the guide which side the canoe should take.

The first proof that the different methods of navigation were based upon the character of the boats came a few minutes after we started. On rounding a bend, we found in the middle of the stream, less than 30 yards away, an immense rock, over which the water was breaking with great force and

against which we threatened to drift broadside, as the current divided. Tom pulled vigorously to the left, quartering upstream, and, although he could not quite stem the current, the boat slowly worked inshore, with a good margin to spare when we dropped past the rock.

Had the boat been going faster than the current, with the oarsman's back to the danger, a smash-up would have been certain. Charlie, on the other hand, in the light and more easily handled canoe, took the inshore channel with a few strokes of his paddle. Thus the lighter boat depended on speed and ease of propulsion, whereas the clumsy and heavily laden skiff, with Tom facing downstream, could be kept in the middle of the river or pulled to either side in time to avoid rocks or rough water

I must concede that there were times when the skiff thus handled had the advantage over the canoe, for when we en tered certain rapids, where the breakers extended from bank to bank, we could by pulling at the oars slightly check the descent. The great curling waves would fall

THESE FEATHERLESS CORMORANTS ARE ABOUT EIGHT DAYS OLD
Their smooth and shiny backs and blunt heads make them resemble turtles in the nest.

HOW THE SAME TWO CORMORANTS LOOKED ONE MONTH LATER
They have acquired plumage to cover their shiny backs of their babyhood and are beginning to take notice of their surroundings.

THESE THREE CORMORANTS ARE TEN DAYS OLDER THAN THE TWO ON PAGE 365

Unlike gulls of a much younger age, they do not leave the nest when alarmed, but groan and disgorge the contents of their stomachs. The cormorants in this picture disgorged two quarts of fish from their pouches when the author appeared to photograph them.

away harmlessly from the flat stern, because they were receding with the same speed as the current. At such times the canoe, drifting rapidly with the stream and often going much faster in order to keep its course, would be deluged with spray, and occasionally a wave would overlap the bow.

To those who have occasion to run swift and crooked streams in backwoods craft that is likely to be one of the easily constructed, box-timbered kind, the stern-first method can be highly recommended as safe and comfortable. Had such a method been in vogue in early gold-rush days on other Alaskan rivers, many a valuable cargo and many a miner's life would undoubtedly have been saved.

At a box canyon, about three miles above the lake, through which the river runs like a mill race between high and perpendicular cliffs for nearly a quarter of a mile, we portaged the canoe and our more valuable

things, since I was unwilling that any risk should be taken. A week before a large boatload of government supplies had been nearly lost here. Half filled with water, it had floated helplessly down the stream.

MOOSE SIGNS UNMISTAKABLE

While we were making this portage, it became apparent to us that we had reached the first great fall and winter range of the moose, for the numerous and well-worn runways, the trees denuded of their bark and lower branches, and an occasional shed antler told the story.

At the foot of the portage we camped for the night near one of the few sloughs connected with the river, in the hope of getting a moose picture or two, but because of the high stage of the water and the fact that the most of these animals were then at the edge of the timber line or in the great swamps west of the river valley, our stop resulted only in giving the mosquitoes an unexpected but welcome meal.

Soon after we started the next afternoon, the canoe, in making a quick rush to avoid going under a log jam, got ahead of us, and when we overtook it 10 minutes later, we found Charlie clinging to a bush with one hand and bailing out with the other. The mishap was due to his having kept to the middle of the stream when rounding a sharp bend. He had run into a stretch of what the natives call "smoky water."

IT REQUIRED A SKYLINE PHOTOGRAPH TO SHOW THEM

Young gulls' coloring harmonized closely with the rocks and gray brush.

His misadventure might have been avoided had we been in advance or had he known the river better. When asked about the matter, he cheerfully remarked that it was now plain why Tom had given him all the canned goods—"because they were waterproof."

At length the boats came to the first slack water, and the next turn revealed the lake, higher by several feet than usual at this season, but smooth and glowing in the quiet hour preceding sunset. For the first time the oars and paddles became necessary for locomotion and, relieved from the continuous strain of watching for rocks, log jams, rough water, and tumultuous whirlpools, we enjoyed the placid surroundings to the utmost.

Dividing the mouth of the river was a low, sandy island ablaze with a solid body of crimson flowers. A semicircular stretch of shore formed by a yellow ribbon of sand was backed by a green fringe of spruce. Still farther back on each side towering snow-capped mountains extended halfway down the lake. Beyond these, rounded hills sank into a great flat that extended to Cook Inlet on the west and to Turnagain Arm on the north.

A wide valley on the left, with a muddy floor resembling a former river course, Tom said was the outwash plain of a great glacier that began a few miles back and extended, he thought, 65 miles to the southwest.

His statement immediately aroused my interest, and during the succeeding days I learned much about the great ice field from which the Skilak glacier flowed. On my return to Seward, and later to Washington, I was able by dint of much inquiry to learn something of its history, with the view of ascertaining in a general way its origin and its probable status among the great ice fields of the northern continent.

THE GATEWAY OF SHEEP COUNTRY

We continued down the lake, and Tom pointed out what he called a "low divide" in the southern range, saying it was the gateway to the sheep country, 10 miles or so in the interior. In the setting sun the distant patches of alders and matted forests looked like smooth greenswards on gently sloping sides.

The climb appeared easy—an impression, however, that was changed considerably when we came to struggle for 3,000 feet up the precipitous sides, where our feet became imprisoned among gnarled limbs and the packs were continually catching in the stiff and unbreakable branches of the dwarf evergreen thickets.

On reaching the lake, we had studied its general contour, and estimated the distance to our first permanent camping site to be some 10 miles to the southwest. My desire to remain for one night at the upper end

ARCTIC TERN ENJOYED A RIDE ON A DEAD LIMB

The birds were loath to leave their floating perch in the center of Skilak Lake even when they were photographed at six feet.

THE KITCHEN AND DINING TENT AT SKILAK LAKE WAS OPEN

With ideal weather and surroundings to charm the eye of the nature lover, camp life was most enjoyable.

OTTERS SEEK SALMON IN A BAY OF SKILAK LAKE

They swim with heads high out of the water and bodies submerged. Thus they can see leaping fish.

of this fine body of water was strengthened by observing two rocky islets ahead, over which gulls, terns, and cormorants were flying in considerable numbers. As we passed these, we saw many nests. In a few minutes the boats were beached in a sheltered bay just opposite the islands.

Here we collected our first wild onions, which we found growing in the shallow waters. Erecting a single tent on the sandy shore, in order to escape a horde of mosquitoes that were buzzing in the forest, we passed a night rather uncomfortable, and noisy with the shrill cries of the gulls and the weird grunts and groans of the black cormorants. Soon after sunrise we visited the bird islands under escort of a great flock of protesting parents.

While the gulls and terns continued to circle just overhead, the cormorants flew short distances on heavy wings, and dropped into the lake to watch with anxiety our visit to their nursery. Some of the scenes are recorded in the accompanying pictures, with explanatory legends.

THE GIANT MOOSE OF THE KENAI PENINSULA

Continuing along the high and rocky northern shore for about seven miles, and finding the direction of the wind to be favorable, though a considerable sea was running, we crossed the lake, where it was about four miles wide, to a beautiful little beach flanked by an open grove of spruces. This site we selected for a two weeks' camp. It was at the end of the longest and most sheltered bay on the lake (see page 360).

The distance across the base of the promontory to the west being less than 75 yards, the canoe could be carried over and launched in the next bay. During the remainder of the stay we had boats in adjoining bays and thus saved considerable time by using either boat in accordance with the direction we wished to take. By this arrangement we were always able to take advantage of a lee shore, an important feature in a country where furious gales that are seldom forecast by the barometer, suddenly spring up in response to local conditions. For purposes of future identification, we called this Double-bay camp.

The erection of the tents, the manufacture of camp furniture, and the setting up of the light sheet-iron Klondike stove took the remainder of the day. Toward evening I ventured back into the forest to look for signs of a moose, for we were now in the home of *Alces gigas,* and several large runways on either side of the tents showed that we were trespassing upon one of its main thoroughfares around the lake. No fresh signs of any kind were in evidence.

At dusk, however, the guides saw, from a nearby knoll, five moose wading in the shallow waters of a pond a mile and a half distant. This sight went far to sustain the accuracy of the information upon which our camp had been located.

Selection of a good game country does not of itself guarantee individual success, though it is, of course, the most important element. Each individual of all our larger wild animals has a particular range often covering an extensive region. Within these ranges they quite often change more or less systematically, according to the season, or arbitrarily, according to the conditions of the weather and the food supply.

BOTH MOOSE AND SHEEP NEAR

If my advance information were correct—and it came from several sources—it meant that I should find moose in an area of less than a square mile, and at a period of the year when they were hardest to locate. The white sheep were to be looked for in several converging ranges, all under easy scrutiny from a single point of observation.

In all my journeys to the wilderness home of hoofed animals, I have only occasionally found an extensive region without animal licks, those resorts where the mineralized waters or soil attract ruminant quadrupeds. True, many of these spots are unknown to the hunters, even those familiar with the locality; nevertheless some hunter or explorer frequently knows of such a place. And here the game photographer should locate for a while, without any fear of the criticism that every true sportsman would voice at the destructive custom of killing visiting animals at a lick, be it natural or artificial (see Volume I, Chapter XII).

An Eastern sportsman had informed me that a mile or so west of the present camp there was a good-sized lick and, from the signs about it, he judged that a number of moose visited it, even in the summer time. Since Tom had been his guide, I knew there would be no trouble finding it. I had also heard of a large lick near the south shore of the lake.

FIRST SIGHT OF GIANT ALASKA MOOSE

What happened the following day is described in extracts from my notebook: *"July 24, 1911—Thermometer, 68-50.*

"At 9 a. m., in a bright sun and a dead calm, we started to look for the moose lick near the shore, and situated, according to directions, at the westerly base of a long point, which I took to be the one heading toward the lower end of Caribou Island. In half an hour the canoe entered the channel between the island and the point, and in a few minutes we swung around toward the bight of the bay. Tom said that the previous winter, while he was crossing the lake with a dog-sled carrying provisions from Cook Inlet to a mining camp, he had run 14 moose, principally bulls, off Caribou Island, but he did not think we would see any bulls at this season, since they were all hiding in the thickets well up toward the mountain-tops.

"A moment later he whispered, 'Gee! there's a bull, and a big one, too!' What I had taken for the brown soil on the roots of an overturned tree was a large moose with antlers that merited attention, but no more than did the tawny color of its coat. I had never seen such antlers before, nor such a color. The moose was quietly watching the canoe, with the greater portion of his antlers shoved up into the lower branches of a spruce. After examining him carefully through a powerful field-glass, I was about to prepare for a picture when Tom, who had been gazing about, said, 'Gee! Two more bulls! Look to the left.'

"There, coming in line toward us, were two big brown-coated beasts with antlers which would have tickled a Maine hunter, but which were somewhat smaller than

A FAIR-SIZED BULL COMES TO THE EDGE OF THE LICK
Note the long, remarkable "bell," which dangles for 18 inches from its neck and looks exactly like
a broken halter end, swinging freely as the animal walked.

those of the first one seen. I got the camera ready for the pair.

"The bulls turned toward the bigger one and for a moment or two rubbed noses in a friendly way. It was the climax of my opportunity, but I missed it by overcaution. The pair passed to the rear and soon were out of sight. They had doubtless been disturbed by us farther down the shore. The big fellow, however, motionless as an image, still gazed at the three heads peering over the edge of the grass."

"No other animal is more obtuse and stolid than the moose appear at times, and no other animal, when he is finally alarmed, is a more helpless victim of an increasing and progressing fear. At times it seems almost impossible to alarm one, but once the alarm is accomplished, one wonders if the moose will ever recover from the shock.

"Getting out of the canoe, I counted on taking a picture of the big bull as he swung clear of the tree. Walking slowly, I got within 50 feet, when he backed a few yards and then peered under the branches from the other side. After taking a picture in this unsatisfactory position, I again advanced, but he slowly turned about and walked away with the spruce intervening.

"Somewhat disappointed, I returned to

THE MOOSE LICK OF SKILAK LAKE WAS HARD TO FIND

The impregnated soil had been eaten several feet below the surrounding marsh, exposing rocks and uncovering many small mineral springs. The view shows the lower half of the lick, looking toward and across the western end of the lake (see text, page 377).

THESE OFFER A NEW SPORT FOR OLD SPORTSMEN

In the picture are some of the finest moose antlers found in the ten days at Double Bay camp. The collection was added to later (see text, page 386).

THE AUTHOR WENT A LITTLE CLOSER

When the cow moose turned toward him, the camera recorded a second picture of her (see text, page 380).

the water, and was about to step into the canoe when I noticed that the bull was coming back. In a minute he was gazing once more at me through the branches of the spruce. Since it was now time for his noonday rest, and since he evidently was determined to see the thing out in a comfortable way, he unconcernedly lay down. For the first time I was able to see, in all their symmetry, the great antlers just above the top of the high grass.

"This led to a change in my plans, and, detaching the smaller and faster lens, I got out a big telephoto to obtain, by a slower exposure, a picture of the antlers. Armed in this way, I began a slight advance to where the footing would be firmer. At this the moose got up with considerable energy,

and all I could see on the focusing mirror was his slowly retreating rear—an unattractive target for the camera, however vulnerable it might be to a ball projected by a modern rifle.

THE BIG MOOSE LICK OF SKILAK LAKE

"Thus, in 10 minutes, three big bulls had offered what would have been easy rifle shots to the veriest tyro; but a single picture, worthless beyond its power to recall the scene to mind, was the only result of my first encounter with the giant moose.

"Pleased by the prospect and disappointed somewhat by the retrospect, I began a search for the lick, which I felt sure was not far away.

"A short distance beyond the canoe, in

THE AUTHOR DELIBERATELY SCARED THIS BULL MOOSE

So unsophisticated was the animal that, after a few pictures, it did not fear man. It had to be given a lesson for its own good (see text, page 381).

THIS LARGE COW MOOSE EDUCATED HERSELF (SEE PAGE 380)

She stood broadside, head up, and unquestionably looking at the photographer out of one eye, but to all appearances she was utterly indifferent to his approach until she caught his scent.

THIS YOUNG BULL MOOSE WAS RECKLESS

HE HAD TO BE EDUCATED BY FORCE

One of the author's amusing adventures involved teaching this animal to beware of man (see text, page 381, and illustration, opposite page).

THE AUTHOR THREW A CLUB AT THE YOUNG BULL

The marksmanship was poor, for the stick struck the ground just this side and, one end flying up, hit the animal in the pit of the stomach. This probably had greater effect than a drubbing on the ribs, however much it violated the ethics of striking below the belt, for he jumped up into the air with his back arched like a scared cat.

the corner of the little bay that lay to our left, we found a large mud hole around which the grass had been trampled for some weeks. The roiled condition of the water showed that one or more moose had been there within a few hours. Looking beyond and through a fringe of trees, I could see a big bare area, the surface of which was plainly several feet below the surrounding marsh.

"Familiar with similar conditions elsewhere, I felt certain that this was one of the greatest resorts of its kind I had seen in many years. Moose had either eaten the

removed soil, or swallowed it in the process of guzzling the mineralized water that oozed out here and there and covered a considerable part of the surface (see page 372).

"It was plain, too, on closer inspection, that the long drought had begun to affect the surface flow; for much of the ground was hard and dry. This accounted for the moose opening up a new lick near the lake by tapping the springs at the base of the sloping shore.

"The number of fresh tracks and the variation in their size finally convinced

A COW MOOSE CAME TOWARD THE AUTHOR
While changing plate-holders, he was surprised to see her turn about and approach on a slow trot.
To the uninitiated this would probably have meant a charge (see text, page 380).

Tom that a good many bulls were regular patrons of this watering place. Since the surrounding country had all been burned over many years before, conditions were somewhat unfavorable for daylight photography. Bull moose, unlike the caribou and elk, are largely nocturnal, especially when visiting licks or exposed feeding places. The ones we had just seen were early morning visitors, and the little patch of spruce would have sheltered them until afternoon or evening but for our unexpected arrival.

FEAR BANISHES STOLIDITY

"While talking over the location of the blind in reference to the position of the sun at different hours and the probable direction of the prevailing winds—the two vital elements in this kind of photography—we saw the big bull a mile away, tearing along the top of a bare ridge that led to the mountain forests. His gait showed that stolidity had at last given way to a belated but overpowering fear. We never saw that animal again in the weeks we spent on the lowlands. As we were cutting brush, a good-sized cow moose walked up within a stone's throw and trotted away unmolested.

"Anxious to learn the number and course of the runways, and the character of the country immediately back of the lake before taking up the daily vigil at the blind, we went inshore half a mile to the pond where the moose had been seen the evening before. Here several acres of pond lilies in shallow waters were untouched—not a leaf or root eaten or disturbed—a condition that was in striking contrast to similar places in the moose country of Maine, New Brunswick, central Canada and Minnesota, where such aquatic plants are considered the choicest summer food.

"Going a mile further, Tom recognized a high mound as the lookout for the other lick, which we examined with great care. It had been used to some extent, but appeared to be only a brief stopping place for the moose en route to the shore lick— as indicated by the runways, but more particularly by the condition of the soil."

Whenever the wind was favorable and the weather was clear, I went to the blind at the main lick, but usually between 9 and 4 o'clock the breeze came in from the lake, carrying my scent across the principal runways, so that within a few days a number of moose suspected, though unjustly, that

JIM JEFFRIES WAS IN ALASKA ON A MOOSE HUNT
Near Skilak Lake, on the Kenai, the author met the former world champion heavyweight pugilist (right). He was out with a guide after fresh meat.

a foe was in ambush near the lick. Altogether I saw some 30 moose in the immediate neighborhood.

One big moose came within easy rifle shot, got the scent and retired, and two others, equally big, were at the lick one morning on my arrival, but could not be photographed from the water. All the others, with one exception, were cows or bulls ranging from one to five years of age.

The exception noted was an enormous bull that came down wind on a rarely used runway to the rear of the blind. The first intimation I had of his presence was a loud grunt behind my back just when I was eating lunch one day, and I nearly choked with surprise. In the excitement he got away, leaving me only a mental picture of a frightened moose and a flustered photographer.

I saw no calves, but only the tracks of a few in some of the heavily forested valleys about the lake. Occasionally large moose could be seen a mile or two away feeding in and out of the willows near the summits of the mountains.

The light-brown color, noticed the first day, was the rule in the case of all the other moose, the shade approaching very closely

that of the great brown bear of the inland. Judging from the shreds of the spring-shed hair and that of several abandoned hides near hunting camps, the winter pelage must be a light buff-brown in color. In the extreme southern range most moose are dark-colored in summer, looking almost black at a distance, with a somewhat lighter shading on the legs and flanks.

HAIR WHITE AT ROOTS

Some of the pelts examined show that all the hair of the narrow abdominal strip was glossy black, while that of the side and back had buff-brown tips, with a pure white body to the root. If the darker tips were clipped, the animal would appear to be white from the ventral strip upward.

The giant moose differs mainly from its counterpart in eastern Canada by its larger size and bigger antlers combined with certain skull and color characters. The largest pair of antlers known had a spread of a little more than 78 inches.

When we returned from our trip into the white sheep country, we camped on Caribou Island in the river opposite the big salt lick where we had made our first observa-

THESE ANTLERS, WITH THE SKULL SPREAD OF FIVE AND A HALF FEET

It is impossible to tell whether the animal died of old age or from wounds. The largest antlers recorded from the Kenai Peninsula ranged between 74 and 77 inches in width (see text, page 386).

tions on moose on our way in. From this location we had several encounters with regular patrons of the lick so much out of the ordinary that they are given below.

A COW MOOSE THAT BECAME SELF-EDUCATED

"Caribou Island Camp, August 17— Thermometer, 74-38.

"Just before noon the wind veered to the south, coming well offshore. Charlie paddled me across the bay to the blind and then went after a mess of partridges.

"I was hardly in ambush before the old cow moose was at a mud hole opposite, drinking a gallon or two of the muddy mixture. So active was the effect upon her salivary glands that long strings of saliva drooled to the ground.

"Determined to try for a close picture and to test her disposition when thus interrupted, I boldly walked into view, crossing the bare and much-trampled field to within 50 feet. She stood broadside, head up, and unquestionably looking at me out of one eye, but to all appearances utterly indifferent to my approach. I took a picture and went a little closer. She turned away without looking, and again the camera recorded the scene (see page 375).

"While changing plate-holders, I was surprised to see the moose turn about and come toward me at a slow trot. To the uninitiated this would probably have meant a bold charge, and to the nature faker sufficient grounds for an exciting story. The animal was now so close that I could notice her nostrils working convulsively, and could see that if let alone she would pass to my leeward about five feet—the first position in which she could get the scent without coming at me directly.

"Wishing to avoid alarming her so soon, I backed across the field to the edge of the

A FEMALE SPRUCE PARTRIDGE MAKES HERSELF AT HOME

She is sitting on an old hawk's nest. She represents a species common in the wooded parts of the Kenai as well as in other forested sections of Alaska.

marsh, but she still followed. Turning my back to the animal, I walked ahead, and upon reaching a place where the ground was almost impassable with fallen timber, I stopped. By this time I noticed that she had crossed my tracks, and thinking perhaps I was mistaken about her wishing to get the scent, I awaited developments. The cow immediately came up, circled almost within reach, and suddenly caught the scent.

"The effect was instantaneous and remarkable. It is unlikely that this animal had come into range of human beings many times in the wilderness that was her home, yet she recognized the scent. As she realized that man was near, she sank back on her haunches, and I noticed that her shoulders trembled violently, just as if a

rifle ball had penetrated her through and through. With a quick, awkward plunge, she made off at her fastest gait. Thus this innocent and apparently impassive animal suddenly revealed her inherited dread of human scent."

A LITTLE BULL MOOSE THAT WAS FORCIBLY EDUCATED

A few days later there occurred another similar scene in the same locality and with a somewhat amusing sequel:

"August 27—Thermometer, 58-34.

"One of my favorite visitors was a little bull moose. At first he always came in company with a five-year-old, but the latter got too much scent on one occasion and ran off, with the smaller one trailing wonderingly behind. But on this particular occa-

A YELLOW-HAIRED PORCUPINE HAD COME TO GNAW THE SHED ANTLERS
It became necessary finally to suspend these trophies on wires from trees to keep them safe from such thieves as these and the squirrels.

sion he was alone. The way he kept eyeing the blind rather indicated that he had visited it in my absence. He came from the long point, where the flies were scarce, and after filling up nearly to the bursting point on lick water, he lay down unconcernedly in the middle of the lick to take a nap.

"Since this was to be the next to my last day in the blind, I concluded to try some more experiments. As I came out of the blind, he saw me at once, but did not get up—simply turned his ears my way and expressing great astonishment in his big, round eyes. When I got very close, he arose and walked to the edge of the marsh, where, getting the sun behind me, I took his picture (see page 376). Later I tried to force him down toward the lake where there was a more effective background. This he objected to, but ran about playfully, showing no concern at the scent.

"After taking a few more pictures, I concluded that I would be doing him a very poor service to leave him in this unsophisticated state of mind. It was plain he now no longer feared the sight or scent of man, and would doubtless soon fall a victim to a party of hunters who were camping half a mile down the shore. Selecting a good-sized club, I got as close as possible, an undertaking in which I was helped by grunting like a bull.

THROWING A CLUB AT A MOOSE

"Throwing the missile with all my force at his well-covered ribs, I gave a piercing yell at the same time. The marksmanship was poor, for the stick struck the ground short and one end flying up hit him in the midriff. This probably had greater effect than a drubbing on the ribs, however much the ethics of such an encounter were violated by the blow below the belt.

"He jumped into the air with his back arched like a scared cat. When he came down, there was no doubt about his intention or ability to get out of that part of the country. Before I could pick up the camera he had vaulted over and beyond the fallen timber."

Only when I blew up the huge grizzly bear with a flashlight machine (page 309), have I known an animal that got its education more quickly, and never, as later events proved, to better purpose.

The following day I came to the blind at an early hour, hopeful that one of the big bulls from the hills would come within photographic range. Just what occurred becomes a sequel to the diary entry of the previous day.

"*August 28—thermometer, 72-38*

"From the start the wind was variable and so light that the mosquitoes became annoying for the first time. Twice I saw a cow moose wandering about, but she was wary. As the hours passed, I was satisfied that the little bull had made his valedictory appearance and was not disappointed by the thought.

"Precisely at 2 I heard the sound of a heavy animal running, then a splash down toward the lake. I could see the little bull struggling out of a mud hole, his feet working like the blades of a water-wheel. Out he got and rushed on without a stop or a glance to the rear. Evidently something was after him—possibly a grizzly bear that looked almost as big as a locomotive.

"Getting out the field glass, I covered what looked like his back tracks for a long distance. I finally noticed the figures of two men coming down the hillside. Since each was armed with a rifle I knew they were not my guides.

"On their approach I arose, and after a greeting found that the larger and heavier of the two was Jim Jeffries, the ex-heavyweight champion of the world. He explained in substance that they were out after a supply of fresh and tender meat, preparatory to hunting big bulls for their heads and had seen in a dense cover the flanks of a small moose. To make sure it was not a cow, the killing of which was prohibited by law, they had crept up very close, and made a slight noise to cause the moose to bring his head into view.

"The animal had given a quick glance out of the corner of one eye and run down the hill as if the devil was after him. Not till the moose was beyond favorable rifle shot did the glass disclose to the hunters the small antlers. They were now pursuing it in hope of a shot. The man of muscle trusted that they had not interfered with my getting a photograph of the little bull. Assuming a slight disappointment, I indicated that I was fully rewarded by the opportunity thus presented of getting a photograph of a *homo gigas,* and snapped him instanter."

THE LITTLE BULL PROFITED BY HIS BAD SCARE

A month later I heard that the little bull had apparently gone through the hunting season unscathed. This year he is proudly growing a pair of Y-shaped horns, and who knows but what in the course of time he will be seen stalking across the ruddy tundra or standing like a sentinel on a granite ridge wearing a polished and serrated crown, so remarkable in size and symmetry that the *Alces gigas* of the Kenai shall have in him an individual that will represent in the future as in the past the largest of the antlered race since the days of the prehistoric Irish elk.

When a sportsman visits the distant

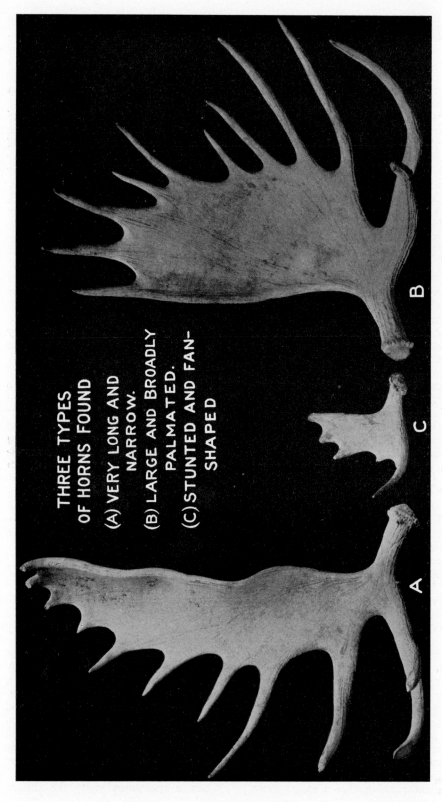

THREE TYPES
OF HORNS FOUND

(A) VERY LONG AND
NARROW.
(B) LARGE AND BROADLY
PALMATED.
(C) STUNTED AND FAN-
SHAPED

THESE THREE DIVERGENT TYPES OF ANTLERS WERE FOUND BY THE EXPEDITION

There was a remarkable resemblance between them and those of the Upper Yellowstone River (page 320). Confinement of the moose in a limited area at a high altitude may account for this resemblance, since elsewhere in Alaska the antlers are normal.

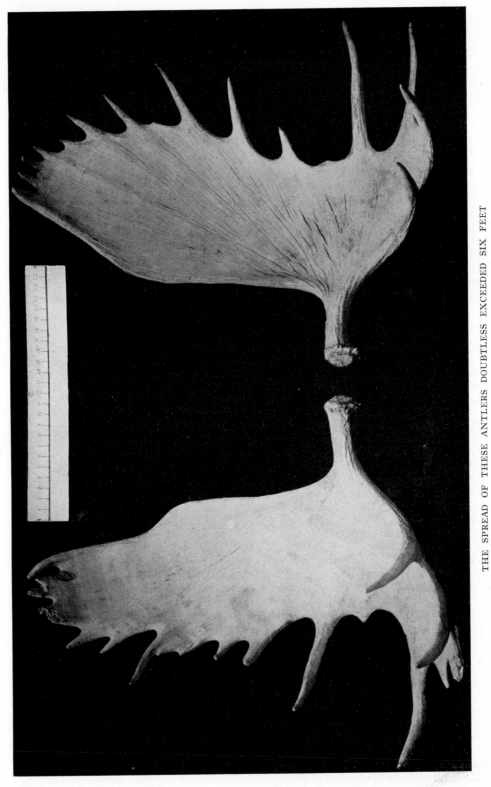

THE SPREAD OF THESE ANTLERS DOUBTLESS EXCEEDED SIX FEET

This large pair of symmetrical antlers is noticeable for the absence of any divisional separation of the brow antlers, the palmation being continuous in each antler.

A MALE WILLOW PTARMIGAN ALIGHTS ON A ROCK IN A ROARING STREAM

wilderness and shoots a big bull elk, moose, or caribou, especially in the rutting season, when they are most easily found and killed, it is seldom that any of the rank flesh is used, and the antlers afford the only trophy. The great carcass, weighing from 400 to 1,200 pounds, according to the species, is left for the ravens and the wolves or coyotes to feed upon. Even though such big beasts are killed at a time when the meat is untainted, its toughness or the great distance from civilization means that it is unused.

Between November 1 and March 1 the larger bull caribou, moose, and elk shed their antlers, and in the order of dates suggested. Unlike the white-tailed deer, which usually drop their antlers in January in the dense coniferous forests and swamps, where porcupines, rabbits, red squirrels, and mice soon destroy or disfigure them, the caribou, when feeding in the winter time on the lichens of the wind-swept barrens, the elk in the open parks and rolling hillsides, and the more northerly moose in the willow thickets or second-growth hardwood forests, usually cast their antlers in places harboring fewer forms of rodent life. In such places one may find many fine antlers.

Such as have become bleached from long exposure can be stained to their natural color, and, when mounted on a wooden base, in simulation of the frontal bone, they resemble in all respects the antlers of freshly killed animals. While it has long been the custom in this country to mount the head and neck, after a lapse of time the shrinking skin, the twisted ears, and the ravages of the moths play havoc with the work of the taxidermist. The old English method of using only the horns and part of the skull has much to recommend it; for many such ancient specimens after centuries of exhibition are superior in appearance to some heads that have been prepared for only a few years.

A NEW SPORT FOR OLD SPORTSMEN

Of course, only the largest and most symmetrical of shed antlers should be mounted, but these will be outstanding in comparison with inferior heads. The network of runways throughout the poplar and birch thickets that were discovered during the several weeks spent in studying the moose near Skilak Lake showed very plainly that this was one of the great winter feeding ranges and that a systematic search would doubtless bring to light many antlers.

In this effort we were successful from the start, and nearly every afternoon one or two especially large or oddly shaped antlers became a part of our canoe cargo. If the camera failed in its quest, here were the discarded crowns of the giant moose, some of them worthy of permanent preservation.

By carefully noting the course of our

A BOAT LOAD OF ANTLERS WAS GATHERED ON THE OPEN MARSHES ON A SINGLE
AFTERNOON

rambles, we found that in less than a week we had pretty well covered a square mile. We had brought to view 26 nearly perfect antlers, besides nearly an equal number, found in the bordering spruce forests, which the porcupines had badly gnawed (see pages 382, 384, and 385).

The members of two hunting parties who visited our camp were surprised and pleased at this collection, and could not understand why they had seen only a few worthless antlers in their long journeys afoot. This was because they were usually content to confine their examination of the more open country to watching it from a knoll with the aid of field glasses, or because they failed, when walking about, to detect the prong or two nearly hidden in the soft moss. Further than this, they did not know the meaning of the great white slabs that were visible here and there on many an exposed hillside.

Three distinct types resembling those of the Rocky Mountain animals were found; first, the so-called normal, or broadly palmated kind; second, one of great length and relatively narrow, and, third, a small fan-shaped variety.

The first type was represented by two rather unusual modifications: (a) great thickness of the lower beams with a second set of brow tines beneath, and (b) broadly palmated antler with no so-called brow tines (see illustration, page 384).

In no other range of the moose have I found such a variety except in the mountain valley of the Upper Yellowstone River, and it suggests the possibility that the northern latitudes and segregation affect and vary the antler growth as do the higher altitudes farther south.

I earnestly contend that it is a false pride that leads a sportsman to pass by a beautiful antler not taken by himself and a false standard that always requires that his antler trophies be removed from the heads of animals he himself has killed. To the public, for the use of museums, and in the comparison and differentiation of the types, shed antlers are just as valuable and just as interesting as if they had been taken from a recently killed animal.

NUMBERS OF MOOSE ON KENAI

Photographing wild animals requires all the skill and endurance demanded by the most ardent and experienced sportsman, and the finding of the discarded antlers of a giant moose adds to the photographic hunt both zest and a valuable trophy. Fortunately for this branch of sport, it requires patience, persistence, and a fair knowledge of the animal's habits and range. When the best antlers only are selected, the collection will represent quite as much skill and value as if they had been secured by killing its unfortunate owner.

THIS FEMALE ROCK PTARMIGAN WAS PHOTOGRAPHED AT A
DISTANCE OF ONLY FIVE FEET

The hen had two warning notes for the young, one causing them to remain stock still or crouch wherever they happened to be—so faithful was the obedience that one could pick them up—and another which caused them immediately to seek an overhead protection, either beneath the broken rocks or under the rims of snow or ice (see text, page 393).

would come and wait for the trees to fall, and would rush forward to appease their hunger before the treetop fairly struck the ground.

In February, 1928, Mr. Van Campen Heilnes published in the *Outlook* some interesting facts regarding the numbers of the moose on the Kenai in 1927. He saw 111 moose, including 29 bulls and 82 cows, in one day, and stated that it was not uncommon to see 60 to 70 in a day. The resident Alaska game warden, Hardy, estimated that at that time the Kenai Peninsula contained from 8,000 to 10,000 moose, and that only about 100 bulls were being killed annually by hunters. In a circumscribed area like the Kenai such an abundance of big game carries with it a distinct menace for its own future. In 1931 it was reported that persistent, year-after-year pursuit of big-antlered animals has reduced their numbers on the Kenai until a really large pair of antlers is now rarely seen.

I have already mentioned the abundance of moose observed by me during my hunt on the Kenai in August, 1911. Since that time many conflicting accounts of conditions there have been spread from year to year, some people even going so far as to assert that this great game animal is in danger of extermination in that area through overkilling by man. As a matter of fact, for years after my visit, moose were more abundant there than in any other area of equal size in the world, and the greatest danger facing them was the starvation that may result from exhaustion of the available winter forage.

While Dr. E. W. Nelson was at Seward the summer of 1920, a local guide guaranteed to show him at least 300 moose in a week, if he would go back into the moose country. During some of the winters following the snow was so deep on the Kenai that the food supply was deeply buried and starvation confronted many of the animals. The hunters and trappers in the region appreciated the situation and cut down many birch trees in order that the moose might feed upon the tops. The animals soon learned the meaning of the sound of the ax, and some of them were so hungry they

THE MOOSE IN GENERAL

The moose, largest of the deer kind, is so curiously proportioned and otherwise different from the existing species of deer that it gives the impression of being a survival from ancient geological times when grotesque forms of animal life roamed the earth. At no distant time, comparatively, the moose was practically circumpolar in distribution, occupying the great forested belt so characteristic of northern lands. It still maintains itself in much of this great range from the Scandinavian Peninsula in Europe eastward through northern Siberia and North America to Nova Scotia.

The moose is neither an astute nor an agile

animal compared with some of the deer, and because of the settlement of parts of its haunts it has disappeared from much of its former range. At one time its decreasing numbers in parts of North America appeared to indicate its approaching doom. It once occurred in considerable numbers in the forests of several of the northern United States, but is now restricted to northern Maine, northern Michigan, northern Minnesota, and limited parts of Wyoming, Montana, and Idaho.

Of recent years in Canada and Alaska the future prospects for the moose have greatly improved. The animals have spread westward in Ontario to occupy the entire northern shore of Lake Superior and northward in Canada to within the watershed of the southern Hudson Bay region and to the Delta of the Mackenzie River, within the Arctic Circle. In Alaska they are continuing to occupy new areas. A part of this extension of range, especially in the Lake Superior region, may be due, in part at least, to the second growth forest on vast cut-over areas which has provided an abundance of browse where little was to be found previously. These factors, with adequate laws, should insure perpetuation of these animals.

A FEMALE AND THREE YOUNG OF THE ROCK PTARMIGAN
The subdued and grayish-brown plumage makes a photograph of the four birds difficult without a background of white.

THE JUNCTION OF THE KENAI AND RUSSIAN RIVERS
The milky, glacial waters of the former commingle with the clear, spring-fed waters of the other.

So far as known, the smallest representatives of the moose with rather insignificant antlers are those of northern Europe. The largest of them all appears to have its headquarters in Alaska. The weight of old bulls in North America ranges from about 900 to more than 1,400 pounds.

To the mountain climber of the northland there are no other birds more interesting than the ptarmigan. One species, the willow ptarmigan, or willow grouse,

PARENT BIRDS OF WILLOW PTARMIGAN GUARD A RETREAT OF THEIR YOUNG

The birds show remarkable cunning in enticing enemies away from their offspring (see text, page 391).

MALE SALMON WORRY THE FEMALES IN KENAI RIVER

In the upper pair the rear fish is rending the tail of the other; in the lower couple the fish to the right has just bitten a piece out of the dorsal fin of the other. Continuously and relentlessly they struggled in couples, rending and tearing the fins and tails, scoring with their sharp teeth the somewhat smoother sides, and occasionally seizing the nose or lower jaw of their victim. In one pool, separated by shallow water from the others, there were ten salmon, and all in fierce contention.

occupies the tundra and scattered thickets bordering the tree limit. A hardier and more humbly plumed kind, the rock ptarmigan, lives a little higher on the rocky slopes. These birds are so numerous and so tame that they may be readily obtained and can be counted upon to supply the larder with a portable and well-flavored article of food. For several weeks we were in their midst, and when making daily rounds to the glassy plateau, where the sheep were apt to be found, I spent a good deal of time following up the smaller streams in order to study and photograph the birds in their natural surroundings.

PTARMIGAN YOUNG IMITATE THEIR MOTHER

She stands erect and the little ones instinctively follow her lead.

Familiar with many other species of grouse, I was particularly impressed by one characteristic of the cock willow ptarmigan. The bird differed from male grouse of the species of the forest and prairie in that he almost invariably accompanied the female during the entire breeding season and, moreover, was the more aggressive parent of the two in times of peril.

WILLOW PTARMIGANS CLEVERLY PROTECT THEIR YOUNG

One's proximity to the family was usually foretold by the sudden fluttering out of the cock, which, with a limp and trailing wing, employed the usual devices of most ground-breeding birds in the effort to coax into futile pursuit any known or suspected enemy. If successful in leading the foe away from the spot where the young crouched by the side of their silent mother, the cock would take wing, uttering loud and raucous notes, to find concealment in a nearby thicket.

If an interloper persisted in trying to locate the young, the female would renew the effort to distract attention. If this did not succeed, she would utter a peculiar note as a signal for the male to return. Between the two of them further efforts would be made to guard against the discovery or injury of the young birds.

In a hundred or more observations we found that the cock was absent only half a dozen times, which might be accounted for by his having met an untimely death in defense of his family or by a temporary absence in search of food.

Two instances of this strategic cooperation of the parents may be quoted from my notebook:

"Following the creek bottom for nearly a mile, we found the ptarmigan unusually abundant, for the day was warm and quiet and the birds were sunning themselves on the gravel bars or dusting their feathers in basins hollowed out in the sloping banks. One brilliantly colored cock rushed out at us from a patch of dried grass, and I followed him down the stream for a few rods with the camera in hand. His gait, however, increased until he took wing, and I returned to the spot where the rest of the family were doubtless concealed. I could see the hen faintly outlined in the thin grass, but overlooked the five or six young, almost at my feet, until the mother bird took flight and they, too, popped up into the air. On their short wings they managed to fly out of the creek bottom and tumble into a willow thicket a few yards away.

A LUCKY SNAP SHOT

"Going to the lower end, I had one of the guides walk through the willows; but before the family were driven out the cock returned in response to the call of the hen. I finally took a picture of him standing boldly on a rock in midstream. The parents then led the young into a bed of blue flowering peas, and when the two returned to guard the retreat I got a portrait of them (see pictures, pages 386 and 390).

"While sitting in a spruce blind waiting for moose, I noticed a large hawk circling the marsh in search of prey. As it passed behind me, there was a roar of wings, and,

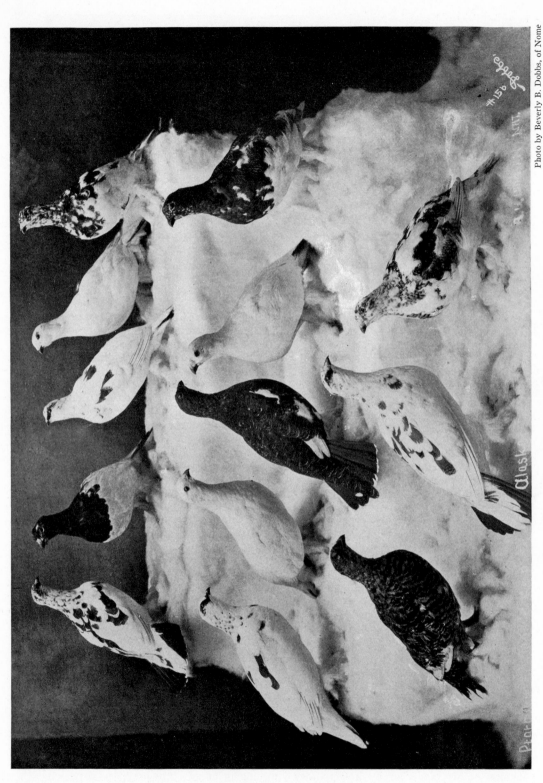

Photo by Beverly B. Dobbs, of Nome

THIS MOUNTED GROUP OF WILLOW AND ROCK PTARMIGAN SHOWS THE WINTER (WHITE) AND SUMMER (DARK) PLUMAGE,
WITH THE INTERMEDIATE SPRING AND FALL DRESS

turning, I saw a brood of willow grouse in the air with the hawk poised above them, apparently uncertain which victim to swoop down upon.

"Before this was determined, the cock shot up straight as an arrow in front of the hawk, and the race was on. For the first 50 yards the two were separated by only a few feet, but the way the cock suddenly increased its speed showed very plainly that its flight had been under check until the hawk was lured away far enough to give the surprised family a chance to find some sort of concealment.

HAWK DEFEATED IN BATTLE

"In a minute or so the hawk returned and carefully circled over the hummocks of moss, looking intently for the slighest trace of one of the covey. Down it suddenly dropped for a distance of 20 feet, undoubtedly seeing the brown feathers of a partly concealed bird. With equal speed the hen darted up and apparently hit the body of the hawk just below the tail.

"Either because the talons could not clutch tight in such a position, or because the hawk was unable to strike with accuracy, the daring mother escaped, with the enemy in fierce pursuit. By flying slowly, she enticed the hawk some 50 yards away, then dropped like a plummet into a bunch of alders. The hawk perched himself on a nearby limb to plan anew how to obtain his breakfast.

"The defeated aviator, however efficient its mathematical processes, knew that two from eight left a substantial remainder, and once more he took wing and returned for a survey of the tangled moss. This time I met him with a shout and a waving hat from the spruce blind; and, much disgruntled, he soared away, doubtless wondering at the intervention of a third party."

On the Kenai Peninsula the timber line is at an altitude of about 2,000 feet, and only twice did we notice willow ptarmigans below it, where they were feeding in an open glade upon the earlier ripening swamp huckleberries. The usual abodes of this bird are the tablelands along upland streams terminating in ravines, where the willows and small bushes succeed the limit of arboreal growth.

The rock ptarmigan stays on the treeless slopes above the main range of the willow ptarmigan, while a third species, the white-tailed ptarmigan, lives in the rocks, where the lichens and patches of grass denote the approaching limit of all vegetation. On the other hand, the spruce partridge remains well within the forested area and is usually to be found in river bottoms or in the second-growth, burnt-over portions of the lowlands.

Thus these four species of northern grouse, whose ranges are complementary, are largely if not wholly controlled by the distribution of plant life, which in turn is dependent on climatic conditions mainly determined by altitude.

One afternoon I saw a small and apparently young red fox coming rapidly down a rock slide, evidently trailing something, but not seeing his quarry. With a field glass I could make out a brood of rock ptarmigan scurrying ahead. When the birds reached the bank of a small ravine, filled nearly to the surface with snow, the hen flew up about 10 feet to alight on the snow, and the little ones with an effort did likewise. Thus concealed from the immediate sight of the fox, they ran a short distance and squatted, where they were practically invisible from their close resemblance to the detached rocks and soil that dotted the edges of the snow.

When the fox reached the bank, he looked intently about and, seeing nothing, descended, sniffing along the surface of the snow below where the birds had alighted. Evidently thinking that they had flown across or had gone farther down, he climbed up the opposite bank. Here a large fat marmot, extracting a root only a short distance away, attracted his attention, and although the fox and the marmot were about the same size, the sudden flight of the latter invited pursuit, which ended unsuccessfully for the fox a few yards away, at the opening of the marmot's burrow.

THE MOTHER ROCK PTARMIGAN HAS TWO WARNING NOTES.

We passed so little time on the mountain summits that I had little chance to observe the habits of the rock ptarmigan and practically none to investigate those of the white-tailed species. In no case that I observed did the cock accompany the brood, and the birds seemed to have no fear whatever of the larger forms of animal life. The hen had two warning notes for the young, one causing them to remain stock still or crouch wherever they happened to be—and so faithful was the obedience that I could

THE IMPRISONED SALMON OF THE UPPER KENAI

This is a gaunt, fierce male, the under portion of the body deep red and that above the surface
of the water a dirty and festering yellow.

pick the young up—and another causing the young immediately to seek protection from overhead, either beneath the broken rocks or under the rims of snow or ice.

Once I saw seven small ptarmigan run beneath the edge of a block of ice, where all I could see of them was the projecting row of small black bills. In another case the young bird, alarmed by the mother's note, squeezed in between my shoes and remained there until relieved by a reassuring call. Hawks and foxes are the principal enemies, while moose, caribou, sheep, or man seem to be regarded in the light of friends.

CHAPTER XVII

Photographing the White Sheep of the Kenai

AFTER obtaining a fairly satisfactory series of photographs of the big moose of the Kenai, I turned my attention to the Alaska white sheep, which had been one of the two main objects of this expedition. While getting information preparatory to my Alaskan trip, I had been struck by the scarcity of photographs representing these sheep.

Since hundreds of the most experienced sportsmen from nearly all countries had pursued these animals, I had considerable doubt of my photographic success among them, even though I had a marked advantage in possessing a better equipment and in making photography my main object. With the others photography had been largely incidental.

STUDY PRECEDES PHOTOGRAPHY

I decided to locate and study the animals first in order to obtain information about their habits, and then, if possible, to make use of the knowledge thus acquired to get within photographing range. If I should at once begin harassing the sheep with the camera at close range, I might get neither pictures nor information.

Ten days were passed in the mountains, four of which were required in going and coming. The six days that I devoted to sheep, with incidental attention to ptarmigan, resulted in a fair collection of pictures. I think the result fully justified the program laid out in advance.

Several days before we started for the interior my old Michigan guide, John Hammer, joined us. The call of the North was irresistible to his Norwegian blood. The addition of a fourth man just as we were about to undertake the hardest part of the journey proved fortunate, especially since the swift waters of the Kenai River had to be overcome on our return to Seward.

At 6 o'clock on the morning of August 5 we were ready to leave Double Bay camp for a 10-days' trip to the sheep country. Tom and John in the heavy skiff and Charlie and I in the canoe made a start for the southeast corner of the lake, just opposite the bird islands. The weather was bright, and the barometer predicted a continuation of fine weather.

On rounding a point, we saw in the morning light the black and frowning features of volcanic Redoubt, and Iliamna's snowy peaks, 100 miles distant on the other side of Cook Inlet. We reached our immediate destination, Cottonwood Creek, in less than two hours, and, after placing our surplus outfit on a porcupine and bear-proof platform, made by Tom the previous season, we started up the mountain creek.

This stream originates in a big snow field just beyond the divide, over which we had to pass on our way to Benjamin Creek, and the cabin in which Tom had lived during a long and vain search for gold. Though Tom found no valuable metals, his effort is commemorated by the creek's being called after the name of his eldest brother.

The ascent was difficult, for the day was hot, the underbrush was a nuisance, and the packs were heavy. Gradually I shed all extra clothing and then lightened my pack, the guides good naturedly picking up the discards as they fell by the wayside. At noon we reached the tree limit half a mile from the divide. There on a rounded knoll where there was plenty of stunted spruce for firewood, we pitched a small tent in which I was to spend the night while the three men returned to the lake to bring up another load in the morning (see page 396).

A LAND OF MOUNTAINS AND RIVERS

After their departure I lay on a cushion of moss for several hours and viewed the landscape through the field glasses, gazing now into the valleys, now upon the foothills and peaks, and now down upon Skilak Lake and across the great untrodden tundra, with its many glistening ponds—the summer nursery of the moose. Most interesting in all this limitless stretch of scenery was Cook Inlet, looking like a giant river and banked on the northern side by the mountains of the Alaska Range, the great cordillera of the Territory, with Mount McKinley as the keystone.

Later my interest became centered in the animals and birds which, in the shadows of the declining sun, came out of thickets of evergreen and willow. At one time I could see a dozen black-haired porcupines, a geographic race of the animal common in east-

THE MOUNTAIN SLOPES ARE STEEP IN THE SHEEP COUNTRY

"Big Pond camp" in the foreground was situated midway between the cabin on Benjamin Creek
on the west and the great ice cap on the east. The author camped alone here several nights while
photographing white sheep. Two Alaskan bears visited the tent one night (see text, page 395).

ern Canada, feeding as stolidly as sloths on
the fresh vegetation that bordered the receding snow banks.

A cock spruce partridge came within five
feet of the tent, evidently mistaking it for
a snow bank; a brood of willow ptarmigan
appeared in the willows just above my
camp, and still higher up a fox brought to
view a covey of rock ptarmigan. Moose
signs were plentiful, but no moose were in
sight. The air resounded with the loud,
clear whistling notes of the hoary marmot,
known to the trappers and traders of the
Rocky Mountains of Canada and the mountains of Alaska as the "whistler" (see
pages 398 and 399).

Then came the mosquitoes, the post-
season crop of the higher altitudes. The
insect-proof tent was a welcome place of
refuge for the night.

On our way over the hills to the sheep
country, we ran into a great swarm of
yellow jackets which attacked us relentlessly. Recalling the Ojibway remedy for
such stings, I applied a tiny portion of wax
(cerumen) from my ear to the puncture I
had received and realized almost instant
relief.

I was somewhat amused when John came
hurrying up, saying in true Norwegian,
"These yellow yackets are mighty bad.
Lend me some of your wax, for mine is all
gone."

Many years ago I had this wax analyzed
to determine the particular element that afforded relief. Although satisfied with the
result of this inquiry, I decided that it was
much better to depend on its natural production, as it would always be at hand. To
some people this subject may seem indeli-
cate, yet this secretion is as pure and clean
as beeswax and its efficiency and availability
should be widely known.

On the following morning I had scarcely
finished breakfast when along came the
men, red-faced and tired from their fight

against gravity and the worst of mountain trails. An hour later we were climbing over the broken rocks that littered the floor of the divide, and thence entered a great plateau that sloped southerly to Benjamin Creek. During the rest of the day we struggled through bushes, stumbling into grass-concealed cracks, leaping from tussock to tussock, and circling around swamps and mud holes.

While we were thus toiling, Tom pointed out a number of round dots of white on a distant ridge that looked like weathered boulders or snowballs from the frozen fields above. These were the white mountain sheep for which we were searching.

NOT SO EASY AS IT SEEMED

When I asked Tom, somewhat hopefully, whether it would not be wise to begin the camera hunt at once, since it made no difference whether we frightened these sheep or not, he politely concealed a negative answer by saying that if I would circle two miles to the left, and ascend to the mountain top from the other side, he would drive the sheep toward me before dark.

This did not promise well for our arrival at Benjamin Creek on scheduled time; and since Tom assured me in a sympathetic tone that I would see four or five sheep in the country near his cabin to one here, we continued the march, and at 6 in the evening came suddenly within sight of the cabin, 200 feet below a terrace that bordered the valley of the creek. John and I were quite exhausted, John still suffering from the after results of typhoid fever contracted on our trip to Mexico the year before.

The restorative effect of a hearty meal and the inspiration of the surroundings soon gave me sufficient energy to climb a hill behind the cabin, and there, at 8 p. m., I could see, at the headwaters of Benjamin Creek, three bands of sheep, all preparing to pass the night on little open benches not much above the meadows. Such a sight told the story of a seldom-visited country in which these wild flocks felt secure by night and day.

At 8 o'clock the next morning the party, with the exception of John, who was left in charge of the commissary department, was ready to start after sheep. After following the creek eastward for half a mile, we went up over a series of sloping meadows for three miles. A little above the cabin three small streams came together to form Benjamin Creek. One flowed in a zigzag course from the snow fields on our side of the low divide above Skilak Lake, where the melting snow was likewise the source of Cottonwood Creek; another carried the overflow waters of a big pond in the highest meadow to the east; and the third drained several large valleys in the southeast.

The last two streams, lying between the highest and steepest mountains in the neighborhood, cut deeply into upland meadows that harbored not only the sheep I had seen the night before, but many others.

On the way up the valley we came to the last stretch of timber—spruce, mountain ash, and a considerable number of cottonwood trees, intermixed with willows and alders. At this terminus of the forest growth there were many trails of moose and numerous fresh beds made by these animals in patches of grass between the willows. It was obvious that the head of this high valley and the smaller ones containing willows were the summer resorts of the bull moose.

We found only two shed antlers in our extensive wanderings, one many years old, a fact that tended to confirm my opinion that all the moose that go to such elevations return to the shores of the lake and the adjoining lowlands in the late fall and mid-winter months. When Tom had hunted sheep here, he had always returned to the cabin at night; but, since to do so meant a waste of time and energy, we deemed it best to erect a tent in the midst of the range, where I could watch the sheep almost continuously during the 18 hours of daylight.

CAMP AT BIG POND

An hour after starting, we came to the pond. It seemed to be the best and most convenient location for my camp, since it commanded a view of three of the best sheep valleys, and yet was not too close to disturb the movements of the animals from one district to another. The tent was placed on a little knoll, close to a fine spring, where a great black mountain rising from the opposite shore of the pond afforded a striking background (see page 396). Numerous adjoining knolls covered with glacial rocks were the homes of many marmots, which viewed my canvas home with surprise and protestation (see page 398).

After luncheon we made a reconnaissance and located an unusually large flock of sheep up a valley to the north. There we passed the rest of the afternoon, with the

THE HOARY MARMOT IS RARELY FOUND BELOW TIMBER

These animals have a remarkable system of signals on the approach of an enemy. This one had just signaled the author's approach with an almost human whistle, as clear as a bell. The sound often confuses hunters who have been separated.

sheep brought within easy inspection by the use of a powerful field glass. The wind was blowing straight up the valley toward the flock, but there was no indication that any of them suspected our presence. I knew of the conflicting views held by sportsmen and guides in reference to the alleged inability of sheep to detect the nearby presence of man through scent, and it was one of my purposes to make every possible experiment to try to learn the facts.

Late in the afternoon Tom and Charlie returned to the cabin, leaving me to pass the night in the tent. Before dark I watched scattered bands of sheep leave the meadows for the higher slopes, where gradually they gathered into several good-sized bunches. At 9:30 o'clock, when distant objects had become obscure, I went into the tent, and while slipping into the sleeping-bag happened to look out the wire ventilator in the rear canvas wall. I saw two large animals

THE ENTRANCE TO THE SHEEP COUNTRY IS A LOW DIVIDE 3,000 FEET ABOVE
SKILAK LAKE

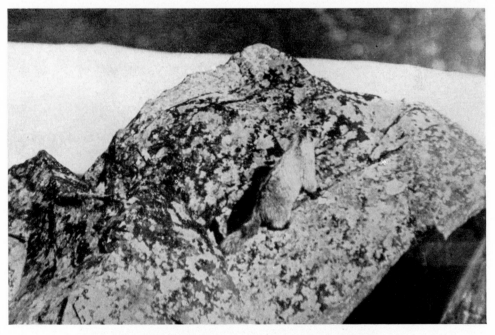

A HOARY MARMOT IS AN ELUSIVE SHADOW SHAPE

The northern type of the American woodchuck offers a good example of protective coloration.
This one was photographed on a mountain at the head of Benjamin Creek.

ALASKA WHITE SHEEP ARE VISIBLE FOR MILES

This is a typical view of them on a high slope bordering the snow fields, where considerable fresh vegetation is found for a short period on spots recently covered with snow. The writer is not a believer in the theory of protective coloration applied to the larger animals of this country. Some of the smaller animals and certain birds, fish, reptiles, and insects, whose enemies are largely the same today as in the past, are undoubtedly preserved by obliterative or deceptive colors, as well as by concealing shapes.

THIS SMALL BAND OF WILD SHEEP HAD JUST COME FROM THE MOUNTAIN TOP

They were in a low meadow covered with the fresh grass and small plants they seek for food. Several lambs were playfully jumping over their mothers.

BADLY FRIGHTENED WHEN PHOTOGRAPHED, THEY RAN UP A ROUGH MOUNTAIN

The author found the mountain sheep exceedingly wary and difficult to approach. It was only by long hours of crouching behind a blind that he obtained this picture of them.

A EWE STOOD SENTINEL

After a long stalk on all fours, the author got within 50 feet of her. Note her extremely long legs. The short black horns and white body have led many of the Alaskan miners from the Rocky Mountain States to mistake the females of these sheep for white mountain goats (see page 413).

THIS BIG RAM WAS PHOTOGRAPHED AT 50 FEET FROM AMBUSH

He jumped the instant after the shutter revolved, but left his picture behind him. Note the fine
poise of the head and the graceful horns (see page 411).

coming down a ridge a hundred yards back
of the tent. My first impression was that
they were sheep, or possibly caribou, but
when one rose on its hind legs and looked
about, I could only conclude that a pair of
the big Alaska brown bears had come to
the meadow to dig out marmots or ground
squirrels.

These animals have a bad reputation
among miners and explorers, due I think
to their immense size and their near relationship to the grizzly, around which many
of the blood-curdling tales of this country
have been woven. From my own experience
and the carefully sifted experience of others,
I had long ago come to the conclusion that
there are no dangerous wild animals whatever in the northern hemisphere, except the
grizzly, and that this is dangerous only occasionally when molested. Having no intention of interfering with these visitors, I
felt little concern, although I quite appreciated that it might be a dearly paid experience if I neglected all precautions.

I closed the opening of the tent and,
when it was too dark to see anything fur-

ther, crawled into the canvas sleeping-bag.
Once I thought I heard something sniffing
behind the tent, but there was no way of
determining the question without going outside. Gradually my nerves quieted and I
heard nothing more until the buzzing of the
mosquitoes greeted the early rising sun.

MANY FLOCKS OF SNOW-WHITE SHEEP

Several hours later Tom arrived with
cooked food sufficient for three meals.
After sampling some of this, we returned
again to the elevated valley, where we had
seen the sheep the afternoon before. The
big band had broken up again into small
flocks, which were feeding on the same
meadows, some of them working down our
way. The wind still continued to blow up
the valley, but since I now wished to get
some views of the sheep grazing on the
meadows and determine just how close one
could get before the scent created alarm, we
cautiously approached.

When we were within 1,000 yards of the
nearest flock, we made a little blind by
cutting out brush in the edge of a thicket

THEY FED FOR HOURS, NONE LOOKING ABOUT SAVE THE SENTINEL (UPPER LEFT)

The keen vision of these sheep is practically their sole reliance for detecting danger. They always feed or rest on open ridges or hillsides devoid of bushes, from which they can have an unhampered view in every direction. They also possess unusual power of inference, detecting danger from the actions of other sheep, however distant the latter may be.

on the top of a mound, and there we went into concealment for several hours. All the sheep were gradually working down wind, and the prospects for obtaining pictures and for determining their scenting power were excellent.

When within 300 yards of us, the nearest flock began showing some uneasiness. The old ewe in front, which had charge of this particular flock, several times raised her head and sniffed the air suspiciously. At 200 yards the leading ewe stopped and looked directly our way.

PICTURES TAKEN JUST IN TIME

I felt sure the limit of the approach had been reached and forthwith took several pictures of the band. None too soon was this accomplished, for the leader turned back, and in a stiff-legged and peculiar way strode through the flock, with her little lamb following obediently.

All the other sheep, some of which were grazing and some lying down, seemed to take immediate notice of what was going on; for when the old ewe reached the end of the flock and began to ascend the steep slope instead of continuing up the valley meadow, the rest fell in behind. In a few minutes a long file was zigzagging up the side of the mountain.

Here occurred another striking incident. Four large rams that had been reclining on the top of a flat rock 200 yards beyond the rest of the sheep all stood up and began looking about, first at the line of sheep ascending the mountain, and then down the valley. Whether their restlessness was due to the flock of sheep leaving the valley at that hour or to the manner or peculiar actions of the ewe, or whether they had got a trace of scent was hard to tell.

Soon the other sheep began working away from us, and finally dropped into a meadow walled in by a stone ridge that ran across the head of the valley, except where it was broken by a narrow opening through which a little stream dashed in a series of pretty cascades.

We saw none of the sheep drink water

THEY ARE CROSSING A SNOW FIELD TO CLIMB THE ADJOINING CLIFFS

Though they have fed all day in the valley meadows, they seek their eyries among the crags when
night draws near. Their bedding places are seldom seen save by intrepid mountain climbers.

either from the streams along which they
grazed or from any of the pools of water
in the green meadows. Whenever the sheep
became thirsty they always went to a snow
field. So noticeable was this habit that I
put in a part of one day getting into a position in which photographs could be taken
of sheep coming to the snow banks to eat
snow (see page 408).

A little later I saw a band of about 20
sheep coming on the dead run down the side
of a distant mountain toward the meadow.
They were jumping rocks, slipping and sliding down the steep sides of the bare mountain, and leaping across little terraces.

So striking was this sight and so certain
was I that these sheep were badly alarmed
that I aroused Tom, who was dozing in the
sun a few feet away, and pointed to the
sheep.

IT'S A WISE PARENT THAT CAN PICK OUT HER OWN YOUNG

In a high meadow still snow-flecked the two ewes on the left are having a disagreement over the ownership of four or five lambs that are playing together.

Looking at them for a moment, he said, "Why, those fellows are just coming to the meadow for their afternoon meal, and, seeing all the others at work, are losing no time in doing it. Just watch them and you will see that on reaching the bottom of the hill they will begin butting one another and cutting up all kinds of capers."

That is exactly what did happen; for when the sheep came to the edge of the little creek, butting matches began, and some of the lambs, in their playfulness, jumped entirely over their mothers. At the creek it was a pretty sight to see them leap from bank to midstream, where rocks amid swirling waters gave a footing, and thence again to the opposite shore.

The bunch of sheep that had come down the mountain in such haste either saw or smelled me when I photographed them, and they immediately departed by the same route they had come. Every sheep in the meadow behind the stone ridge left immediately for the mountain top. I was curious now to know just how this little meadow looked. We walked up and crossed over the top, to look down upon a beautiful spot. Below us was a circular meadow, containing a small but beautifully clear pond, and its trampled condition showed that every day the sheep came there for grass, which was unusually green and abundant. At one corner of the pond a good-sized mudhole was a possible indication of the presence of a lick, but I could not be sure of this at the time. I was sorry that I did not investigate it later.

This seemed an ideal place for close-range pictures, and we immediately began the construction of a blind on the face of the cliff overlooking the meadow. A narrow ledge gave just room enough for us to make a wall of flat stones behind which three of us could squeeze while we pointed the cameras downward. Our experiences in the blind the following day are described in my notebook:

A MORNING IN THE SHEEP BLIND

"August 12—Thermometer 75-52.

"Today was selected for a visit to the stone blind above the little basin meadow, regardless of wind or weather. The three of us passed a rather uncomfortable night in the small tent, and at an early hour I heard the men breaking the stunted willows for a fire and a cup of hot coffee. The fog for the first time had descended into the valley, and no object more than 50 yards away could be seen. This condition resulted in a later start than we had intended.

"When we were half a mile below the blind, the fog lifted suddenly and the warm, bright sunlight so illuminated the valley and the mountain sides as to accentuate the obscurity it had replaced.

"Above us on the left, near the summit of the mountain, were about 40 ewes and lambs, all lying down, but evidently looking at us. Two hundred yards above the blind, and on the same side as the others, were two big rams a little distance apart. One was watching us most intently, and in a moment it began the ascent. The other, apparently alarmed by his companion's going up instead of down at the feeding hour, began to scan the bottom. He soon saw us, although we were standing motionless. Instead of retreating, he walked to the edge of a cliff and, standing like a marble image, gazed in our direction.

TOO LATE TO GET NEAR THE FLOCK

"Soon our positions became irksome and we started for the blind, while the ram immediately trailed after his more cautious companion and disappeared over the mountain top. Had we arrived an hour sooner, none of these sheep would have been disturbed, and probably others would have been attracted from more distant points.

"Entering the blind, we soon made everything ready for an instant or continuous bombardment. An hour passed and nothing came down any of the many runways radiating like gray ribbons from the green meadow.

"Finally Tom, who thought that the big flock of ewes was past due, climbed cautiously to the top of the cliff behind the blind. On his return he said that not a single sheep was in sight. Among this flock were many that had seen us slipping up the valley. They had received additional warning by the hasty departure of the rams.

"The 'sure thing' counted upon, like most predetermined results, had missed a cog somewhere. At length, four sheep appeared on the skyline two miles away and started down one of the big runways leading to the valley. They came rapidly and soon were standing on a bare plateau a quarter of a mile above the meadow. Here they stopped and looked below, but in a few minutes began grazing on the sparse grass. After remaining half an hour they took a

THESE SHEEP REFUSED TO DRINK WATER, BUT ATE SNOW INSTEAD

They had spent the entire afternoon on a meadow well supplied with water. Life on the high mountains, where most of the year there is no water, and what there is in the summer swiftly cascades from the snow fields, seems to have been the cause of this taste.

ALASKA WHITE SHEEP TRAVEL TOWARD THE LARGEST SNOW FIELD IN THE VICINITY

Note the four big rams on the upper edge, and how inconspicuous they are when compared with the smaller sheep on the dark soil. The curved and bulky horns of the four rams can be clearly seen. The rams spent most of the summer on the extreme mountain tops, rarely accompanying the ewes.

THE BAND OF SHEEP SHOWN ON PAGE 408 TOOK ITS TIME EATING SNOW

The flesh of a young ram is quite the equal of the best Southdown mutton. It is appetizing whether fried, roasted, or stewed. The carcass will remain in excellent condition for many days.

trail toward the head of the valley, where there were doubtless many other sheep.

"It was then that the idea occurred to me that the photographer might take advantage of this 'follow-the-leader' habit of the sheep by using a few light and portable life-size silhouette decoys of white paper or canvas, similar to those used for geese and cranes in parts of the West. Such decoys could be placed at strategic points near a blind before the sheep were astir in the morning, or near their trails back to their bedding ground before the time for them to return in the afternoon.

"They could be set at any desired angle where they could be seen a long distance and might save uncertain and wearisome hours in the blind. We had noticed how quickly and unsuspiciously small and scattered bands of sheep descended and joined flocks already feeding in the valley.

"At noon we opened the lunch box, but before we had fairly made a start at it I saw a big ram approaching along a ridge from the direction of our camp. He came

rapidly, with head up and steps mincing, looking very much like a small and sturdy caribou stag. When in sight of the meadow, he stopped and looked down for fully five minutes, occasionally scanning the mountains on our side.

"We feared that, like the others, he would turn away at the sight of the deserted meadow. Tom, however, thought that he was anxious to join a band of his fellows, and might cross to our side in order to look for them beyond. At any rate, the ram soon started down toward the creek. We were in doubt as to his final destination.

"At the edge of the bank he disappeared. We felt sure that he would come along our ridge, but on which side was the question. Several moments passed, and I feared he was then passing behind the blind, cut off from our vision by a wall of rock against which our backs were resting.

"Slipping over my neck the camera strap, I was in the act of climbing over the top of the blind when Tom seized my arm, whispering: 'Good Lord, here he comes right at us.'

"There was the ram, not 40 yards away, stalking along most unconcernedly in a direction that would bring him to a point where he could gaze down into the blind. The several portholes that we had made for the camera all faced the meadow, for an invasion from any other quarter had not been looked for. When the ram was within 75 feet of us, I was in a quandary. If I should rise up nearly full length above the low wall of the blind, he would be instantly alarmed, and I would have no time to obtain the sharp focus necessary for such a big lens.

"Holding my fire, I trusted to fate. When within 50 feet of us, the ram stopped, turned broadside, and nibbled at a sprig of vegetation. Silently and quickly in one steady motion, I arose, with my eyes fixed on the focusing mirror instead of looking directly at the ram. In the ground glass I saw his head raised suddenly and turned my way. Quickly the milled head of the focusing screw brought him in focus and the focal-plane shutter clanged harshly.

"His white form had vanished when I raised my head, and, to Tom's and Charlie's inquiring glances, I could say only that the effort was successful provided the ram was not in the air when the shutter revolved."

It was two days before I went to Tom's cabin. When darkness finally came at 10 p. m., I dropped the negative into the developer and in a few minutes saw on the plate the big ram, broadside, head up, gazing at the camera (see page 403).

PECULIARITIES OF THE SHEEP

Our last day at the head of Benjamin Creek was reserved for studying and photographing a large flock of sheep which heretofore had occupied the end of a ridge west of our tent, and which always fed on a large circular meadow nearly surrounded by small canyons. At no time did the daily program of the sheep vary. By 7 o'clock in the morning the entire flock of about 50 descended the mountain, crossed a little creek, and then in bunches of six to a dozen scattered out over the meadow, feeding not only on grass, but on small bushes.

Often some of these bands, containing many lambs, would work their way out to the edge of the meadow, fully three-quarters of a mile from the base of the mountains so that their retreat could readily have been cut off by a man with a rifle or by any fleet-footed predaceous animal. This, of course, meant that they had enjoyed entire absence

NAVIGATION WAS ON FOOT

In swift shallows the adventurers had to get out and drag the boat. It took only three hours to go down the stream but three days to ascend it.

of molestation during the season and probably for years.

I noticed that in coming down the steeper mountains the sheep usually took earth trails, however loose the soil or treacherous the shaly rocks. On their return, the steepest cliffs, if they afforded a good foothold, were ascended in preference to the nearby trails used on the descents. The probable reasons, if my brief observations warrant an opinion, were that on the descent the loose soil and tumbling rocks accelerated instead of retarded the progress of these sure-footed animals.

On the return, such conditions had the opposite effect. In jumping down from ledge to ledge, an animal weighing from 100 to 250 pounds might slip or break off a fragment of the ledge much more readily than when ascending. The sheep makes each upward jump lightly as a bird.

I had noticed, moreover, that at noon some of the sheep often returned for a rest on a lower slope of the ridge. We could not make a blind on the meadow without alarming them all, unless we built it at night, a difficult undertaking. I planned to

A TYPICAL HEAD OF A WHITE RAM

In 1884 E. W. Nelson first described a pure white species of mountain sheep inhabiting Alaska and northwestern Canada, naming it *Ovis dalli,* in honor of Prof. Wm. H. Dall, the well-known scientist and Alaskan explorer. While the horns of this species are not so massive as those of the Rocky Mountain Big Horn, or the base circumference equal to that of the Big Horns or of the southern California species, the extensive spread and graceful symmetry, in connection with the beauty of the head, make them a prized trophy. The greatest spread of a Kenai ram's horns has been recorded as 27½ inches.

get on the ridge in the morning after all the sheep had gone to the meadow, when there would be some chance to obtain pictures in case any returned at noon and, a greater certainty, toward night as they assembled in the vicinity of the blind.

After we broke camp in the morning, Charlie continued with his pack down the valley to the cabin. Tom and I left our packs near the pond, where we intended wading the outlet stream so as to reach the base of the ridge at a point where nothing could see us from the meadow. The stream proved much deeper and swifter than it looked at a distance. Although we did not

object to a wetting, we feared being carried off our feet, with resultant injury or loss to the photographic outfit. A rifle will stand much more ill-usage than a camera. We put in nearly an hour gathering and throwing flat stones into the swift water before we obtained a footing that we felt was safe.

On reaching the edge of the ridge about 200 feet above the meadow, we could see many scattered bands of sheep; but, to our disappointment, a dozen sheep were now coming along in single file toward the ridge. They were already too close for us to pass around and get in a position to meet them on their ascent. There was nothing to do but to await developments. In a few minutes they had jumped the creek, one lamb falling over backward into the water, much to the indignation of its mother, who stamped her feet vigorously as her bedraggled offspring endeavored to climb the steep bank. With a single and later exception, this was the only time we saw any sheep, big or little, prove awkward or careless.

When the band finally came up the slope they were soon lost to sight, and we waited until they had time to reach a resting place. On climbing to the rim, I saw the flock about 200 yards to the left and on the same level. All were lying down, save one which acted like a sentinel.

PHOTOGRAPHING THE SENTINEL EWE

After carefully studying the approach and figuring on the possibilities of remaining concealed, Tom assured me "that with ordinary crawling ability one could get within 50 feet." Tom could crawl like a serpent and climb like a squirrel. He had the equipoise and jumping ability of a mountain sheep. Consequently his encouragement was of doubtful character.

Experience had taught me that, although it was important not to be seen approaching, it was equally important, when armed with a camera, to know the exact position of the animals in relation to the last cover sought. I started on all fours, a mode of travel rendered more difficult by my being obliged to push the heavy camera ahead.

When I reached the final rock, I carefully pushed a piece of small brush to the top of it and, raising my head, looked through the branches. This method might excite a puzzled interest if any movement should be observed by animals at close range, but even so it was safer than to let my head appear suddenly to their view a few yards away.

All the sheep were in a row less than 20 yards away, the sentinel ewe standing with a little lamb at her feet, and the rest lying down nearby. I could see that it was impossible for the plate to cover them all in proper focus. I would photograph the sentinel ewe and her lamb to supplement the picture of the big ram and complete a family group.

In a moment I arranged the camera at a focus that would probably require no further change when brought to bear upon the sheep. Lowering my eyes into the hood surrounding the focusing mirror, I slowly

arose, and when the camera cleared the top of the rock I found the sentinel looking directly at me and in sharp focus. Without a moment's hesitation I pressed the button, and the shutter revolved. What the camera saw is reproduced on page 402.

Before the frightened sheep had time to gather their wits, I had reversed the plateholder. I caught the band as it struggled in a disordered way over the broken rocks above me (see photograph, page 402).

We set about constructing a comfortable blind between rocks that concealed us from animals coming from below or above, and where we could remain the rest of the day watching the scattered bands of sheep on the meadow below. It seemed that practically every such band had a leader, readily picked out when the sheep were moving from one locality to another or were feeding. And this today is a predominating characteristic of domestic sheep that has survived from primitive times. A dread, growing out of their exposed position and distance from the mountains, was manifested by the way the sentinel sheep continuously surveyed the country (see page 404).

Mr. Charles Sheldon, who is accepted, and properly so, as the leading authority on northern sheep, inclined strongly to the belief that such bands of sheep have no sentinel in a strict sense, but rather that the more alert or experienced of the members at times give the appearance of prearrangement for guard duty.

SHEEP REALLY HAVE A LOOKOUT

Such a conclusion is undoubtedly true in the case of caribou and elk, but in the case of sheep, where gregarious ties are very strong, it seems to me that the selection of a leader or the voluntary assumption of leadership by an individual, who watches over the flock for days and perhaps seasons, presupposes responsibility for lookout duties, unless such a leader is thoroughly satisfied that every condition is favorable to the security of the flock.

While I was making observations, Tom was devoting himself to watching the mountains above. He finally discovered coming down toward us a ewe, which he thought was one of the sheep that might not have seen us clearly when the stampede took place and was anxious now to join the other sheep feeding in the meadows. Its course would bring it some 20 yards to the left of us, and well out of way of the quartering wind blowing up the mountainside.

When within 75 feet of us, the sheep turned to the right, and, since we knew that its course would bring it across the line of our scent, I was most anxious to note the results, even if I lost the picture. When the animal was between two rocks, with only its head and shoulders visible to us, our scent struck it suddenly. The ewe winced as if shot and dashed upward again with the speed of a deer. Her action showed pretty conclusively that a sheep at close range has a good nose, at least when it has been previously alarmed.

A PROPITIOUS MOMENT

At length the animals on the meadow turned toward us, and as band after band came up our side of the hill, we thought the time right for a series of pictures.

The leader of the first flock began watching the side of the mountain, advancing 10 or 15 feet and then stopping for a minute or two; during such intervals the rest of the band continued to graze and some of them would lie down. By the time the leader reached the creek, she had apparently become suspicious for some reason, and stood eyeing the entire side of the mountain. She finally lay down with the others, but with her head turned toward the mountain side. Unquestionably the absence of sheep from the place in which they were accustomed to gather in the afternoon, and possibly the ascent of the first flock, had something to do with her uncertainty.

Meanwhile, within 50 yards of the first, had come another band, also led by a ewe, which acted very much like the first. In a few minutes the two bunches commingled, and, to our regret, soon began retreating toward the meadow, where they stood in an uncertain way for a long time. Then the two bands separated, one continuing up the little creek.

The manner of the leader, which was looking steadily at a distant point on the side of the mountain, led me to turn the glass in that direction, and I saw four sheep on the edge of a cliff. Toward these the band was evidently going. Soon the others were on the move across the meadows, all, with the exception of one distant flock, headed for the same spot. We saw our chances of obtaining photographs fading away.

In a short time these flocks had joined the four sheep at the other end of the ridge, a portion, doubtless, of the flock which we had previously photographed, and which had sought out a new place for the night. At 4 o'clock the little band of sheep that had been feeding at the extreme western end of the meadow came trotting back on a well-defined trail bordering a canyon, and I felt almost certain that none of them would come to our blind, although on five previous days all the sheep had gathered every afternoon just above it.

Now, more than ever, I was convinced that a set of sheep decoys, as suggested previously, would have brought most of these sheep within photographing range. Tom thought that even a white linen nightshirt would have answered if he would have been permitted to trot about in it in front of the blind.

While the last flock continued to approach, it seemed best to slip down the side of the slope as close to the creek as possible and try for a picture as they went by. When we had gone a third of the way down, I found that they were coming more rapidly than I expected. In an effort to pass an exposed place between two rocks—a crossing that should have been made by slow crawling—I carelessly jumped across. As I landed behind the sheltering rock, I heard Tom's warning whistle.

Looking down on the meadows, I saw that all the sheep had reversed ends and were rushing back again. Since these animals were more than a quarter of a mile away, their behavior was a good illustration of their acuteness of sight and their quickness in realizing the character of the danger.

THE SHEEP WERE TOO QUICK

Not knowing how these sheep could escape in the direction they were going, I called to Tom for advice. He yelled that they were headed for an ice bridge across the canyon, and he thought they would swing toward us again after crossing this to ascend the mountain slope behind.

I exercised all the energy at my command, but the sheep won. I could see them 200 yards below quartering up the mountain. In a few minutes they reached a ledge of rock within a hundred feet of the crest of the great black cliff opposite the site of our former camp. This was our last view of the white mountain sheep until two days later, when we entered the pass of the low divide above Skilak Lake.

Our visit had made the sheep considerably wilder, and the flocks that formerly had rested each night on the lower benches now whitened the ledges of many a high cliff. No red had dyed the white and woolly sides, however, and no flock looked for an absent one within its ranks. The next morning we left for Skilak Lake, and camped half a mile from the low divide, giving the men an opportunity to make a further trip to the cabin that day.

At an early hour the next morning we took down the little tent and cached it with other articles to be called for the following day. With heavy packs we began trudging along the slight rise to the low divide, through which Cottonwood Creek ran on its short and rapid career to Skilak Lake, 3,000 feet below.

It was here that I obtained my last photographs of rock ptarmigan, and before we climbed up on the broken masses of rock that littered the pass between the cliffs of the divide, I put away the lenses and boxed the camera in case some one should suffer a fall on the insecure footing.

A LAST VIEW OF THE WHITE SHEEP

Halfway through the pass we noticed, almost overhead, seven or eight sheep lying on a narrow ledge with a perpendicular drop of nearly 300 feet beneath them. To one who had seen large white gannets nesting here and there upon the face of a maritime cliff, the resemblance to them was a striking one. Before I could get the camera out and arranged, the sheep, noticing that we had stopped and were gazing upward, became alarmed. In a series of awe-inspiring leaps they took ledge after ledge until they reached the top, where they all lined up and looked down at us. My last but still lingering mental picture of these graceful creatures shows them poised on the highest summit above Skilak Lake.

Impressed once more with the agility and self-confidence of these nomads of the crags, I asked Tom whether he had ever seen the remains of any that indicated that sometimes sheep paid forfeit with their lives for a careless gambol or a desperate effort to avoid pursuit. He replied that in nearly 16 years in the sheep ranges of Alaska he had never seen a single case of the kind, although several times he had found carcasses at the ends of snow avalanches.

Within a few short hours and at the same spot a tragedy occurred that constituted a most remarkable answer to my inquiry. After returning to the lake and remaining overnight, Tom and Charlie started back the next morning for the tent and the remainder of our outfit. In passing through the same divide Tom saw, hanging partly over a ledge and midway between top and bottom, the crumpled body of a large, fine ewe. Running about below was a little lamb, which, whimpering and bleating, continued to look up toward the spot no feet could reach.

A TRAGEDY OF THE CLIFFS

How this accident happened is, of course, a matter of surmise. However it may have occurred, we know that when time passed and the mother failed to return, the little fellow by a circuitous trail reached the bottom of the pass, to be no nearer than before to the only one it loved. Let us trust that before the day had passed the little lamb saw a white line zigzagging into the valley, which he dimly knew was the pastoral range of his mother's clan, and that he found a welcome within the ranks.

All animals develop the abilities and characteristics necessary for their safety and for the other requirements of their lives. Mountain sheep are agile, sure-footed, and keen of eye. Experience and practice are their spelling book and primer. Every one has seen a kitten chase the end of a string in motion, or even the tip of its own tail, or run up and down the trunk of a tree apparently in sheer aimlessness. By these motions it is educating its muscles to play the part it must take as a member of the cat family.

The young lambs we saw among the flocks on the mountain slopes were very playful. They frolicked about, jumping over one another's backs, and sometimes leaped from shelving rock slopes to the tips of little pinnacles so small there was hardly room for their little feet. They often appeared in danger of bad falls as they turned about on such precarious footholds in order to leap back, but they never lost their footing. This youthful play of course fitted them for their future life among the gigantic mountain crags where a single misstep might be fatal.

The snowy-white sheep of the Alaskan ranges, with its slender, gracefully curved and often waxy, yellowish horns, is probably the most beautiful of its kind in the world. At the time of my visit they were

TRAILS ARE OFTEN HARSH WORK

The worst part of tracking requires the men to wade in swift water of uncertain depth to avoid log jams and overhanging trees.

to weigh from about 200 to 250 pounds and the ewes much less. In 1907 a ram with horns measuring 14¼ inches around the base and having a spread of 27¼ inches was killed on the Kenai. The horns of the ewes and yearling rams extend up and back in curves that, seen at a distance, have given rise to the unwarranted opinion by numerous hunters and prospectors that ibex also occur in the Alaskan mountains.

Man is the most destructive enemy of the white sheep, but it is a victim also of wolves, coyotes, lynxes, wolverines, an occasional big bear, and many golden eagles.

abundant in the mountains of the Kenai Peninsula and in the Alaska Range westerly toward the head of Bristol Bay as well as on the little-known Endicott Range paralleling the coast of the Arctic Ocean on the north. From these mountains they range eastward into the northern Rocky Mountains of Yukon Territory.

COLORS OF THE WHITE SHEEP VARY WITH CLIMATE

Throughout the range of the sheep in the Kenai, in the Mount McKinley region and the Endicotts, the freshly grown winter pelage is snowy-white, with now and then a black hair on the top of the tail. These black hairs become more numerous in the sheep found in the mountains near Yukon Territory and through the southern part of that area into northern British Columbia, the tops of the tails sometimes becoming all black and the fronts of the forelegs dusky until, through an area in which the sheep have an amazingly varied amount of dark colors on the back and elsewhere, the dark-colored Stone sheep (*Ovis dalli stonei*) are developed in Northern British Columbia. During the months following their assumption of the winter coat, contact with the earth in their bedding places stains the pure white sheep to a dingy or dirty white.

The white sheep is a lighter, more gracefully proportioned animal than the well-known Rocky Mountain bighorn of ranges farther south. The large bucks are reported

Although so numerous and widely distributed in the northern mountains of Alaska and western Canada, these sheep remained unknown to science until specimens were obtained for E. W. Nelson from the upper Yukon region, through the cooperation of the well-known northern pioneer, Jack McQuesten. Doctor Nelson, who described the species in 1882, named it *Ovis dalli*, in honor of the early Alaskan explorer, Dr. W. H. Dall.

When they are on a snow-covered slope, or on one of the many scattered patches of snow in their summer haunts, the white sheep are very difficult to see. Their color blends so perfectly with their background that only when the sun is at such an angle that it casts their shadows on the snow may they be located easily. When they are on bare ground, the reverse of this becomes true and they are conspicuous. Their white forms stood out so strongly when they were grazing on green slopes that I could see them sometimes at a distance of two miles.

On our return from the mountain country our camp was located at the farther end of Caribou Island, a few miles west of Doublebay camp, and opposite the moose lick.

This island has a length of about three-quarters of a mile, and has a maximum width of one-third of a mile. Except for a few acres of pine, it is covered with a vigorous second growth and some swamp land, the result, probably, of the same fire that cleared so much of the shore opposite.

And here it may be remarked that, however wasteful in a commercial sense may have been many of the forest fires in the wilder portions of our continent, they nevertheless have often been of corresponding benefit to the game and range stock.

The replacement of dense and often stunted and useless conifers with poplar, birch, cherry, oak, beech, and maple, and the subsequent appearance also of meadows and

OCCASIONALLY THE GOING BECOMES EASIER

This was a restful half mile where the original forests on the bank had been cut down by Russians in 1857.

glades covered with grass, moss, bushes, and small herbage, have done much to supply an abundant and nutritious variety of winter and summer food, valuable alike to the larger game animals, domestic stock, pack horses, many game birds, and small quadrupeds, few of which resort to or can thrive throughout the year in the dense, dark evergreens of the North.

In recent years hundreds of thousands of acres of such second growth have sprung up in Alaska, and nowhere has it been of greater advantage to game and the pack trains than throughout the interior of the Kenai Peninsula. Caribou Island, subjected to easy examination, showed that on the coming of the ice it was visited by many moose, and the abundance of spruce partridges indicated their appreciation of the berries and swelling buds, just as the rabbits thrived on the tender bark and great variety of smaller plants.

In its isolation the Kenai Peninsula is like a great island, allowing a marked segregation of northern game, for it is naturally favorable to their existence and is now much improved by physical changes, the ease with which the game laws can be enforced, the concentration of Indian settlements near the canneries, and the practical extermination of the wolf.

Reports of those best acquainted with present conditions show that the moose have been increasing steadily in recent years, that the white sheep are thriving,

and that all other game animals except the small fur bearers and the caribou are holding their own. Just why the caribou was approaching extinction on the peninsula no one seems to know, but I am glad to report that a good-sized stag was seen south of Benjamin Creek by a party of surveyors in July, 1910. Since much of the peninsula is well adapted for caribou, an effort should be made to introduce them into the region, the interior of which will readily support many thousands.

CHARLES SHELDON AND THE MOUNT MC KINLEY AREA

During this expedition my interest and enjoyment of brief and distant glimpses of majestic Mount McKinley were enhanced by my recollection that my friend, Charles Sheldon, had passed a year—1906-7—near its northern base. There he trod little known valleys and climbed many dangerous mountain slopes hunting and studying the white sheep, caribou, moose, bears, and smaller forms of wild life. On his daily expeditions he hunted alone, and with rare persistence wrote his diary records in detail each night. For some reason that I never understood, this valuable and interesting description of an almost unknown region did not appear in print until two years after his death, when it was issued with a foreword by Dr. C. Hart Merriam.

This work bears the title "The Wilderness of Denali," the name by which the

THE WRECK OF THE "RAMONA"

This lifeboat loaded with people from the lost ship arrived at the *Northwestern* on which the author was traveling home from Alaska.

mountain was known among the Indians living near its northern base. It seems a pity that this spectacular eminence has not been called by its picturesque Indian name, as was so much desired by Sheldon, instead of being named after a political leader who never was in Alaska and who knew little or nothing of the far North.

As a result of his several visits to Alaska, Sheldon became impressed with the idea that the region about this mountain should become a national park. The completion of the Alaska railroad extending from Seward to Fairbanks made this mountain area readily accessible to the public by a comparatively short highway. Soon thereafter Sheldon initiated the movement that resulted in the establishment of the Mount McKinley National Park and thus created a permanently protected home for some of Alaska's big-game animals.

The National Park Service informs me that in 1931 this area contained approximately 13,250 Dall sheep, 25,000 caribou, 60 moose, 50 grizzly, and 15 black bears.

Many know that this mountain is the highest on the North American continent, but the fact that it rises higher above its base than any mountain in the world is not generally known. The great peaks of the Andes and the Himalayas rise from bases already well up in altitude, whereas McKinley rears its 20,300 feet of height from a base only 2,500 feet above sea level.

The ease with which even the least experienced and venturesome of travelers may now reach many of the wild places of the earth and enjoy the spiritual uplift that comes from viewing magnificent scenery is well illustrated by the history of Mount McKinley. This highest peak of North America, located in the wild interior of Alaska, was the last of our great mountains to be discovered. For years following this it was considered a feat of skill and hardihood merely to reach its base. Even as late as 1906 Charles Sheldon found it a strenuous task to enter this area and return from his camp using dog sleds or pack horses according to the season.

Today, as a result of the establishment of McKinley National Park, such conveniences for travel have been provided that I venture to say that one might leave the city of Washington, and by the use of railroad trains, steamships, and motor vehicles, arrive at Copper Mountain Camp, fronting one of the greatest glaciers on the base of McKinley, and commanding a superb view of this majestic mountain, without the necessity of walking 1,000 feet.

CHAPTER XVIII

Hunting Great Brown Bears in Alaska

THE trip to the Kenai Peninsula in 1911 proved to be so interesting that in 1913 I undertook another Alaskan venture. This time I was accompanied by my son George and, as before, by my Michigan guides, John Hammer and Charles Anderson. During the first journey, the purpose of which was to photograph the giant moose and the white sheep, I had enjoyed no opportunity to study the great bears that are so numerous in some localities. My son was particularly eager to hunt the great brown bear and the diminutive Sitka black-tailed deer.

AN UNPROPITIOUS START

The beginning of our journey from Marquette was not propitious, for the first night out the train was wrecked by running into a large white pine that had been blown across the tracks during a terrific thunderstorm. The engine rolled over two or three times, killing the engineer and firemen and two trainmen in the adjoining car. All the lights in the train were extinguished, and we made our way forward by the intermittent illumination of lightning to view the harrowing sight. Learning that the road would be blocked until the next morning and that the next train would get us to Seattle only a few hours before the departure of our steamer, we returned to Marquette and changed our reservations to a boat that was to sail a week later.

During our voyage north from Seattle the weather was fair, and the trip through the inside passage was most enjoyable. In the absence of fog or rain the abrupt mountainous slopes that rise from the water's edge beside the narrow channels between the islands stood out clearly. To take advantage of the long hours of daylight at this season we remained most of the time on deck. The perils of navigation in these parts were impressed upon us by the sight of the hulks of several passenger steamers that had met their fate in fog or snow storms when the swift tides had carried them out of their narrow courses. Our plan was to hunt first on the lower Copper River, where bears were said to be numerous, and then to return to Admiralty Island. On reaching Juneau we called upon the superintendent of the Copper River railroad to arrange for our transportation up the river. He was in bed as the result of a peculiar accident in which he and a companion had been thrown from their railroad track cycle when it collided with a stray horse. His companion had been killed.

The superintendent was propped up in bed reading the July number of the NATIONAL GEOGRAPHIC MAGAZINE, which contained my article on "Wild Animals that Took Their Own Pictures by Day and by Night." He was therefore in a mood to help us on our trip.

From Juneau we went by steamer to the end of the railroad at Cordova. There, in addition to our canoe, we hired a heavier boat for the outboard motor. An old and water-soaked craft, weighing probably 300 pounds, it set so deep in the water that progress in shallow places was difficult.

Our destination on the railroad was "Mile 84," near a section house, where our mail could be delivered. At this point we crossed Copper River, which there was more than half a mile wide, to a camping place a short distance above the mouth of a smaller tributary known as Bremner River (see page 422). It is about the mouth of this stream that many bears gather each year during the run of the salmon that ascend the smaller streams to spawn. It was not until the day after pitching camp that we discovered we were on an island.

NO BEARS, BUT MANY TRACKS

Naturally, after landing, and while the guides were putting up the tents, I looked about for bear signs. I was amazed to see hundreds of tracks, big and little, on the mud flats; but all of them appeared to be more than two weeks old. The skeletons of salmon and the uprooted skunk cabbage along the shores showed that many bears had been active here only a short time before; but all the salmon had gone upstream and the bears had followed. This meant that we must try to locate them nearer the headwaters. Since the stream came out of one of the highest mountain ranges in this region, we expected to find good trout fishing, for there the water would be clear and cold.

GEORGE SHIRAS, 4TH, PROVIDED GAME FOR THE POT

The youngest member of the party brought a welcome offering of ptarmigan into camp near the
mouth of Bremner River (see also page 430).

Willow ptarmigan were numerous about camp, but were very wild, although they were seldom shot at. This condition I attributed to the presence of many hawks. The ptarmigan rarely ventured more than a rod or so from cover and took refuge promptly when alarmed, so that it required quick and accurate wing-shooting to bag them. My son enjoyed this sport very much, and it kept him busy supplying our needs. We were delayed for several days trying to work out a method of going up the stream, for unusual difficulties beset us.

The water in Copper River was lower than it had been for many years, with the result that the Lower Bremner, instead of being banked up by the larger stream, was also drained to a low stage. We managed to get our motor boat some distance upstream, but the water was so muddy that it was hard to find a channel. Most of our

time was devoted to getting free from mud bars over which two or three inches of water flowed with the same speed as in the channel.

Half a mile above the Copper we came upon a flat-bottomed boat with its bow buried deeply in the muddy water. On the stern was an outboard motor. Who its occupants had been and whether they had escaped death we never learned.

It required both of our boats to move us and our outfit, and after persistent efforts we became convinced that we could make only slow and uncertain progress. We decided to return to Juneau and to outfit for Admiralty Island, on which bears were known to be numerous and accessible.

As we were breaking camp the next day, the first rain of the trip began to fall. While we were crossing the river, the little motor boat was caught in what appeared to be a dangerous eddy, caused partly by a heavy wind that blew down the river. The boat seemed about to upset, and Anderson, who was in the bow, jumped overboard into the chilly water so as to lighten the load. We all let out a loud shout of laughter when we saw him land in about 18 inches of water. He looked back at us with a sheepish grin, but nevertheless he got the credit for a courageous act in an apparent emergency.

The bed of the Copper River railroad was laid in places on earth-covered glaciers, which in the summer were continually melting so that the rails sagged at times sufficiently to interrupt traffic. This was the situation the afternoon we loaded our outfit on a car to return to Cordova on our way to Juneau. The section men on the road worked for several hours propping up the track before we could go on.

Near here is the famous Childs Glacier, which can readily be seen from the train. At other points along this coast are large glaciers, from which huge pieces of ice now and then topple into the water, but they rarely float out into the open sea as they do off the Greenland coast.

Although at that time the coyotes had not invaded the Upper Copper River Valley, they had already entered Alaska, and since then they have reached the sheep ranges along the headwaters of this river. It seems justifiable to make reference here to the northward spread of these carnivores because of the possible disastrous effect they may have on certain valuable northern birds and mammals.

COYOTES INVADE ALASKA

At the time of the Klondike gold rush coyotes are said to have followed the overland trail northward through British Columbia to Yukon Territory, being attracted by the carcasses of pack animals that perished there. This brought them to a region that supported so much game and other wild life that they have spread over enormous areas. They are now found about the upper drainage of Copper River and beyond the Yukon Valley to the north and west. They occur yearly throughout Yukon Territory, and some have reached even to the Lower Mackenzie River Valley.

They are the most dangerous enemy of Alaska game, both great and small, that could have appeared in that region, for they menace the big game throughout the year, including lambs of the mountain sheep along the crests of at least some of the ranges, and they have already begun depredations among nesting migratory wild fowl to an extent that may prove disastrous to some of the geese and other species.

A cooperative campaign to control them is being conducted by the Biological Survey and the Alaska Game Commission, and many coyotes and wolves have been destroyed. The country is so vast, so thinly populated, and so lacking in means of communication, and the coyotes are so difficult to capture, that their control has become a serious problem in the maintenance of Alaska game. It is possible that the long, severe winters of interior Alaska and far northern Canada may prove a determining factor in controlling their numbers. Some evidence of this appears to be indicated by their decrease in the Upper Copper River country during 1930 and 1931.

WE LEAVE JUNEAU FOR ADMIRALTY ISLAND

From Cordova, after our fruitless search for bears on the Copper River, we went direct to Juneau by steamer. The morning following our arrival at the capital of the Territory we met the well-known local guide, Allan Hasselborg, who had over a period of several years collected many specimens for Dr. C. Hart Merriam, former chief of the Biological Survey, long engaged in a monumental study of North American bears.

Hasselborg was just recovering from severe injuries inflicted by a grizzly. He had mortally wounded the animal at close range on a steep hillside, but the dying bear had seized him and badly lacerated his arm as they rolled together to the bottom of the gulch.

Apropos of Doctor Merriam's work, I may add that before we left for Alaska a friend in Washington remarked, "For heaven's sake don't bring back with you a new species of bear, or Merriam will never finish his book." This very thing happened as regards the bear, and Doctor Merriam gave it due attention.

On our first meeting with Hasselborg we discovered some of the eccentricities for which he is noted. He refused to enter the hotel to talk over plans for our trip, saying that he always took cold in a house, especially a public one. For years he had lived on his little launch, and if anyone wished

THEY TOOK TO BOATS ON THE COPPER RIVER

The party left the railroad at Mile 84 to cross over and camp near the mouth of the Bremner River, a reputed gathering place for big bears.

UNUSUAL WEATHER MADE UNUSUAL SCENERY

As the little craft passed down Frederick Sound, from Juneau to Admiralty Island, the detached and stranded ice from a nearby glacier glistened blue and white beneath a sun that was celebrating its farewell appearance, for thereafter fog and rain screened the island camp for days at a time.

THE PARTY'S LOCATION ON ADMIRALTY ISLAND PROVED FORTUNATE

The new species of bear was first sighted on Admiralty as it came to the beach opposite this camp. On the mountain slopes the author saw hundreds of the little Sitka blacktail deer.

CAMP IN SHELTON COVE, ADMIRALTY ISLAND, WAS WET

Here the party hunted bears while rain fell for nearly 18 consecutive days. The great cedars deluged the tents on each heavy puff of wind. There was an attractive and convenient spring-fed fresh-water pool in front of the camp site.

HERRING AND GLAUCOUS GULLS FISH FOR SALMON EGGS

to talk to him under cover there he would have to go.

We later found that his boat was small, it being intended for only a guide and one hunter. Before our return we had some trying experiences with the overcrowded craft. The morning we left Juneau for Admiralty Island the weather was perfect, and the trip along the passage to Frederick Sound was most interesting, the sunlight bringing out with fine effect the blue-white of the glaciers and the varying shades and tints of the forested mountain slopes.

ADMIRALTY ISLAND

It was long after dark when we entered Sheldon Cove in Pybus Bay at the south end of Admiralty Island, one of the largest and finest of the Alexander Archipelago. Our confinement all day in the small cabin of the motor boat had nearly stifled us, and we proceeded at once to put up the tent. The tide was high and the launch was anchored only about a hundred feet away from the camp site. It was the identical site occupied by Charles Sheldon and his bride in September, 1909.

As we groped about we discovered the foundation logs of their camp, the walls of which had been built up about four feet and then topped with a canvas roof. Sheldon's account of this visit had been published in 1912, the year after my first trip to Alaska, and his description of the rugged wilderness, with its many bears and deer, had so impressed me that Admiralty Island was the place I most desired to visit on this trip.

CHARLES SHELDON

It gives me pleasure to present here the valuation placed by Doctor Merriam on the work and activities of this fine man and good friend, whose untimely death in 1927 was so sincerely regretted by all who knew him.

"Among the hunter-naturalists of America Charles Sheldon occupied a unique position. For, notwithstanding his attitude of self-effacement so well expressed by George Bird Grinnell—'he was our most famous big-game hunter.' Choosing his hunting grounds in some of the most remote and inaccessible parts of the continent; possessed of physical strength and endurance almost beyond belief, of unbounded enthusiasm, of powers of observation second to none; and endowed with a conscience intolerant of exaggeration, he gave accounts of his hunts that abound in vivid descriptions of localities not previously explored.

"His circumstantial studies of the habits of animals rank among the most valuable of the contributions thus far made to the life histories of many species—particularly the mountain sheep, caribou, moose, grizzly bear and wolverine."

On the coming of daylight we viewed our surroundings with much interest. The launch was now lying about a hundred yards from the shore, for the tide was low. Since the rise and fall of the tide amounted to 18 feet, it was sometimes possible to row up to the front of our tents. At other times we had to struggle through a long stretch of mud, over which, when necessary, we pulled the smaller boat. The sky was cloudless and the temperature agreeable.

HASSELBORG PREDICTS FOG

As we were putting some finishing touches to the camp, Hasselborg said to me: "If you want to take some pictures of the surroundings, you'd better do it now, for rain and fog can soon be expected."

I recalled the Sheldons' experiences here of 18 days of continuous rain, often mixed with fog. Hasselborg's warning was timely, for later we broke the Sheldon record by a day.

Before noon on September 2, I went with Hasselborg in the rowboat to a small salmon stream that entered the bay about half a mile to the east. When we were half way across, I saw three bears leave the brush and come to the beach, and I whispered to the oarsman: "There are three black bears on the beach."

Without turning his head to look, he replied, with marked irritation, "There are no black bears on this island."

To this I retorted, "I did not mean the American black bear, but bears of a black color, and coal black at that."

At this he turned his head quickly and then gave a surprised whistle. Just then all three animals rose on their hind legs, evidently looking at the approaching boat.

"They are getting ready to leave," Hasselborg said, and a moment later they hurried into the brush. "Those were the strangest bears I have ever seen," he continued, "and I have been up north a good many years. . . . It was a large female and two two-year-old cubs. The only bears known on this island are the big brown bears, and the three we saw must belong to an unknown color phase of this animal."

It may be said at this point that in the next two weeks we saw four more big adult black-colored bears. We felt sure that these animals must represent a black phase of the big brown bear common on the island, just as there is a brown phase of our common black bear that is usually called the cinnamon bear. Later, when Doctor Merriam examined our black specimen, he found from its skull characters that it was a new species.

True to Hasselborg's predictions, a hard rain began the next day and continued for 19 days, with one let-up of five hours and another of nine. We had so-called waterproof tents, but they all leaked badly except the paraffined cook tent. This was not surprising, for our canvas was spread under some huge red cedars, and these would collect many gallons of water, which would be precipitated upon the tents whenever a gust of wind struck the treetops. The continual hammering soon forced the water through the canvas.

Although our tents did not keep out the water, they held it excellently after it entered. The floor cloth of each tent was of heavy waterproofed material that held the water that penetrated the roof until it was bailed out each morning.

After three days of the downpour I became worried about a camera and flashlight machine that I had placed up the stream at a pool where the bears were making daily raids on the salmon. The camera had been set several feet above the stream and was wired to a log as a matter of precaution. The lens with it was the one that I valued highly, for with it I had taken my first series of flashlight pictures of deer more than 25 years before.

THE CAMERA SUBMERGED

Upon arrival at the place where the camera was set, we found it submerged and bounding up and down in the swift current, but it was held securely by the wire. The camera box was ruined, but the lens, when cleaned, proved to be uninjured. Weather conditions continued to prevent daylight photography, except during five hours of sunlight, when, in addition to pictures of gulls, I obtained several showing surf birds and black turnstones.

The numerous salmon streams of Admiralty Island are interesting; for, after descending in beautiful cascades from the hills, many of them have courses only a few hundred yards long. Four of these

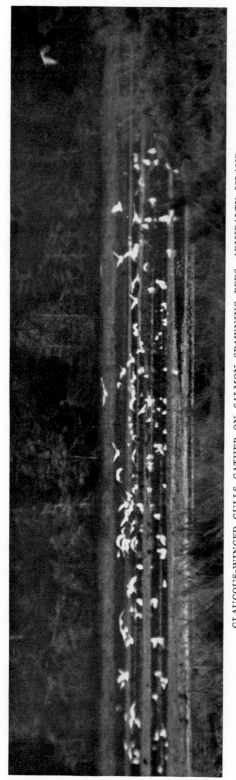

GLAUCOUS-WINGED GULLS GATHER ON SALMON SPAWNING BEDS, ADMIRALTY ISLAND

THESE GLAUCOUS-WINGED GULLS ARE TRAVELING TO THE FEEDING GROUND SHOWN ABOVE

streams enter Pybus Bay within easy distance of our camping place, and in the more remote parts of the island are many others.

To rivers like the Yukon or the Columbia, where salmon often ascend more than a thousand miles to spawn, these streams afford a remarkable contrast. That a sufficiently regular supply of water can be maintained in these streams to support the several species of spawning fish that frequent them throughout the summer seems incredible to one accustomed to more southern waters.

STREAMS ABUNDANTLY FED BY RAIN AND MELTING SNOW

Their regular supply, however, is due to two alternating causes—the almost continuous rainfall at this season and the powerful effect that an all-day sun exerts on the snow fields and glaciers when the sky clears for a day or two. In such short streams the salmon are naturally confined to a few pools, with the result that the visiting bears are concentrated in a comparatively small area near the ocean; and the gulls, ducks, eagles, and ravens, seeking the spawn or the remains of the fish that are carried ashore by the bears or by the current, create a scene of activity very interesting to the visitor, whether he comes armed with a gun, with a camera, or with a field glass.

The bird most active at the salmon streams was an old favorite of mine—the Bonaparte gull. These birds came from the tidal mud flats in flocks of a dozen or more, and each would hang suspended a few feet above a spawning fish. As the eggs were laid, the little gulls would plunge down with sufficient force to penetrate the water a foot or so, and thus obtain some of the eggs from the gravel bottoms. They would then retire to digest their food and prepare for another raid.

Once when the sun broke through the clouds for an hour, I made a brush blind at the edge of the stream and succeeded in getting a series of pictures of the diving birds engaged in a method of feeding I had never noticed elsewhere. Gulls usually find their food on or near the surface of the water.

That gulls in turn sometimes become the victim of voracious fish we noticed as our steamer passed along the coast near Ketchikan. Within 10 minutes I saw four gulls that were at rest on the water pulled, struggling, beneath the surface. This would indicate a possible widespread destruction from a source that previously I had not seen or heard mentioned.

The almost continuous rainfall on Admiralty Island was in striking contrast to the bright, dry weather we had enjoyed on the Kenai Peninsula two years before, when in more than a month we had only one brief shower. The explanation I worked out for the almost incessant downpour may account for the situation.

Practically every day we could see rifts of sunlight a few miles back of the main shore. There the currents of air evidently flowed upward on account of the heat of the sun on the land. This upward current drew in the moist air from the ocean, which in passing over the mountains of Admiralty Island had its moisture condensed and precipitated in rains.

The low and even temperature day and night on the island was due to winds off the ocean. Whenever heavy winds blew in from the Pacific, the rains increased in volume and fell night and day. The few times the wind came from the mainland, or blew up and down the coast, we had lighter rainfall and warmer weather.

This seems to corroborate my theory, particularly since there was usually less rainfall after sundown. The weather from day to day from this time forward is recorded mainly in my son's diary, for he bore the brunt of many hardships while hunting persistently regardless of weather conditions.

The photographer of the party being weather bound most of the time, it fell to the lot of my son to supply the most interesting events of our outing. Rain could not prevent hunting deer, bears, and wild fowl. The following extracts from his diary tell the story of his hunts and how they resulted.

DIARY OF ADMIRALTY TRIP BY GEORGE SHIRAS, 4TH

"September 1.—We left Juneau about 9.30 a. m. and decided to go all the way to Pybus Bay. The day was beautiful, and we enjoyed the trip very much. Arrived at Pybus Bay, 9.30 p. m., so late and it was so dark that we pitched only one tent and slept four in a row, Hasselborg staying on his boat.

"September 2.—It was a fine day. About 9 a. m. Hasselborg and I went out after

CHARLIE ANDERSON BRINGS IN A GOOSE

The camp table was well supplied with game of many different sorts.

"About 1 o'clock we turned back for camp by a way different from our route up the mountain. My shoe packs were too large, and this made awkward going for me on steep slopes. In places it was so steep that it was impossible for me to retain my foothold and I would slide 15 or 20 feet at a time, clutching wildly at the bushes as I went.

"In places here and there the slope dropped away sheer for from 150 to 200 feet and we had to work cautiously around these cliffs. This was nervous work for me, unaccustomed as I was to mountains and having on utterly unsuitable footgear. At the bottom we forced our way through tangled bushes and found ourselves on the shore of the little cove near the mouth of which camp was located. The cove is an arm of Pybus Bay, and is about half a mile long.

deer. Through the field glasses we saw some browsing on the mountain slopes, but first we tried for a shot at one in the small lowland meadows. We saw no fresh signs there, so decided to climb the nearest mountain. It took about two hours to reach the top, where there was an irregular plateau with little meadows at slightly different elevations and numerous small ponds.

"Finally we spied a deer feeding on a slope, but could not determine whether it was a buck or a doe, for we had left the field glasses at camp. We were out mainly after camp meat, but did not wish to shoot a doe. After going a few hundred yards farther, we made out a deer across a gully. I raised the sights for 200 yards and fired, but the bullet went high.

"The tide was high, and we had to force our way through the dense vegetation bordering it, making only about 300 yards in an hour. Hasselborg reached camp well ahead of me, and Charlie came to meet me about 3 p. m. and took me back to camp in the small boat.

"After having something to eat, Charlie and I took the boat out to try for ducks. We had no success in our search for ducks, but we saw a few geese too far away to warrant shooting at them.

"September 3.—I had planned to climb the mountain again today, but rain in the morning prevented this, and Charlie rowed me across the cove to look for bears. Many salmon were in a small stream there, and plenty of bear signs were along the banks.

It appeared that I would probably be as successful in getting a shot at one of the animals by quietly waiting where signs were plentiful as when moving about. Soon a bear was heard making a great noise in the thickets to our left—possibly two cubs fighting—but nothing appeared. Nearly an hour later another was heard much closer and near the stream, but it also failed to come into the open.

"About 7 p. m. we decided to return to camp, and were startled to discover that the tide had run down until it had left our boat stranded several hundred yards from the water, although we supposed we had left it in a place safe from such a mishap. Fortunately, we had to drag it only about 70 yards to a little drainage way through the tide flat, which enabled us to reach open water without great exertion. It was practically dark when we reached camp at 8 o'clock. Our only game for the whole trip was a single teal.

A WISE OLD RAVEN INSPECTS THE CAMP

These birds were common about the shores of Admiralty Island. In summer they feed largely on dead salmon along streams.

DIFFICULT COUNTRY

"September 4.—Left camp with Charlie soon after 5 o'clock, and we began climbing the mountain slope very soon instead of waiting until we came to a long ridge that, as we learned later, made an easier way. The slope was exceedingly steep, and we had literally to pull ourselves up by our hands, as in a prolonged 'chinning' exercise, using our feet mainly for toe-holds. After about an hour of this going, the difficulties were increased by a dense growth of scrubby alders and devil's club, and loose stones under foot. Here Charlie was

ahead, and several small boulders started by him barely missed me as they fell.

"Suddenly an extraordinary commotion began above me. It seemingly was made by a combination of snorting, growling, and hissing sounds from some big animal. Accompanying it sounded the cracking of branches and the rattle of rolling rocks, which began to pass me. It was evident that Charlie had started a bear in my direction.

"As I cocked my rifle, Charlie shouted for me to get my gun ready. Then the bushes began to move and I could hear the bear going away to the left. The bushes were so dense that I could not get a glimpse of it, although it was very near. If I had not called in reply to Charlie's warning,

A NEW SPECIES OF BIG BEAR (URSUS SHIRASI)

This huge beast was encountered in the brush and went down under some well-directed shots by George Shiras, 4th. Because of the reflection of the light from its glossy hairs the animal appears somewhat gray, but in reality it is dead black. In coloring it shows strong contrast to the big brown bears also found on Admiralty Island and previously supposed to be the sole occupants of the bear family there.

the bear would have come directly down upon me.

"An extremely awkward situation would have been the result, for I could not have seen the creature in the brush until it was fairly at the muzzle of my gun, and whatever the result of the shot, we should have pitched down the abrupt mountain slope together. I had been told by bear hunters that these animals, when alarmed, always go up the slope. Consequently the course taken by this animal at first surprised me. A few minutes later we found immediately above us an overhanging cliff; it became evident that the bear was cornered and forced down.

"About 9 o'clock we came to the mountain top. A spike-horn buck dashed from the cover on my left, and I missed him at 40 feet. He stopped a moment at the crack of the gun, but was gone so quickly there was not time for a second shot. We saw no more deer, and about 11 o'clock we began our return to camp.

BAD WEATHER MADE HARD HUNTING

"For three days the rain had fallen and the brush was soaked. All this morning the rain had continued; we had become wet to the skin soon after we started out. The constant exertion of climbing kept us warm, but as soon as we stopped to rest for a minute we became badly chilled and our teeth would begin to chatter despite every effort.

"Being unfamiliar with these mountains, we descended the wrong slope and struggled for five hours through a heart-breaking tangle of dense brush until I finally became so exhausted that it was all I could do to break through the brush and fall over hidden logs. Whenever we paused for a moment we became so chilled it was evident that if we failed to make camp before dark our plight would be serious. We had neglected to carry our matches in a waterproof container and they were as wet as we were.

"At length we broke through the brush on the border of Pybus Bay, and there about 400 yards away was the welcome sight of Hasselborg's boat at anchor. Our relief was tremendous. Six hours after we left the mountain top, we were in dry clothes before the camp fire enjoying a fine, hot clam chowder. Father and Hasselborg had become uneasy about our prolonged absence and were out looking for us when we came in, but a rifle shot in the air brought them back.

"September 5.—None the worse for yesterday's strenuous 11 hours on the mountain side, I remained in camp part of the day and went out for shore birds with father. It did not take long for us to obtain a bag of 17, all we desired, consisting largely of surf birds and black turnstones. Hasselborg and Charlie went up the mountain for deer by an easier way, but failed to get one. Rain all day.

"September 6.—In the morning the rain stopped for about five hours and then began again. Hasselborg and John looked over the set cameras, but found none of the flashes fired, although the bait had been taken at one place. The cameras and flashlight apparatus are covered with waterproof material, but the steady downpour of rain has spoiled some of the flashlight powder. I fear the general moisture will spoil the plates, but the cool temperatures may save them.

A WET CAMP

"In the afternoon Hasselborg went out with me for ducks. I killed three, but lost them in thick grass. We were thoroughly soaked by the rain, as were also father, John, and Charlie, who were out for a time. It is fortunate that we have a small stove in the cook tent; otherwise our situation would be hopeless. Most of our things are wet all the time and we lack enough changes of clothing. Waterproof articles in such a situation give much trouble, for they are difficult to dry.

"September 7.—Rain continued all last

THE FEET OF THE SHIRAS BEAR

These were cut off to be presented to the museum along with the head pictured on page 437.

night. The tent leaks in a few places only, but wet some of my possessions including my diary in which these notes are being recorded. My sleeping-bag rested in a pool of water, but the dampness did not penetrate to the blankets inside. In the afternoon Charlie took me out for an hour in the small boat after geese, which we failed to get, since they flew when we were too far away for my shot to be effective.

"I took the rifle and went across the bay to look for bears. As we were about to land, the wind became almost a small tornado, blowing great rain-laden gusts across the water. It did not look promising for bear hunting, and we returned to camp.

"September 8.—After breakfast at daybreak Hasselborg and I started out for deer. We went in his launch to another cove near the head of Pybus Bay. After landing, we at once climbed a mountain. At the top were a doe and a fawn, which stood looking innocently at us. We were out for camp meat but did not wish to shoot anything but bucks. We whistled and they bounded away. Two other deer were seen that did not afford good shots.

"After eating some sandwiches in the downpour, we continued our hunt along the ridge. We walked some distance apart and Hasselborg saw 14 deer and I counted 10, with not a single buck in the lot. Finally we were forced to give up our search for a buck, and took into camp the meat of a doe and a fawn. Meanwhile Charlie had

YOUTHFUL REPRESENTATIVES OF THE NEW BEAR (URSUS SHIRASI)

This picture of two-year-old twins shows them at the edge of a salmon stream. Their noticeably dark colors contrast with the light yellowish brown of the huge bears that previously had the island as an exclusive family home.

killed a white-cheeked goose and a willow ptarmigan.

"September 9.—Early in the morning Hasselborg and I crossed to the other side of the bay. To our pleased surprise it was not raining, and I took some photographs of gulls and of the mountains. Through the glasses we saw deer on the mountain side, which we hoped were bucks. When we stalked within gun-shot, however, they proved to be does, and we went on.

"On the way up we came within 25 feet of a small buck with rather good antlers, but I refrained from shooting it when Hasselborg assured me that I could get a much better one a little later. I took three unsuccessful shots at an albino buck that was with several other deer across a small valley. It was raining hard at the time and my shots all went high. In our wandering over the mountain today we walked within a short distance of between 15 and 20 deer, all does except two spike-horn bucks. Not a single fawn was in sight.

ENCOUNTER WITH A BEAR

"From the foot of the mountain we followed down a small salmon stream and encountered a big brown bear fishing. He was on the right bank looking up and across at us. Dropping to one knee I took careful aim at the middle of his neck and fired. He immediately fell on his back and rolled over and over several times, roaring and bellowing with rage and pain.

"Hasselborg shouted, 'He's a dead bear'; then, 'Shoot again.'

"Just then the bear regained his feet, and as he rose I fired at his shoulder. Off he went up the bank to the right, continuing his roars. I should have shot again, but felt confident the two shots already given were enough. Down by the stream where the bear had been shot there was much blood on the bank, and the leaves and ground where we trailed him were covered with it.

"The brush was so dense that it was necessary to follow the trail cautiously with rifles ready for instant use should our victim rise suddenly before us. Finally it began to grow dark and Hasselborg assured me that the bear was so badly wounded that we were certain to find his trail easy to follow in the morning. Rain was the only thing to fear, and the stars were shining. Never before in my life had I such an intense desire for no rain.

"September 10.—It began raining about midnight, and in the morning we found the blood along the bear's trail all washed away except here and there on the underside of devil's club leaves. The trail led us to another stream where, despite all our efforts, we lost it completely.

"September 11.—Last night the rain fell more heavily than ever before at our camp, and in the morning my sleeping-bag had a good-sized pool in a depression on its top. The thermometer usually registered 52 degrees but one morning it showed 49. One advantage of this coolness here over the warmer Copper River camp is the absence of black flies and mosquitoes. Although I wear a waterproof hat, slicker, and rubber boots here, I become soaked with water every time I go out, but we find game. Our cook serves us venison, geese, ducks, shore birds, blue grouse, and ptarmigan.

"This proved to be the stormiest day we have experienced, with a heavy northeaster. Hasselborg kept under cover on his boat and the rest of us remained in the tents. When I started to get into my sleeping-bag, I found the blankets soaking wet. During the hard downpour of the day the tent had leaked a steady stream, and the water had entered the opening of the bag. Taking it over to the really waterproof cook tent, I spread my slicker over the bag and crept into the soggy mess, but did not enjoy a very good night's rest.

"September 12.—Father, Charles, and I went to the lower bay, from which father and Charles returned to camp in the small boat, while the launch was anchored and I walked up the salmon stream with Hasselborg looking for bears. From an open place up over the mountain slope I caught a glimpse of the albino buck. On our way back to camp we ran upon a reef but without damage and arrived before 5 p. m. This has been our first day without rain here.

RAIN AND FOG AGAIN

"September 13.—At 9 o'clock last evening began a steady rain that continued all night. During the entire day the mountains back of us were lost in a heavy bank of fog, and it was necessary for Hasselborg and me to abandon our proposed hunt on them. For a while in the early morning Charlie went with me to the salmon stream. I walked ahead looking for bears, and he followed with a rod fishing for trout. We saw some fresh bear tracks, some salmon

Photograph courtesy Nature Magazine

URSUS SHIRASI STANDS AND ANNOUNCES HIS PRESENCE

In the summer of 1933 Mr. Arthur N. Pack, at the head of an expedition, visited Admiralty Island to study and photograph the great brown bear and especially a black phase of this animal described and named *Ursus shirasi* by Dr. C. Hart Merriam many years before (see text, page 437).

"About 9 in the morning, Hasselborg set out with me in a hard rain after bears. I wore my rubber boots and a slicker that had become badly torn and had lost all but the top button. We circled around the base of the mountain back of camp and were following down a large salmon stream when we saw a big brown bear in the water with a fish held crosswise in its mouth. I crept to within 100 yards of it and opened fire; the first two shots were high, but the third hit it in the rump.

"To my surprise it gave a jump and tried to climb a tree beside it. At least it stood up full length and appeared to be doing its best to climb. At this time another shot struck its right paw, and dropping to the ground it disappeared so quickly I could not get another shot. Hasselborg crossed the stream on a wet and slippery log, but in trying to follow I slipped off into the water. Fortunately it was only up to my waist, but the current was so strong it nearly carried me away.

working up the stream, some gulls, a pair of harlequin ducks, and a merganser, but obtained no game. The trout refused to take flies or bait made either of salmon meat or of eggs.

"September 14.—Hard rain all night. The tent leaked badly and in the morning I was awakened by a splash of cold water on my face. I discovered that water had been falling on me until my head and shoulders were very wet, and water had penetrated to the middle of the sleeping-bag. Although very wet, I was comfortable enough, for the blankets had held the warmth of my body.

"The bark of the tree that the bear tried to climb showed deep claw marks, and blood was on the tree trunk and on the ground at its base. We trailed the bear a long distance, here and there finding much blood and then for a considerable distance no sign of it. In places the signs indicated that the bear had started to lie down and then our scent or the noise of our approach had sent it on again.

"The trail led us along a crooked route through the dense brush. It was completely lost on the bank of a creek. On our way back along the trail we found that the rain had already washed away all trace of the blood.

"We arrived at camp at 5 o'clock, wet through, cold, tired, discouraged, and hungry. After a hearty meal of roast goose, boiled potatoes, apple sauce, prunes, and rice pudding, with two cups of coffee, I felt more cheerful and began to think that I might yet get one of these elusive bears.

"September 15.—Heavy rain fell all night, and our tent leaked so badly that I carried my sleeping-bag over to the cook tent and laid it beside the guides. There I appreciated a dry night. Nothing worthy of record today.

GETTING A BIG BEAR

"September 16.—About 9 o'clock Hasselborg and I began another bear hunt. We went up the basin at the foot of which our camp is set, and then up along the salmon stream, passing the place where, on September 14, I had wounded the bear. Above this we came to some beautiful waterfalls.

"As we were climbing along the slope through dense alders, I heard a stick break directly to my left and below. At this instant Hasselborg beckoned and in about two steps I was beside him, just as a big bear appeared about 15 feet below us. He turned toward us, apparently to learn what was making the noise near him, and I fired four shots into his side and rump, and one through the brush that struck him in the lower jaw. He went about 30 feet along the slope and was dead when we reached him.

"He was a large example of the big bears of this region, measuring 6 feet 8 inches from the tip of the nose to the tail. This is the only accurate method of measuring the length of a bear, for after the skin is taken off it can be stretched far beyond the length of the animal. His hind foot with the claws was 14 inches long, and his forefoot 13 inches long and 7 inches broad.

"He was entirely black, but his fur was not in such good condition as it would have attained in another month. After disemboweling him, we returned to camp to wait until tomorrow before preparing the trophy. During the day father and Charlie had been out for surf birds and black turnstones, minute game as compared with mine; but these certainly made delicious additions to our camp fare.

"September 17.—In the morning father, Charlie, Hasselborg, and I went up to the dead bear. The head, cape, and front feet were removed and taken back to camp by father and Charlie, while Hasselborg and I continued on to the big mountain beyond the ridge lying back of camp, a trip that we had been planning for days.

"After leaving the carcass of the bear, we had climbed about 2,500 feet when a buck with a fine pair of antlers appeared about 100 yards up the slope. I was so completely out of breath that my first shot was a clean miss, and my second caught him in the hind quarters. Steadying down somewhat I tried for his shoulders, but hit his neck. Still another struck him back of the shoulders. At the last shot he dropped on the steep slope and went rolling over and over until he disappeared.

"Leaving him to be found on our return, we continued on our way. It was hard labor to force a way up through gnarled alders and thorny devil's club with almost no foothold. Near the summit the bushes gave way to bare rocks and moss.

"This was the first entirely pleasant day since our arrival on the island, and the outlook from the summit was wonderful. All the surrounding region was visible, many wooded, mountainous islands, with Frederick Sound to the south, and a little patch of the open Pacific miles away through a notch in the distant mountains.

HARD WORK TO GET THE KILL

"The descent was difficult, and even dangerous in places, where it was all I could do to hold on above small precipices. The buck killed in the morning had rolled down about 500 feet and lay among some alders that saved him from a further drop of several hundred feet, clear. As it was, two prongs were broken from the antlers.

"September 18.—Last night the weather turned cool and this morning the temperature stood at 40 degrees. Hasselborg took my bear head on his boat to clean it for preservation, and I put in the time alternately watching him and reading parts of Sheldon's account of his hunt on Admiralty. Later, on a walk up to some ponds at the head of the cove, I flushed four mallards.

"Charlie returned early in the afternoon from a fishing trip with five fine trout measuring from 15 to 20 inches. The large ones appeared to weigh about three pounds. Hasselborg calls them "sea trout," but they are probably what are usually called salmon trout. In a general way they resemble big brook trout, but their backs are darker—almost black—and their tails are slightly forked instead of being cut straight across at the end. The meat was firm and pink.

"Charlie had landed and fastened his boat at low tide and when he returned from fishing up the stream he found the water so high that the boat was inaccessible. He was forced to return to camp on foot along shore, wading in some places up to his waist. It was foggy all day and rain began again in the afternoon.

"I have been feeling a little off for the last two days. On Saturday Charlie and I went out after geese in the pouring rain, but on the way I was taken with a chill and we had to turn back to camp. The sea was so rough that it was all Charlie could do with the oars to make camp."

THE AUTHOR RESUMES HIS NARRATIVE

One afternoon in camp we heard several shots in rapid succession well up on the mountain side where George and Hasselborg had gone hunting bears. Upon their return later it was apparent at a glance that my son had been successful. He had killed an old male of the big black-colored animals which we had been seeing but which previously had been unknown to Hasselborg.

Early the following morning the camp was astir, and we set out for the scene of the previous encounter. Fortunately, for the first time in many days, the morning was clear and favorable for photography. The walk up the forested valley was fairly easy along the trails made by bears in summer and deer in winter. These trails made convenient passageways through a dense undergrowth of matted brush and prickly devil's club. A dry creek bottom led us up a ravine for about a quarter of a mile to within about 10 steps of the bear's carcass.

We soon formed an interested circle about the great black form where it lay in a dense mass of alder brush. As we came to the spot we were put on the alert by the sound of breaking bushes as a heavy animal plunged down one side of the ravine we had ascended. It was apparently another bear, but probably not the mate of the dead animal. Bears do not mate permanently. Many ravens were gathered in surrounding treetops waiting for the feast in store for them. After clearing away some of the undergrowth, I took photographs of the bear from several angles.

Several characteristics of this big bear impressed me as I saw it in the flesh—its large size, its glossy blackish coat, the exceptionally broad skull, and an uptilted muzzle with a porcine cast as if it was built for rooting out mice and turning over sod and earth in search of roots.

Although there were five of us, we had difficulty in turning over the body so that the skin of the head, neck, and back could be removed. We took the skull for scientific study and the front feet as trophies. When this had been done, George and Hasselborg went up the mountain to try to get a fine buck that had been seen the day before, and the rest of us, carrying parts of the bear, made our way back to camp.

We were rather uneasy as we descended the ravine near the route followed by the bear earlier in the morning, for our only equipment consisted of a hatchet and a small camera. In the abstract we know that even the biggest and fiercest bears are slow to attack man unless wounded or cornered, or in defense of their young; but while we were unarmed, in the midst of the dense growth harboring such great beasts, we might be forgiven for having had the feeling that morning that we might prove victims to the exception that proves the rule.

Hasselborg told us that if we would return to the bear's carcass in a week or so we should find it buried under broken branches, roots, sod, and rocks. He had previously pointed out several mounds where lay bodies of bears he had killed.

HASSELBORG'S BEAR CEMETERY

I had seen on various other occasions the temporary caches of meat made by bears and other predatory animals. These mounds on Admiralty Island were larger and flatter than a beaver house, and had well-marked trails about them.

These, Hasselborg solemnly assured me, represented a ceremonial custom of burial quite apart from any food-storing habit. He said that for a year or more these places would be visited by the bears. This weird tale of prolonged mourning by bears was not well authenticated by several of the mounds that I examined. They contained only the bones of deer and evidently had been food caches.

HEAD OF THE NEW BEAR, URSUS SHIRASI, FROM ADMIRALTY ISLAND, SHOT BY
GEORGE SHIRAS, 4TH

This animal measured 6 feet and 8 inches from the tip of its nose to the root of its tail. The forefeet, skull, and skin are now in the Biological Survey Collection in Washington, D. C. The tailpiece used at some chapter ends is from a drawing of this trophy by Hashime Murayama.

For the sake of continuity I will introduce here the information we received after our return to Washington. The skull, skin, and front feet of the bear shot by George had been submitted to Dr. C. Hart Merriam for examination. Doctor Merriam compared them with the unequaled series of Alaskan bear material in the Biological Survey collection and decided that our animal was an unknown species. Under date of July 1, 1914, he wrote me in part as follows:

"Your bear turned out to be a splendid new species, which it has given me pleasure to name *Ursus shirasi.* We previously had several young specimens of it but none old enough to show the adult skull characters. Since you were here, two additional older specimens have come in, one not quite so old as yours, the other very much older but smaller. Your specimen I have made the type of the species to remain in our National Collection for all time as the unit of comparison for this bear. It is a great pity that the skin and claws could not be preserved with the skull to show their distinctive characters. However, I appreciate your desire to keep the mounted head as a trophy. If you do not need both of the fore feet we should be mighty glad to have one of them for the collection in order to prove by the claws as well as the skull that

Ursus shirasi is a Big Brown Bear and not a Grizzly."

Doctor Merriam published a technical description of this bear on page 195 of the *Proceedings of the Biological Society of Washington,* issued August 13, 1913. In this the animal is described as entirely black except for the full brown muzzle and a brownish wash along the middle of the back.

He adds: *"Ursus shirasi* is a very large member of the Brown Bear group. Whether or not it is always black, like the type specimen, is not known. But of all the American bears it has a skull the most striking and distinctive. The short, broad frontal shield rising on each side into huge postorbital processes which arch broadly over the orbits serve to distinguish it at a glance from all other species, rendering close comparison unnecessary.

"In this connection it is interesting to observe that *shirasi* and its neighbor *eulophus,* an inhabitant of the same island, present opposite extremes of departure from the normal ursine type—*eulophus* having a long narrow skull with slender elongate rostrum, long and narrow frontal shield, and insignificant postorbital processes, while *shirasi* has an exceptionally broad skull, with broad short rostrum, excessively broad and short frontal shield, and huge massive postorbital processes."

LATER REPORTS CONCERNING THE BEARS OF ADMIRALTY ISLAND

After some twenty years, another expedition under the leadership of Mr. Arthur N. Pack visited Admiralty Island for the purpose of studying and photographing the Great Brown Bear or any new form of the same. Mr. Pack was successful in getting a fine series of the island bears in the vicinity of the streams where the salmon spawn. It is a pleasure to note that pictures of the black-garbed ones predominated in his collection.

In the origin of species, it has long been recognized that where wild animals are confined on a large island inaccessible from the main shore there is often presented a favorable opportunity for any abnormal offspring to develop permanently into a newly established form. This appears to have happened on Admiralty Island.

I am glad to welcome Mr. Pack into the ranks of those who successfully hunt with the camera, and to express my appreciation for the use of several of his pictures, which will greatly aid in establishing the origin and history of this newcomer among the giant bears of Alaska.

In addition to the several species of gulls, heretofore mentioned, and the mallards, and Canada geese in the fresh-water ponds near camp, I had a chance to observe a number of other aquatic birds in the bays and channels of the western side of Admiralty Island. Among these were the red-breasted merganser, and the bald-pate, the pintail and both species of scaup. In some of the narrow channels were golden-eyes and buffleheads.

WATER BIRDS ABOUT ADMIRALTY ISLAND

Further out from shore were old-squaws, whose varied and penetrating notes reminded me of winters spent on Long Island Sound. Numerous but more or less separated were white-winged scoters and surf scoters, which in the spring gather in large flocks. Near rocky islands and reefs, out toward Frederick Sound, were many scattered harlequin ducks whose brighter plumage was in contrast to the other deep-water ducks of this region.

Because of the warm waters of the Japanese current along the shore and about the islands of southeastern Alaska many of the wild fowl, including even hundreds of mallards, remain in the open waters throughout all, or the greater part of, the winter. At the time of our visit to the island the shore birds were moving southward and, in addition to the surf birds and black turnstones, so numerous in Pybus Bay, I saw a few yellowlegs, northern phalaropes, and two or three species of sandpipers. In flight I also noticed semi-palmated plover and black-bellied plover, as well as a small flock which looked like the Pacific golden plover, but which were too distant for certain identification. One evening a small flock of little brown cranes passed overhead, their loud croaks attracting my attention skyward. These birds, however, were flying northeasterly instead of south.

Usually the man who hunts birds with the camera has a decided advantage over the gunner, for he can see many species that nature did not design to be served on the table. On Admiralty Island, however, the reverse was true. With the skies almost continually overcast and the air filled with rain or fog, I had little chance to picture the birds on or about the island. Many of

DESERTED TRAPPER'S CABINS AFFORD TEMPORARY LODGING

During the return of the author and his party from Admiralty Island to Juneau a severe storm forced them to take refuge on a small island for two days. There they were fortunate to find good shelter awaiting them.

these appeared on a different kind of plate, where a knife and fork instead of developing powder came into use.

A great comfort during the almost continuously bad weather was our use of the so-called gunny-sack camp beds, described in the previous volume. It may be restated that this light and convenient bed consisted of a 6 x 3 foot canvas bag open at each end, through which ran supporting saplings nailed or otherwise fastened on logs at each end of the bed. It mattered not whether rain made its way beneath the tent or covered the floor cloth with puddles from a leaking roof, we were elevated above these troubles, and with a waterproof sleeping bag on each of these cots escaped the hardships of a bed on the floor (see Volume I, page 167).

The large camp umbrella, so seldom seen in the wilderness, was also particularly useful on this trip. At mealtime it was suspended over the kitchen fire whenever it rained, thus sheltering the attendant and the cooking utensils and providing a service that would otherwise have been extremely difficult.

On several occasions this umbrella, which

was made of dark green waterproof canvas, was suspended from a lower limb of a tree by a cord running to a ring at the end of the shaft. Here, beneath the dripping trees along the banks of a salmon stream, I could watch for bears or feeding gulls with myself and camera amply protected.

RETURN TO JUNEAU WAS ACCOMPLISHED
UNDER DIFFICULTIES

September 20 ended our stay on Admiralty Island. Although we have been beset by almost continuous rain that interfered seriously with my photographic work, the conditions as a whole were so novel and interesting that both George and I have greatly enjoyed the experience. Soon after we put to sea a severe storm of wind and rain forced us to run for the nearest shelter on a little wooded island, on which we could see the deserted hut of some Indian fisherman or trapper. The island was only about 350 yards long and gave no safe anchorage for the launch. After landing the four passengers with their bedding and provisions, Hasselborg went on to seek refuge behind some sheltering point along the nearby shore of the main island we had just left.

On September 21 the sea and wind had subsided and, according to our agreement with Hasselborg, we were on the beach very early in the morning with our outfit packed and ready to go, but he failed to appear. We waited impatiently for him until, finally, in view of the favorable weather, we feared he had suffered some mishap. Charlie and John passed some hours in the afternoon in the small boat looking for him, but without success.

HASSELBORG TAKES HIS TIME

There was no sign of the launch the morning of September 22, and later in the day the guides again set out to search for the missing boat. Just at sundown we heard the welcome chugging of the exhaust, and the launch appeared with our men on board and their boat in tow. When we expressed to Hasselborg the anxiety we had undergone because of his delay in returning, he said that he did not suppose anyone was so interested in his welfare. We made it plain that our anxiety had more to do with our own situation. The only reason he gave for causing us to lose two fair days was that it was too rough for the return trip. This is an example of the curious and often irritating difficulties of exploration.

The next morning in the face of an increasing wind and rain we made an early start from our little island of refuge. Before we had gone far, the engine suddenly stopped and the boat rolled so heavily that the necessary adjustments to start the motor again were made with much difficulty. The little launch, only 27 feet long, was badly overloaded with four passengers and several hundreds of pounds of cargo, besides some heavy timbers which Hasselborg had cut while held up by the storm. The timbers were for use in a new boat he was building.

The launch was clearly so overloaded that I was doubtful about the outcome if the engine should give out when we were farther out in the open water. When I suggested a possible return to our camp site on Admiralty Island not many miles away, where we might await better weather, Hasselborg laughed and said, "We've got to meet our fate sometime, so why worry?"

As the waves increased in force, the launch labored so heavily that it became necessary to put overboard our two small boats fastened to a tow line. Hasselborg said that if the sea became too rough, he would cut them loose. This idea failed to

appeal to me very much, for if the poorly balanced and heavily rolling launch should turn over, as it seemed inclined to do now and then, we should be without any means of escape. When we were midway in the open passage, the steamer *Northwestern,* on which we were to go south on her return to Juneau, passed on her way to Seward.

I must confess that I had a great desire to be on board her; for just at that time our tow line broke and it was necessary for the launch to make a wide circle amid the breaking waves to recover the boats. Finally we secured the line and entered the shelter of a little bay to readjust it just as the engine stopped again. It required four hours of hard work by Hasselborg to repair it.

Had the accident occurred half an hour earlier, while we were in the open sound, it is doubtful if the boat could have survived until the repairs were made. It is needless to say that all the members of our party were much relieved when we finally came alongside the wharf at Juneau, although Hasselborg had appeared quite unconcerned at the time. He had the reputation of being a very skillful, but exceedingly eccentric guide, and this was demonstrated especially during the last part of our expedition.

THE SITKA BLACK-TAILED DEER

The coastal islands along the panhandle of southeastern Alaska are inhabited by a small and dark geographic race of the well-known black-tailed deer of the wooded northwestern coast region of the United States and British Columbia. In comparatively recent years these small deer have been introduced on a number of islands along the southern coast of Alaska. On Hinchinbrook and Hawkins islands they have prospered and increased. They are reported also to have swum from Hawkins Island, lying west of Cordova, to the wooded adjacent mainland, and to be thriving there. Attempted introductions of these deer on the Kenai Peninsula and on Kodiak Island seem to be failures, so far as I can learn.

The abundance of these deer on the coastal islands of southeastern Alaska appears to vary greatly from time to time. In a series of favorable seasons they become very abundant, but one or two winters of unusually heavy snowfall may bury their forage so deeply on the abrupt slopes they

A WHALE ADRIFT ATTRACTS HUNGRY BIRDS

At a distance the author thought he was sighting a wreck, but nearer approach showed it to be a dead whale with a long shaft planted on top of it bearing a lantern and a small flag as finding and identification marks. Apparently it had been carried away by wind and currents until lost by the whaling ship to which it belonged. It was being escorted by a swarm of shearwaters, relatives of the petrels, intent on the oily food the carcass provided.

frequent that they cannot reach it. They then are forced down to the barren beaches along shore, where they try to sustain life by eating the seaweed exposed at low tide. This plant seems not to have any food value, and in such seasons so many deer perish from starvation that they are scarce for a few years following. They are so prolific, however, that a few favorable years result in their being as numerous as before.

One winter some years ago the Biological Survey, with the financial aid of the National Association of Audubon Societies, the American Game Association, and the National Humane Society, assisted by numerous Alaskans, provided hay along the beaches for the starving deer with such success that similar action continues to save hundreds of these animals from an unhappy fate.

From prehistoric times these little deer have been of the utmost value to the Indians along the coast they frequent. Their flesh furnished food, their skins clothing, and their sinews thread, and other parts of them served primitive needs in many ways.

The existence of deer on the southernmost Alaskan island accounts for the presence of the big, dark-colored timber wolves that swim the narrow channels separating certain islands from the mainland of British Columbia, which they cross from island to island. There they prey upon the deer, which constitute their main food supply— for rabbits and other game that are found on most of the mainland do not occur on these islands.

THE DEVELOPMENT OF ALASKA

On my two trips to Alaska I found great local enthusiasm over the proposed building of a railroad by the Government that would extend from the town of Seward, on the Kenai Peninsula, to Fairbanks, on the Tanana River, a distance of more than 400 miles. After making inquiries on the ground and giving the matter considerable thought, I failed to find any economic justification for such a heavy investment.

I had known for many years Franklin Lane, then Secretary of the Interior, under whose direction the road would be built, and after returning from my second trip to the Territory I felt so strongly on the subject that I went to see him regarding it. The project was then in a formative stage, and I gave the Secretary such information as I had gathered bearing on the economics of the proposed road and strongly urged that he disapprove it and thus save a wasteful expenditure of public funds. My conviction was made plain that such a railroad could not pay its way, either when completed or at any future time, so far as could reasonably be foreseen.

The original incentive to build this railroad was the supposed value of the Matanuska coal fields. Later investigation proved this coal to have practically no commercial value on account of its being so thoroughly scattered by the seismic disturbances common in this volcanic region.

It was my opinion, as expressed to Secretary Lane, that instead of spending the great sum necessary to build the railroad from a small port on the coast to an even smaller terminal more than 400 miles in the interior, and the huge annual amount necessary for operating it, a part of the money could be used far more effectively in developing the Territory by properly surveying the coastal waters, to lessen the heavy toll in vessels and human lives under present conditions, and by otherwise improving the coastwise traffic. An extensive system of good roads for automobile and sled traffic could also be built wherever they were needed.

To these suggestions Secretary Lane replied that so much pressure had been brought to bear by Alaskans and by people from the northwestern States and elsewhere, who were personally interested in exploiting the Territory, that the building of the railroad had been forced upon the administration as one of its policies. At the time the railroad was being strenuously advocated the then Governor of the Territory declared that the building of the road would raise the population of Alaska to several million people.

THE ROAD A FINANCIAL FAILURE

The road was completed in 1923. It has since been operated at a heavy loss each year. The effect of the railroad on increasing the population of the Territory is best shown by the fact that in 1920, three years before the railroad was completed, the white population was 27,883, and in 1930 it is reported as being 28,640. These figures are from the census reports, and show that the white population has increased only slightly. The population of Seward and of Anchorage, at the southern end of the road, in 1930 was 835 and 2,227, respectively, and that of Fairbanks, the northern terminus, was 2,101.

These facts yield a striking confirmation of the opinions of those who opposed the building of the road on the strongest and most obvious economic grounds before the Government took any action in the matter. The outlook for the road at present appears to be hopeless so far as any adequate return on the investment is concerned. One bright spot in the situation developed by the building of the railroad has been the establishment of the McKinley National Park, which contains such a wealth of wild life and magnificent scenery that it should attract an increasing number of summer visitors.

LIGHTS AND SHADOWS ON ALASKA

In considering some of the economic conditions in Alaska the author has no desire to reflect upon the Territory and its possibilities, but wishes to express his friendly opinion on the subject. It is a fact that agriculture, except on a very limited scale, offers little inducement, for there is a lack of a large local demand for agricultural products and the cost of exporting any surplus and competing with products grown under more favorable conditions in the northwestern States is prohibitory. In fact, grain and vegetables grown in the State of Washington are sold at such low prices on the coast of southern Alaska as to make local competition difficult.

Another economic handicap is the absence of coal of a good commercial quality. In other directions, however, Alaska has valuable resources, such as its timber, favorably located on tidewater, its salmon and other fisheries, its reindeer herds, its fur bearers (including the fur seal), and its splendid game animals, as well as its gold, silver, copper, and other minerals. Last and not least is its unequaled combination of magnificent scenery, an asset of increasingly great value.

The greatest danger to Alaska's future is a tendency to exploit destructively some of its natural resources. It has required a constant war to save the fisheries from destruction. It has been difficult also to protect the game, and especially the fur bearers. Alaskans should bear in mind that visitors are drawn by scenic attractions and by hunting and fishing. With these assets properly conserved, Alaska stands potentially supreme.

INDEX TO VOLUME I

Page

Page

INDEX TO VOLUME II